FREQUENTLY ASKED QUESTIONS

Other UNSHELVED collections by Bill Barnes & Gene Ambaum:

Unshelved
What Would Dewey Do?
Library Mascot Cage Match
Book Club
Read Responsibly

FREQUENTLY ASKED QUESTIONS

an UNSHELVED® collection
by Bill Barnes and Gene Ambaum

OVERDUE
MEDIA
Seattle

Reprinting *Unshelved* comic strips originally published on the *Unshelved* website from February 19, 2007 to February 16, 2008, the American Library Association website, and *ALA CogNotes* newspapers in June 2007 and January 2008.

ISBN-10: 0-9740353-5-1
ISBN-13: 978-0-9740353-5-2

First printing: May 2008

Printed in Canada.

Your Malville Public Library Staff

Branch manager **Mel** enjoys reading biographies, human resources manuals, and office supply catalogs. She likes fly-fishing, new policies, and endlessly reorganizing the desk schedule.

Young adult librarian **Dewey** prefers to read comics, sci-fi, and fantasy. His colorful interactions with the public have earned the sobriquet "Dewey Moments." No relation to Thomas, John, George or Melvil.

Children's librarian **Tamara** loves upbeat stories of positivism and triumph. She asks that her "pint-sized patrons" eschew spilling their cruelty-free snacks on the floor of her section. They can do it anywhere else, but please not where she works. She is a black belt in Aikido.

Reference librarian **Colleen** reads comprehensive scholarly works of all kinds, the more volumes the better. She is confident that the "online catalog" fad will pass. Her blog has been optioned by a major studio. Colleen's work-schooled daughter **Doreen** is always around somewhere.

Library page/summer reading mascot **Buddy The Book Beaver** avidly listens to audiobooks of an adult nature. He complies with all state laws regarding costume laundering. He is sorry about the times he fell on your laptop, shredded your term paper, and whitewashed your service dog.

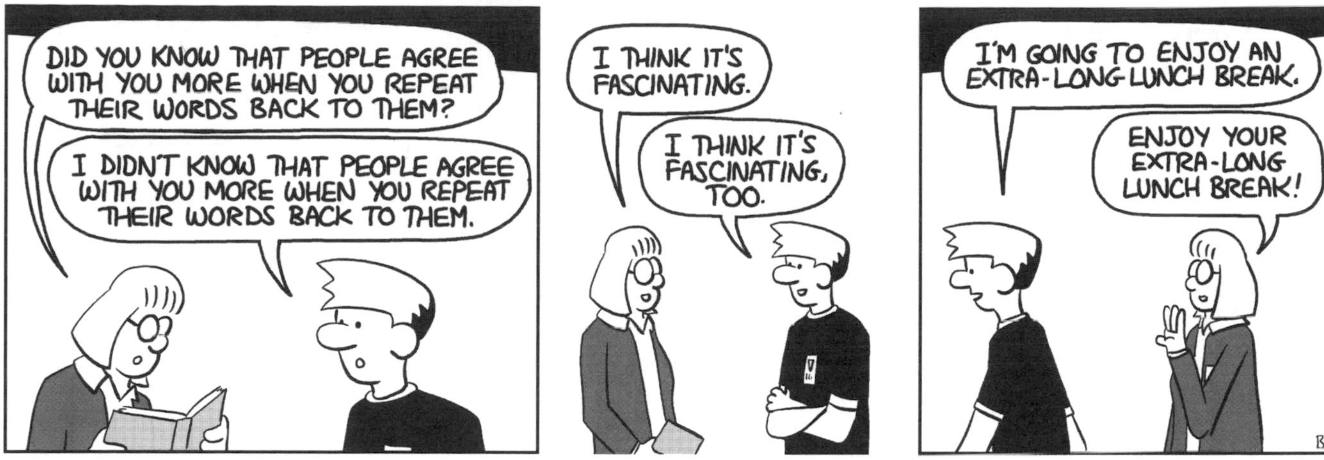
DID YOU KNOW THAT PEOPLE AGREE WITH YOU MORE WHEN YOU REPEAT THEIR WORDS BACK TO THEM?
I DIDN'T KNOW THAT PEOPLE AGREE WITH YOU MORE WHEN YOU REPEAT THEIR WORDS BACK TO THEM.
I THINK IT'S FASCINATING.
I THINK IT'S FASCINATING, TOO.
I'M GOING TO ENJOY AN EXTRA-LONG-LUNCH BREAK.
ENJOY YOUR EXTRA-LONG LUNCH BREAK!
BB

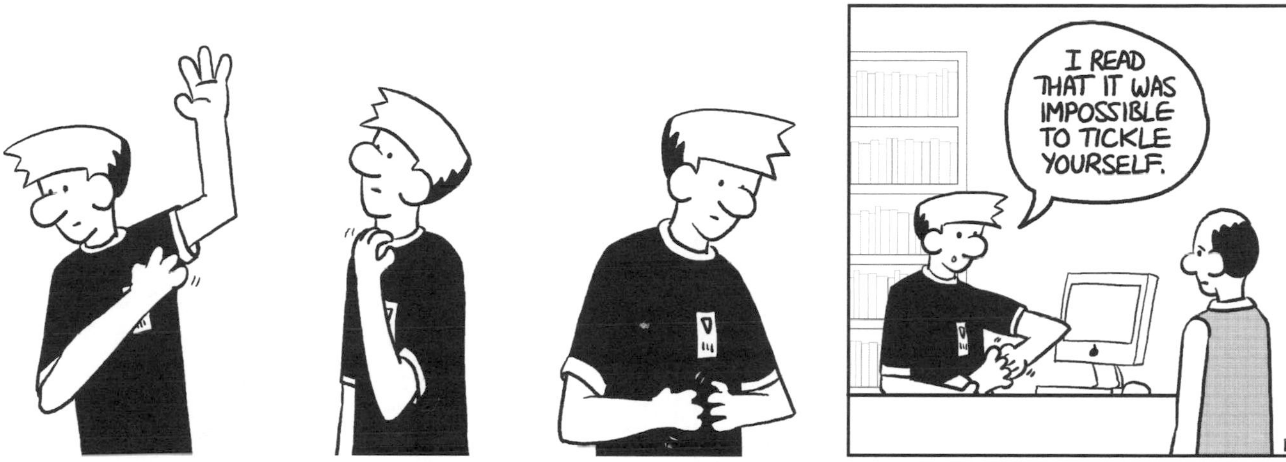
I READ THAT IT WAS IMPOSSIBLE TO TICKLE YOURSELF.
BB

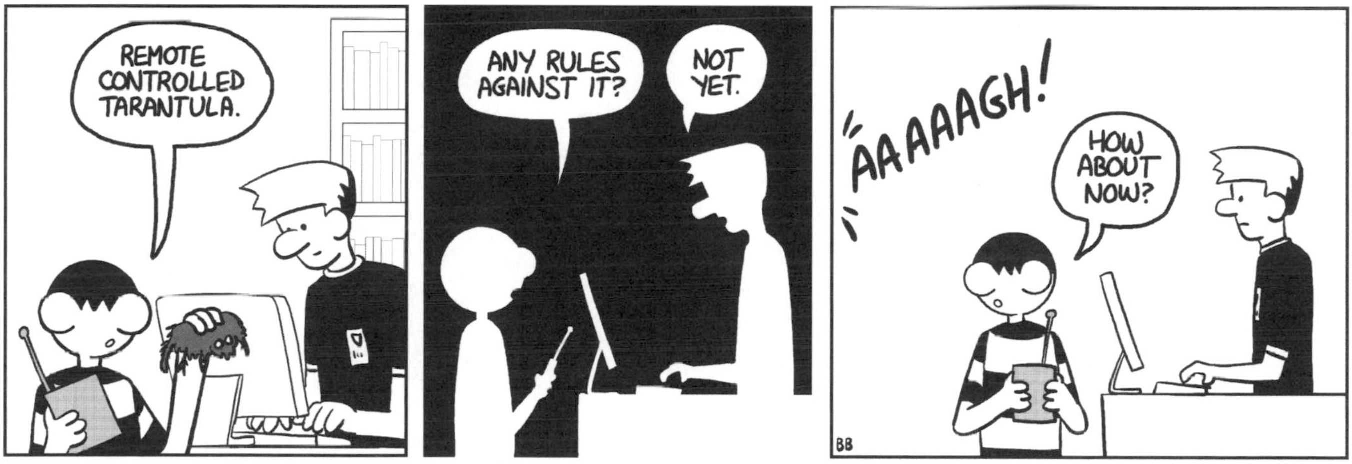
REMOTE CONTROLLED TARANTULA.
ANY RULES AGAINST IT?
NOT YET.
AAAAAGH!
HOW ABOUT NOW?
BB

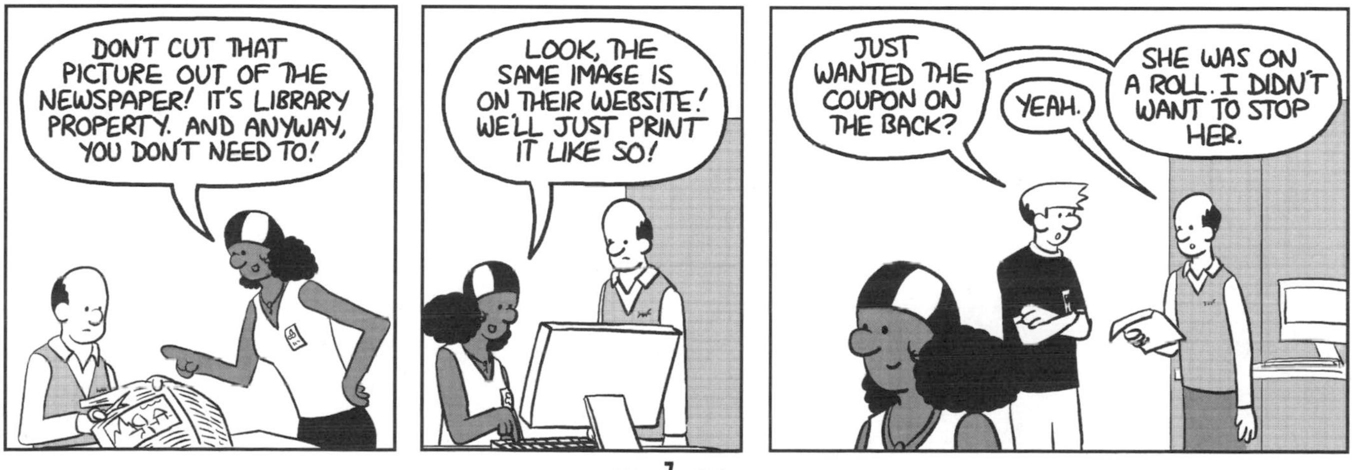
DON'T CUT THAT PICTURE OUT OF THE NEWSPAPER! IT'S LIBRARY PROPERTY. AND ANYWAY, YOU DON'T NEED TO!
LOOK, THE SAME IMAGE IS ON THEIR WEBSITE! WE'LL JUST PRINT IT LIKE SO!
JUST WANTED THE COUPON ON THE BACK?
YEAH.
SHE WAS ON A ROLL. I DIDN'T WANT TO STOP HER.

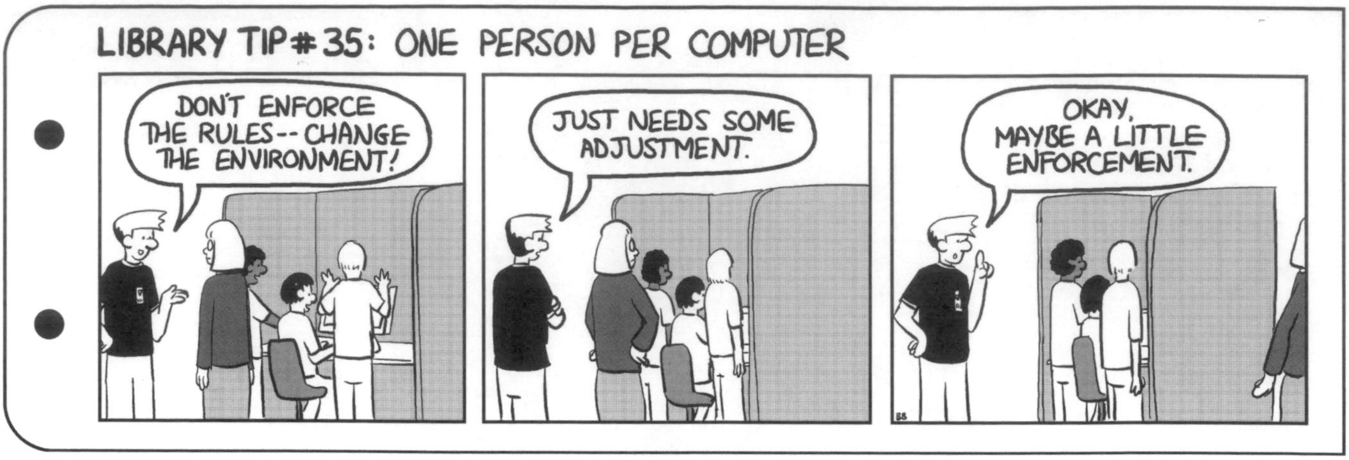
LIBRARY TIP #35: ONE PERSON PER COMPUTER
DON'T ENFORCE THE RULES-- CHANGE THE ENVIRONMENT!
JUST NEEDS SOME ADJUSTMENT.
OKAY, MAYBE A LITTLE ENFORCEMENT.
BB

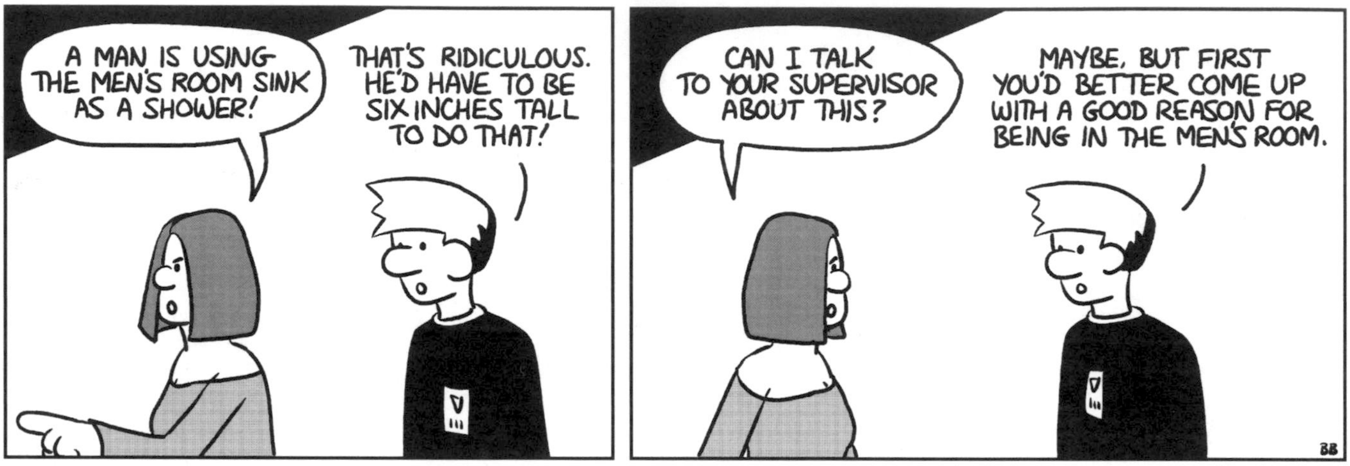
A MAN IS USING THE MEN'S ROOM SINK AS A SHOWER!
THAT'S RIDICULOUS. HE'D HAVE TO BE SIX INCHES TALL TO DO THAT!
CAN I TALK TO YOUR SUPERVISOR ABOUT THIS?
MAYBE, BUT FIRST YOU'D BETTER COME UP WITH A GOOD REASON FOR BEING IN THE MEN'S ROOM.
BB

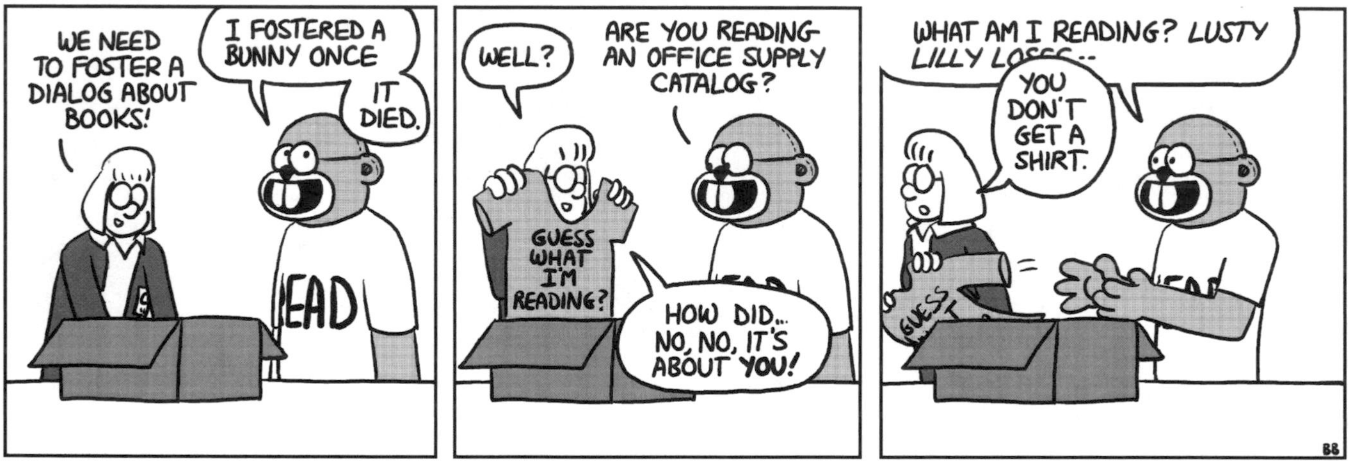
WE NEED TO FOSTER A DIALOG ABOUT BOOKS!
I FOSTERED A BUNNY ONCE
IT DIED.
EAD
WELL?
ARE YOU READING AN OFFICE SUPPLY CATALOG?
GUESS WHAT I'M READING?
HOW DID... NO, NO, IT'S ABOUT **YOU**!
WHAT AM I READING? *LUSTY LILLY LO*--
YOU DON'T GET A SHIRT.
BB

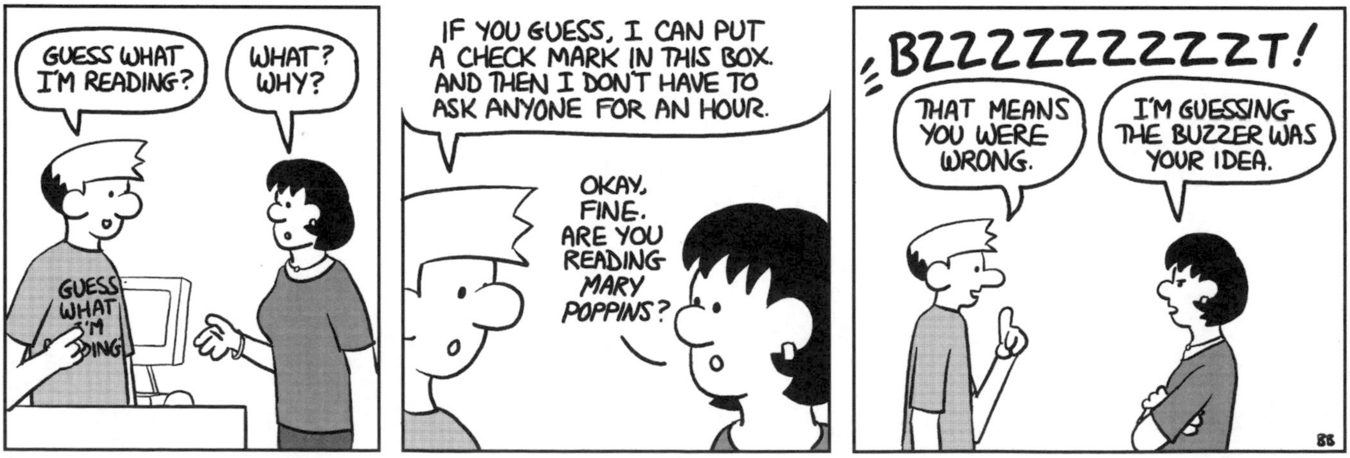
GUESS WHAT I'M READING?
WHAT? WHY?
IF YOU GUESS, I CAN PUT A CHECK MARK IN THIS BOX. AND THEN I DON'T HAVE TO ASK ANYONE FOR AN HOUR.
OKAY, FINE. ARE YOU READING *MARY POPPINS*?
BZZZZZZZZZT!
THAT MEANS YOU WERE WRONG.
I'M GUESSING THE BUZZER WAS YOUR IDEA.
BB

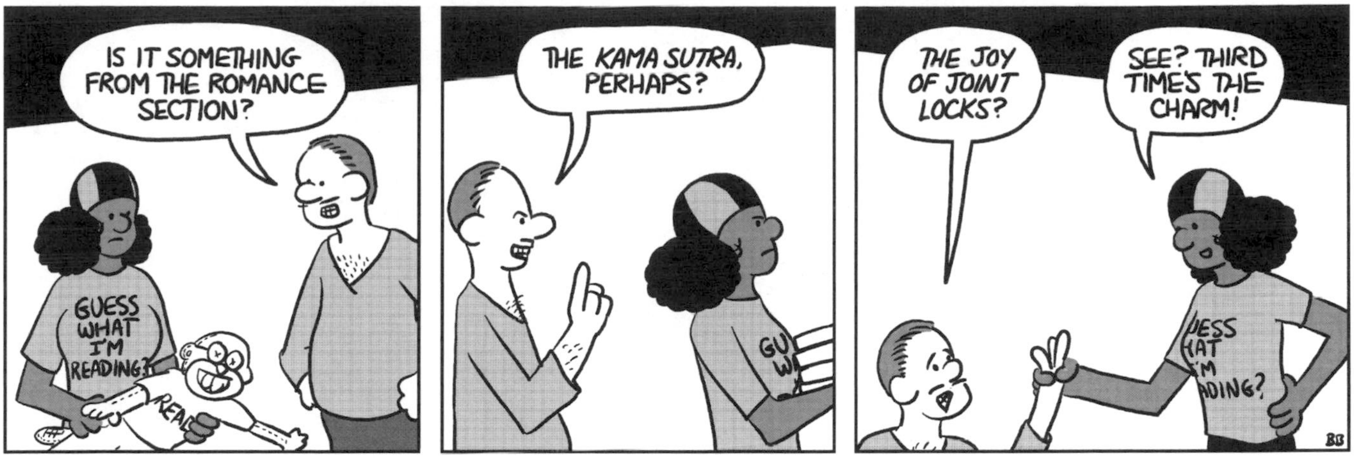
IS IT SOMETHING FROM THE ROMANCE SECTION?
THE *KAMA SUTRA*, PERHAPS?
THE JOY OF JOINT LOCKS?
SEE? THIRD TIME'S THE CHARM!
GUESS WHAT I'M READING?

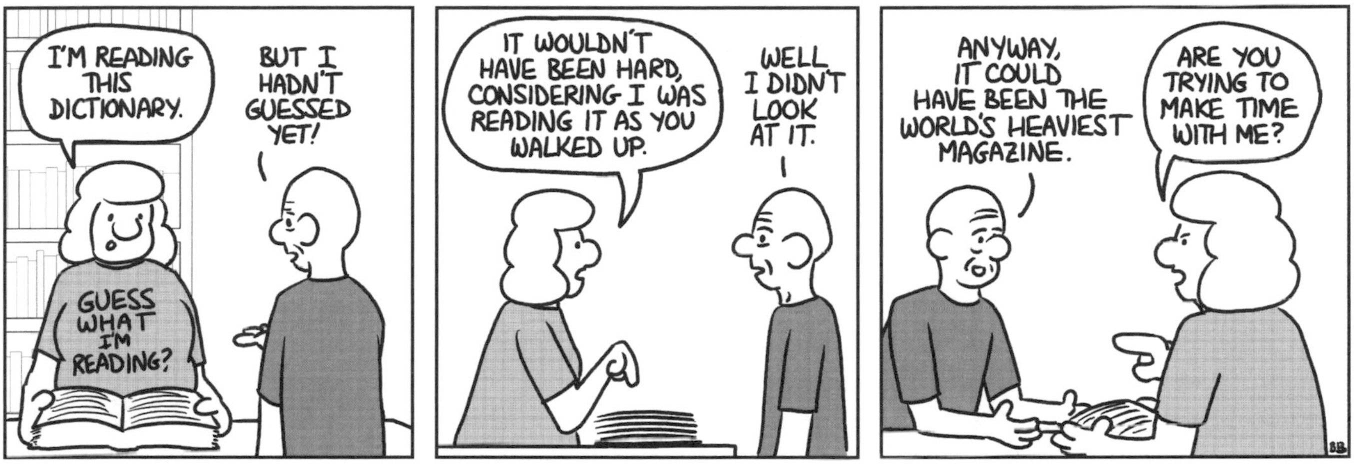
I'M READING THIS DICTIONARY.
BUT I HADN'T GUESSED YET!
GUESS WHAT I'M READING?
IT WOULDN'T HAVE BEEN HARD, CONSIDERING I WAS READING IT AS YOU WALKED UP.
WELL I DIDN'T LOOK AT IT.
ANYWAY, IT COULD HAVE BEEN THE WORLD'S HEAVIEST MAGAZINE.
ARE YOU TRYING TO MAKE TIME WITH ME?

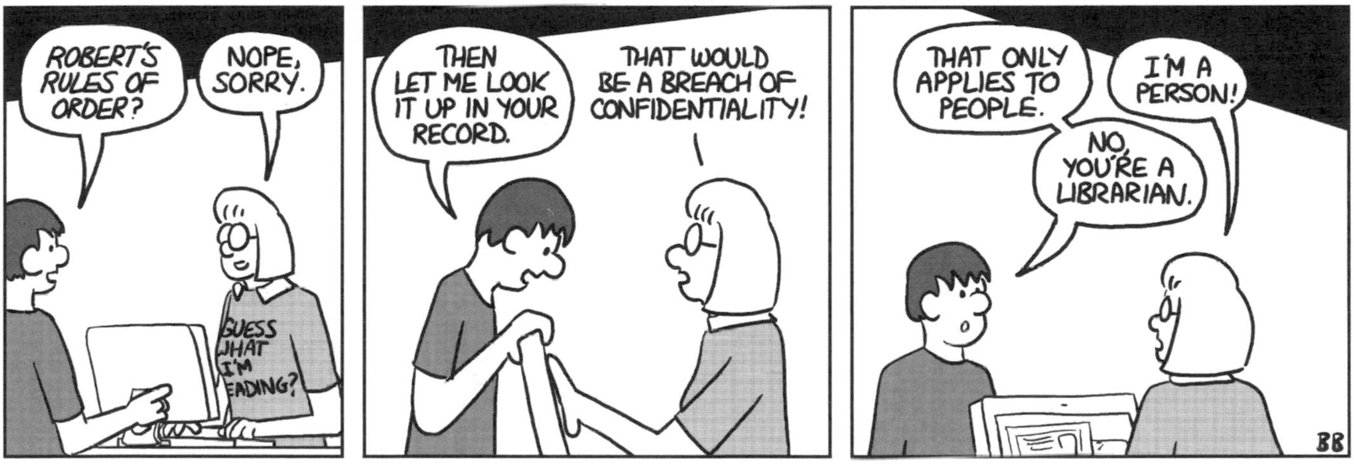
ROBERT'S RULES OF ORDER?
NOPE, SORRY.
THEN LET ME LOOK IT UP IN YOUR RECORD.
THAT WOULD BE A BREACH OF CONFIDENTIALITY!
THAT ONLY APPLIES TO PEOPLE.
I'M A PERSON!
NO, YOU'RE A LIBRARIAN.

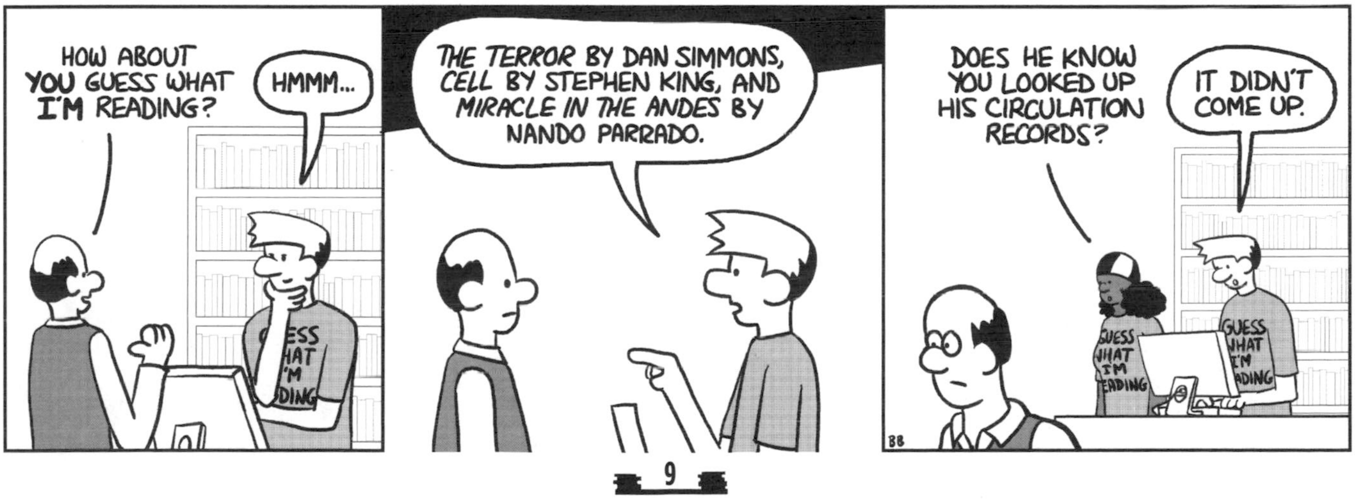
HOW ABOUT **YOU** GUESS WHAT **I'M** READING?
HMMM...
THE TERROR BY DAN SIMMONS, *CELL* BY STEPHEN KING, AND *MIRACLE IN THE ANDES* BY NANDO PARRADO.
DOES HE KNOW YOU LOOKED UP HIS CIRCULATION RECORDS?
IT DIDN'T COME UP.

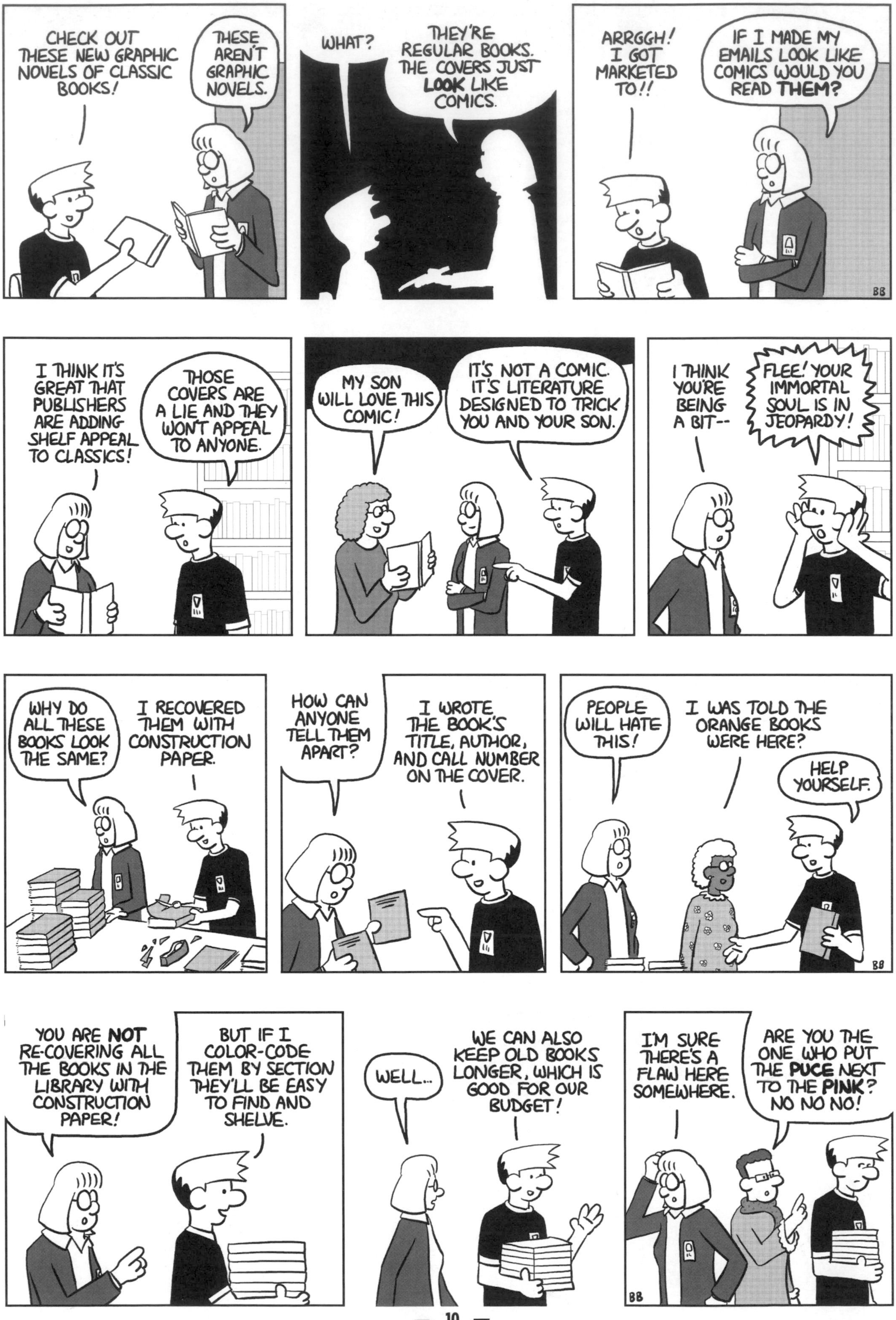
CHECK OUT THESE NEW GRAPHIC NOVELS OF CLASSIC BOOKS!
THESE AREN'T GRAPHIC NOVELS.
WHAT?
THEY'RE REGULAR BOOKS. THE COVERS JUST **LOOK** LIKE COMICS.
ARRGGH! I GOT MARKETED TO!!
IF I MADE MY EMAILS LOOK LIKE COMICS WOULD YOU READ **THEM?**
BB
I THINK IT'S GREAT THAT PUBLISHERS ARE ADDING SHELF APPEAL TO CLASSICS!
THOSE COVERS ARE A LIE AND THEY WON'T APPEAL TO ANYONE.
MY SON WILL LOVE THIS COMIC!
IT'S NOT A COMIC. IT'S LITERATURE DESIGNED TO TRICK YOU AND YOUR SON.
I THINK YOU'RE BEING A BIT--
FLEE! YOUR IMMORTAL SOUL IS IN JEOPARDY!
WHY DO ALL THESE BOOKS LOOK THE SAME?
I RECOVERED THEM WITH CONSTRUCTION PAPER.
HOW CAN ANYONE TELL THEM APART?
I WROTE THE BOOK'S TITLE, AUTHOR, AND CALL NUMBER ON THE COVER.
PEOPLE WILL HATE THIS!
I WAS TOLD THE ORANGE BOOKS WERE HERE?
HELP YOURSELF.
BB
YOU ARE **NOT** RE-COVERING ALL THE BOOKS IN THE LIBRARY WITH CONSTRUCTION PAPER!
BUT IF I COLOR-CODE THEM BY SECTION THEY'LL BE EASY TO FIND AND SHELVE.
WELL...
WE CAN ALSO KEEP OLD BOOKS LONGER, WHICH IS GOOD FOR OUR BUDGET!
I'M SURE THERE'S A FLAW HERE SOMEWHERE.
ARE YOU THE ONE WHO PUT THE **PUCE** NEXT TO THE **PINK**? NO NO NO!
BB

I'M THE SMARTEST PERSON IN THIS LIBRARY!

NEXT TO ME YOU ARE ALL INTELLECTUAL LILLIPUTIANS!

I NEED A BOOK. BUT IT'S GOT TO BE CHALLENGING!

THEN LET ME SHOW YOU THE BOOKS ON MANNERS.

ISN'T THAT A "GIRL COMIC"?

IT'S MY RESPONSIBILITY TO GIVE IT A SHOT.

WHAT'S WITH THE GLASSES? IS THE COMIC 3-D?

NO, IT'S JUST VERY PINK. SO I RE-TASKED THE GLASSES THAT CAME WITH MY SPY KIDS DVD.

I'M CONFUSED BY THE EFFORT YOU'RE PUTTING INTO THIS.

IF I CAN'T TAKE IT I'M GOING TO STUFF THE "GIRL-FRIENDLY" SECTION WITH ZOMBIE COMICS.

THE WELL OF SOULS IS LOCATED IN BARTLETT'S FAMOUS QUOTATIONS!

I NEVER KNOW WHAT HE'S TALKING ABOUT.

HE SEEMS TRIUMPHANT. THAT'S USUALLY A BAD SIGN.

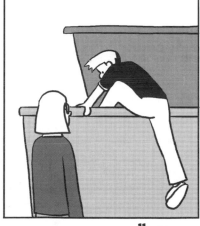

THAT DOESN'T LOOK SAFE.

3PO! SHUT DOWN ALL THE GARBAGE MASHERS ON THE DETENTION LEVEL!

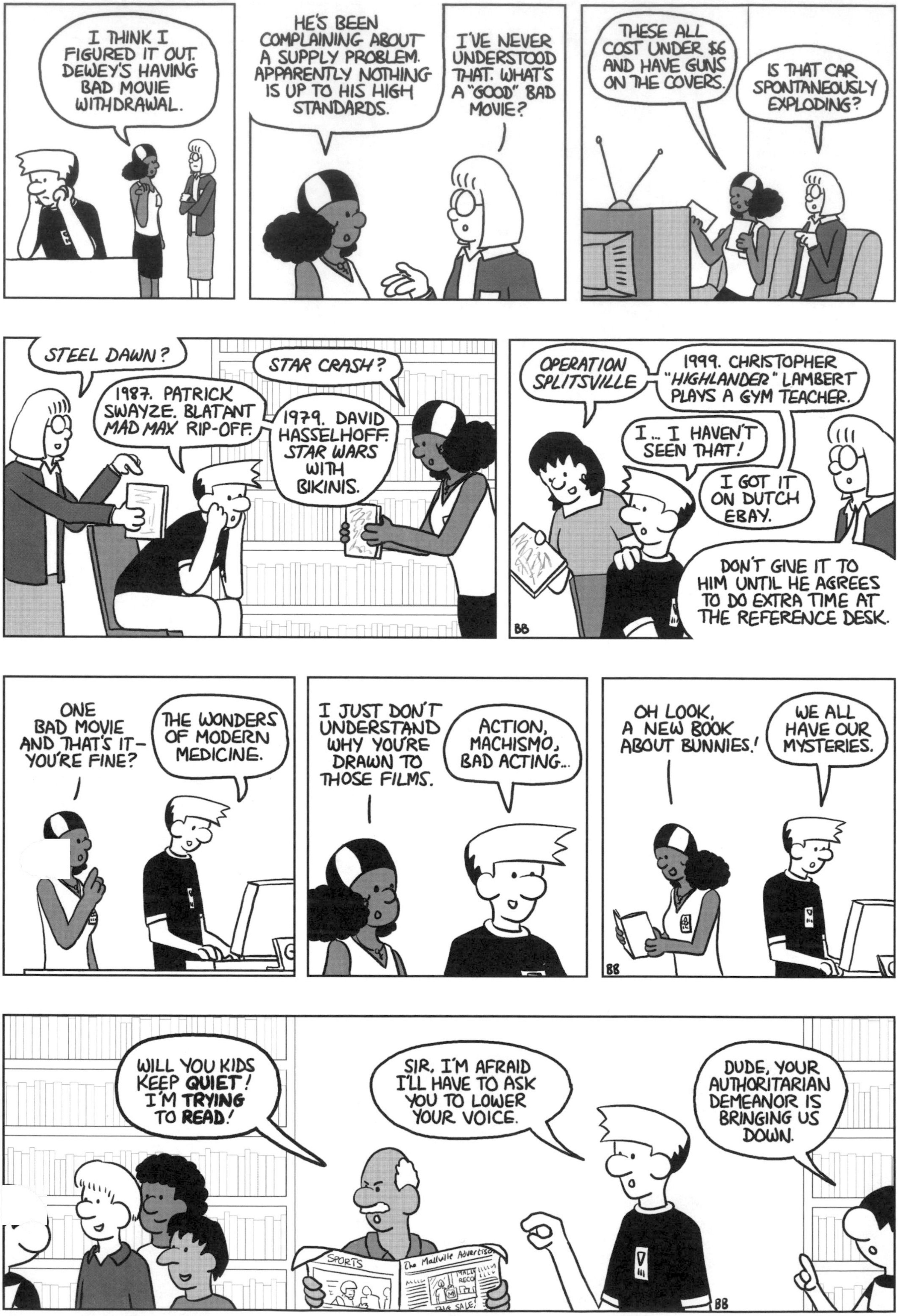
I THINK I FIGURED IT OUT. DEWEY'S HAVING BAD MOVIE WITHDRAWAL.
HE'S BEEN COMPLAINING ABOUT A SUPPLY PROBLEM. APPARENTLY NOTHING IS UP TO HIS HIGH STANDARDS.
I'VE NEVER UNDERSTOOD THAT. WHAT'S A "GOOD" BAD MOVIE?
THESE ALL COST UNDER $6 AND HAVE GUNS ON THE COVERS.
IS THAT CAR SPONTANEOUSLY EXPLODING?
STEEL DAWN?
1987. PATRICK SWAYZE. BLATANT MAD MAX RIP-OFF.
STAR CRASH?
1979. DAVID HASSELHOFF. STAR WARS WITH BIKINIS.
OPERATION SPLITSVILLE
1999. CHRISTOPHER "HIGHLANDER" LAMBERT PLAYS A GYM TEACHER.
I... I HAVEN'T SEEN THAT!
I GOT IT ON DUTCH EBAY.
DON'T GIVE IT TO HIM UNTIL HE AGREES TO DO EXTRA TIME AT THE REFERENCE DESK.
BB
ONE BAD MOVIE AND THAT'S IT— YOU'RE FINE?
THE WONDERS OF MODERN MEDICINE.
I JUST DON'T UNDERSTAND WHY YOU'RE DRAWN TO THOSE FILMS.
ACTION, MACHISMO, BAD ACTING...
OH LOOK, A NEW BOOK ABOUT BUNNIES!
WE ALL HAVE OUR MYSTERIES.
BB
WILL YOU KIDS KEEP QUIET! I'M TRYING TO READ!
SIR, I'M AFRAID I'LL HAVE TO ASK YOU TO LOWER YOUR VOICE.
DUDE, YOUR AUTHORITARIAN DEMEANOR IS BRINGING US DOWN.
SPORTS
The Mallville Advertiser
BB

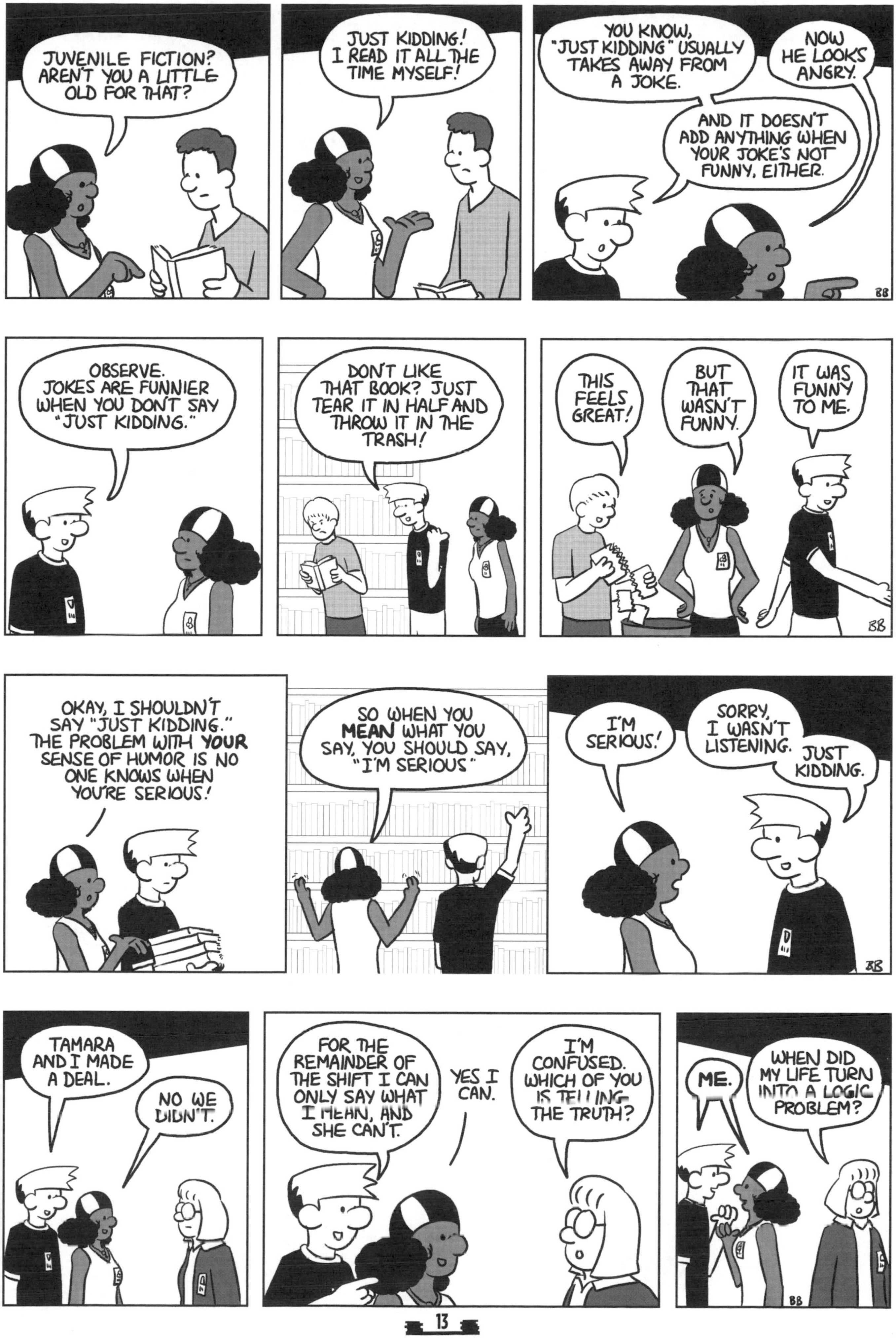
JUVENILE FICTION? AREN'T YOU A LITTLE OLD FOR THAT?
JUST KIDDING! I READ IT ALL THE TIME MYSELF!
YOU KNOW, "JUST KIDDING" USUALLY TAKES AWAY FROM A JOKE.
NOW HE LOOKS ANGRY.
AND IT DOESN'T ADD ANYTHING WHEN YOUR JOKE'S NOT FUNNY, EITHER.
BB
OBSERVE. JOKES ARE FUNNIER WHEN YOU DON'T SAY "JUST KIDDING."
DON'T LIKE THAT BOOK? JUST TEAR IT IN HALF AND THROW IT IN THE TRASH!
THIS FEELS GREAT!
BUT THAT WASN'T FUNNY.
IT WAS FUNNY TO ME.
BB
OKAY, I SHOULDN'T SAY "JUST KIDDING." THE PROBLEM WITH **YOUR** SENSE OF HUMOR IS NO ONE KNOWS WHEN YOU'RE SERIOUS!
SO WHEN YOU **MEAN** WHAT YOU SAY, YOU SHOULD SAY, "I'M SERIOUS"
I'M SERIOUS!
SORRY, I WASN'T LISTENING.
JUST KIDDING.
BB
TAMARA AND I MADE A DEAL.
NO WE DIDN'T.
FOR THE REMAINDER OF THE SHIFT I CAN ONLY SAY WHAT I MEAN, AND SHE CAN'T.
YES I CAN.
I'M CONFUSED. WHICH OF YOU IS TELLING THE TRUTH?
ME.
WHEN DID MY LIFE TURN INTO A LOGIC PROBLEM?
BB

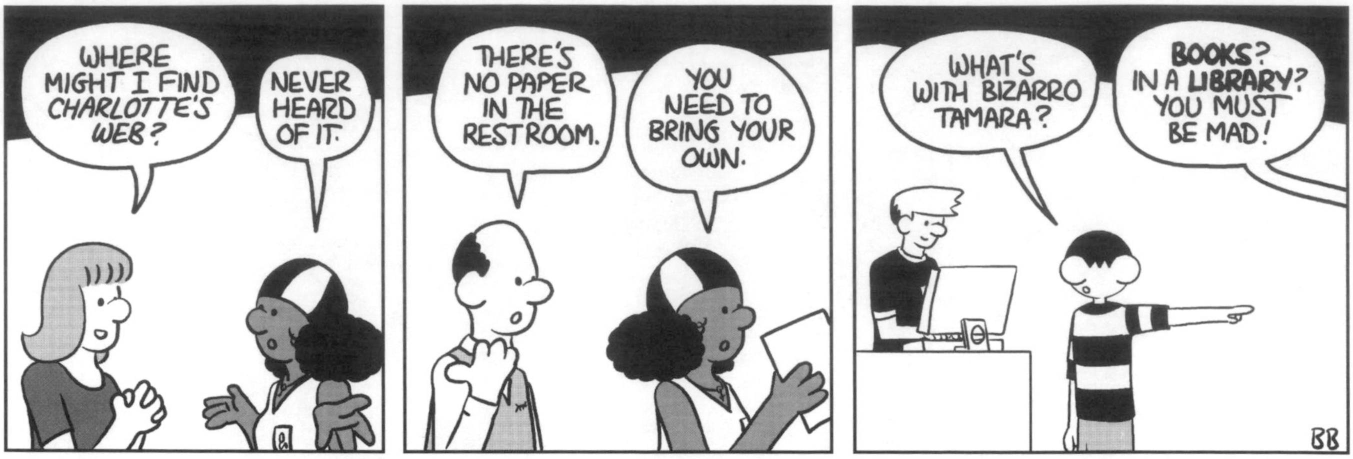
WHERE MIGHT I FIND CHARLOTTE'S WEB?
NEVER HEARD OF IT.
THERE'S NO PAPER IN THE RESTROOM.
YOU NEED TO BRING YOUR OWN.
WHAT'S WITH BIZARRO TAMARA?
BOOKS? IN A LIBRARY? YOU MUST BE MAD!
BB

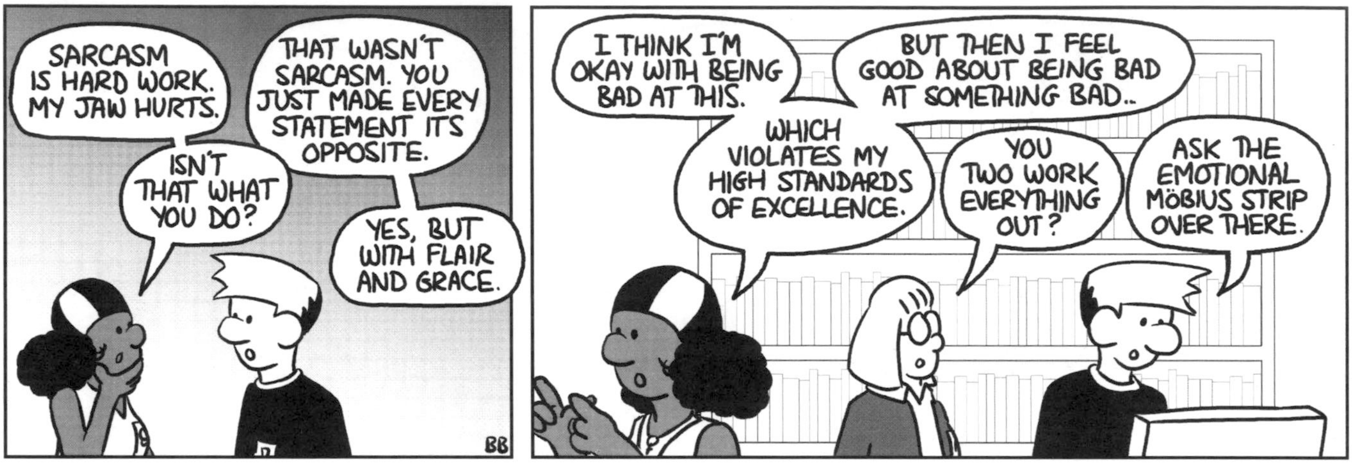
SARCASM IS HARD WORK. MY JAW HURTS.
THAT WASN'T SARCASM. YOU JUST MADE EVERY STATEMENT ITS OPPOSITE.
ISN'T THAT WHAT YOU DO?
YES, BUT WITH FLAIR AND GRACE.
BB
I THINK I'M OKAY WITH BEING BAD AT THIS.
BUT THEN I FEEL GOOD ABOUT BEING BAD AT SOMETHING BAD..
WHICH VIOLATES MY HIGH STANDARDS OF EXCELLENCE.
YOU TWO WORK EVERYTHING OUT?
ASK THE EMOTIONAL MÖBIUS STRIP OVER THERE.

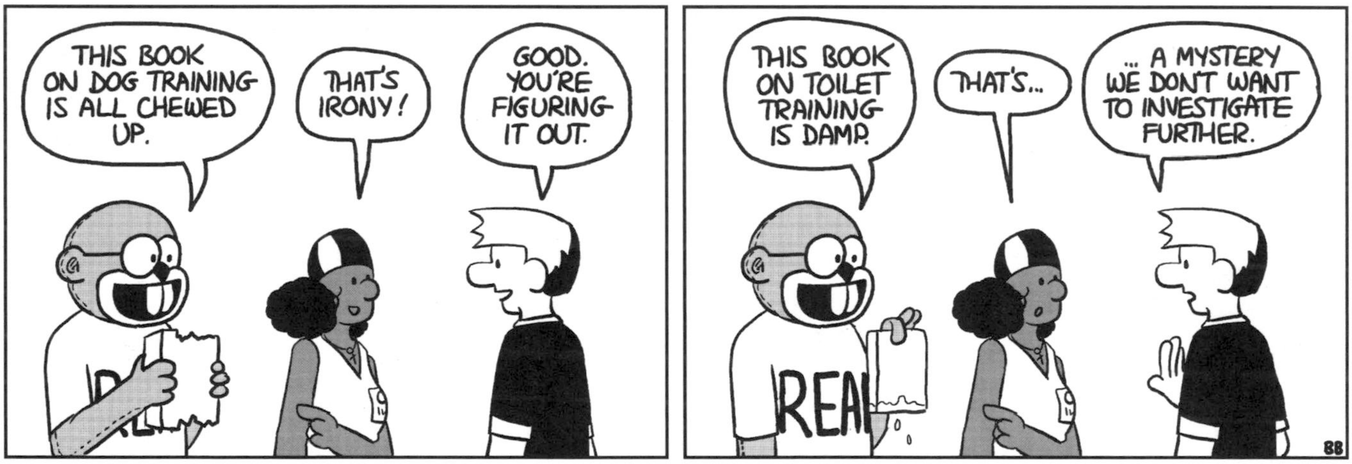
THIS BOOK ON DOG TRAINING IS ALL CHEWED UP.
THAT'S IRONY!
GOOD. YOU'RE FIGURING IT OUT.
THIS BOOK ON TOILET TRAINING IS DAMP.
THAT'S...
... A MYSTERY WE DON'T WANT TO INVESTIGATE FURTHER.
REA
BB

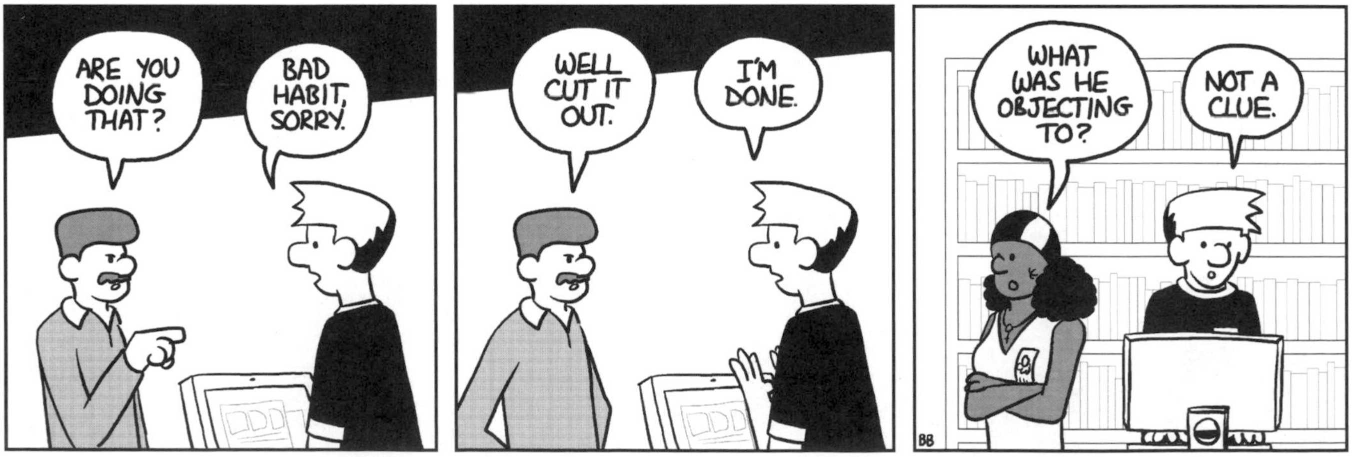
ARE YOU DOING THAT?
BAD HABIT, SORRY.
WELL CUT IT OUT.
I'M DONE.
WHAT WAS HE OBJECTING TO?
NOT A CLUE.
BB

The Great Plastic Coffee Cup Lid Comic Strip Challenge

It all started with Gene's hatred of the nasty things, and his attempt to channel that passion into an Unshelved *sequence. Said attempt was a spectacular failure, but we observed that it was just the sort of leaden subject that Dave Kellett alchemically turns into comedy gold every day in* Sheldon (www.sheldoncomics.com). *That got us feeling competitive, and before we knew it we had challenged him to a duel of comic strippery, now collected together here for the very first time.*

We felt some color commentary was in order, so we called upon esteemed (and enmustached) webcomics journalist Gary Tyrrell. Take it away, Gary.

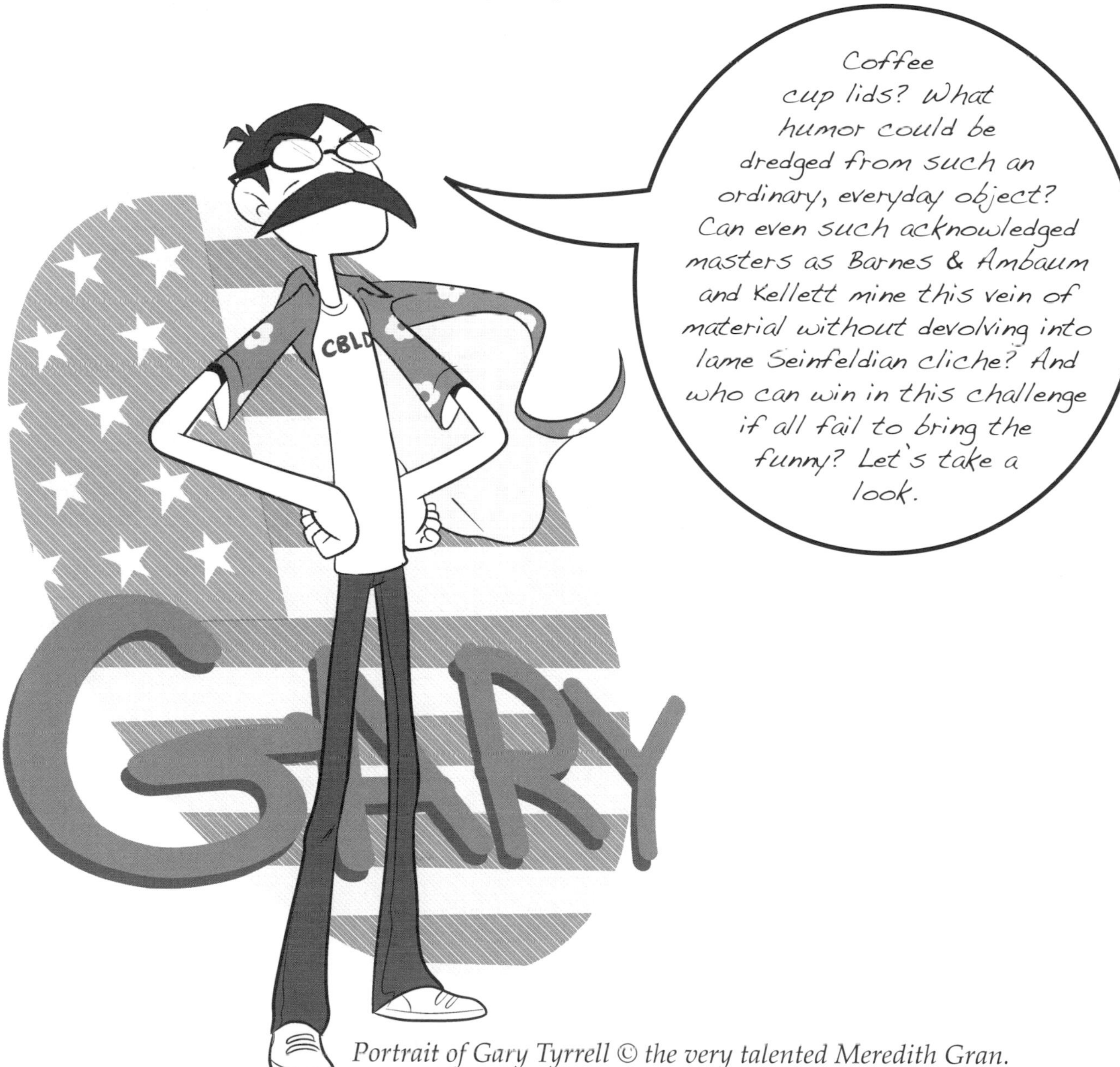
Coffee cup lids? What humor could be dredged from such an ordinary, everyday object? Can even such acknowledged masters as Barnes & Ambaum and Kellett mine this vein of material without devolving into lame Seinfeldian cliche? And who can win in this challenge if all fail to bring the funny? Let's take a look.
CBLD
GARY

Portrait of Gary Tyrrell © the very talented Meredith Gran. Read her comic strip Octopus Pie (www.octopuspie.com).

I SENSE A TIRADE COMING ON.
IS IT ABOUT STAR WARS AGAIN? BECAUSE IF IT IS I'M GOING HOME SICK.

Unshelved takes a sidelong approach to the topic at hand (indeed, one might suspect that the theme for the week was actually "Star Wars"), treating the lids themselves as catalyst for (one would hope) future laugh-chuckles. While not about coffe cup lids per se, one may hope that this strip is merely to intrigue the comedic palate and prime it for what is to come. An amuse bouche, indeed.

LET'S COMPARE, SHALL WE? THE COFFEE CUP LID VS. THE SIPPY CUP
BOTH HAVE TINY, IMPOSSIBLE HOLES TO DEAL WITH
BOTH INVARIABLY DRIBBLE DOWN YOUR CHIN
BOTH ARE DESIGNED TO AVOID SPILLS WITH PEOPLE WHO DON'T KNOW BETTER ("CAUTION! THE DRINK YOU'RE ABOUT TO ENJOY IS EXTREMELY HOT. ...YOU DOOFUS. IT'S COFFEE.")
BOTH ARE DESIGNED FOR PEOPLE IN SIMILAR EMOTIONAL STATES
MA-MA!! I WANT MEEEELK!
MA-MA! I WANT DOUBLE-TALL LATTE WITH CREEEEEAM!

Sheldon, by contrast, forgoes the subtle mise-en-scene and tackles the topic head on and by name. Coffee cups are contrasted directly to the also-ubiquitous "sippy cup", leading to the classic humor trope of comparing things that are unalike (babies and old people) to show how truly similar they are. Plus it has Grover. Grover's cool.

WINNER: sheldon

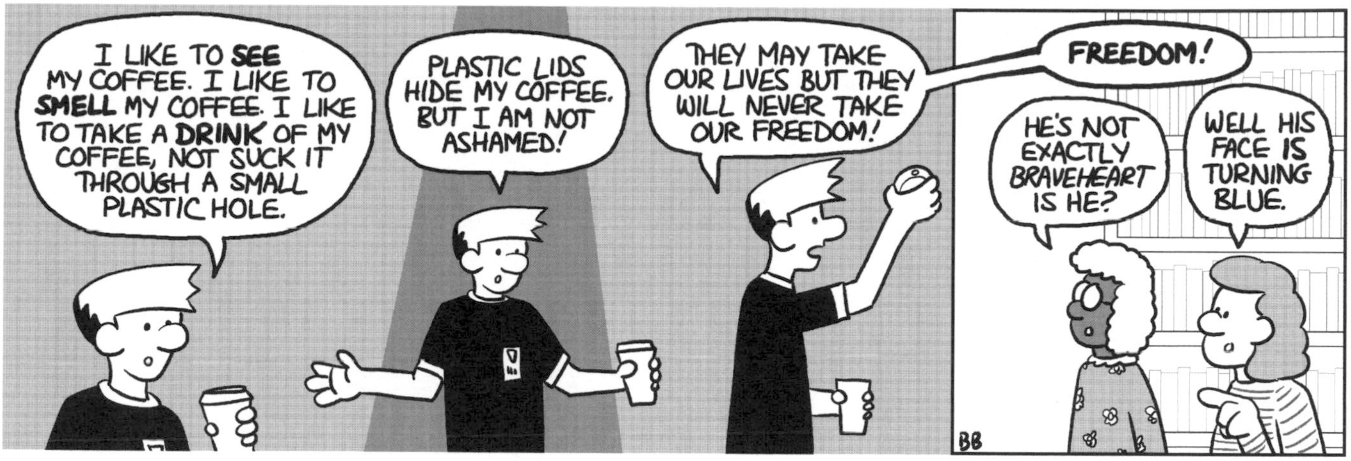
I LIKE TO SEE MY COFFEE. I LIKE TO SMELL MY COFFEE. I LIKE TO TAKE A DRINK OF MY COFFEE, NOT SUCK IT THROUGH A SMALL PLASTIC HOLE.
PLASTIC LIDS HIDE MY COFFEE. BUT I AM NOT ASHAMED!
THEY MAY TAKE OUR LIVES BUT THEY WILL NEVER TAKE OUR FREEDOM!
FREEDOM!
HE'S NOT EXACTLY BRAVEHEART IS HE?
WELL HIS FACE IS TURNING BLUE.
BB

Unshelved moves to directly reference coffee cups, but in a surprise move also keeps with the movie theme brought up yesterday. Indeed, the bombastic, over-the-top histrionics of "Braveheart" are most appropriate as a model here, as one can only hope that Dewey remembers what happened to Mel Gibson at the end of that movie. Yelling your head off in a library, Dewey? YOUR library? Disembowelment's too good for you.

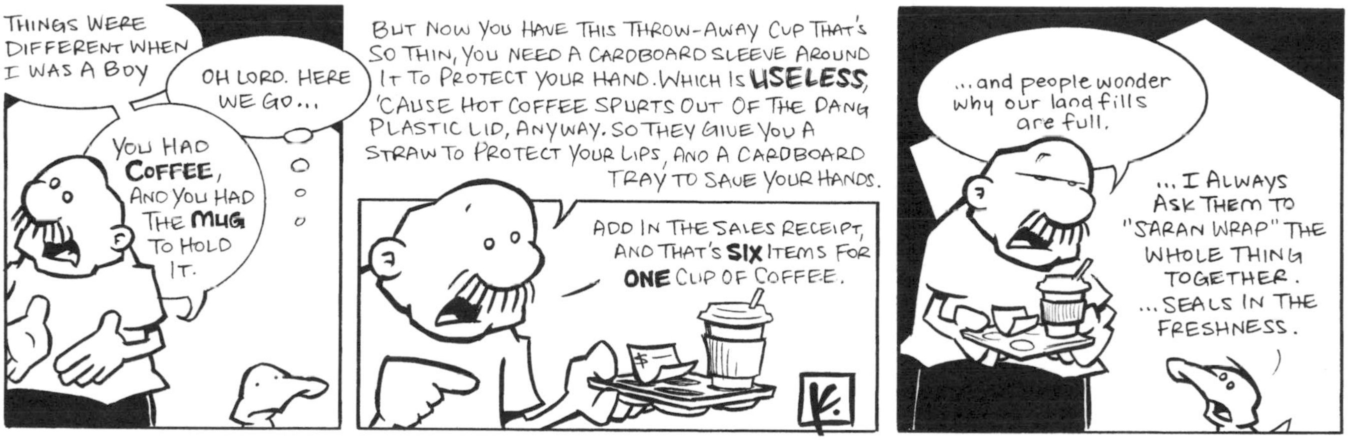
THINGS WERE DIFFERENT WHEN I WAS A BOY
OH LORD. HERE WE GO...
YOU HAD COFFEE, AND YOU HAD THE MUG TO HOLD IT.
BUT NOW YOU HAVE THIS THROW-AWAY CUP THAT'S SO THIN, YOU NEED A CARDBOARD SLEEVE AROUND IT TO PROTECT YOUR HAND. WHICH IS USELESS, 'CAUSE HOT COFFEE SPURTS OUT OF THE DANG PLASTIC LID, ANYWAY. SO THEY GIVE YOU A STRAW TO PROTECT YOUR LIPS, AND A CARDBOARD TRAY TO SAVE YOUR HANDS.
ADD IN THE SALES RECEIPT, AND THAT'S SIX ITEMS FOR ONE CUP OF COFFEE.
...and people wonder why our landfills are full.
...I ALWAYS ASK THEM TO "SARAN WRAP" THE WHOLE THING TOGETHER. ...SEALS IN THE FRESHNESS.

Sheldon also looks to complement the primary theme with the secondary theme of classic comedy tropes, here launching into the classic, "When I was a kid" approach. Unfortunately, crusty old Gramp undercuts the effectiveness of this as, instead of pining for the good old days of the Eisenhower administration, he reduces himself to a hippie tree-hugger whining about ecological sustainability. Get a job and a haircut, hippie!

WINNER: UNSHELVED®

NO LID? BUT THE BEVERAGE YOU'RE ABOUT TO ENJOY IS EXTREMELY HOT!
YOU MIGHT SCALD YOURSELF, EXPOSING OUR CORPORATION TO MASSIVE LAWSUITS!
BUT DON'T WORRY, I'LL HELP ENSURE YOUR PERSONAL SAFETY.
HAVE A LITIGATION-FREE DAY!
BB

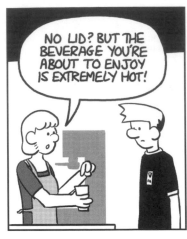

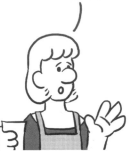

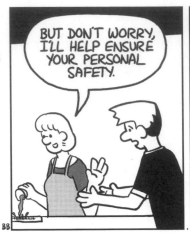

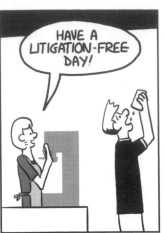

No more time for movie linkages at Unshelved as Dewey, seeking to take back what little control he has over his life, demands his coffee without a lid! Tragically, his attempt to transform himself into Master of his Existence via indomitable Will is derailed by a curiously tattoo- and piercing-free barrista. You have run headlong into the Immovable Object to your Will's Irresistable Force, Dewey: the threat of a personal-injury lawsuit. Enjoy what little coffee The Man will permit you, knowing that those few drops represent you, an insignificant cog in the omnipresent machine.

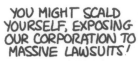

A filmed presentation by:
CROTCHLEY LABS
COPY-RIGHT 1955

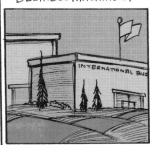

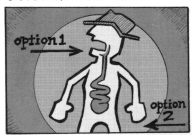

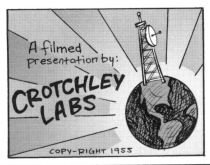

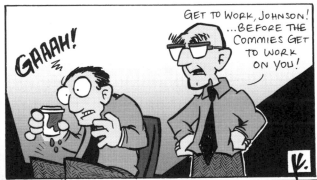

EVER WONDER WHERE THE COFFEE CUP LID CAME FROM? WHY, IT CAME FROM THE GOOD FOLKS AT INTERNATIONAL BUSINESS MACHINES!
INTERNATIONAL BUS
IN 1952, IBM MANAGERS REALIZED IT TOOK LAZY EMPLOYEES 35 MINUTES TO "WAKE UP" BY DRINKING COFFEE. BUT IT TOOK MERE SECONDS IF THEY SPILLED JET-HOT, MOLTEN COFFEE ON THEIR GROIN
option 1
option 2
SO IBM COMMISSIONED CROTCHLEY LABS TO DESIGN A COFFEE CUP LID THAT COULD DO JUST THAT!
GAAAH!
GET TO WORK, JOHNSON! ...BEFORE THE COMMIES GET TO WORK ON YOU!

Meanwhile, at Sheldon, did somebody say "Eisenhower administration"? Kellett busts open the traditional four-panel strip template and takes us on a journey of newsreel exposition to a better time, a better place, to explore the origins of coffee cup lids.

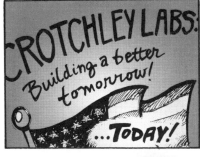

CROTCHLEY LABS:
Building a better tomorrow!
...TODAY!

Black and white visuals, flapping flags, a scratchy soundtrack, men in fedoras, and the ever-present threat of the international communist conspiracy all collude to construct an unassailable fortress of funny. Plus, he totally said "crotch".

WINNER: sheldon

THURSDAY

I HEARD YOU WERE GIVING UP PLASTIC! YOU MUST FEEL GRAND!
I'M ONLY GIVING UP COFFEE LIDS.
YOU'RE TAKING YOUR FIRST STEPS TOWARD ENVIRONMENTALISM!
I'M ESCHEWING AN UNNECESSARY ANNOYANCE.
YOU'RE SAVING THE WORLD, WHETHER YOU WANT TO OR NOT!
TELL YOU WHAT. EVERY TIME I BUY COFFEE I'LL THROW OUT AN UNUSED LID.
THAT'S... THAT'S...
NOW I FEEL GRAND.
BB

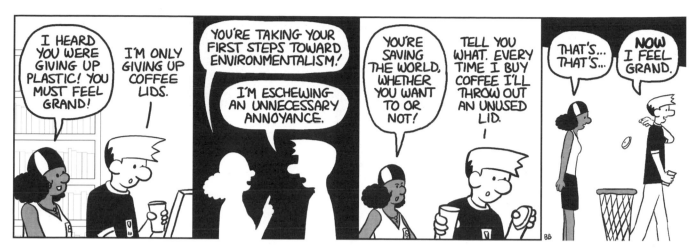

In a curious reversal, Unshelved takes up the abandoned environmental theme from Sheldon, and again uses the agreed-upon theme of the week ("coffee cup lids", for those coming in late) almost as a background element. Here the intent seems more for Dewey to again annoy Tamara with his cruel barbs, leading one to wonder if he might be brutally injured in retaliation in the remaining two days of the challenge. One can only hope!

A filmed presentation by:
"CROTCHLEY LABS trade-mark"
FILMED IN KODAK VISI-TRUE TECNA-SCOPE!

ONCE THE FLIMSY COFFEE CUP LID MADE ITS WAY INTO THE AMERICAN WORKFORCE, PRODUCTIVITY SOARED!
I JUST INVENTED THE AUTOMATIC TRANSMISSION!
YES — PROGRESS! SCIENCE! INDUSTRY! THAT'S THE AMERICAN WAY, AND THAT'S THE CROTCHLEY LABS WAY!
DON'T BUY CANADIAN!
....AND IT'S THAT SAME GO-GO SPIRIT THAT WILL GET US A PERMANENT MOONBASE BY 1959!
HUZZAH! THANKS, COFFEE-CUP LID!

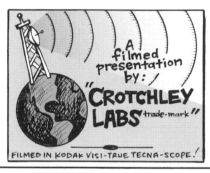

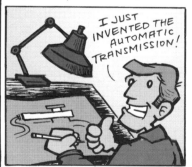

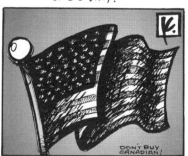

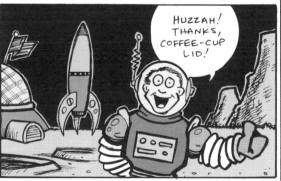

Sheldon, knowing a good thing when it sees one, stays with the "Crotchley Labs" leitmotif, reminding us with a misty-teared nostalgia how big our country's dreams once were. Oh, how we

CROTCHLEY LABS...
A BRIGHTER FUTURE THROUGH SPILLED COFFEE!!
KNOW A COMMUNIST? CALL KLONDIKE-5-5-1

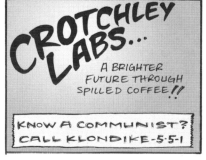

dreamed as we bestrode the world like unto a colossus. Oh, that we might shape all we that beheld once again.

WINNER: sheldon

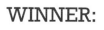

LIBRARY POLICY. BEVERAGES NEED LIDS!
THIS ISN'T A BEVERAGE. IT'S A LIFE-SUSTAINING THERAPEUTIC INFUSION!
YOU MAKE IT SOUND LIKE SOMETHING YOU'D PUT IN AN I.V. DRIP.
NO, NO... TOO HOT.
BUT KEEP THOSE IDEAS COMING!
BB

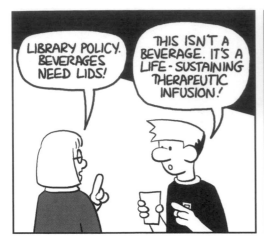

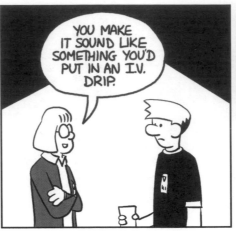

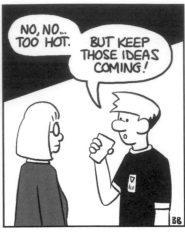

Slowly and with much deliberation, the disparate threads of the week have resolved themselves at Unshelved. As was hinted on Wednesday, the week is less about coffee cup lids and more about Dewey's Quixote-like quest to assert some measure of control in his life, to have that little scrap of dignity in his day-to-day existence. It is, of course, denied by Mel's insistence on the status quo, and Dewey's casual disregard of those in power will cost him dearly. The dramatic underscore is rising to a blistering crescendo, and the reader can only wonder breathlessly where it will all end.

A film by
CROTCHLEY LABS
MAKERS OF LUNGLY CIGARETTES
THEY'RE GOOD FOR YOU!

COFFEE! IT'S THE ALL-AMERICAN DRINK! GROWN IN IOWA, IT'S AS AMERICAN AS MOM AND APPLE PIE!
JOHN VALDEZ
AND AT CROTCHLEY LABS, WE'RE DESIGNING BETTER COFFEE CUP LIDS THAT SPILL YOUR COFFEE FASTER! BECAUSE SPILLS EQUAL PRODUCTIVITY... AND "PRODUCTIVITY" IS JUST ANOTHER WAY TO SPELL "AMERICA"*
NO DAMES IN THE OFFICE
*IN YOUR HEART
YES.... IT'S THE FUTURE! AND CROTCHLEY LABS IS DRIVING YOU THERE FASTER!
USE BURMA SHAVE!

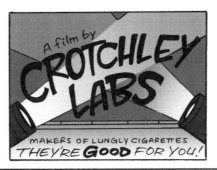

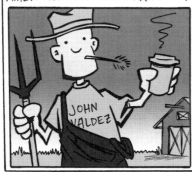

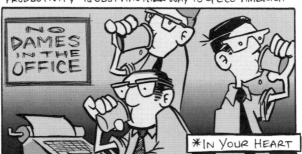

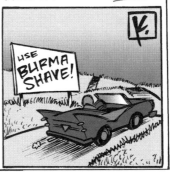

Sheldon, still stuck in the '50s, almost seems to have overstayed its welcome in that storied decade. Whereas one, or even two installments of past glories would stir the soul and drive all to regain that Utopian vision, a third merely reminds us of all we have lost. The Great Iowa Coffee Blight, the disastrous loss of tail-fins, the fact that every one of those office workers wound up replaced by robots built by 12 year olds from Bolivia ... the weight of nostalgia has become too great. The taste of this Proustian madeleine has become too bitter to bear.

THE END
AND REMEMBER, ADAM THE A-BOMB SEZ:
...I CAN'T HURT YOU WHEN YOU DUCK AND COVER!

WINNER: UNSHELVED

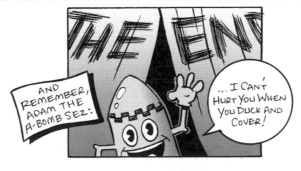

SATURDAY

AH-CHOO!
BLOOP!
WHERE ARE YOU GOING?
TO GET A COVERED CUP OF COFFEE.
BB

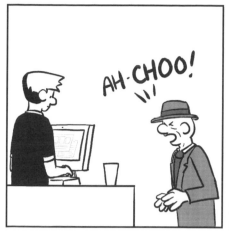

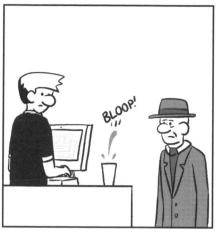

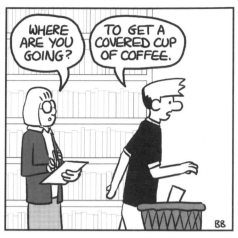

And when Dewey's Hero's Journey comes to an end, having endured travail and hardship, the prize of wisdom is his at last: coffee cup lids, far from being an unnecessary encumbrance, are a vital part of our everyday life as long as there exist disgusting old guys who won't cover their damn mouths when they sneeze. Somewhere in the distance, a lonely trumpet plays the stinger: wah wah wah-waaaaaaaaaaaah.

"COFFEE CUP LIDS"
HEY-O!

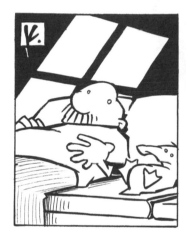

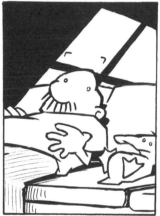

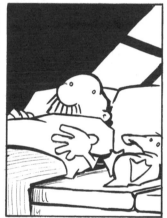

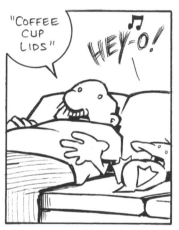

And in Sheldon, perhaps having spent all of the creative energy reserves on a trip back in time, there is nothing left to do but invoke the loveably affable Ed McMahon. But isn't Ed McMahon dead? Because if he is, that's in terrible taste. Or maybe I'm thinking of Abe Vigoda? DAMMIT SOMEBODY TELL ME IF I SHOULD BE ENJOYING THIS OR NOT.

WINNER: UNSHELVED

And so we come to the end of the week and find the competition all tied up. But really, when two of the best webcomics duel in such a fashion, can there really be a winner other than the reading public? I think not.

Gary Tyrrell doesn't make webcomics, but he writes about them on the internet. Enjoy his semi-abusive opinion-mongering at Fleen (www.fleen.com).

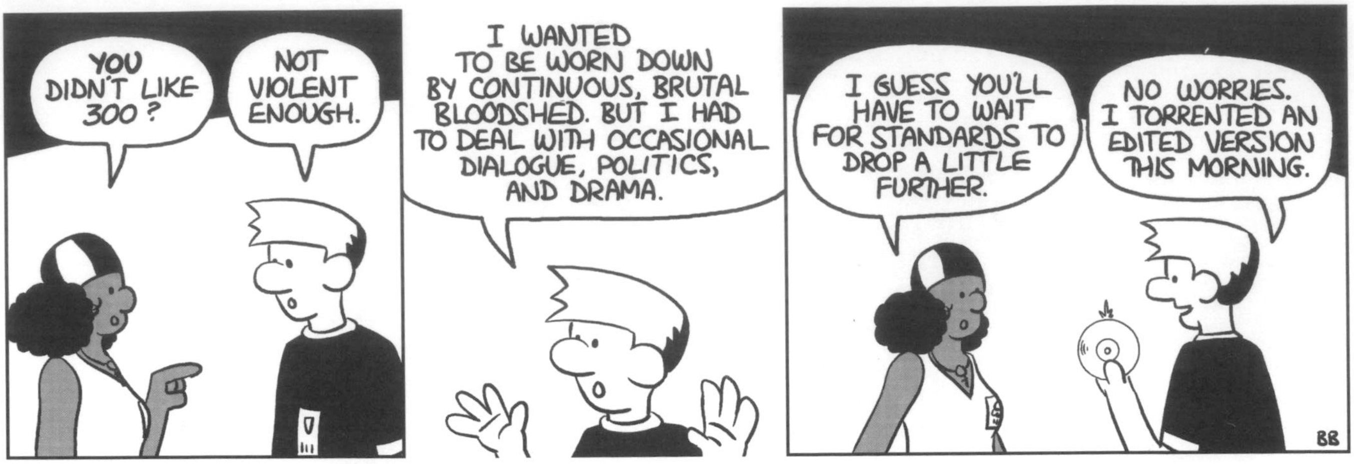
YOU DIDN'T LIKE 300?
NOT VIOLENT ENOUGH.
I WANTED TO BE WORN DOWN BY CONTINUOUS, BRUTAL BLOODSHED. BUT I HAD TO DEAL WITH OCCASIONAL DIALOGUE, POLITICS, AND DRAMA.
I GUESS YOU'LL HAVE TO WAIT FOR STANDARDS TO DROP A LITTLE FURTHER.
NO WORRIES. I TORRENTED AN EDITED VERSION THIS MORNING.
BB

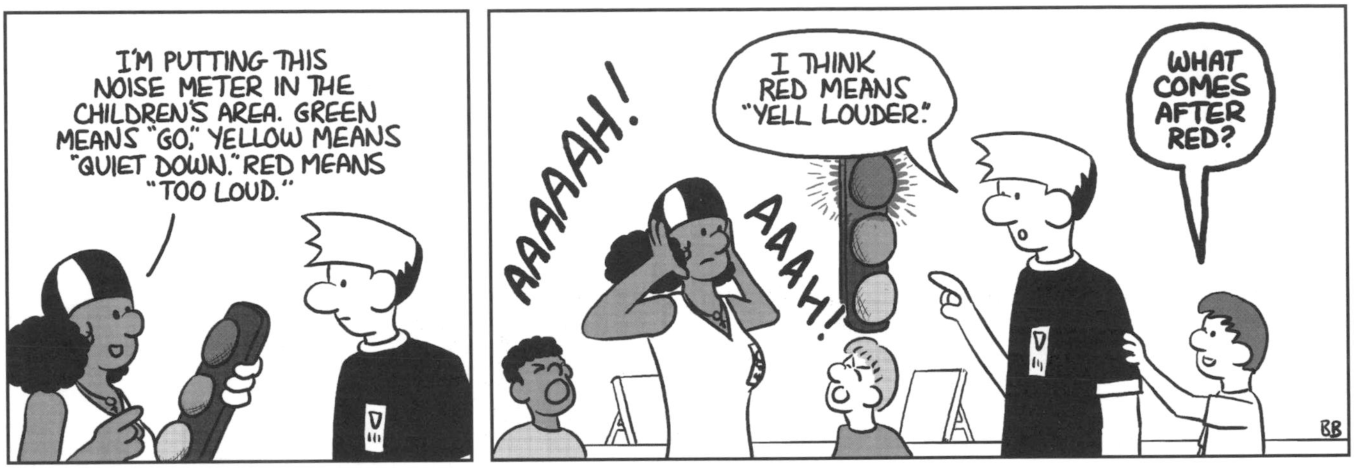
I'M PUTTING THIS NOISE METER IN THE CHILDREN'S AREA. GREEN MEANS "GO," YELLOW MEANS "QUIET DOWN." RED MEANS "TOO LOUD."
AAAAAH!
AAAAH!
I THINK RED MEANS "YELL LOUDER."
WHAT COMES AFTER RED?
BB

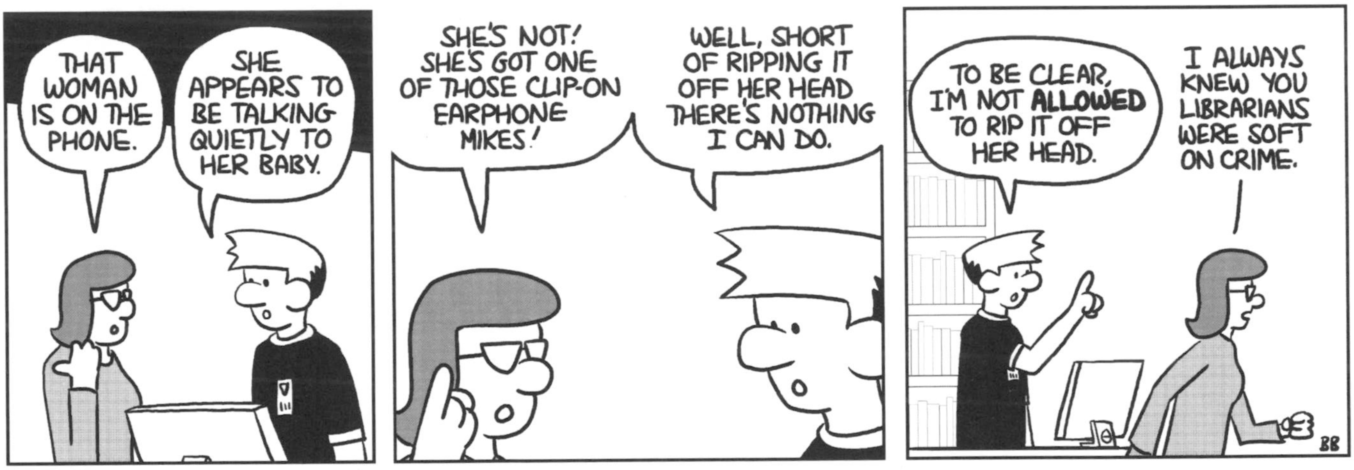
THAT WOMAN IS ON THE PHONE.
SHE APPEARS TO BE TALKING QUIETLY TO HER BABY.
SHE'S NOT! SHE'S GOT ONE OF THOSE CLIP-ON EARPHONE MIKES!
WELL, SHORT OF RIPPING IT OFF HER HEAD THERE'S NOTHING I CAN DO.
TO BE CLEAR, I'M NOT ALLOWED TO RIP IT OFF HER HEAD.
I ALWAYS KNEW YOU LIBRARIANS WERE SOFT ON CRIME.
BB

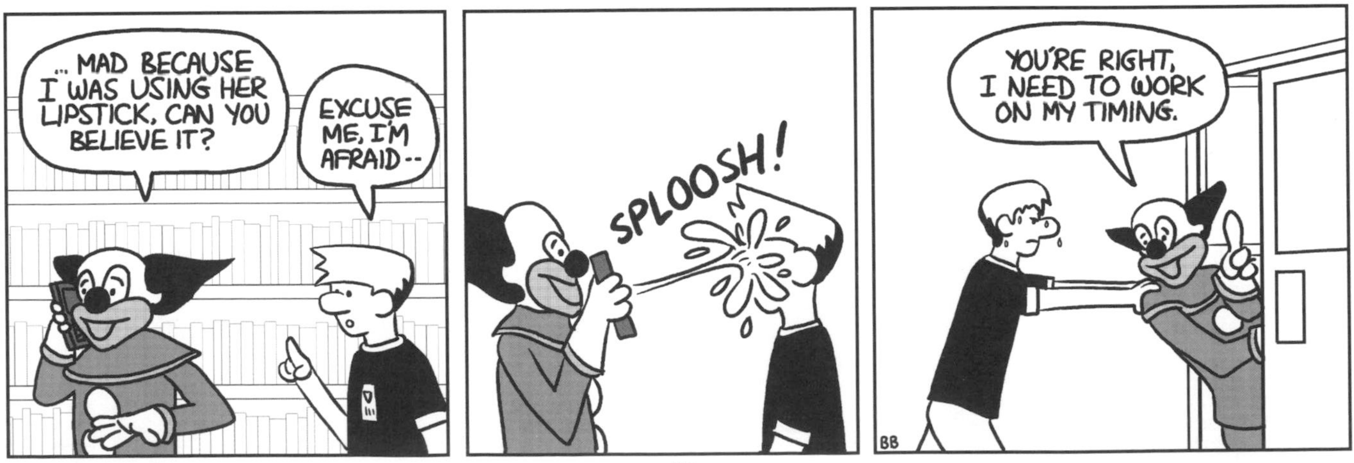
... MAD BECAUSE I WAS USING HER LIPSTICK. CAN YOU BELIEVE IT?
EXCUSE ME, I'M AFRAID--
SPLOOSH!
YOU'RE RIGHT, I NEED TO WORK ON MY TIMING.
BB

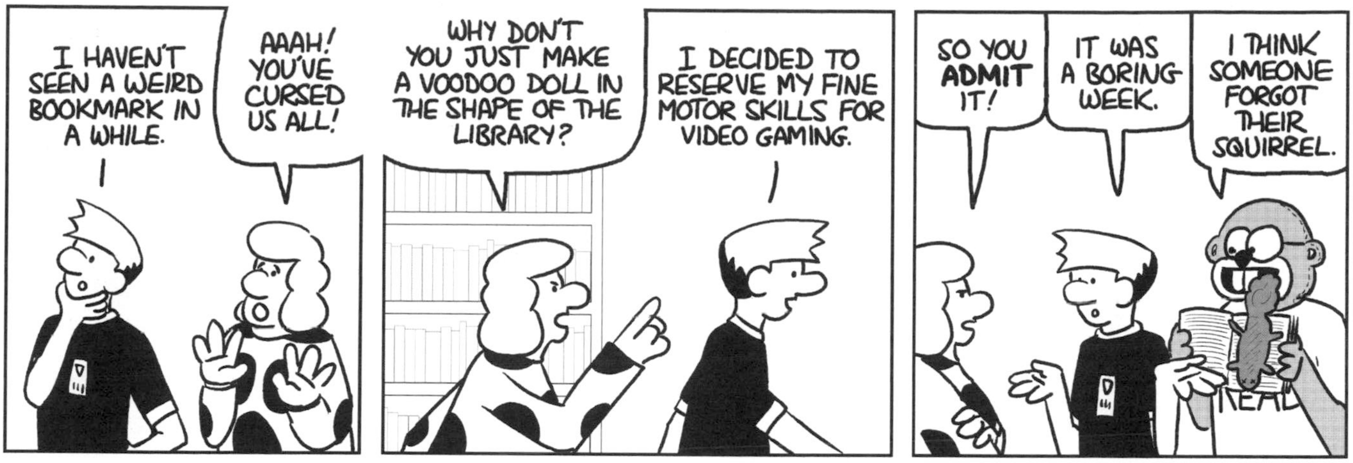
I HAVEN'T SEEN A WEIRD BOOKMARK IN A WHILE.
AAAH! YOU'VE CURSED US ALL!
WHY DON'T YOU JUST MAKE A VOODOO DOLL IN THE SHAPE OF THE LIBRARY?
I DECIDED TO RESERVE MY FINE MOTOR SKILLS FOR VIDEO GAMING.
SO YOU **ADMIT** IT!
IT WAS A BORING WEEK.
I THINK SOMEONE FORGOT THEIR SQUIRREL.

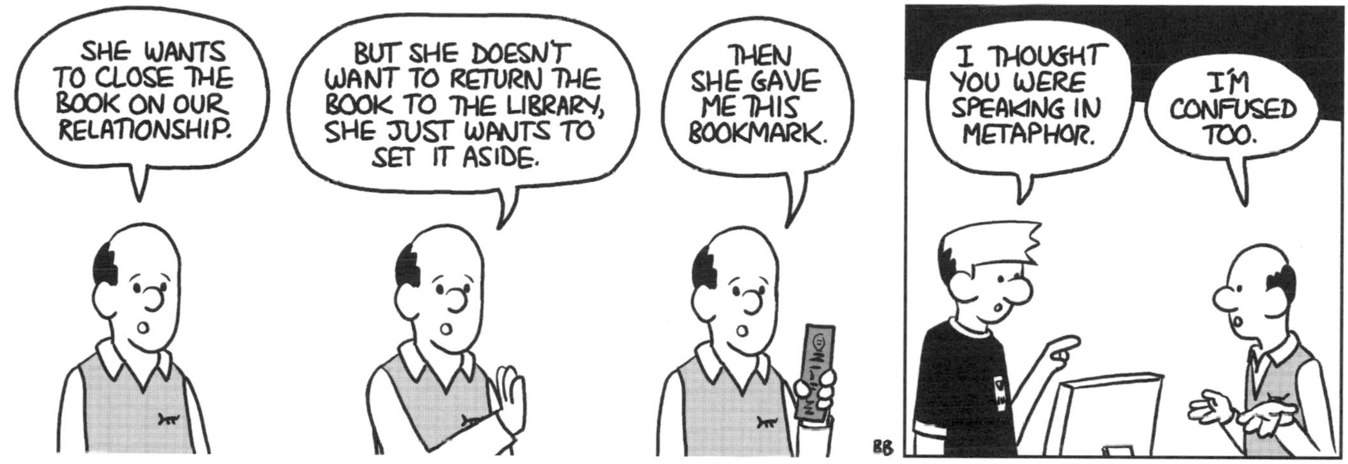
SHE WANTS TO CLOSE THE BOOK ON OUR RELATIONSHIP.
BUT SHE DOESN'T WANT TO RETURN THE BOOK TO THE LIBRARY, SHE JUST WANTS TO SET IT ASIDE.
THEN SHE GAVE ME THIS BOOKMARK.
BB
I THOUGHT YOU WERE SPEAKING IN METAPHOR.
I'M CONFUSED TOO.

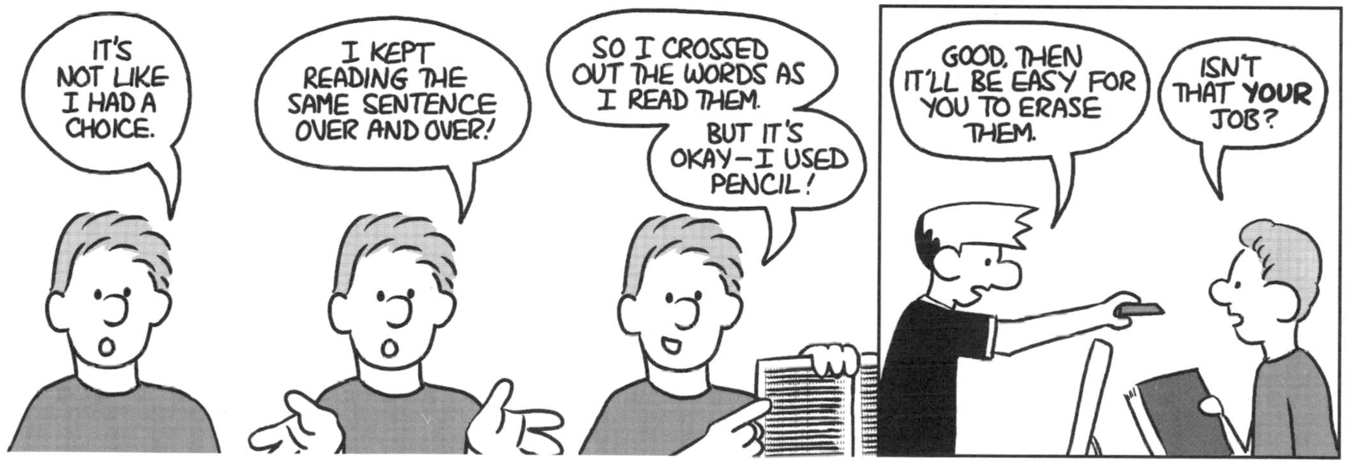
IT'S NOT LIKE I HAD A CHOICE.
I KEPT READING THE SAME SENTENCE OVER AND OVER!
SO I CROSSED OUT THE WORDS AS I READ THEM.
BUT IT'S OKAY—I USED PENCIL!
GOOD, THEN IT'LL BE EASY FOR YOU TO ERASE THEM.
ISN'T THAT **YOUR** JOB?

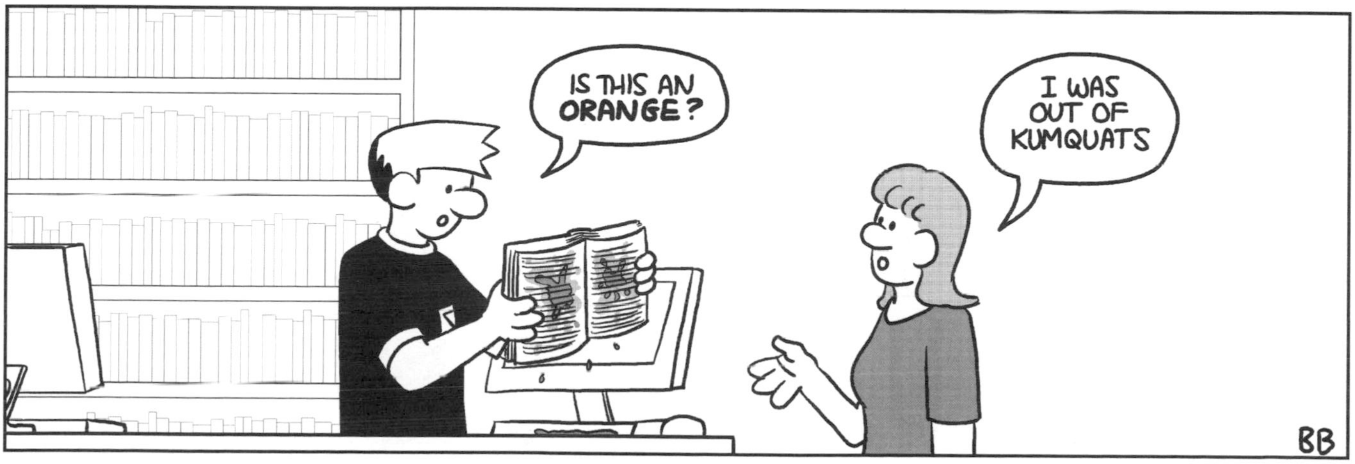
IS THIS AN **ORANGE**?
I WAS OUT OF KUMQUATS
BB

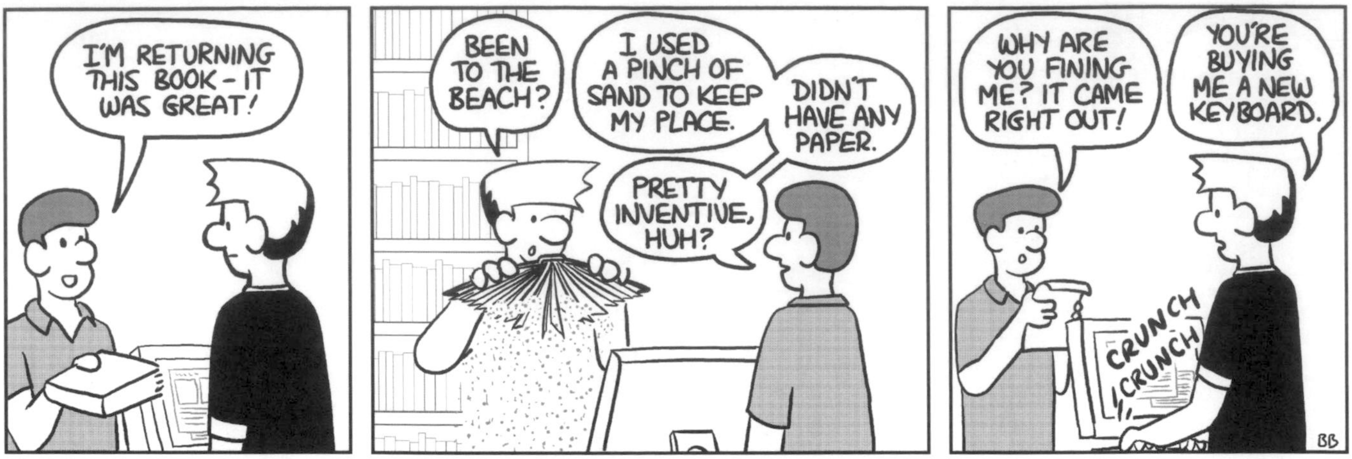
I'M RETURNING THIS BOOK - IT WAS GREAT!
BEEN TO THE BEACH?
I USED A PINCH OF SAND TO KEEP MY PLACE.
DIDN'T HAVE ANY PAPER.
PRETTY INVENTIVE, HUH?
WHY ARE YOU FINING ME? IT CAME RIGHT OUT!
YOU'RE BUYING ME A NEW KEYBOARD.
CRUNCH
CRUNCH
BB

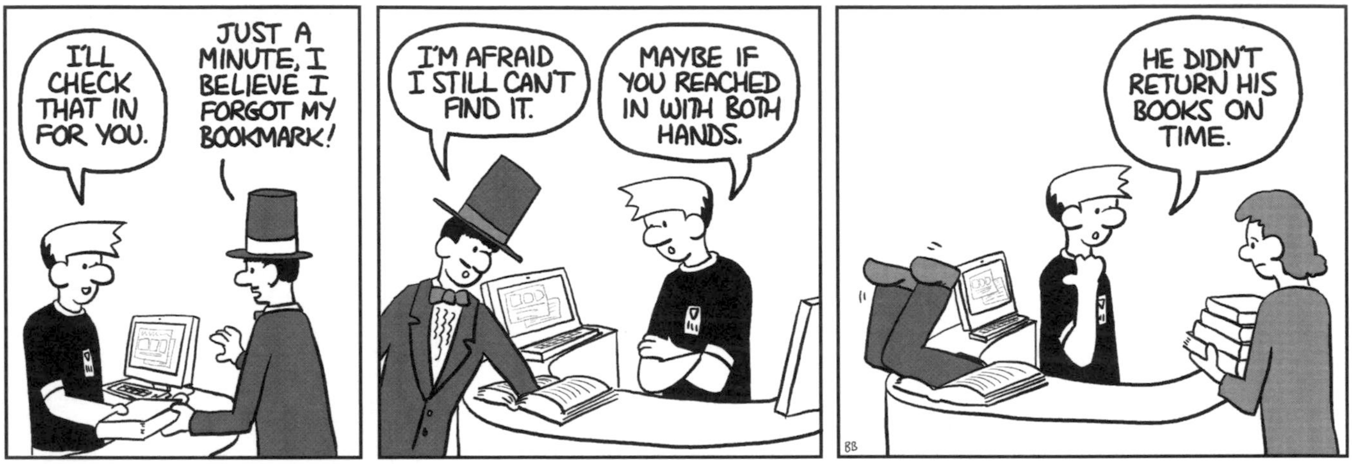
I'LL CHECK THAT IN FOR YOU.
JUST A MINUTE, I BELIEVE I FORGOT MY BOOKMARK!
I'M AFRAID I STILL CAN'T FIND IT.
MAYBE IF YOU REACHED IN WITH BOTH HANDS.
HE DIDN'T RETURN HIS BOOKS ON TIME.
BB

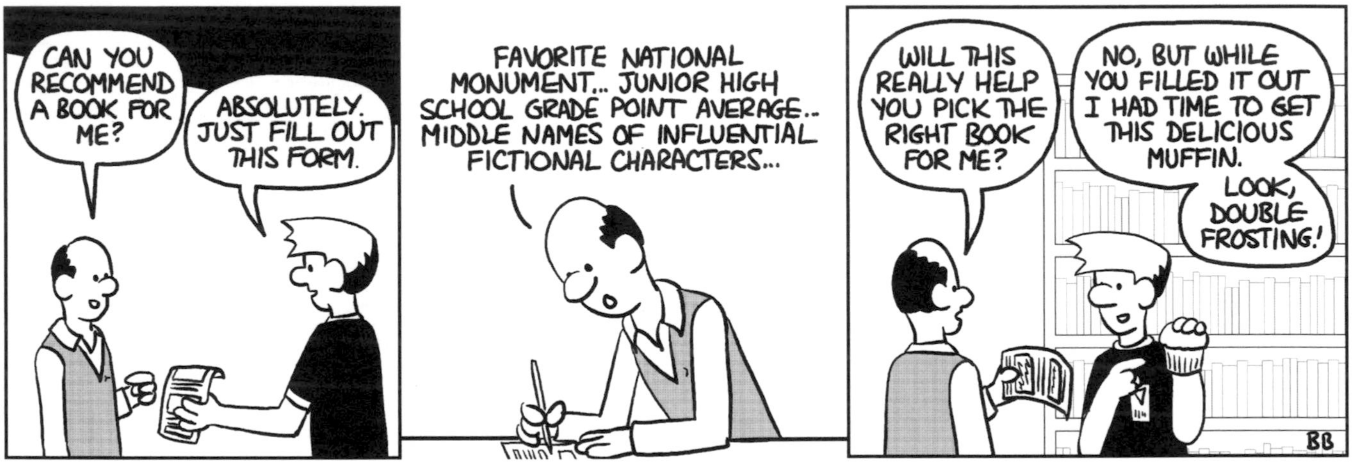
CAN YOU RECOMMEND A BOOK FOR ME?
ABSOLUTELY. JUST FILL OUT THIS FORM.
FAVORITE NATIONAL MONUMENT... JUNIOR HIGH SCHOOL GRADE POINT AVERAGE... MIDDLE NAMES OF INFLUENTIAL FICTIONAL CHARACTERS...
WILL THIS REALLY HELP YOU PICK THE RIGHT BOOK FOR ME?
NO, BUT WHILE YOU FILLED IT OUT I HAD TIME TO GET THIS DELICIOUS MUFFIN.
LOOK, DOUBLE FROSTING!
BB

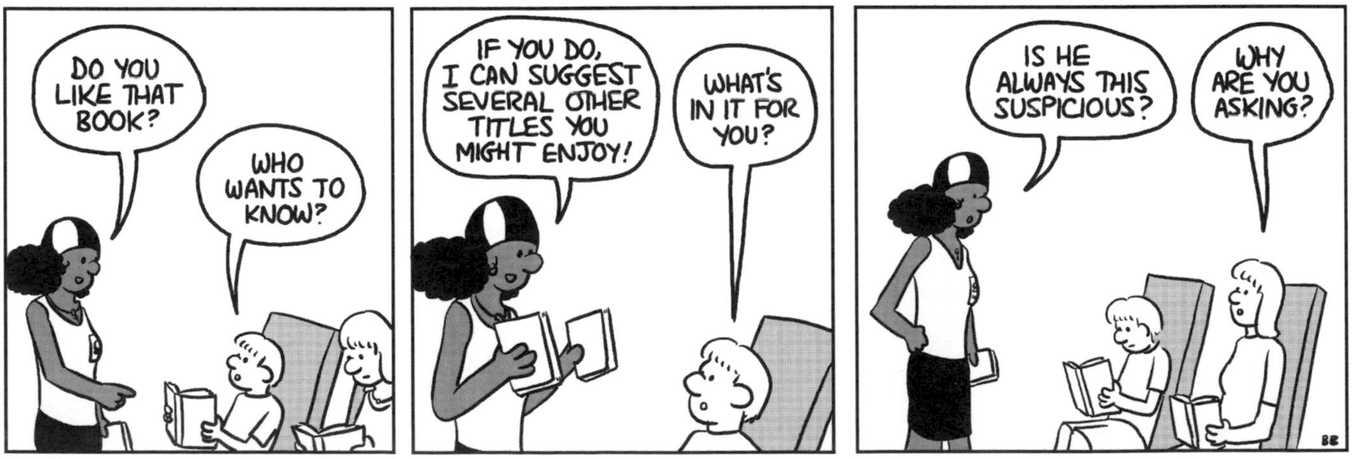
DO YOU LIKE THAT BOOK?
WHO WANTS TO KNOW?
IF YOU DO, I CAN SUGGEST SEVERAL OTHER TITLES YOU MIGHT ENJOY!
WHAT'S IN IT FOR YOU?
IS HE ALWAYS THIS SUSPICIOUS?
WHY ARE YOU ASKING?
BB

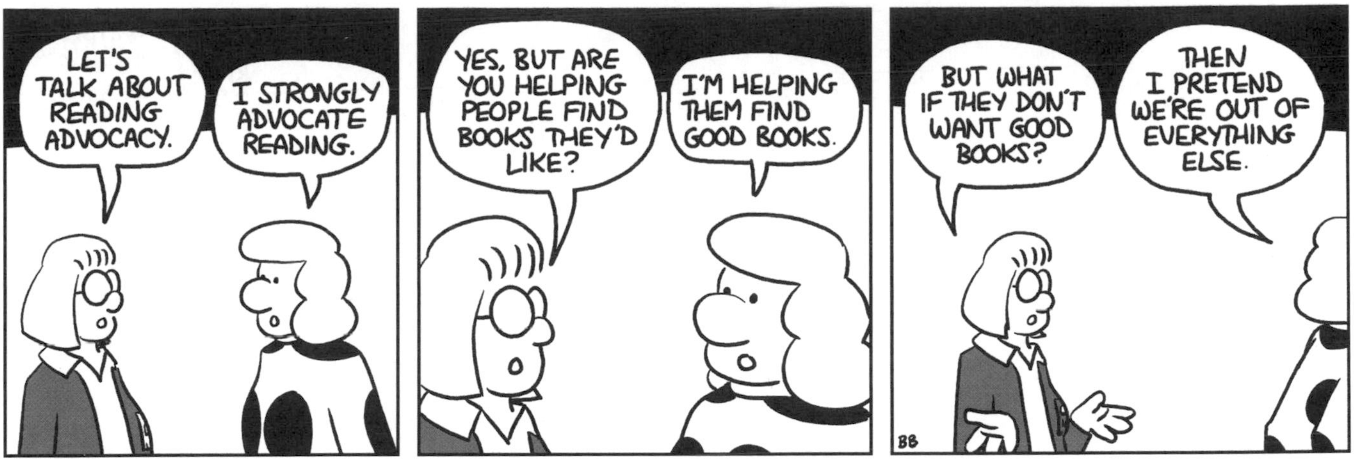

LET'S TALK ABOUT READING ADVOCACY.
I STRONGLY ADVOCATE READING.
YES, BUT ARE YOU HELPING PEOPLE FIND BOOKS THEY'D LIKE?
I'M HELPING THEM FIND GOOD BOOKS.
BUT WHAT IF THEY DON'T WANT GOOD BOOKS?
THEN I PRETEND WE'RE OUT OF EVERYTHING ELSE.
BB

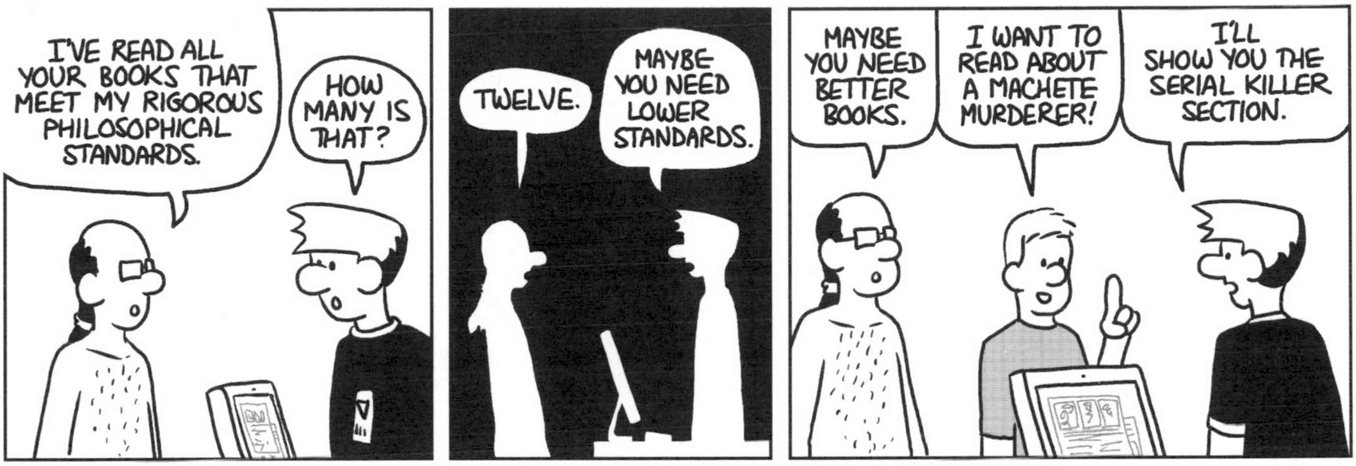

I'VE READ ALL YOUR BOOKS THAT MEET MY RIGOROUS PHILOSOPHICAL STANDARDS.
HOW MANY IS THAT?
TWELVE.
MAYBE YOU NEED LOWER STANDARDS.
MAYBE YOU NEED BETTER BOOKS.
I WANT TO READ ABOUT A MACHETE MURDERER!
I'LL SHOW YOU THE SERIAL KILLER SECTION.

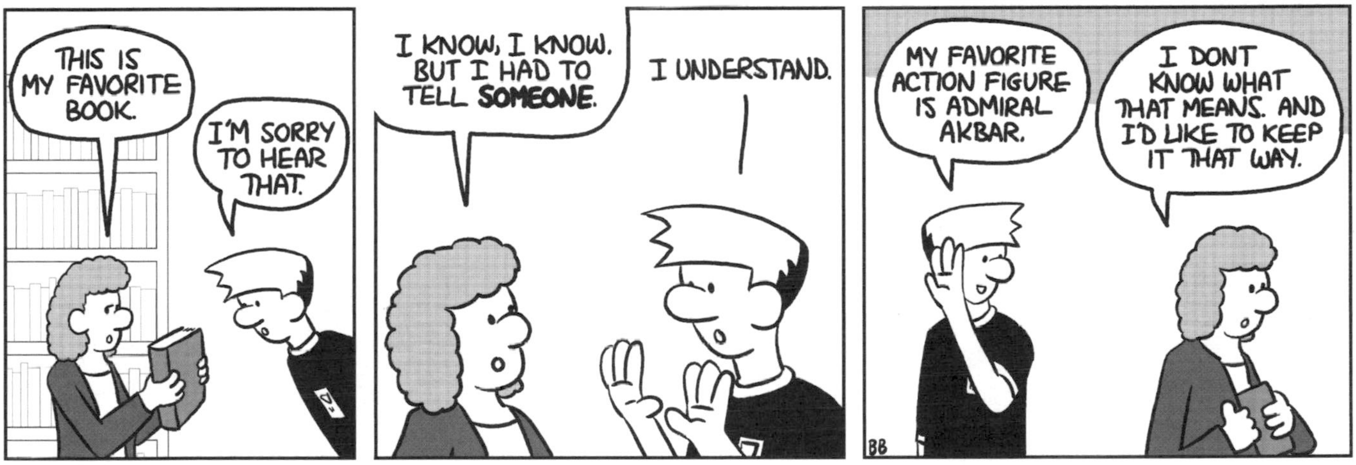

THIS IS MY FAVORITE BOOK.
I'M SORRY TO HEAR THAT.
I KNOW, I KNOW. BUT I HAD TO TELL **SOMEONE**.
I UNDERSTAND.
MY FAVORITE ACTION FIGURE IS ADMIRAL AKBAR.
I DONT KNOW WHAT THAT MEANS. AND I'D LIKE TO KEEP IT THAT WAY.
BB

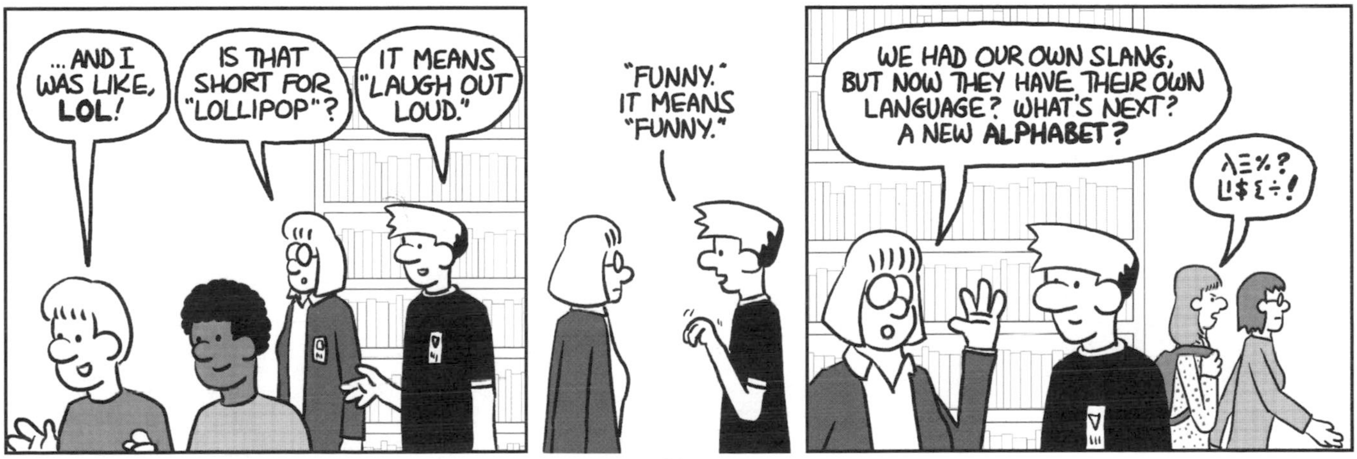

...AND I WAS LIKE, **LOL**!
IS THAT SHORT FOR "LOLLIPOP"?
IT MEANS "LAUGH OUT LOUD."
"FUNNY." IT MEANS "FUNNY."
WE HAD OUR OWN SLANG, BUT NOW THEY HAVE THEIR OWN LANGUAGE? WHAT'S NEXT? A NEW **ALPHABET**?

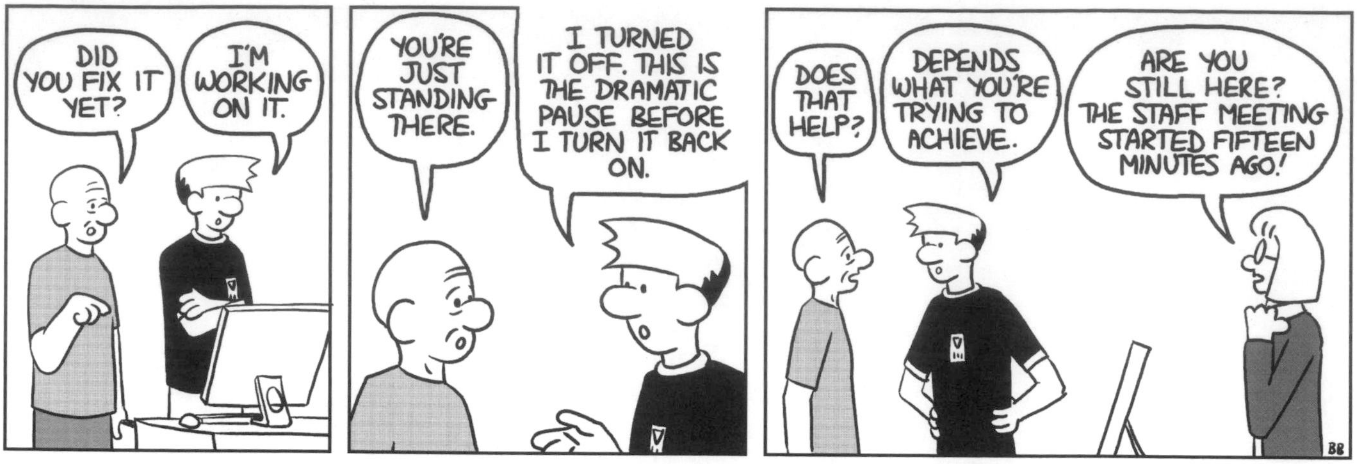
DID YOU FIX IT YET?
I'M WORKING ON IT.
YOU'RE JUST STANDING THERE.
I TURNED IT OFF. THIS IS THE DRAMATIC PAUSE BEFORE I TURN IT BACK ON.
DOES THAT HELP?
DEPENDS WHAT YOU'RE TRYING TO ACHIEVE.
ARE YOU STILL HERE? THE STAFF MEETING STARTED FIFTEEN MINUTES AGO!
BB

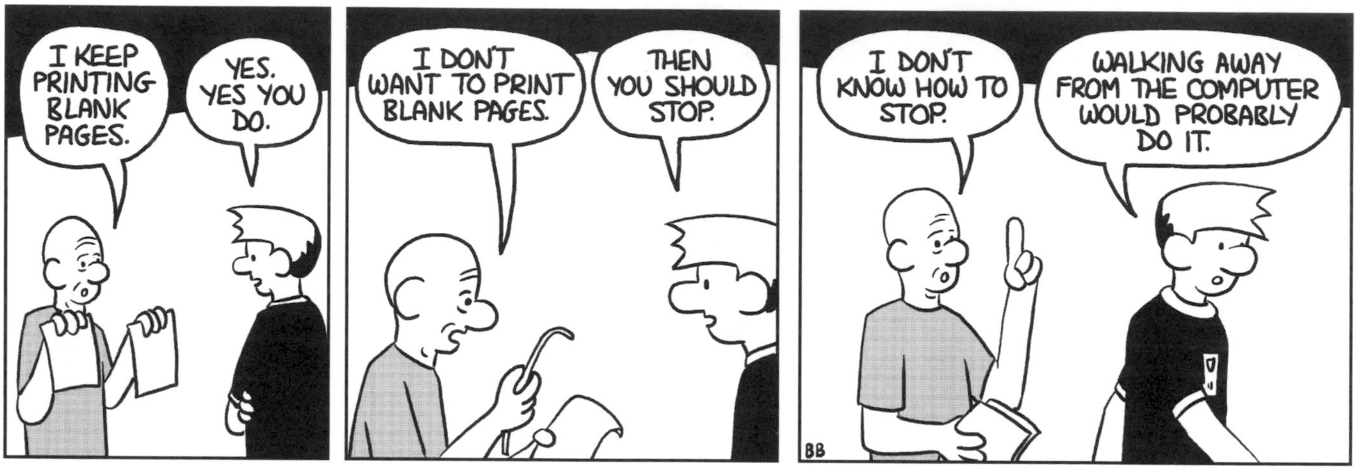
I KEEP PRINTING BLANK PAGES.
YES. YES YOU DO.
I DON'T WANT TO PRINT BLANK PAGES.
THEN YOU SHOULD STOP.
I DON'T KNOW HOW TO STOP.
WALKING AWAY FROM THE COMPUTER WOULD PROBABLY DO IT.
BB

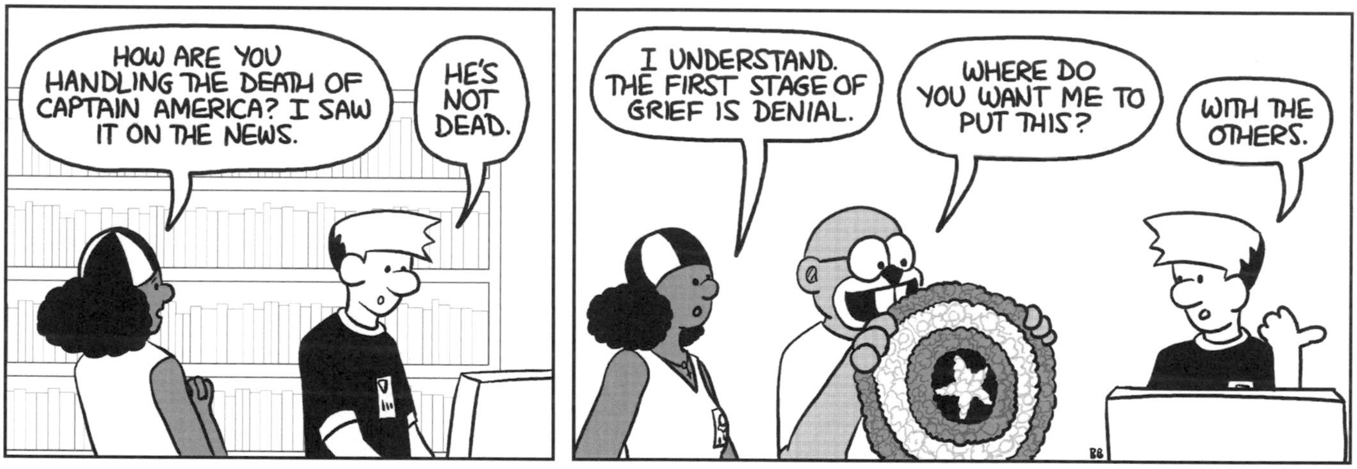
HOW ARE YOU HANDLING THE DEATH OF CAPTAIN AMERICA? I SAW IT ON THE NEWS.
HE'S NOT DEAD.
I UNDERSTAND. THE FIRST STAGE OF GRIEF IS DENIAL.
WHERE DO YOU WANT ME TO PUT THIS?
WITH THE OTHERS.
BB

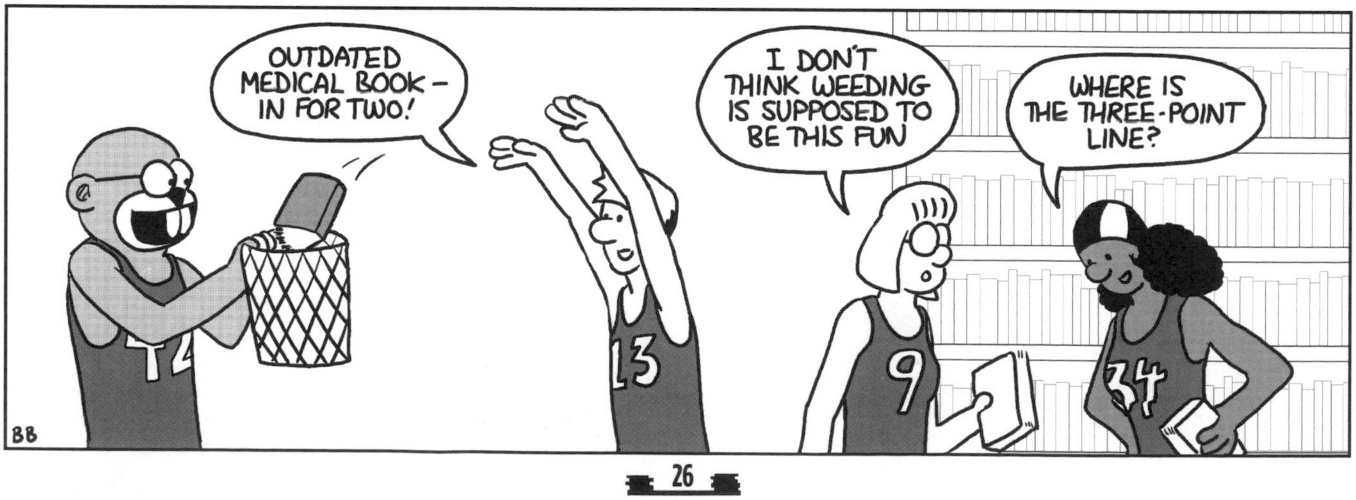
OUTDATED MEDICAL BOOK - IN FOR TWO!
I DON'T THINK WEEDING IS SUPPOSED TO BE THIS FUN
WHERE IS THE THREE-POINT LINE?
42
13
9
34
BB

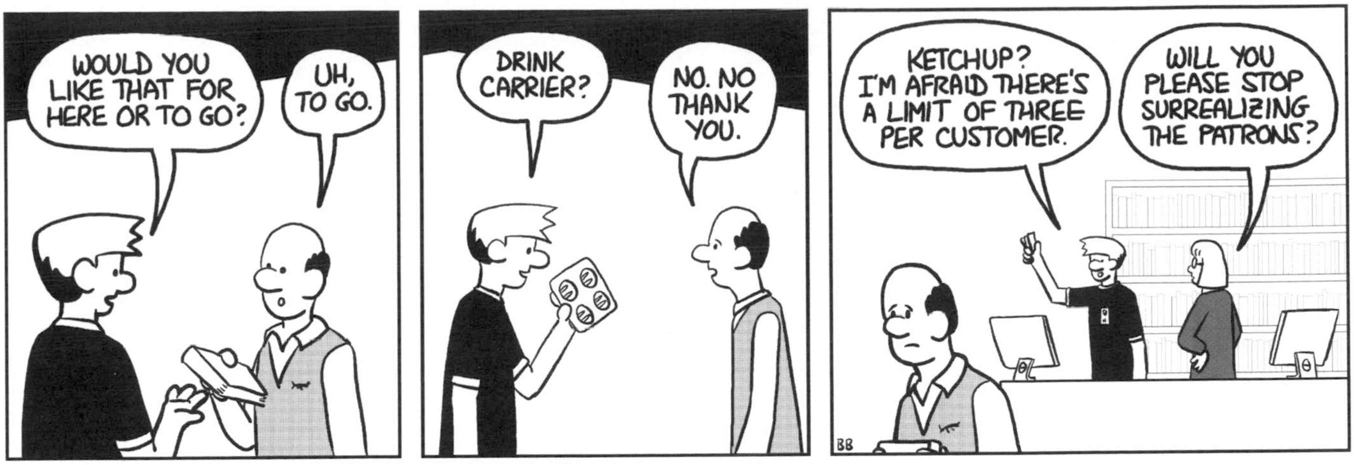
WOULD YOU LIKE THAT FOR HERE OR TO GO?
UH, TO GO.
DRINK CARRIER?
NO. NO THANK YOU.
KETCHUP? I'M AFRAID THERE'S A LIMIT OF THREE PER CUSTOMER.
WILL YOU PLEASE STOP SURREALIZING THE PATRONS?
BB

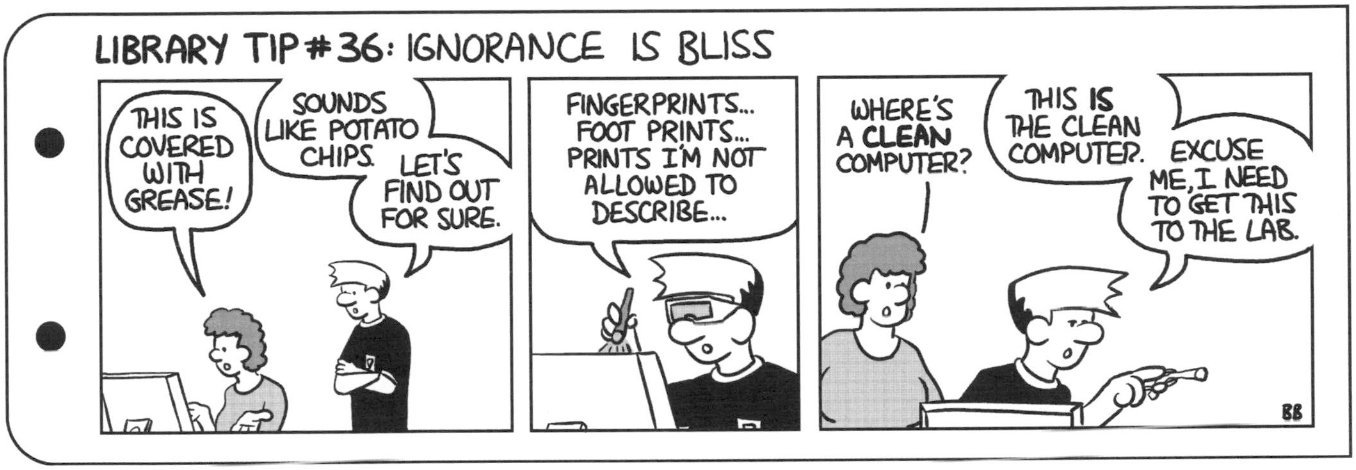
LIBRARY TIP #36: IGNORANCE IS BLISS
THIS IS COVERED WITH GREASE!
SOUNDS LIKE POTATO CHIPS.
LET'S FIND OUT FOR SURE.
FINGERPRINTS... FOOT PRINTS... PRINTS I'M NOT ALLOWED TO DESCRIBE...
WHERE'S A CLEAN COMPUTER?
THIS IS THE CLEAN COMPUTER.
EXCUSE ME, I NEED TO GET THIS TO THE LAB.
BB

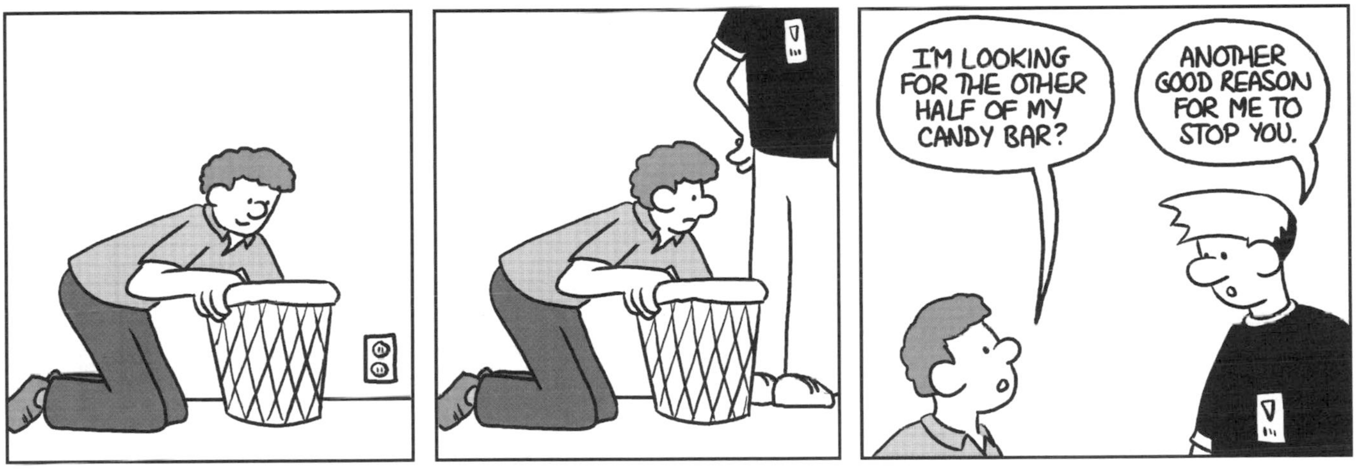
I'M LOOKING FOR THE OTHER HALF OF MY CANDY BAR?
ANOTHER GOOD REASON FOR ME TO STOP YOU.

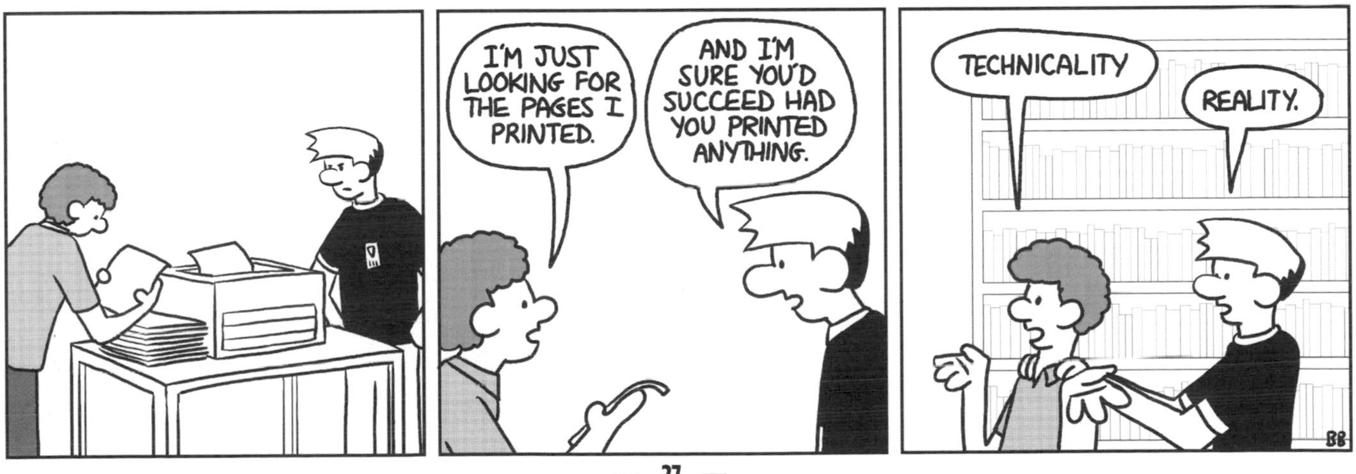
I'M JUST LOOKING FOR THE PAGES I PRINTED.
AND I'M SURE YOU'D SUCCEED HAD YOU PRINTED ANYTHING.
TECHNICALITY
REALITY.
BB

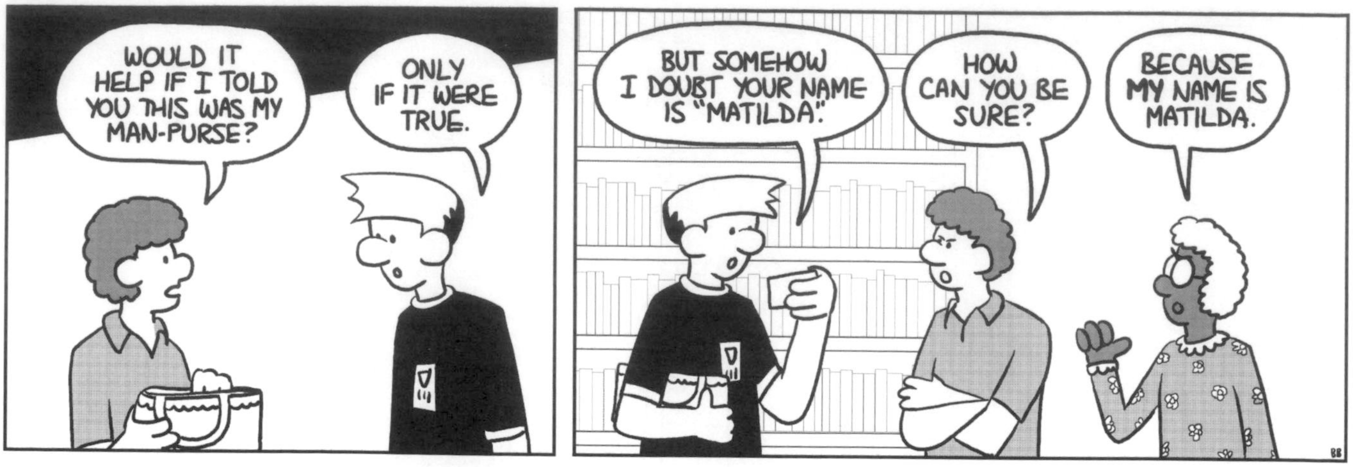
WOULD IT HELP IF I TOLD YOU THIS WAS MY MAN-PURSE?
ONLY IF IT WERE TRUE.
BUT SOMEHOW I DOUBT YOUR NAME IS "MATILDA".
HOW CAN YOU BE SURE?
BECAUSE MY NAME IS MATILDA.
BB

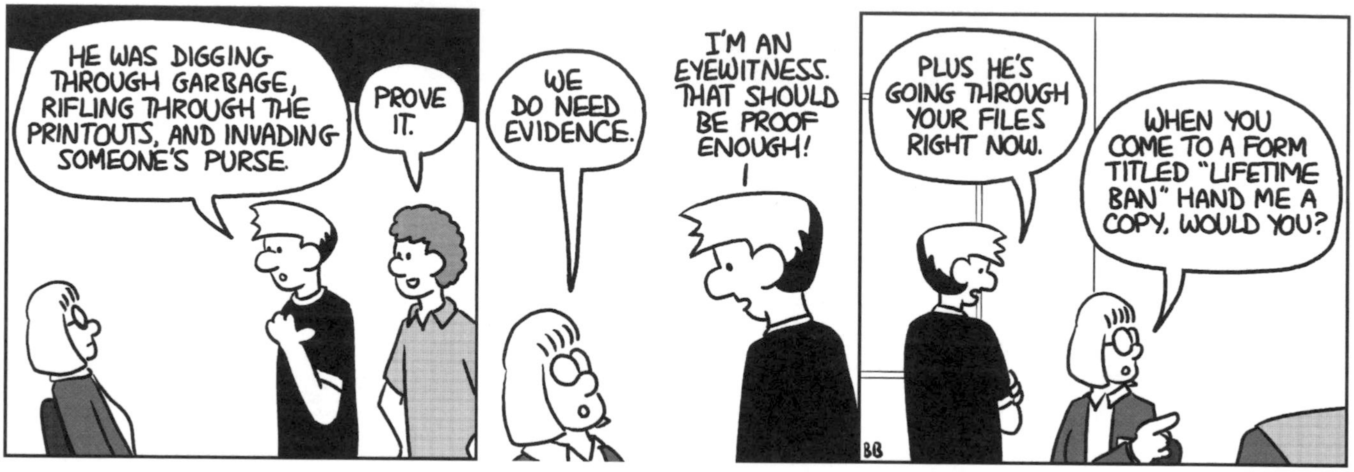
HE WAS DIGGING THROUGH GARBAGE, RIFLING THROUGH THE PRINTOUTS, AND INVADING SOMEONE'S PURSE.
PROVE IT.
WE DO NEED EVIDENCE.
I'M AN EYEWITNESS. THAT SHOULD BE PROOF ENOUGH!
PLUS HE'S GOING THROUGH YOUR FILES RIGHT NOW.
WHEN YOU COME TO A FORM TITLED "LIFETIME BAN" HAND ME A COPY, WOULD YOU?
BB

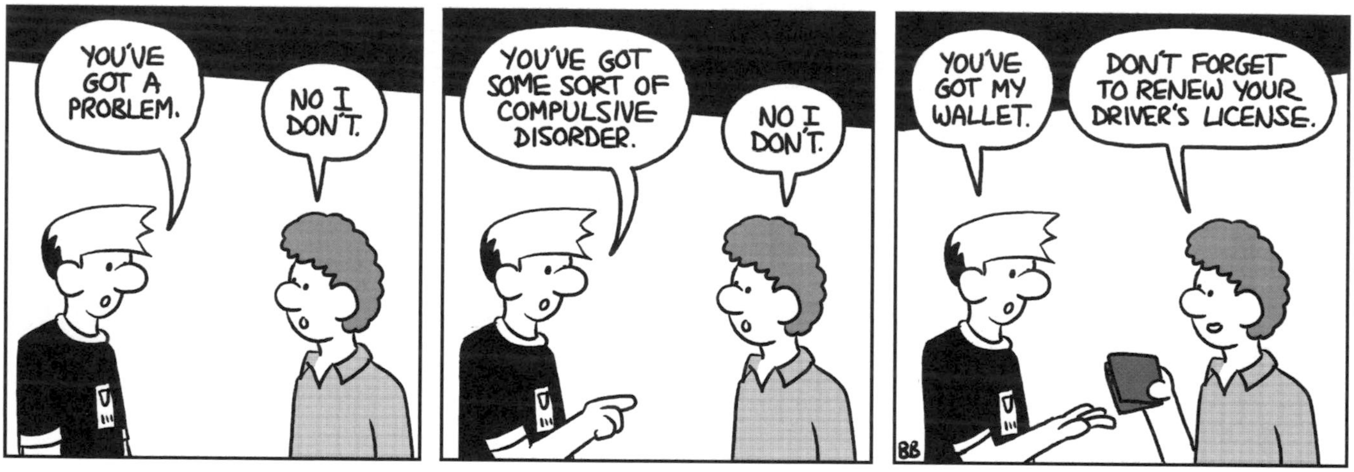
YOU'VE GOT A PROBLEM.
NO I DON'T.
YOU'VE GOT SOME SORT OF COMPULSIVE DISORDER.
NO I DON'T.
YOU'VE GOT MY WALLET.
DON'T FORGET TO RENEW YOUR DRIVER'S LICENSE.
BB

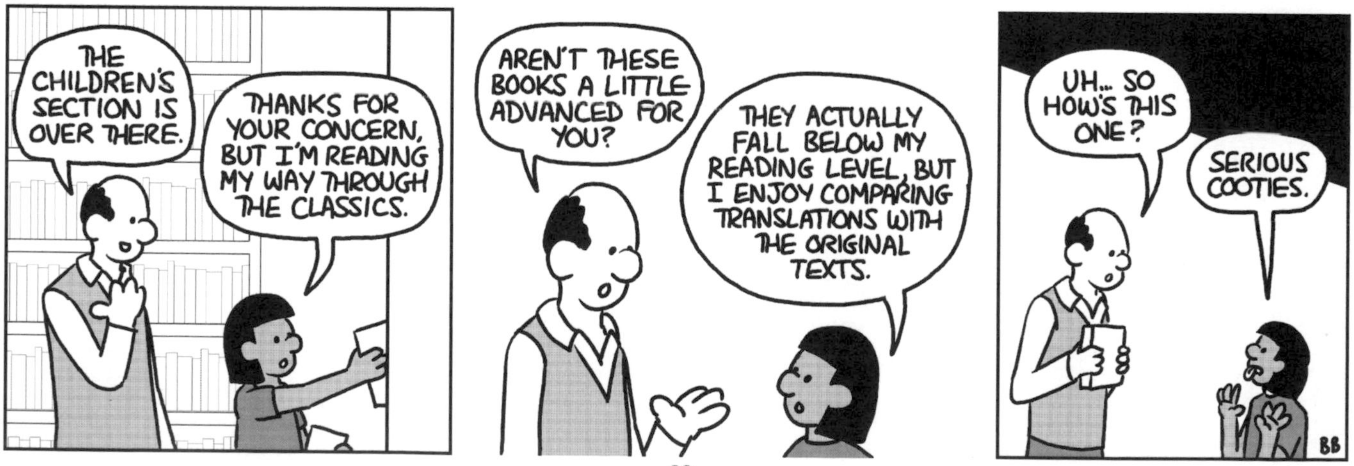
THE CHILDREN'S SECTION IS OVER THERE.
THANKS FOR YOUR CONCERN, BUT I'M READING MY WAY THROUGH THE CLASSICS.
AREN'T THESE BOOKS A LITTLE ADVANCED FOR YOU?
THEY ACTUALLY FALL BELOW MY READING LEVEL, BUT I ENJOY COMPARING TRANSLATIONS WITH THE ORIGINAL TEXTS.
UH... SO HOW'S THIS ONE?
SERIOUS COOTIES.
BB

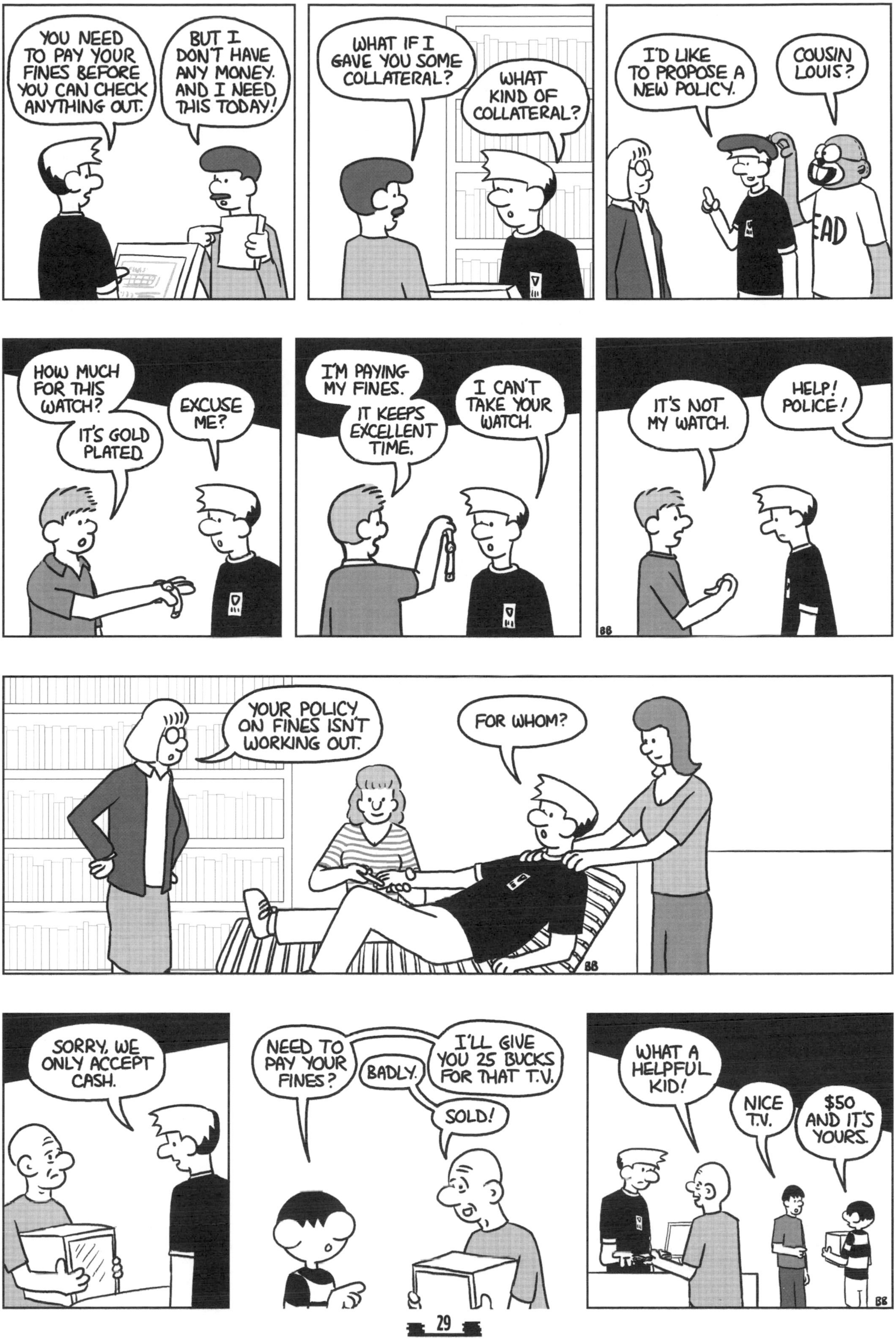
YOU NEED TO PAY YOUR FINES BEFORE YOU CAN CHECK ANYTHING OUT.
BUT I DON'T HAVE ANY MONEY. AND I NEED THIS TODAY!
WHAT IF I GAVE YOU SOME COLLATERAL?
WHAT KIND OF COLLATERAL?
I'D LIKE TO PROPOSE A NEW POLICY.
COUSIN LOUIS?
HOW MUCH FOR THIS WATCH?
IT'S GOLD PLATED.
EXCUSE ME?
I'M PAYING MY FINES.
IT KEEPS EXCELLENT TIME.
I CAN'T TAKE YOUR WATCH.
IT'S NOT MY WATCH.
HELP! POLICE!
YOUR POLICY ON FINES ISN'T WORKING OUT.
FOR WHOM?
SORRY, WE ONLY ACCEPT CASH.
NEED TO PAY YOUR FINES?
BADLY.
I'LL GIVE YOU 25 BUCKS FOR THAT T.V.
SOLD!
WHAT A HELPFUL KID!
NICE T.V.
$50 AND IT'S YOURS.

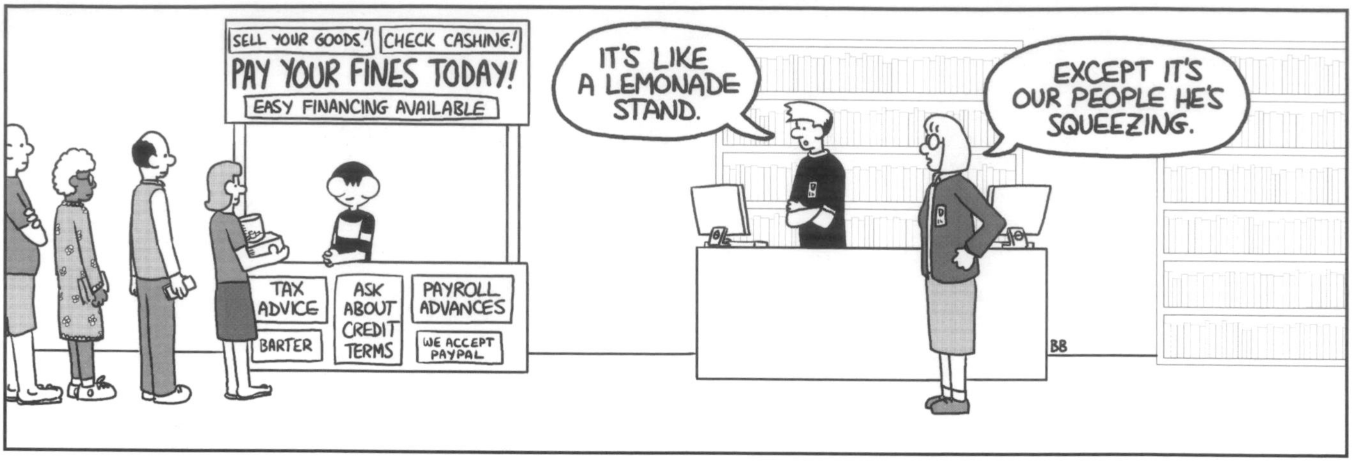
SELL YOUR GOODS!
CHECK CASHING!
PAY YOUR FINES TODAY!
EASY FINANCING AVAILABLE
TAX ADVICE
BARTER
ASK ABOUT CREDIT TERMS
PAYROLL ADVANCES
WE ACCEPT PAYPAL
IT'S LIKE A LEMONADE STAND.
EXCEPT IT'S OUR PEOPLE HE'S SQUEEZING.
BB

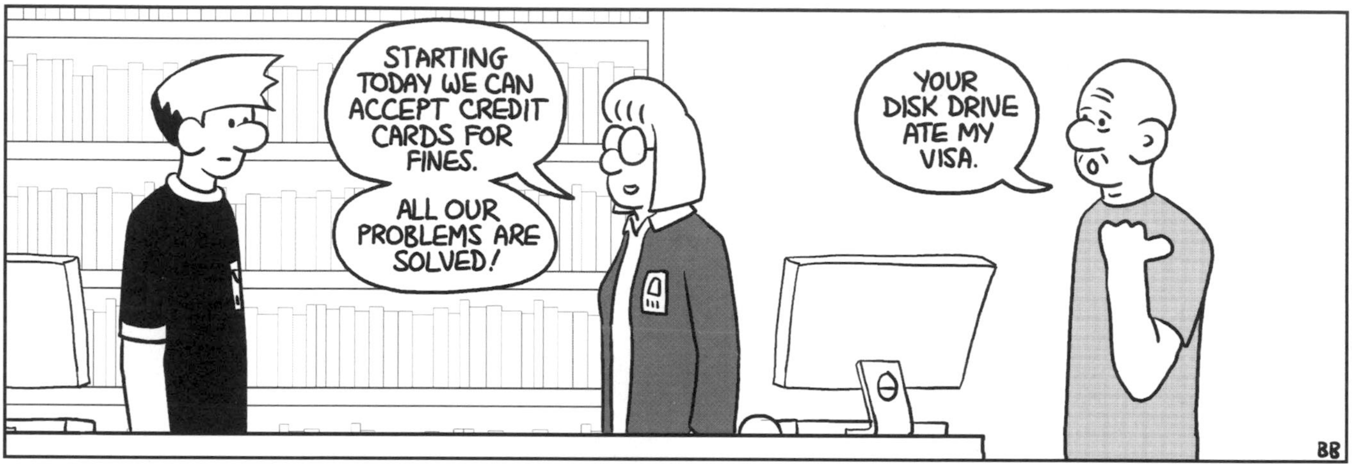
STARTING TODAY WE CAN ACCEPT CREDIT CARDS FOR FINES.
ALL OUR PROBLEMS ARE SOLVED!
YOUR DISK DRIVE ATE MY VISA.
BB

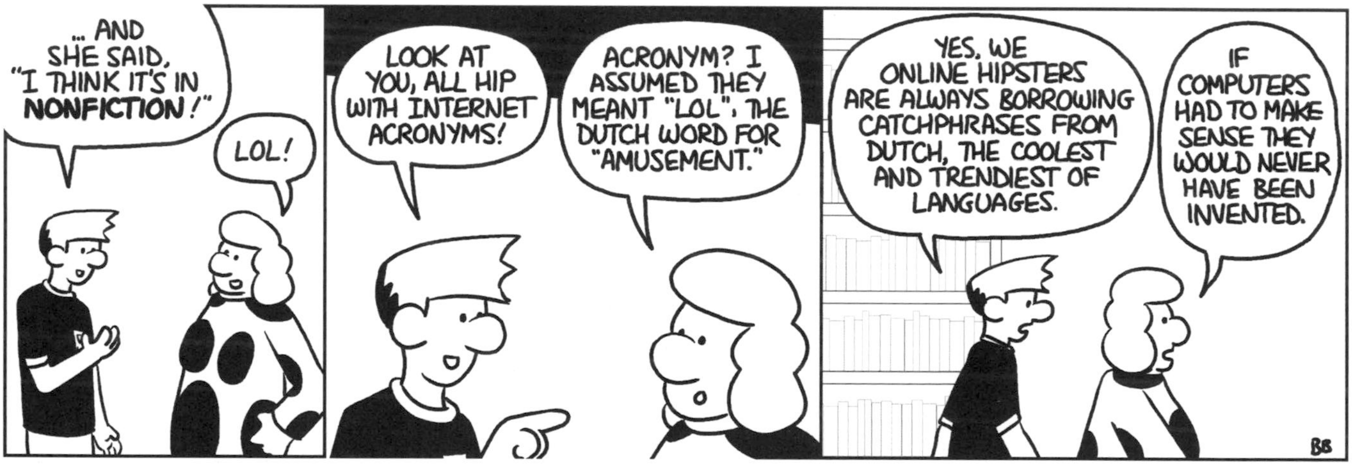
... AND SHE SAID, "I THINK IT'S IN **NONFICTION**!"
LOL!
LOOK AT YOU, ALL HIP WITH INTERNET ACRONYMS!
ACRONYM? I ASSUMED THEY MEANT "LOL", THE DUTCH WORD FOR "AMUSEMENT."
YES, WE ONLINE HIPSTERS ARE ALWAYS BORROWING CATCHPHRASES FROM DUTCH, THE COOLEST AND TRENDIEST OF LANGUAGES.
IF COMPUTERS HAD TO MAKE SENSE THEY WOULD NEVER HAVE BEEN INVENTED.
BB

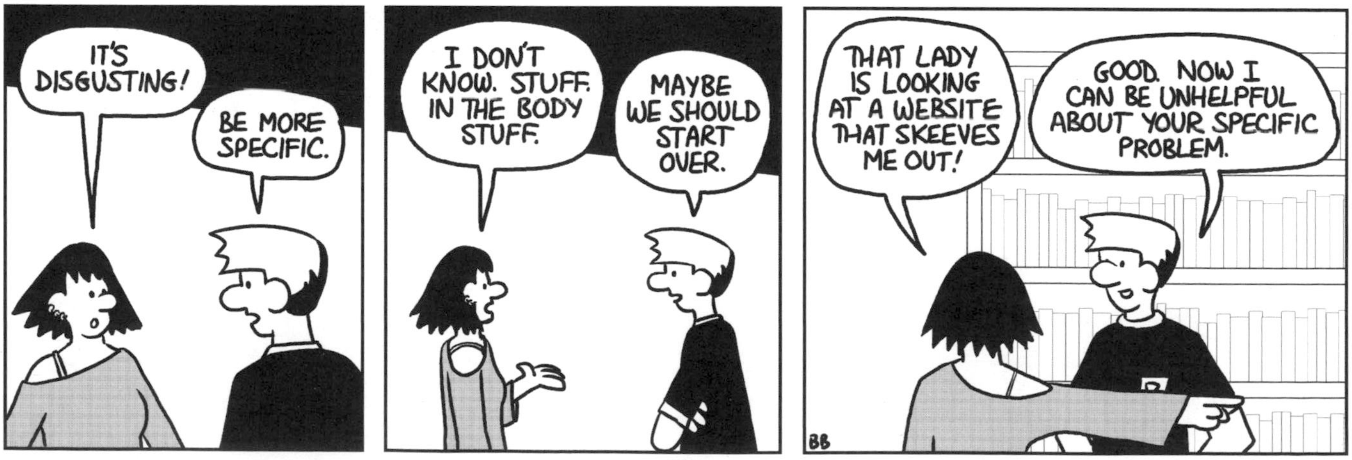
IT'S DISGUSTING!
BE MORE SPECIFIC.
I DON'T KNOW. STUFF. IN THE BODY STUFF.
MAYBE WE SHOULD START OVER.
THAT LADY IS LOOKING AT A WEBSITE THAT SKEEVES ME OUT!
GOOD. NOW I CAN BE UNHELPFUL ABOUT YOUR SPECIFIC PROBLEM.
BB

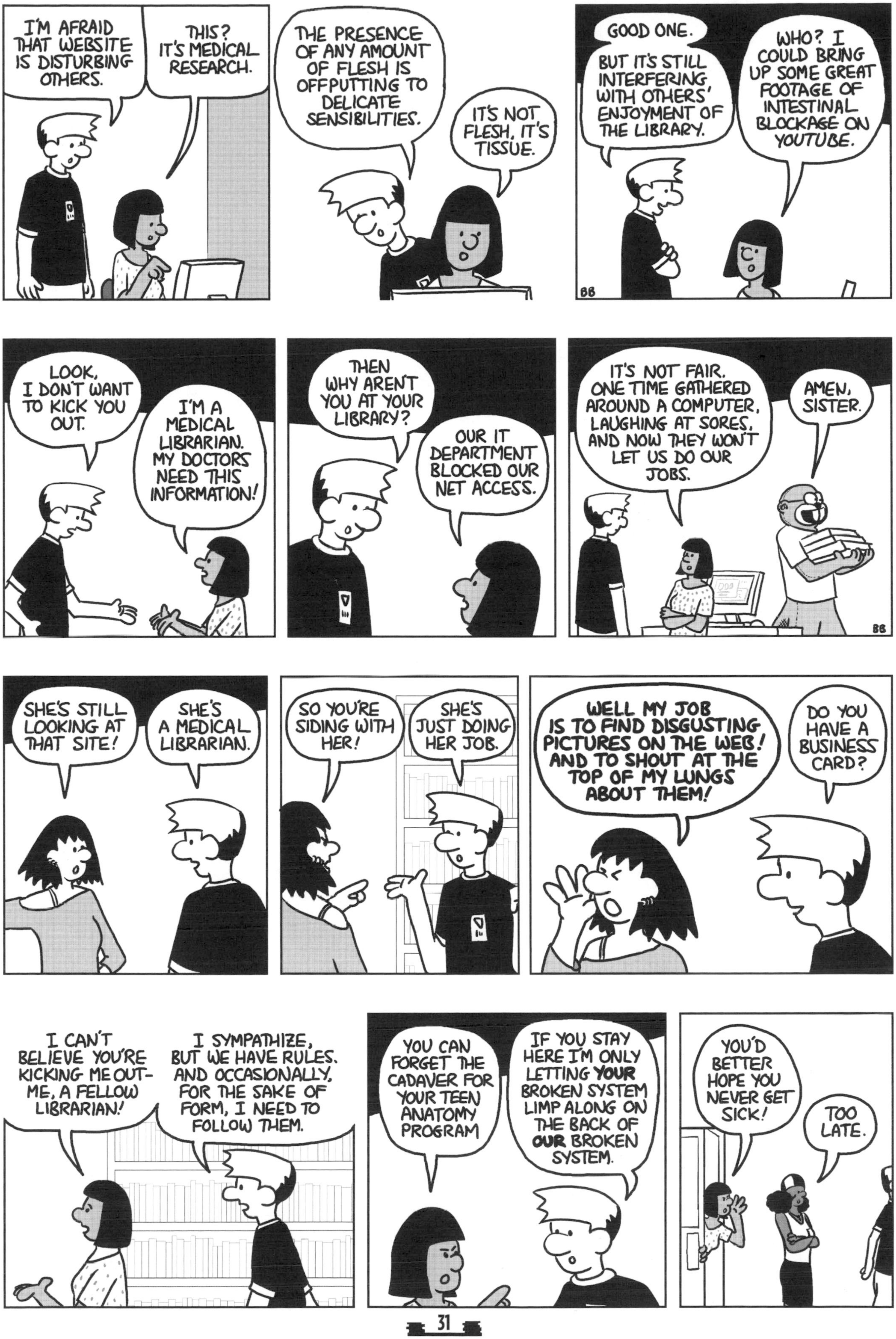
I'M AFRAID THAT WEBSITE IS DISTURBING OTHERS.
THIS? IT'S MEDICAL RESEARCH.
THE PRESENCE OF ANY AMOUNT OF FLESH IS OFFPUTTING TO DELICATE SENSIBILITIES.
IT'S NOT FLESH, IT'S TISSUE.
GOOD ONE.
BUT IT'S STILL INTERFERING WITH OTHERS' ENJOYMENT OF THE LIBRARY.
WHO? I COULD BRING UP SOME GREAT FOOTAGE OF INTESTINAL BLOCKAGE ON YOUTUBE.
BB
LOOK, I DON'T WANT TO KICK YOU OUT.
I'M A MEDICAL LIBRARIAN. MY DOCTORS NEED THIS INFORMATION!
THEN WHY AREN'T YOU AT YOUR LIBRARY?
OUR IT DEPARTMENT BLOCKED OUR NET ACCESS.
IT'S NOT FAIR. ONE TIME GATHERED AROUND A COMPUTER, LAUGHING AT SORES, AND NOW THEY WON'T LET US DO OUR JOBS.
AMEN, SISTER.
BB
SHE'S STILL LOOKING AT THAT SITE!
SHE'S A MEDICAL LIBRARIAN.
SO YOU'RE SIDING WITH HER!
SHE'S JUST DOING HER JOB.
WELL MY JOB IS TO FIND DISGUSTING PICTURES ON THE WEB! AND TO SHOUT AT THE TOP OF MY LUNGS ABOUT THEM!
DO YOU HAVE A BUSINESS CARD?
I CAN'T BELIEVE YOU'RE KICKING ME OUT- ME, A FELLOW LIBRARIAN!
I SYMPATHIZE, BUT WE HAVE RULES. AND OCCASIONALLY, FOR THE SAKE OF FORM, I NEED TO FOLLOW THEM.
YOU CAN FORGET THE CADAVER FOR YOUR TEEN ANATOMY PROGRAM
IF YOU STAY HERE I'M ONLY LETTING YOUR BROKEN SYSTEM LIMP ALONG ON THE BACK OF OUR BROKEN SYSTEM.
YOU'D BETTER HOPE YOU NEVER GET SICK!
TOO LATE.

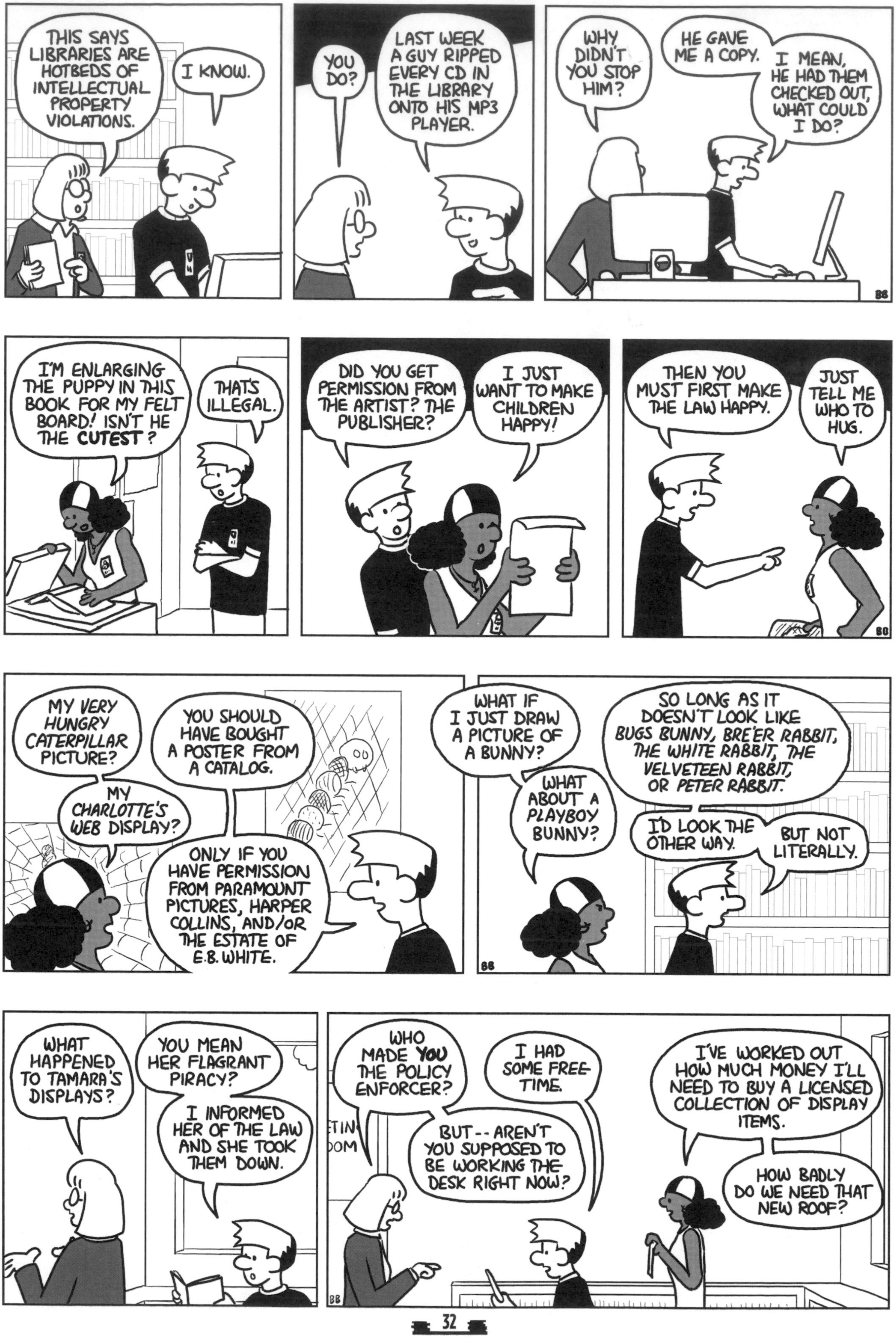
THIS SAYS LIBRARIES ARE HOTBEDS OF INTELLECTUAL PROPERTY VIOLATIONS.
I KNOW.
YOU DO?
LAST WEEK A GUY RIPPED EVERY CD IN THE LIBRARY ONTO HIS MP3 PLAYER.
WHY DIDN'T YOU STOP HIM?
HE GAVE ME A COPY.
I MEAN, HE HAD THEM CHECKED OUT, WHAT COULD I DO?
BB
I'M ENLARGING THE PUPPY IN THIS BOOK FOR MY FELT BOARD! ISN'T HE THE **CUTEST**?
THAT'S ILLEGAL.
DID YOU GET PERMISSION FROM THE ARTIST? THE PUBLISHER?
I JUST WANT TO MAKE CHILDREN HAPPY!
THEN YOU MUST FIRST MAKE THE LAW HAPPY.
JUST TELL ME WHO TO HUG.
BB
MY *VERY HUNGRY CATERPILLAR* PICTURE?
YOU SHOULD HAVE BOUGHT A POSTER FROM A CATALOG.
MY *CHARLOTTE'S WEB* DISPLAY?
ONLY IF YOU HAVE PERMISSION FROM PARAMOUNT PICTURES, HARPER COLLINS, AND/OR THE ESTATE OF E.B. WHITE.
BB
WHAT IF I JUST DRAW A PICTURE OF A BUNNY?
SO LONG AS IT DOESN'T LOOK LIKE *BUGS BUNNY, BRE'ER RABBIT, THE WHITE RABBIT, THE VELVETEEN RABBIT,* OR *PETER RABBIT.*
WHAT ABOUT A *PLAYBOY* BUNNY?
I'D LOOK THE OTHER WAY.
BUT NOT LITERALLY.
WHAT HAPPENED TO TAMARA'S DISPLAYS?
YOU MEAN HER FLAGRANT PIRACY?
I INFORMED HER OF THE LAW AND SHE TOOK THEM DOWN.
WHO MADE **YOU** THE POLICY ENFORCER?
I HAD SOME FREE TIME.
BUT-- AREN'T YOU SUPPOSED TO BE WORKING THE DESK RIGHT NOW?
I'VE WORKED OUT HOW MUCH MONEY I'LL NEED TO BUY A LICENSED COLLECTION OF DISPLAY ITEMS.
HOW BADLY DO WE NEED THAT NEW ROOF?
BB

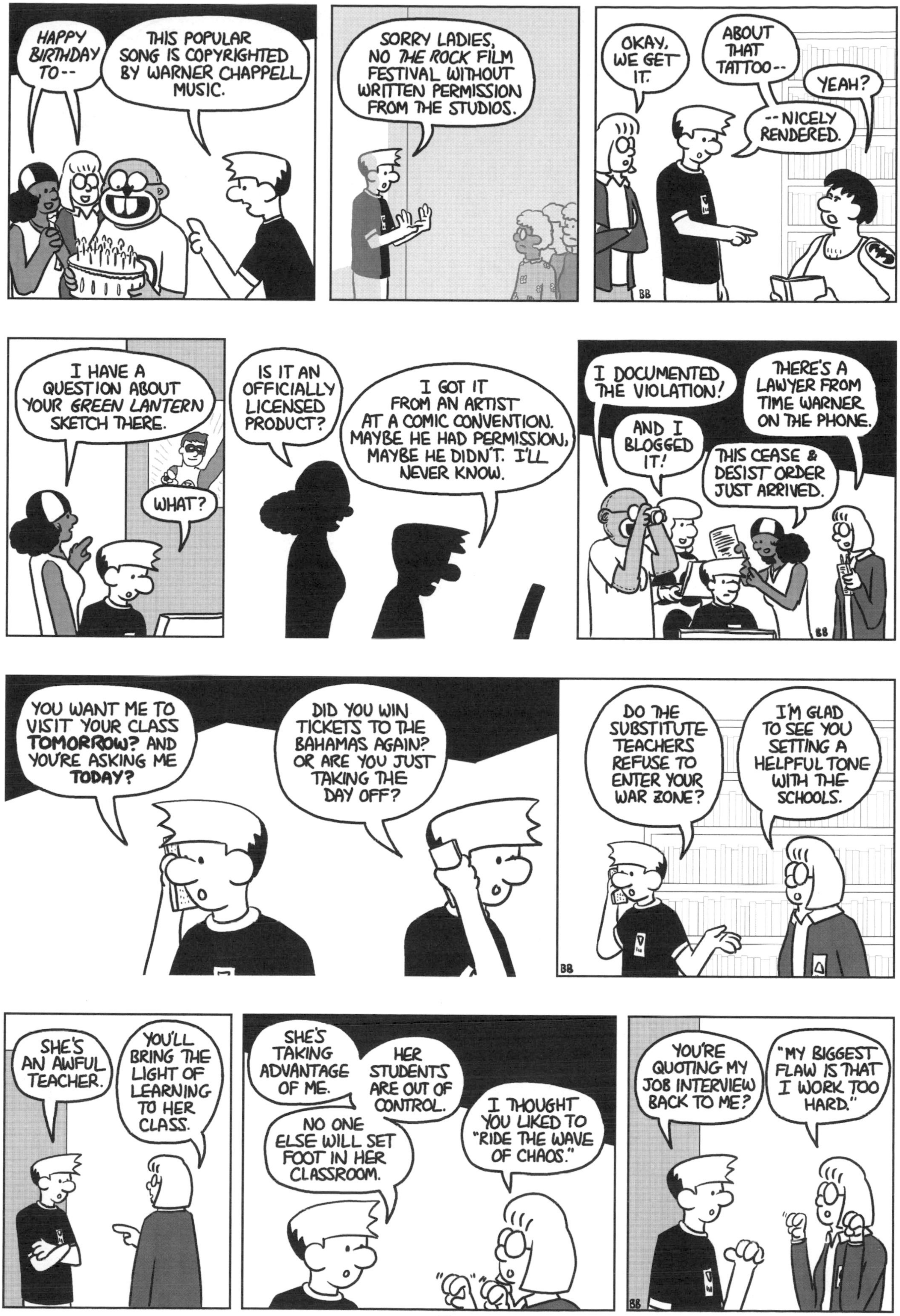
HAPPY BIRTHDAY TO--
THIS POPULAR SONG IS COPYRIGHTED BY WARNER CHAPPELL MUSIC.
SORRY LADIES, NO *THE ROCK* FILM FESTIVAL WITHOUT WRITTEN PERMISSION FROM THE STUDIOS.
OKAY, WE GET IT.
ABOUT THAT TATTOO--
YEAH?
--NICELY RENDERED.
BB
I HAVE A QUESTION ABOUT YOUR *GREEN LANTERN* SKETCH THERE.
WHAT?
IS IT AN OFFICIALLY LICENSED PRODUCT?
I GOT IT FROM AN ARTIST AT A COMIC CONVENTION. MAYBE HE HAD PERMISSION, MAYBE HE DIDN'T. I'LL NEVER KNOW.
I DOCUMENTED THE VIOLATION!
AND I BLOGGED IT!
THERE'S A LAWYER FROM TIME WARNER ON THE PHONE.
THIS CEASE & DESIST ORDER JUST ARRIVED.
BB
YOU WANT ME TO VISIT YOUR CLASS **TOMORROW?** AND YOU'RE ASKING ME **TODAY?**
DID YOU WIN TICKETS TO THE BAHAMAS AGAIN? OR ARE YOU JUST TAKING THE DAY OFF?
DO THE SUBSTITUTE TEACHERS REFUSE TO ENTER YOUR WAR ZONE?
I'M GLAD TO SEE YOU SETTING A HELPFUL TONE WITH THE SCHOOLS.
BB
SHE'S AN AWFUL TEACHER.
YOU'LL BRING THE LIGHT OF LEARNING TO HER CLASS.
SHE'S TAKING ADVANTAGE OF ME.
HER STUDENTS ARE OUT OF CONTROL.
NO ONE ELSE WILL SET FOOT IN HER CLASSROOM.
I THOUGHT YOU LIKED TO "RIDE THE WAVE OF CHAOS."
YOU'RE QUOTING MY JOB INTERVIEW BACK TO ME?
"MY BIGGEST FLAW IS THAT I WORK TOO HARD."
BB

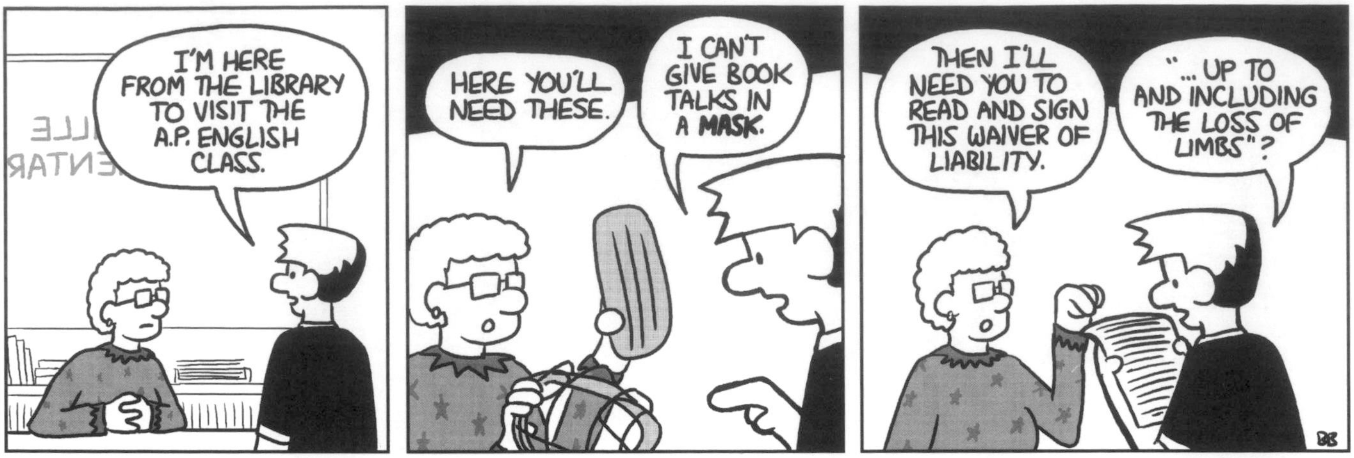
I'M HERE FROM THE LIBRARY TO VISIT THE A.P. ENGLISH CLASS.
HERE YOU'LL NEED THESE.
I CAN'T GIVE BOOK TALKS IN A **MASK**.
THEN I'LL NEED YOU TO READ AND SIGN THIS WAIVER OF LIABILITY.
"... UP TO AND INCLUDING THE LOSS OF LIMBS"?
BB

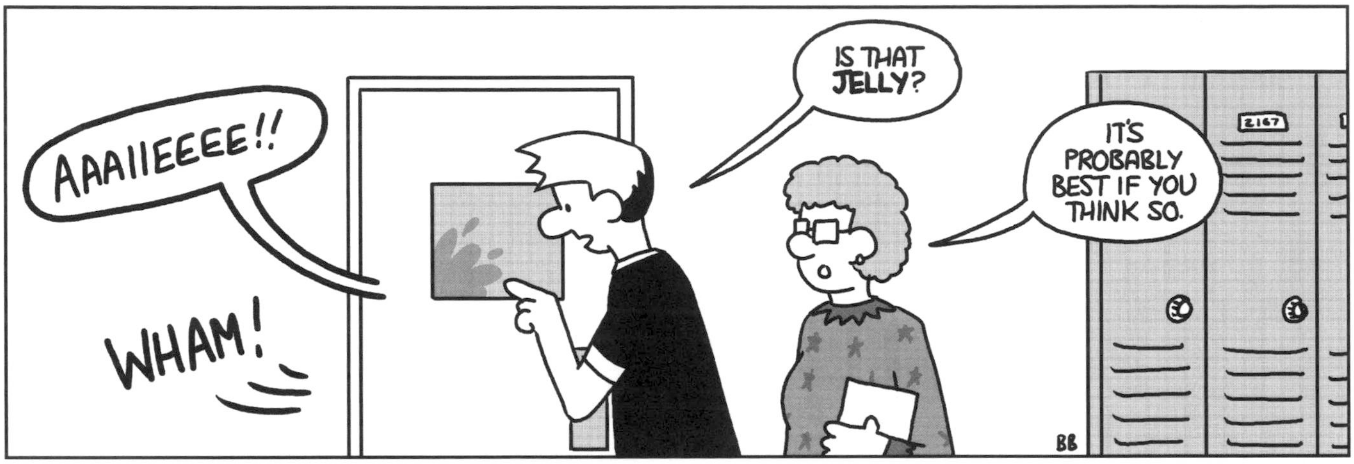
AAAIIEEEE!!
WHAM!
IS THAT **JELLY**?
IT'S PROBABLY BEST IF YOU THINK SO.
2167
BB

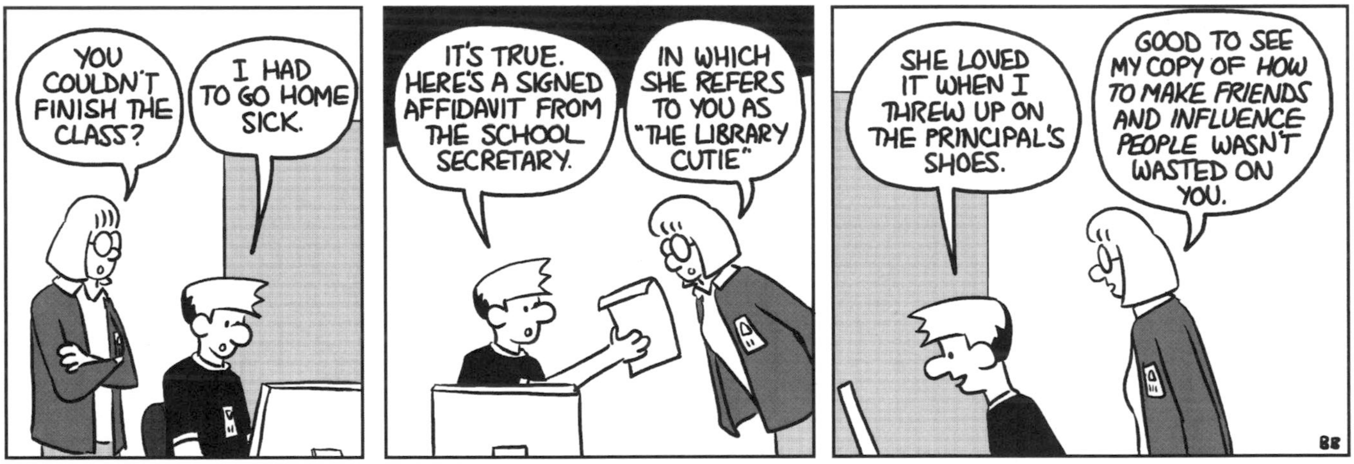
YOU COULDN'T FINISH THE CLASS?
I HAD TO GO HOME SICK.
IT'S TRUE. HERE'S A SIGNED AFFIDAVIT FROM THE SCHOOL SECRETARY.
IN WHICH SHE REFERS TO YOU AS "THE LIBRARY CUTIE"
SHE LOVED IT WHEN I THREW UP ON THE PRINCIPAL'S SHOES.
GOOD TO SEE MY COPY OF *HOW TO MAKE FRIENDS AND INFLUENCE PEOPLE* WASN'T WASTED ON YOU.
BB

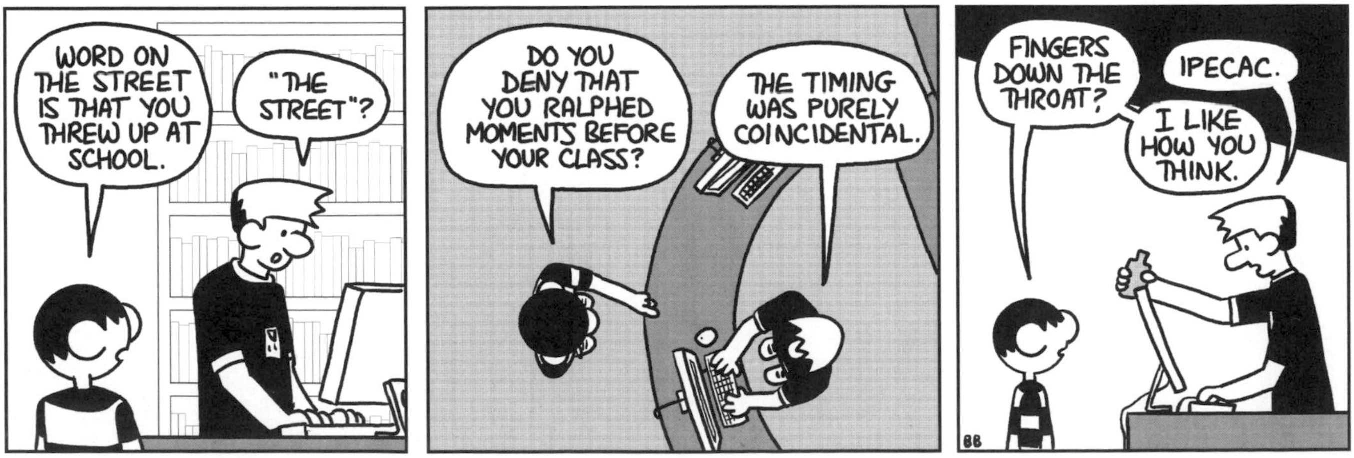
WORD ON THE STREET IS THAT YOU THREW UP AT SCHOOL.
"THE STREET"?
DO YOU DENY THAT YOU RALPHED MOMENTS BEFORE YOUR CLASS?
THE TIMING WAS PURELY COINCIDENTAL.
FINGERS DOWN THE THROAT?
IPECAC.
I LIKE HOW YOU THINK.
BB

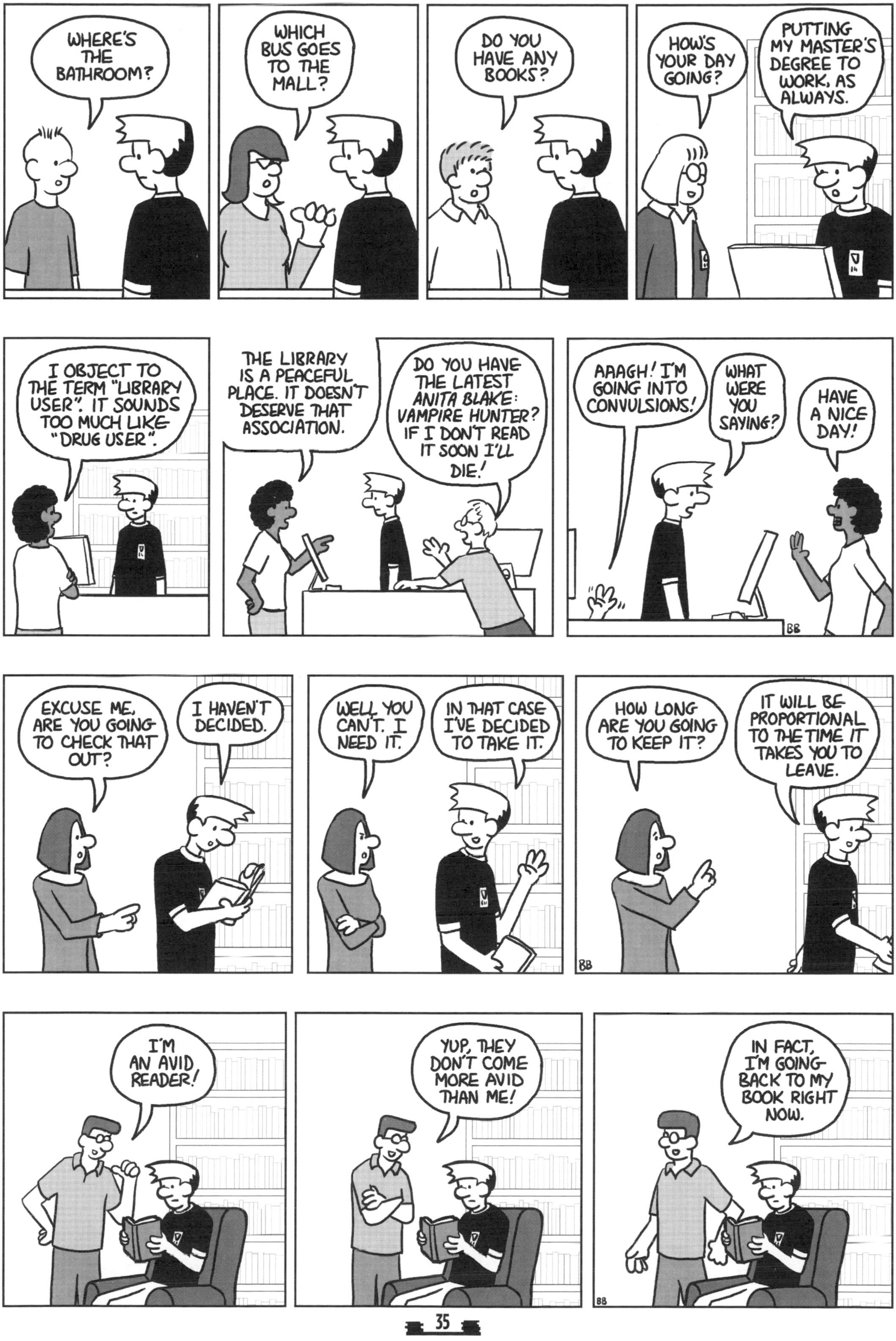
WHERE'S THE BATHROOM?
WHICH BUS GOES TO THE MALL?
DO YOU HAVE ANY BOOKS?
HOW'S YOUR DAY GOING?
PUTTING MY MASTER'S DEGREE TO WORK, AS ALWAYS.
I OBJECT TO THE TERM "LIBRARY USER". IT SOUNDS TOO MUCH LIKE "DRUG USER".
THE LIBRARY IS A PEACEFUL PLACE. IT DOESN'T DESERVE THAT ASSOCIATION.
DO YOU HAVE THE LATEST ANITA BLAKE: VAMPIRE HUNTER? IF I DON'T READ IT SOON I'LL DIE!
AAAGH! I'M GOING INTO CONVULSIONS!
WHAT WERE YOU SAYING?
HAVE A NICE DAY!
BB
EXCUSE ME, ARE YOU GOING TO CHECK THAT OUT?
I HAVEN'T DECIDED.
WELL YOU CAN'T. I NEED IT.
IN THAT CASE I'VE DECIDED TO TAKE IT.
HOW LONG ARE YOU GOING TO KEEP IT?
IT WILL BE PROPORTIONAL TO THE TIME IT TAKES YOU TO LEAVE.
BB
I'M AN AVID READER!
YUP, THEY DON'T COME MORE AVID THAN ME!
IN FACT, I'M GOING BACK TO MY BOOK RIGHT NOW.
BB

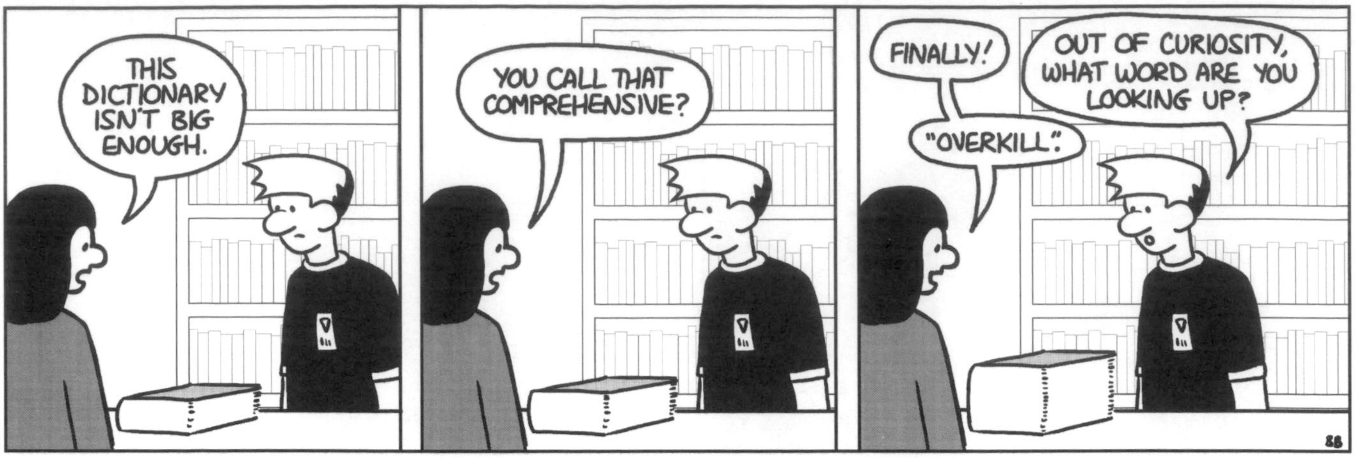
THIS DICTIONARY ISN'T BIG ENOUGH.
YOU CALL THAT COMPREHENSIVE?
FINALLY!
OUT OF CURIOSITY, WHAT WORD ARE YOU LOOKING UP?
"OVERKILL."
BB

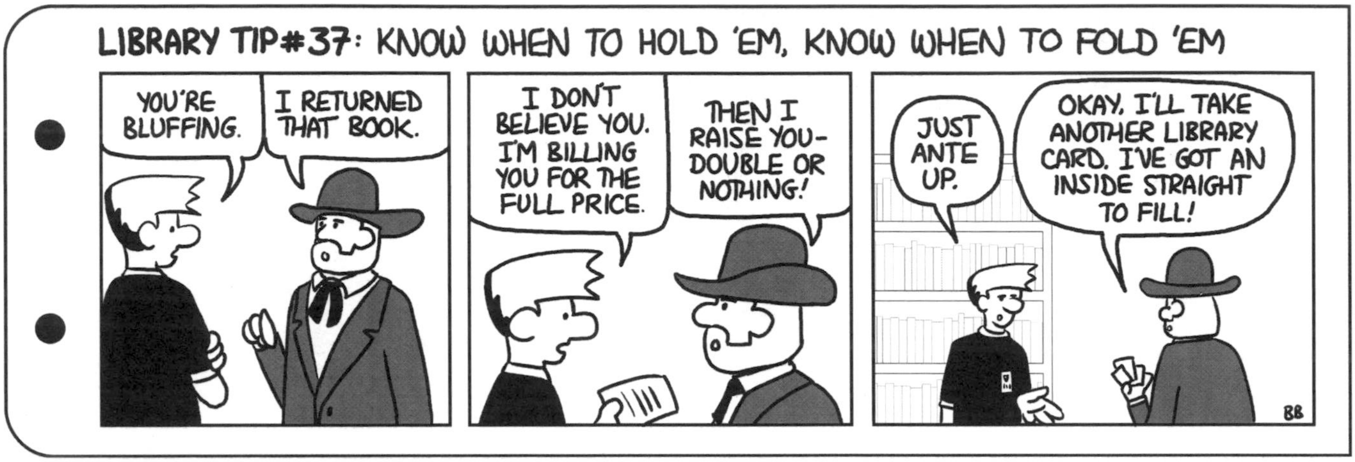
LIBRARY TIP#37: KNOW WHEN TO HOLD 'EM, KNOW WHEN TO FOLD 'EM
YOU'RE BLUFFING.
I RETURNED THAT BOOK.
I DON'T BELIEVE YOU. I'M BILLING YOU FOR THE FULL PRICE.
THEN I RAISE YOU- DOUBLE OR NOTHING!
JUST ANTE UP.
OKAY, I'LL TAKE ANOTHER LIBRARY CARD. I'VE GOT AN INSIDE STRAIGHT TO FILL!
BB

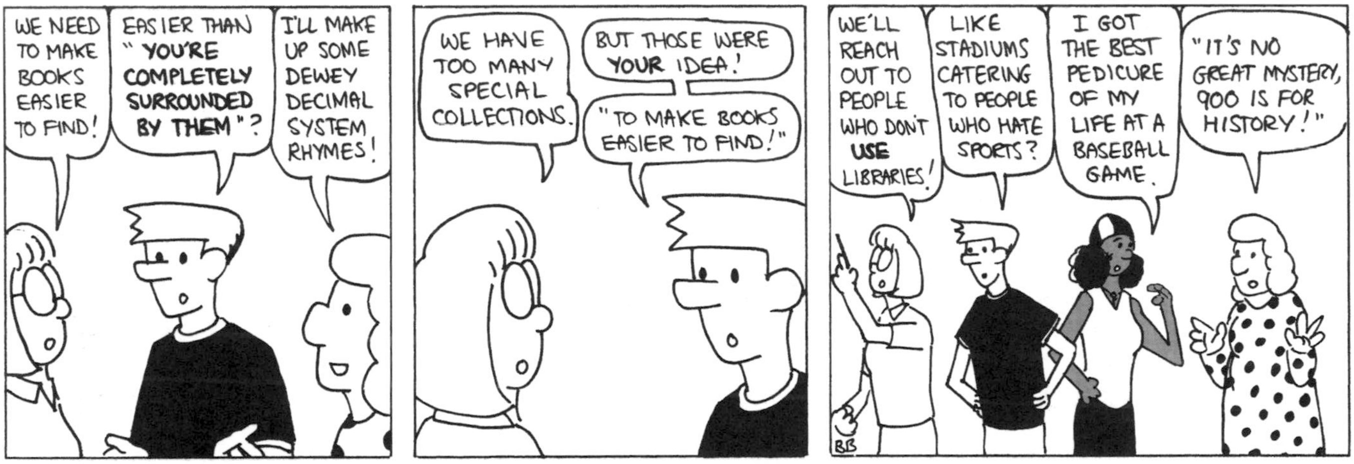
WE NEED TO MAKE BOOKS EASIER TO FIND!
EASIER THAN "YOU'RE COMPLETELY SURROUNDED BY THEM"?
I'LL MAKE UP SOME DEWEY DECIMAL SYSTEM RHYMES!
WE HAVE TOO MANY SPECIAL COLLECTIONS.
BUT THOSE WERE YOUR IDEA!
"TO MAKE BOOKS EASIER TO FIND!"
WE'LL REACH OUT TO PEOPLE WHO DON'T USE LIBRARIES!
LIKE STADIUMS CATERING TO PEOPLE WHO HATE SPORTS?
I GOT THE BEST PEDICURE OF MY LIFE AT A BASEBALL GAME.
"IT'S NO GREAT MYSTERY, 900 IS FOR HISTORY!"
BB

One day Bill was behind the eight-ball on strips and we found this one, which for some reason we had never run. We want to hear that rap.

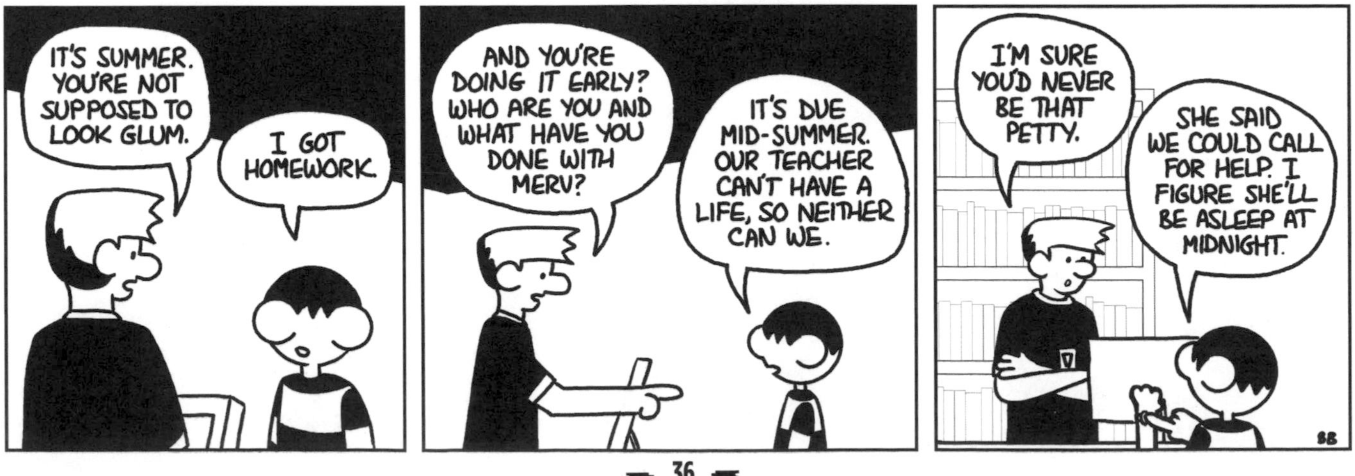
IT'S SUMMER. YOU'RE NOT SUPPOSED TO LOOK GLUM.
I GOT HOMEWORK.
AND YOU'RE DOING IT EARLY? WHO ARE YOU AND WHAT HAVE YOU DONE WITH MERV?
IT'S DUE MID-SUMMER. OUR TEACHER CAN'T HAVE A LIFE, SO NEITHER CAN WE.
I'M SURE YOU'D NEVER BE THAT PETTY.
SHE SAID WE COULD CALL FOR HELP. I FIGURE SHE'LL BE ASLEEP AT MIDNIGHT.
BB

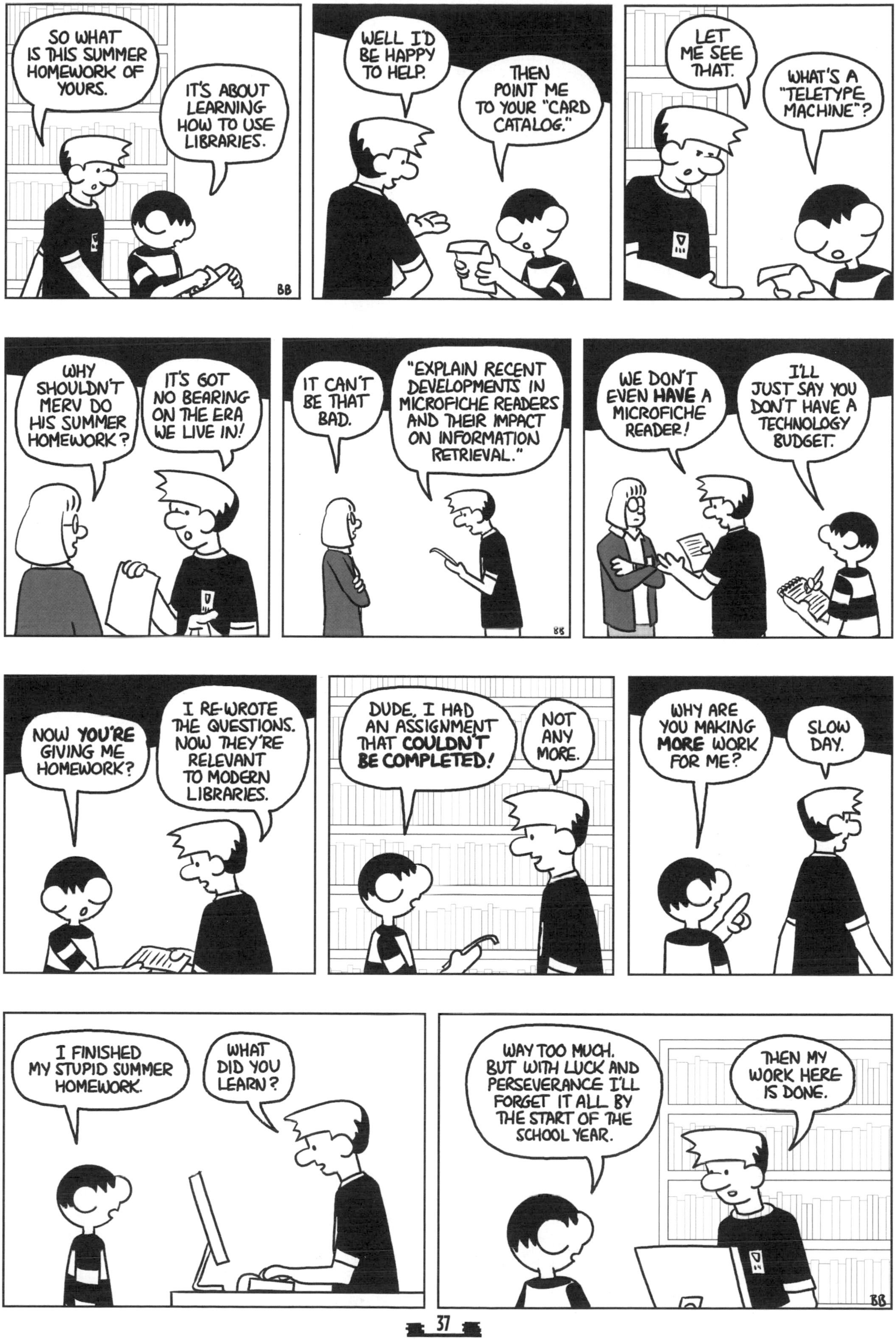

SO WHAT IS THIS SUMMER HOMEWORK OF YOURS.
IT'S ABOUT LEARNING HOW TO USE LIBRARIES.
BB
WELL I'D BE HAPPY TO HELP.
THEN POINT ME TO YOUR "CARD CATALOG."
LET ME SEE THAT.
WHAT'S A "TELETYPE MACHINE"?
WHY SHOULDN'T MERV DO HIS SUMMER HOMEWORK?
IT'S GOT NO BEARING ON THE ERA WE LIVE IN!
IT CAN'T BE THAT BAD.
"EXPLAIN RECENT DEVELOPMENTS IN MICROFICHE READERS AND THEIR IMPACT ON INFORMATION RETRIEVAL."
BB
WE DON'T EVEN **HAVE** A MICROFICHE READER!
I'LL JUST SAY YOU DON'T HAVE A TECHNOLOGY BUDGET.
NOW **YOU'RE** GIVING ME HOMEWORK?
I RE-WROTE THE QUESTIONS. NOW THEY'RE RELEVANT TO MODERN LIBRARIES.
DUDE, I HAD AN ASSIGNMENT THAT **COULDN'T BE COMPLETED**!
NOT ANY MORE.
WHY ARE YOU MAKING **MORE** WORK FOR ME?
SLOW DAY.
I FINISHED MY STUPID SUMMER HOMEWORK.
WHAT DID YOU LEARN?
WAY TOO MUCH. BUT WITH LUCK AND PERSEVERANCE I'LL FORGET IT ALL BY THE START OF THE SCHOOL YEAR.
THEN MY WORK HERE IS DONE.
BB

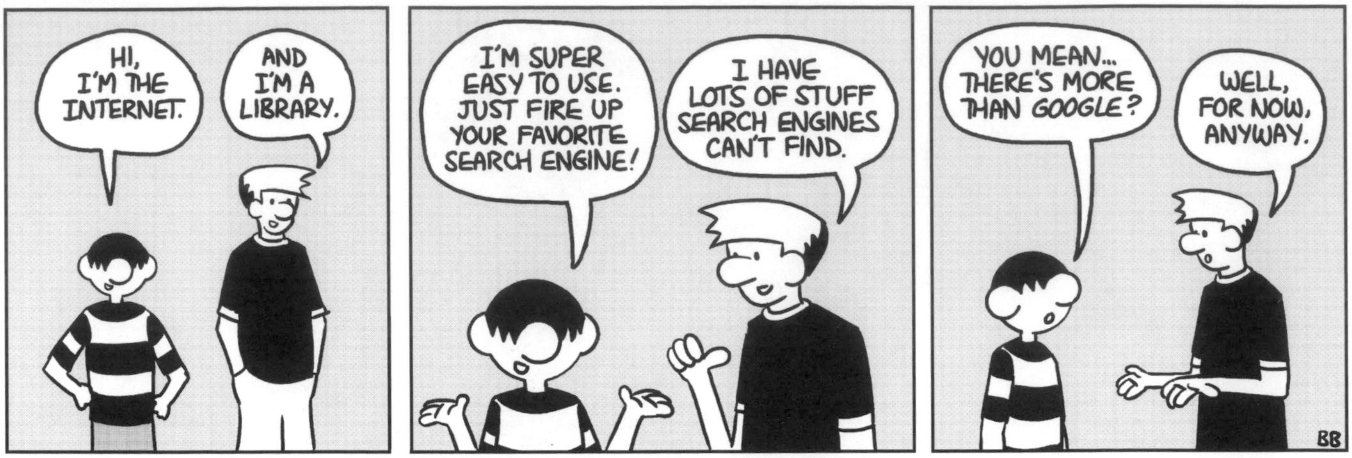
HI, I'M THE INTERNET.
AND I'M A LIBRARY.
I'M SUPER EASY TO USE. JUST FIRE UP YOUR FAVORITE SEARCH ENGINE!
I HAVE LOTS OF STUFF SEARCH ENGINES CAN'T FIND.
YOU MEAN... THERE'S MORE THAN *GOOGLE*?
WELL, FOR NOW, ANYWAY.
BB

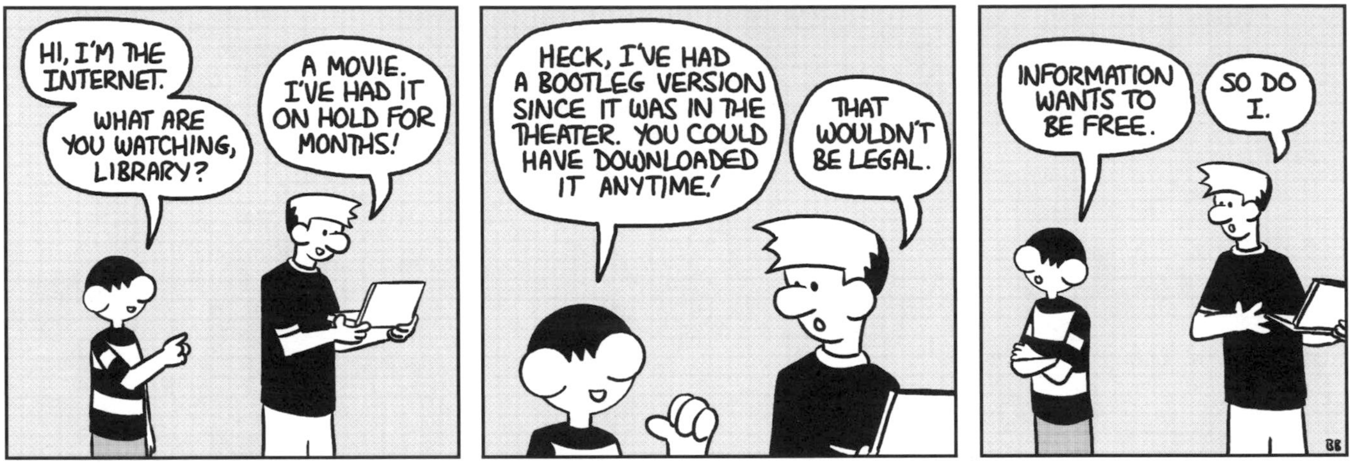
HI, I'M THE INTERNET.
WHAT ARE YOU WATCHING, LIBRARY?
A MOVIE. I'VE HAD IT ON HOLD FOR MONTHS!
HECK, I'VE HAD A BOOTLEG VERSION SINCE IT WAS IN THE THEATER. YOU COULD HAVE DOWNLOADED IT ANYTIME!
THAT WOULDN'T BE LEGAL.
INFORMATION WANTS TO BE FREE.
SO DO I.
BB

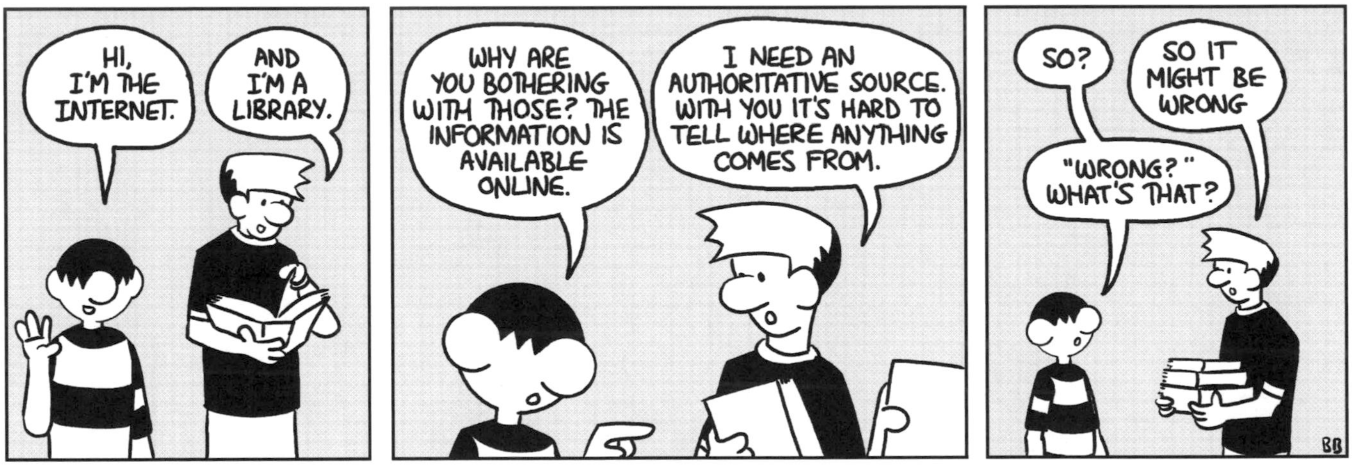
HI, I'M THE INTERNET.
AND I'M A LIBRARY.
WHY ARE YOU BOTHERING WITH THOSE? THE INFORMATION IS AVAILABLE ONLINE.
I NEED AN AUTHORITATIVE SOURCE. WITH YOU IT'S HARD TO TELL WHERE ANYTHING COMES FROM.
SO?
SO IT MIGHT BE WRONG
"WRONG?" WHAT'S THAT?
BB

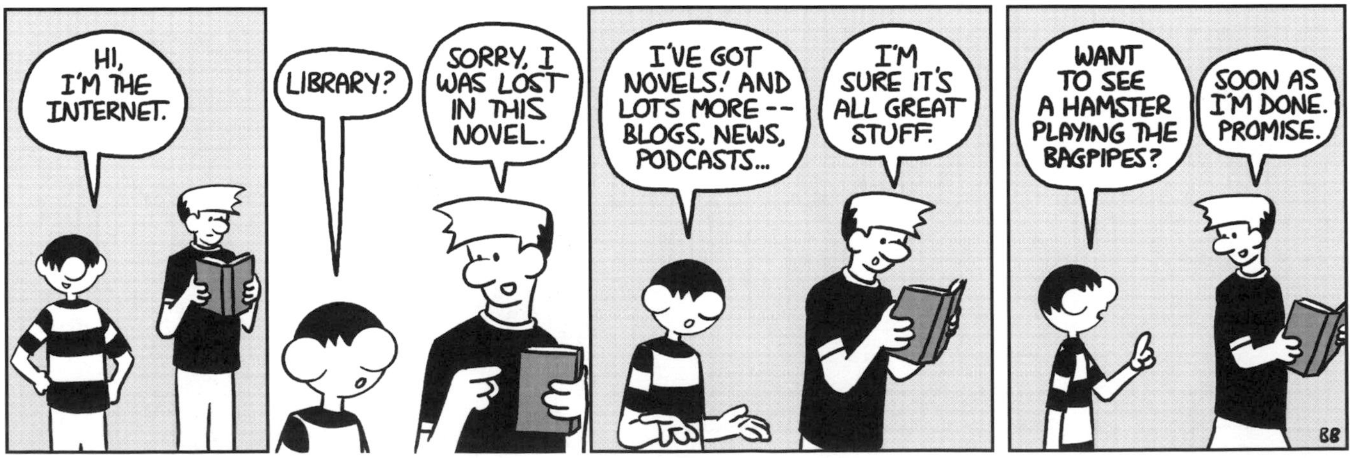
HI, I'M THE INTERNET.
LIBRARY?
SORRY, I WAS LOST IN THIS NOVEL.
I'VE GOT NOVELS! AND LOTS MORE -- BLOGS, NEWS, PODCASTS...
I'M SURE IT'S ALL GREAT STUFF.
WANT TO SEE A HAMSTER PLAYING THE BAGPIPES?
SOON AS I'M DONE. PROMISE.
BB

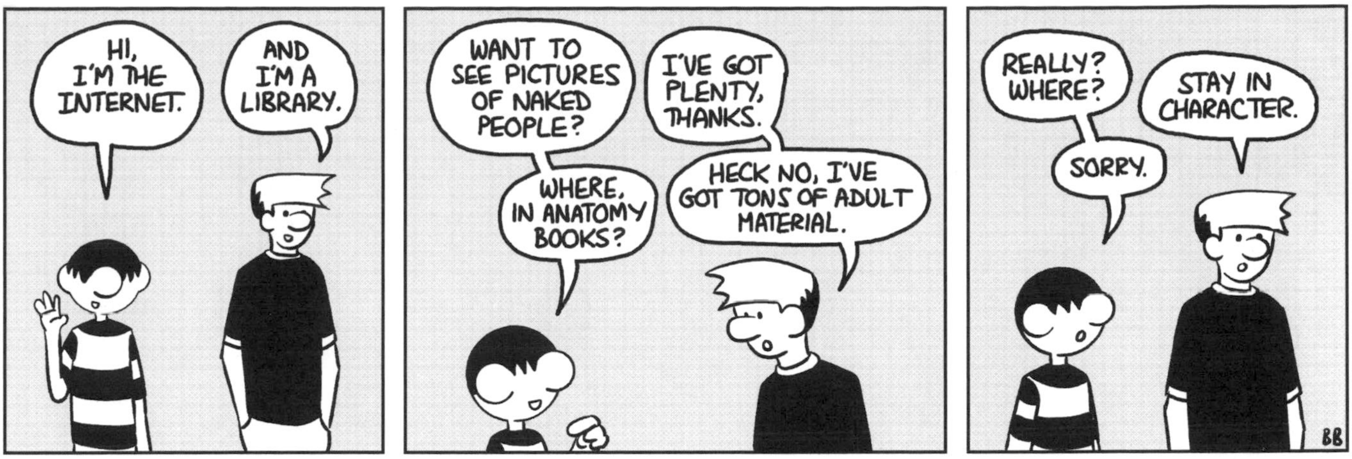
HI, I'M THE INTERNET.
AND I'M A LIBRARY.
WANT TO SEE PICTURES OF NAKED PEOPLE?
I'VE GOT PLENTY, THANKS.
WHERE, IN ANATOMY BOOKS?
HECK NO, I'VE GOT TONS OF ADULT MATERIAL.
REALLY? WHERE?
SORRY.
STAY IN CHARACTER.
BB

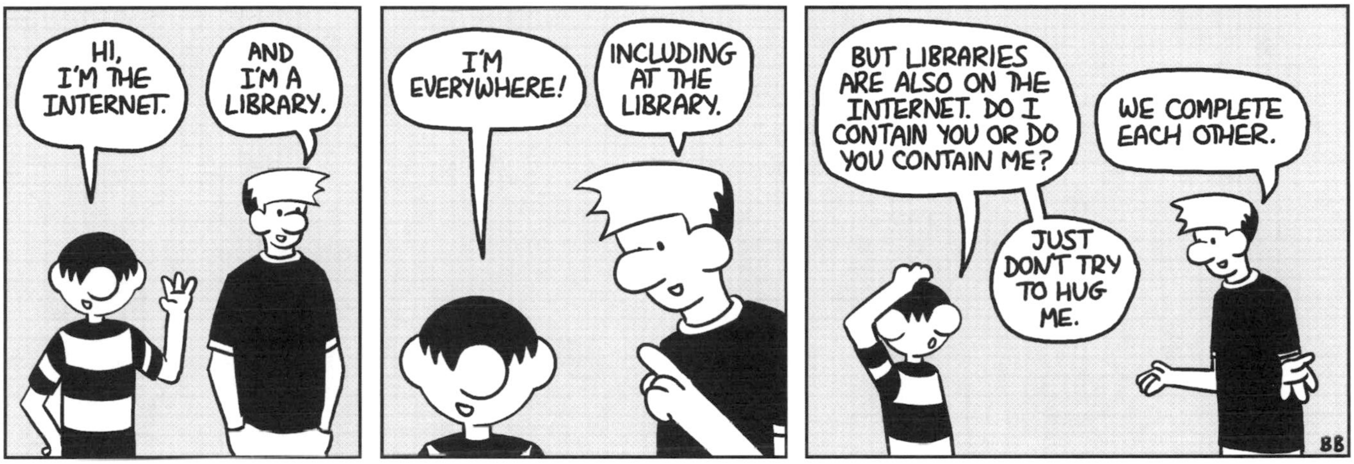
HI, I'M THE INTERNET.
AND I'M A LIBRARY.
I'M EVERYWHERE!
INCLUDING AT THE LIBRARY.
BUT LIBRARIES ARE ALSO ON THE INTERNET. DO I CONTAIN YOU OR DO YOU CONTAIN ME?
JUST DON'T TRY TO HUG ME.
WE COMPLETE EACH OTHER.
BB

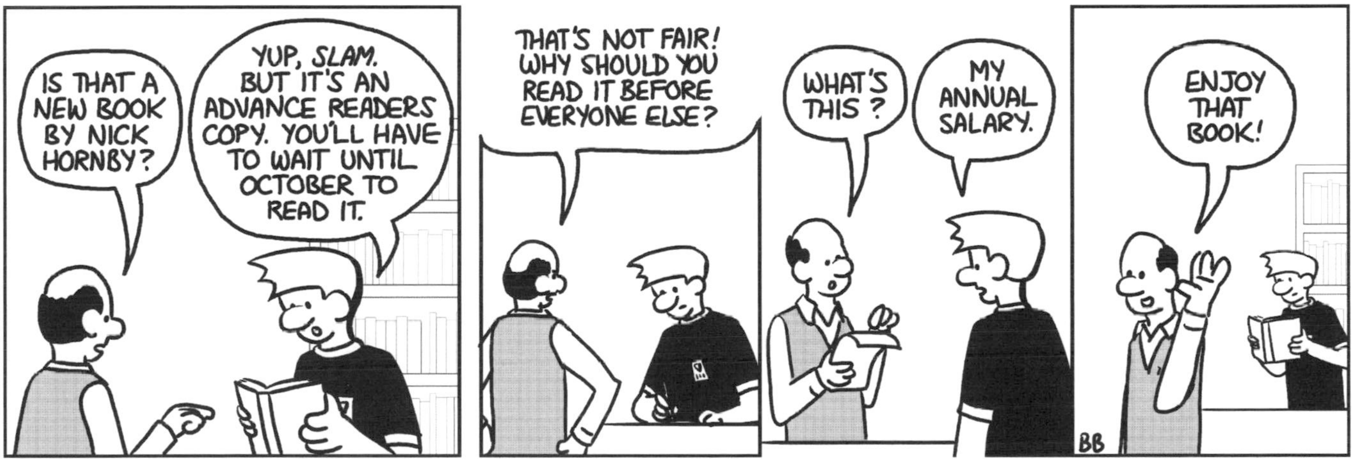
IS THAT A NEW BOOK BY NICK HORNBY?
YUP, SLAM. BUT IT'S AN ADVANCE READERS COPY. YOU'LL HAVE TO WAIT UNTIL OCTOBER TO READ IT.
THAT'S NOT FAIR! WHY SHOULD YOU READ IT BEFORE EVERYONE ELSE?
WHAT'S THIS?
MY ANNUAL SALARY.
ENJOY THAT BOOK!
BB

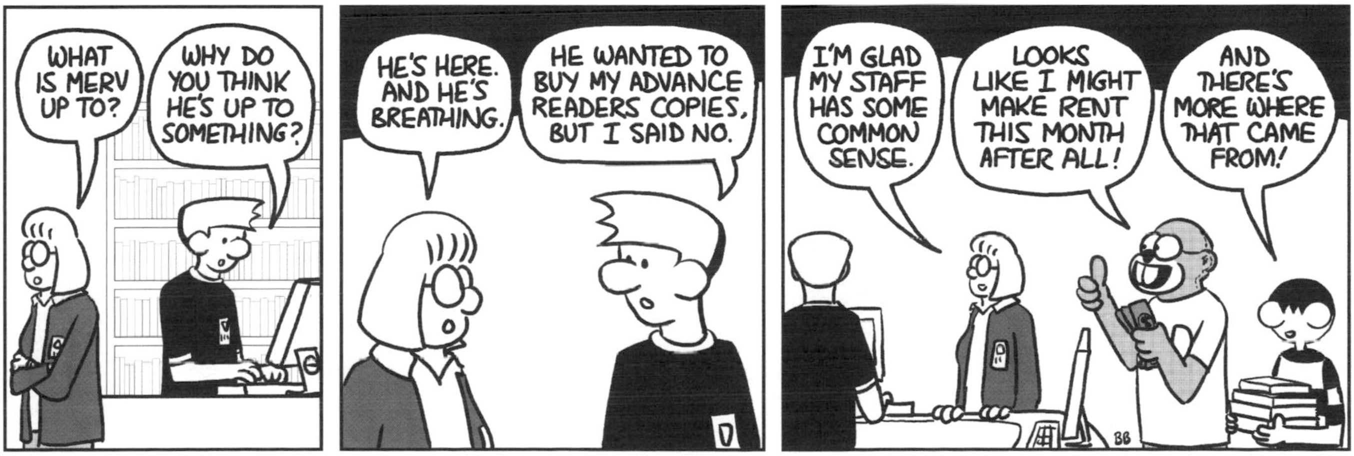
WHAT IS MERV UP TO?
WHY DO YOU THINK HE'S UP TO SOMETHING?
HE'S HERE. AND HE'S BREATHING.
HE WANTED TO BUY MY ADVANCE READERS COPIES, BUT I SAID NO.
I'M GLAD MY STAFF HAS SOME COMMON SENSE.
LOOKS LIKE I MIGHT MAKE RENT THIS MONTH AFTER ALL!
AND THERE'S MORE WHERE THAT CAME FROM!
BB

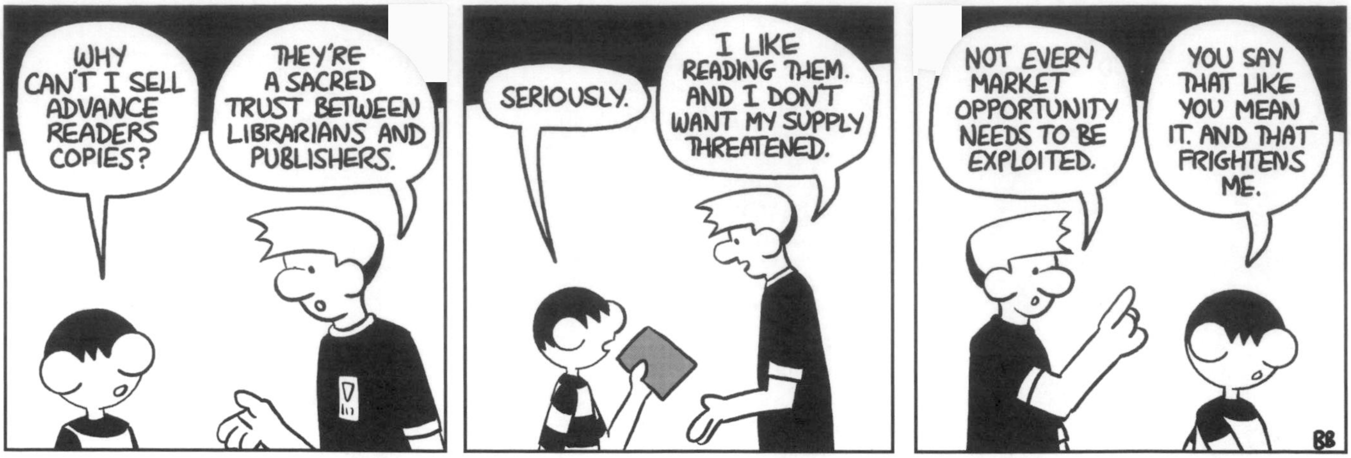
WHY CAN'T I SELL ADVANCE READERS COPIES?
THEY'RE A SACRED TRUST BETWEEN LIBRARIANS AND PUBLISHERS.
SERIOUSLY.
I LIKE READING THEM. AND I DON'T WANT MY SUPPLY THREATENED.
NOT EVERY MARKET OPPORTUNITY NEEDS TO BE EXPLOITED.
YOU SAY THAT LIKE YOU MEAN IT. AND THAT FRIGHTENS ME.
BB

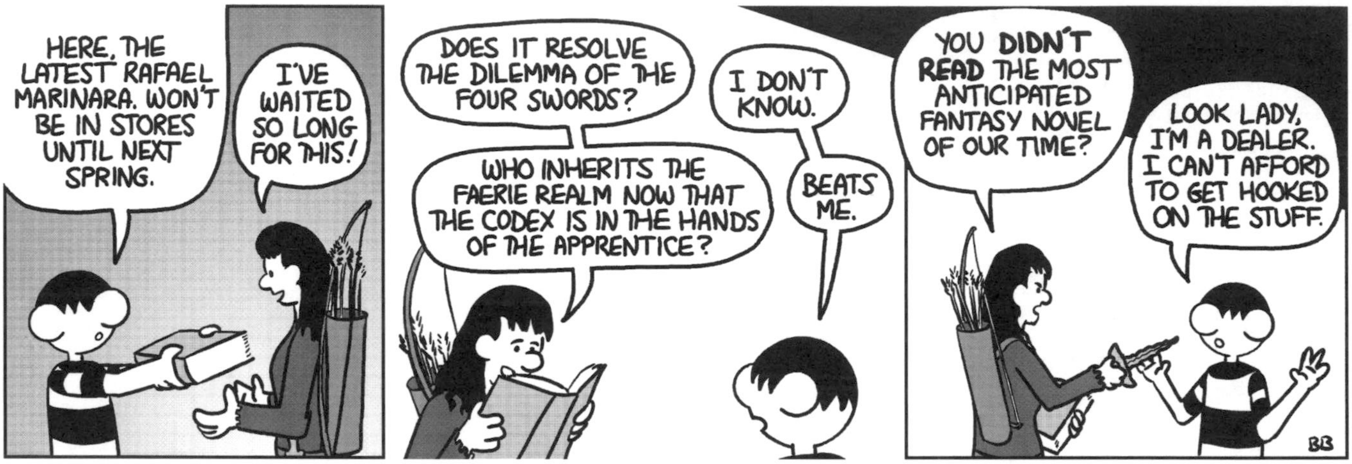
HERE, THE LATEST RAFAEL MARINARA. WON'T BE IN STORES UNTIL NEXT SPRING.
I'VE WAITED SO LONG FOR THIS!
DOES IT RESOLVE THE DILEMMA OF THE FOUR SWORDS?
WHO INHERITS THE FAERIE REALM NOW THAT THE CODEX IS IN THE HANDS OF THE APPRENTICE?
I DON'T KNOW.
BEATS ME.
YOU **DIDN'T READ** THE MOST ANTICIPATED FANTASY NOVEL OF OUR TIME?
LOOK LADY, I'M A DEALER. I CAN'T AFFORD TO GET HOOKED ON THE STUFF.
BB

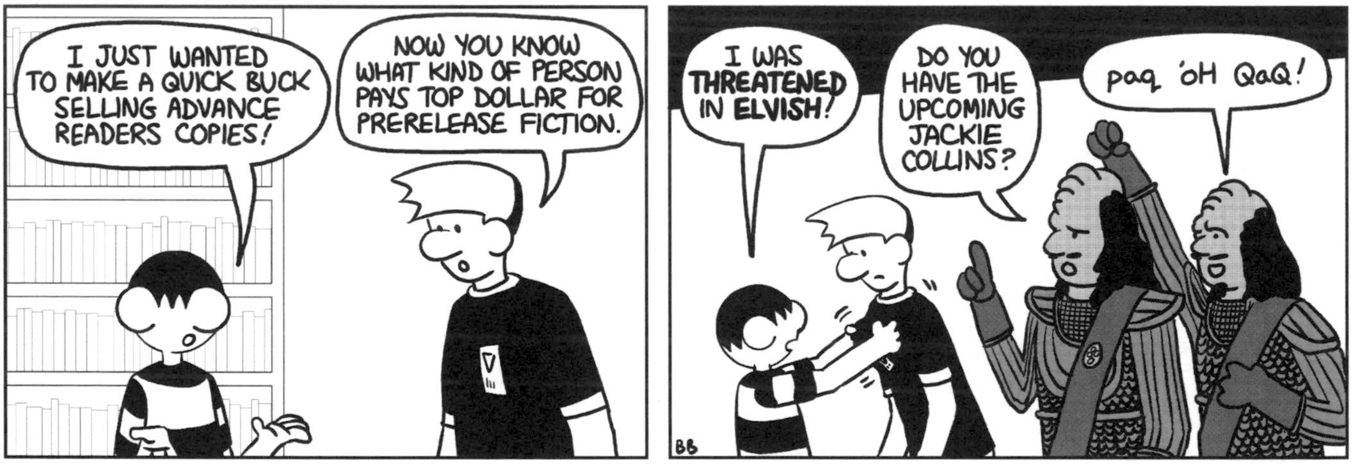
I JUST WANTED TO MAKE A QUICK BUCK SELLING ADVANCE READERS COPIES!
NOW YOU KNOW WHAT KIND OF PERSON PAYS TOP DOLLAR FOR PRERELEASE FICTION.
BB
I WAS **THREATENED** IN **ELVISH**!
DO YOU HAVE THE UPCOMING JACKIE COLLINS?
paq 'oH QaQ!

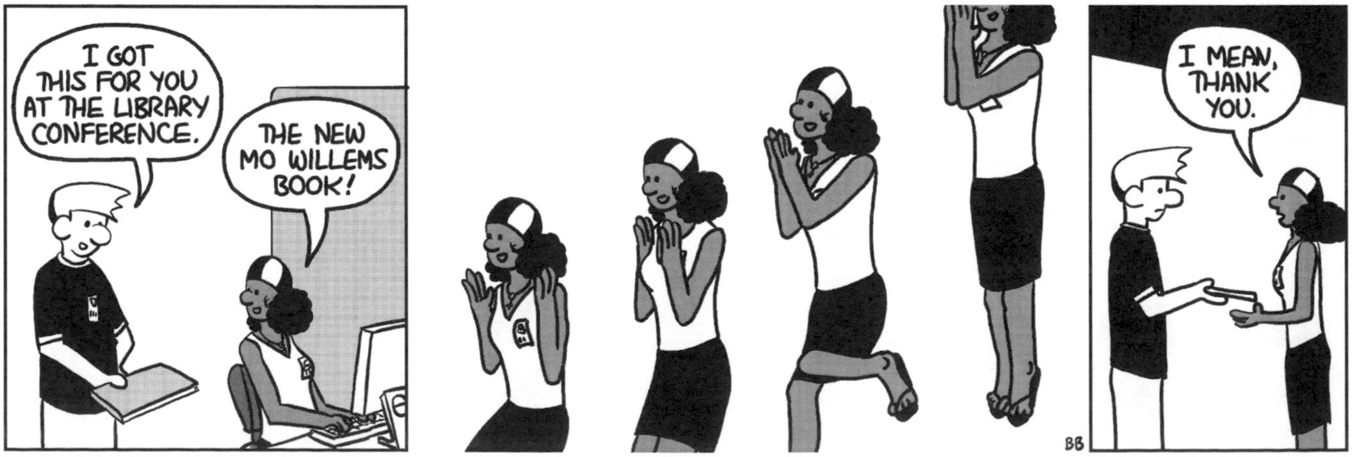
I GOT THIS FOR YOU AT THE LIBRARY CONFERENCE.
THE NEW MO WILLEMS BOOK!
I MEAN, THANK YOU.
BB

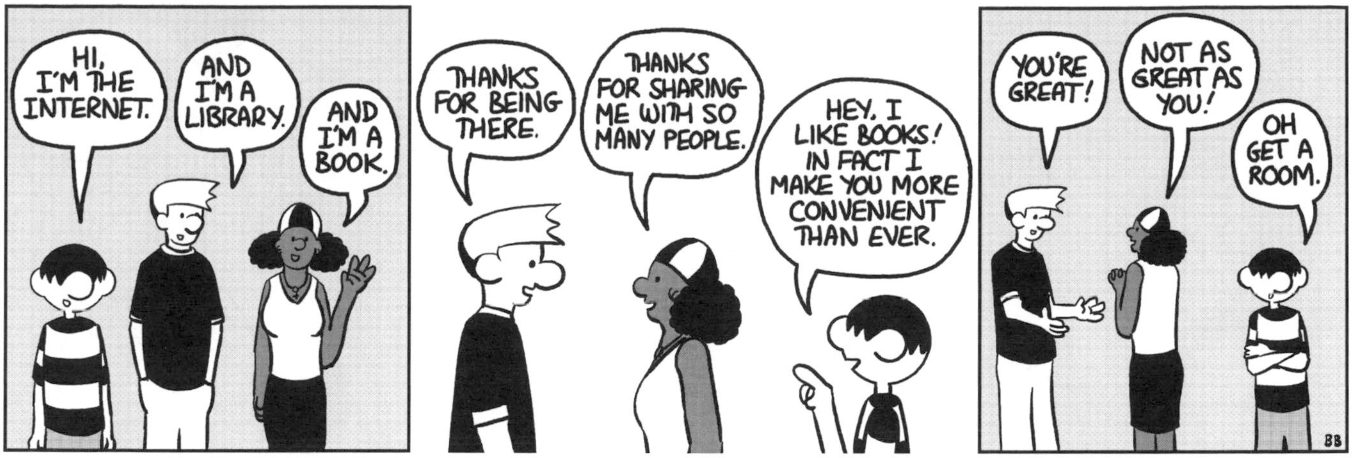
HI, I'M THE INTERNET.
AND I'M A LIBRARY.
AND I'M A BOOK.
THANKS FOR BEING THERE.
THANKS FOR SHARING ME WITH SO MANY PEOPLE.
HEY, I LIKE BOOKS! IN FACT I MAKE YOU MORE CONVENIENT THAN EVER.
YOU'RE GREAT!
NOT AS GREAT AS YOU!
OH GET A ROOM.
BB

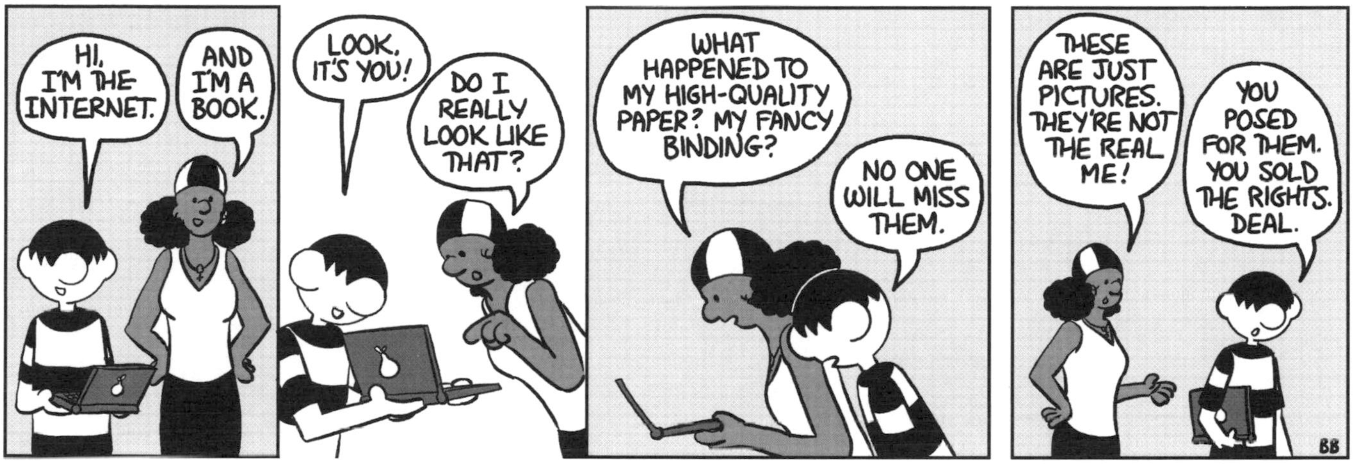
HI, I'M THE INTERNET.
AND I'M A BOOK.
LOOK, IT'S YOU!
DO I REALLY LOOK LIKE THAT?
WHAT HAPPENED TO MY HIGH-QUALITY PAPER? MY FANCY BINDING?
NO ONE WILL MISS THEM.
THESE ARE JUST PICTURES. THEY'RE NOT THE REAL ME!
YOU POSED FOR THEM. YOU SOLD THE RIGHTS. DEAL.
BB

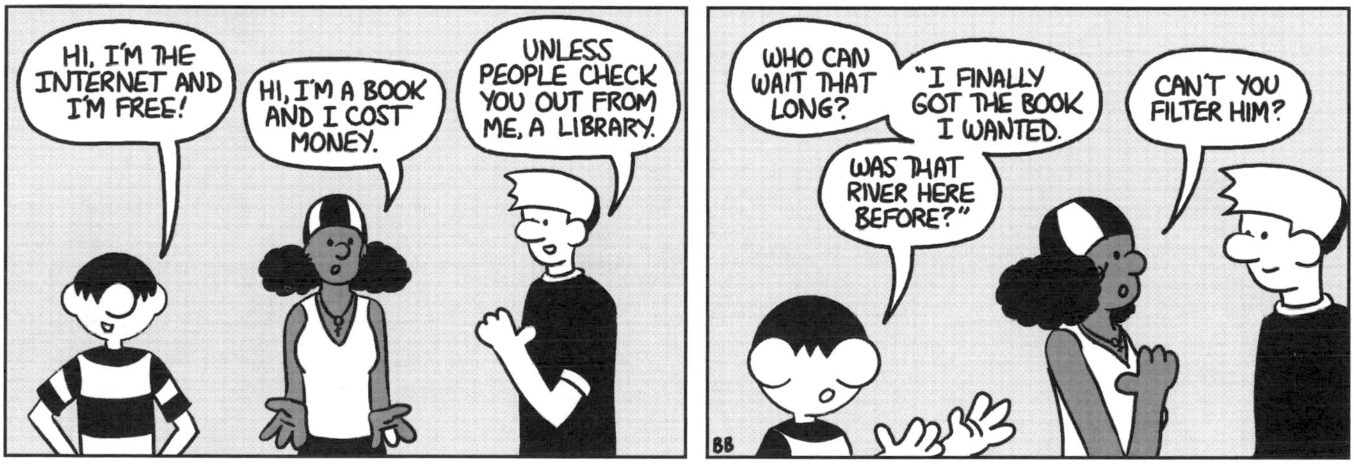
HI, I'M THE INTERNET AND I'M FREE!
HI, I'M A BOOK AND I COST MONEY.
UNLESS PEOPLE CHECK YOU OUT FROM ME, A LIBRARY.
BB
WHO CAN WAIT THAT LONG?
"I FINALLY GOT THE BOOK I WANTED.
WAS THAT RIVER HERE BEFORE?"
CAN'T YOU FILTER HIM?

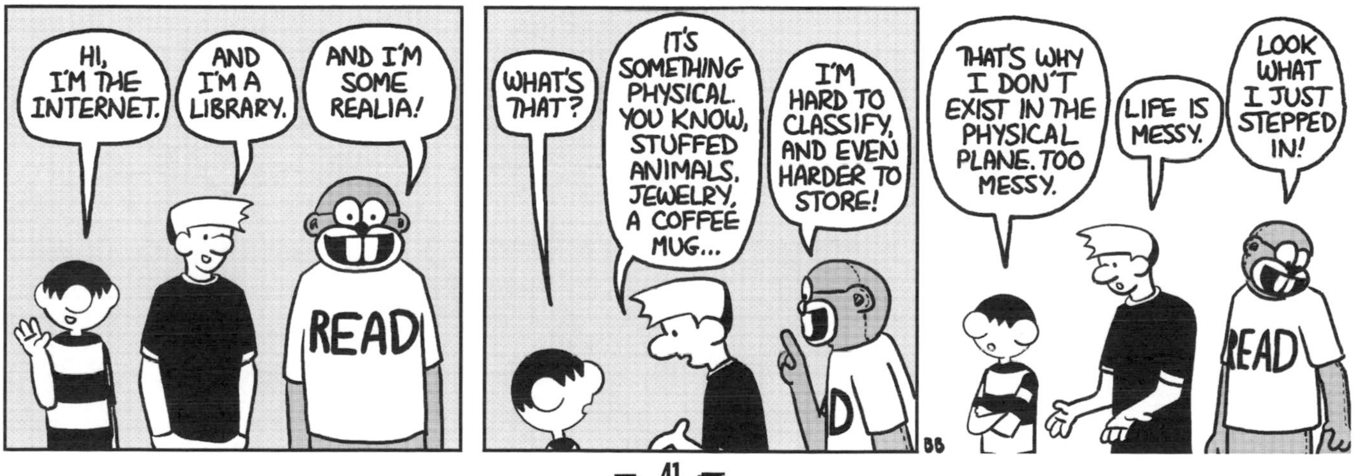
HI, I'M THE INTERNET.
AND I'M A LIBRARY.
AND I'M SOME REALIA!
READ
WHAT'S THAT?
IT'S SOMETHING PHYSICAL. YOU KNOW, STUFFED ANIMALS, JEWELRY, A COFFEE MUG...
I'M HARD TO CLASSIFY, AND EVEN HARDER TO STORE!
BB
THAT'S WHY I DON'T EXIST IN THE PHYSICAL PLANE. TOO MESSY.
LIFE IS MESSY.
LOOK WHAT I JUST STEPPED IN!
READ

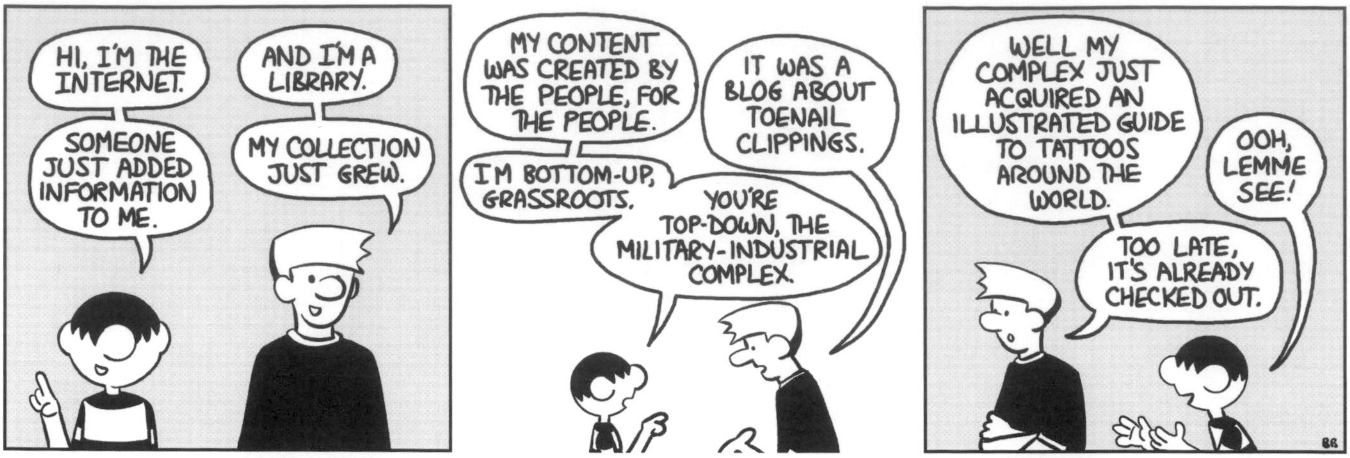
HI, I'M THE INTERNET.
SOMEONE JUST ADDED INFORMATION TO ME.
AND I'M A LIBRARY.
MY COLLECTION JUST GREW.
MY CONTENT WAS CREATED BY THE PEOPLE, FOR THE PEOPLE.
I'M BOTTOM-UP, GRASSROOTS.
YOU'RE TOP-DOWN, THE MILITARY-INDUSTRIAL COMPLEX.
IT WAS A BLOG ABOUT TOENAIL CLIPPINGS.
WELL MY COMPLEX JUST ACQUIRED AN ILLUSTRATED GUIDE TO TATTOOS AROUND THE WORLD.
OOH, LEMME SEE!
TOO LATE, IT'S ALREADY CHECKED OUT.
BB

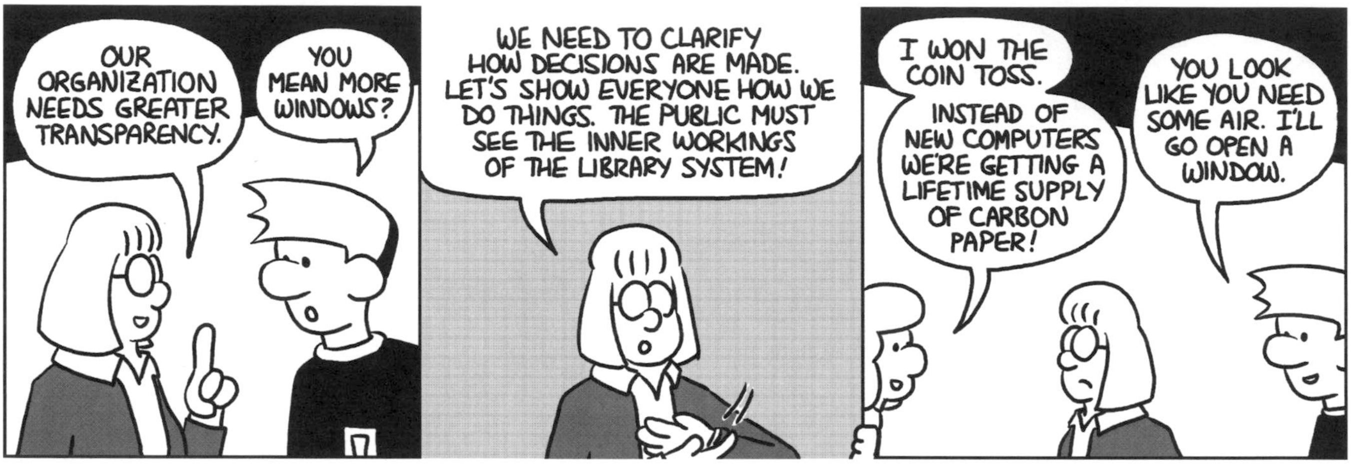
OUR ORGANIZATION NEEDS GREATER TRANSPARENCY.
YOU MEAN MORE WINDOWS?
WE NEED TO CLARIFY HOW DECISIONS ARE MADE. LET'S SHOW EVERYONE HOW WE DO THINGS. THE PUBLIC MUST SEE THE INNER WORKINGS OF THE LIBRARY SYSTEM!
I WON THE COIN TOSS.
INSTEAD OF NEW COMPUTERS WE'RE GETTING A LIFETIME SUPPLY OF CARBON PAPER!
YOU LOOK LIKE YOU NEED SOME AIR. I'LL GO OPEN A WINDOW.

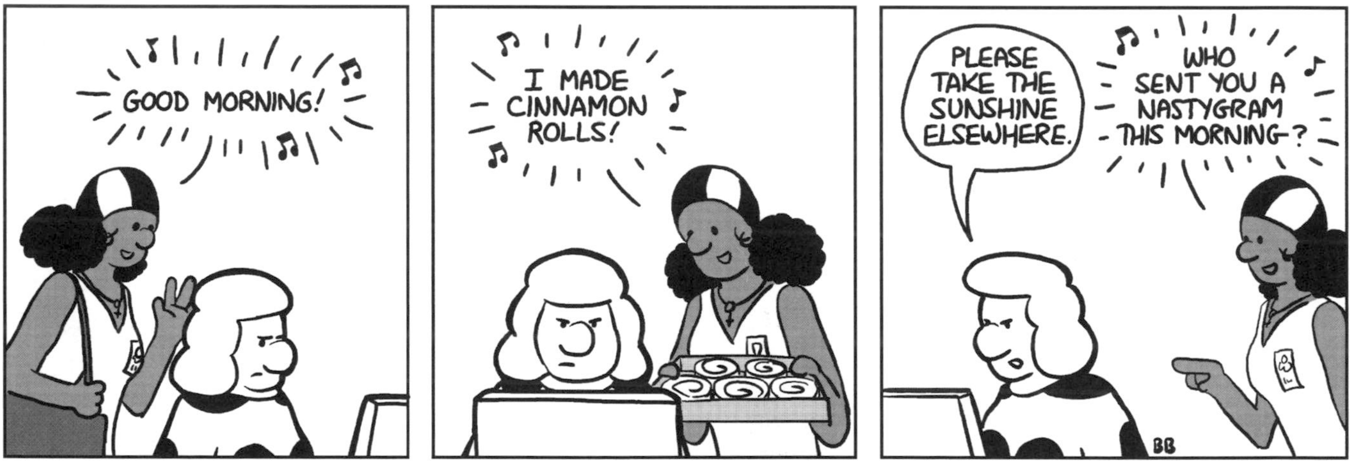
GOOD MORNING!
I MADE CINNAMON ROLLS!
PLEASE TAKE THE SUNSHINE ELSEWHERE.
WHO SENT YOU A NASTYGRAM THIS MORNING?
BB

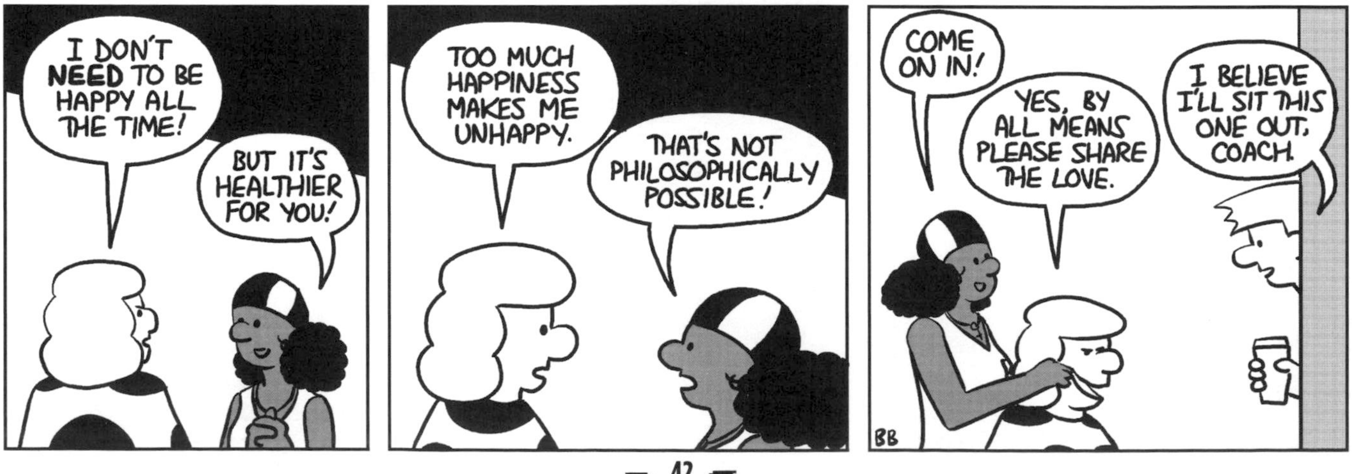
I DON'T **NEED** TO BE HAPPY ALL THE TIME!
BUT IT'S HEALTHIER FOR YOU!
TOO MUCH HAPPINESS MAKES ME UNHAPPY.
THAT'S NOT PHILOSOPHICALLY POSSIBLE!
COME ON IN!
YES, BY ALL MEANS PLEASE SHARE THE LOVE.
I BELIEVE I'LL SIT THIS ONE OUT, COACH.
BB

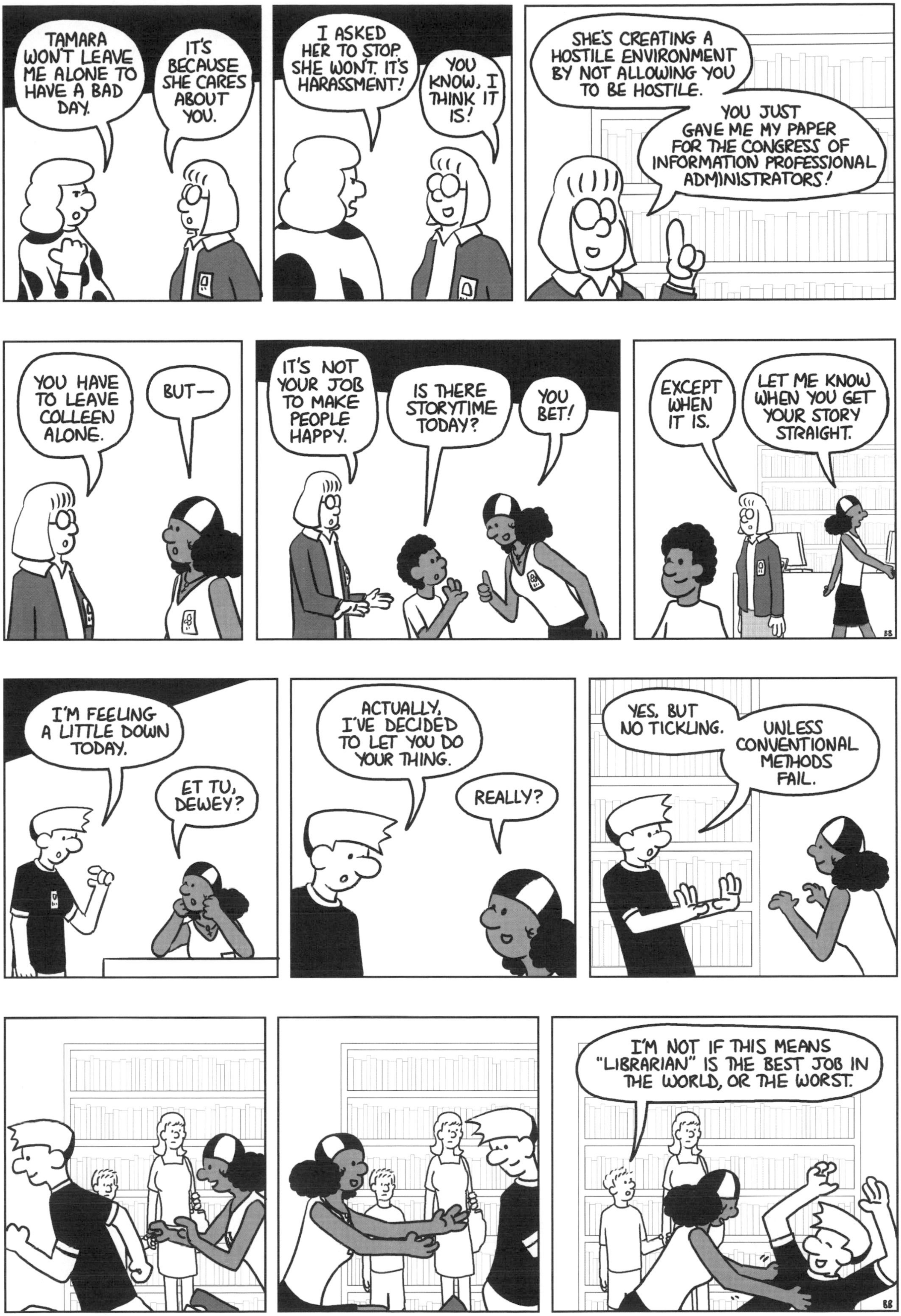
TAMARA WON'T LEAVE ME ALONE TO HAVE A BAD DAY.
IT'S BECAUSE SHE CARES ABOUT YOU.
I ASKED HER TO STOP. SHE WON'T. IT'S HARASSMENT!
YOU KNOW, I THINK IT IS!
SHE'S CREATING A HOSTILE ENVIRONMENT BY NOT ALLOWING YOU TO BE HOSTILE.
YOU JUST GAVE ME MY PAPER FOR THE CONGRESS OF INFORMATION PROFESSIONAL ADMINISTRATORS!
YOU HAVE TO LEAVE COLLEEN ALONE.
BUT—
IT'S NOT YOUR JOB TO MAKE PEOPLE HAPPY.
IS THERE STORYTIME TODAY?
YOU BET!
EXCEPT WHEN IT IS.
LET ME KNOW WHEN YOU GET YOUR STORY STRAIGHT.
BB
I'M FEELING A LITTLE DOWN TODAY.
ET TU, DEWEY?
ACTUALLY, I'VE DECIDED TO LET YOU DO YOUR THING.
REALLY?
YES, BUT NO TICKLING.
UNLESS CONVENTIONAL METHODS FAIL.
I'M NOT IF THIS MEANS "LIBRARIAN" IS THE BEST JOB IN THE WORLD, OR THE WORST.
BB

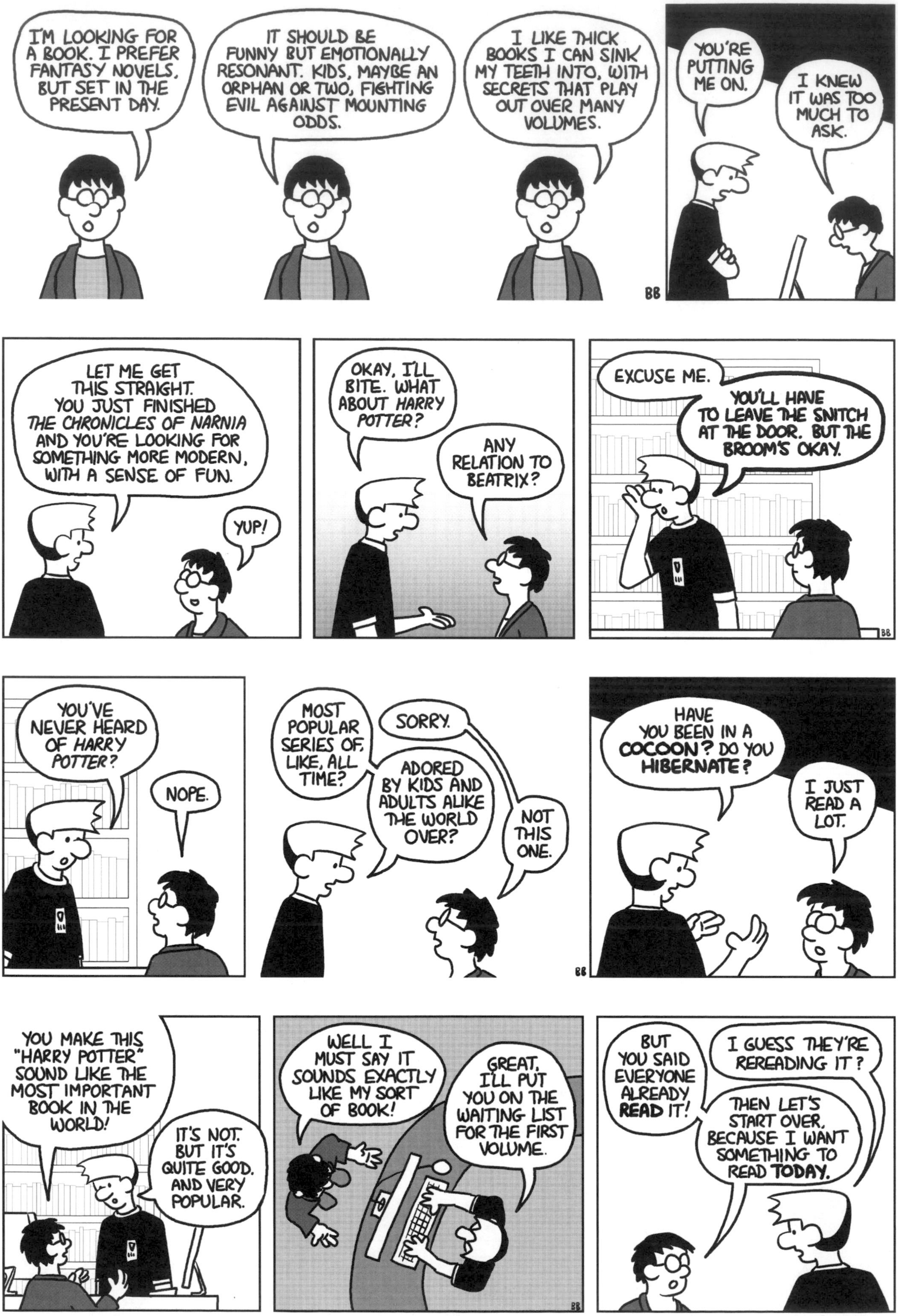
I'M LOOKING FOR A BOOK. I PREFER FANTASY NOVELS, BUT SET IN THE PRESENT DAY.
IT SHOULD BE FUNNY BUT EMOTIONALLY RESONANT. KIDS, MAYBE AN ORPHAN OR TWO, FIGHTING EVIL AGAINST MOUNTING ODDS.
I LIKE THICK BOOKS I CAN SINK MY TEETH INTO, WITH SECRETS THAT PLAY OUT OVER MANY VOLUMES.
YOU'RE PUTTING ME ON.
I KNEW IT WAS TOO MUCH TO ASK.
BB
LET ME GET THIS STRAIGHT. YOU JUST FINISHED *THE CHRONICLES OF NARNIA* AND YOU'RE LOOKING FOR SOMETHING MORE MODERN, WITH A SENSE OF FUN.
YUP!
OKAY, I'LL BITE. WHAT ABOUT *HARRY POTTER*?
ANY RELATION TO BEATRIX?
EXCUSE ME.
YOU'LL HAVE TO LEAVE THE SNITCH AT THE DOOR. BUT THE BROOM'S OKAY.
BB
YOU'VE NEVER HEARD OF *HARRY POTTER*?
NOPE.
MOST POPULAR SERIES OF, LIKE, ALL TIME?
SORRY.
ADORED BY KIDS AND ADULTS ALIKE THE WORLD OVER?
NOT THIS ONE.
BB
HAVE YOU BEEN IN A **COCOON**? DO YOU **HIBERNATE**?
I JUST READ A LOT.
YOU MAKE THIS "HARRY POTTER" SOUND LIKE THE MOST IMPORTANT BOOK IN THE WORLD!
IT'S NOT. BUT IT'S QUITE GOOD. AND VERY POPULAR.
WELL I MUST SAY IT SOUNDS EXACTLY LIKE MY SORT OF BOOK!
GREAT, I'LL PUT YOU ON THE WAITING LIST FOR THE FIRST VOLUME.
BB
BUT YOU SAID EVERYONE ALREADY **READ** IT!
I GUESS THEY'RE REREADING IT?
THEN LET'S START OVER, BECAUSE I WANT SOMETHING TO READ **TODAY**.

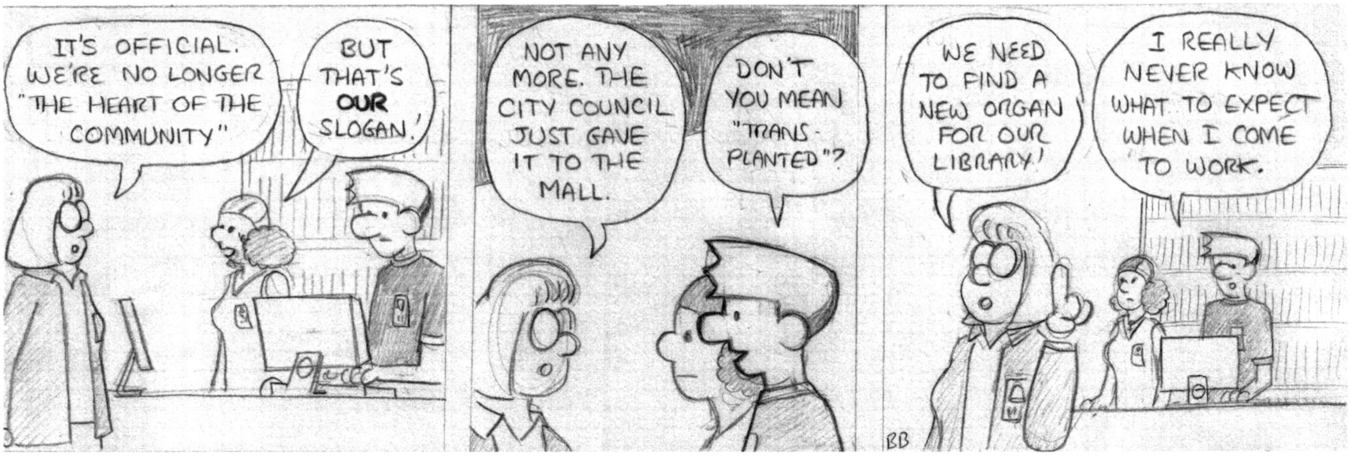
IT'S OFFICIAL: WE'RE NO LONGER "THE HEART OF THE COMMUNITY"
BUT THAT'S **OUR** SLOGAN!
NOT ANY MORE. THE CITY COUNCIL JUST GAVE IT TO THE MALL.
DON'T YOU MEAN "TRANS-PLANTED"?
WE NEED TO FIND A NEW ORGAN FOR OUR LIBRARY!
I REALLY NEVER KNOW WHAT TO EXPECT WHEN I COME TO WORK.
BB

Bill usually draws the strip on his computer, but he drew these in classic pencil at Comic Con International in San Diego.

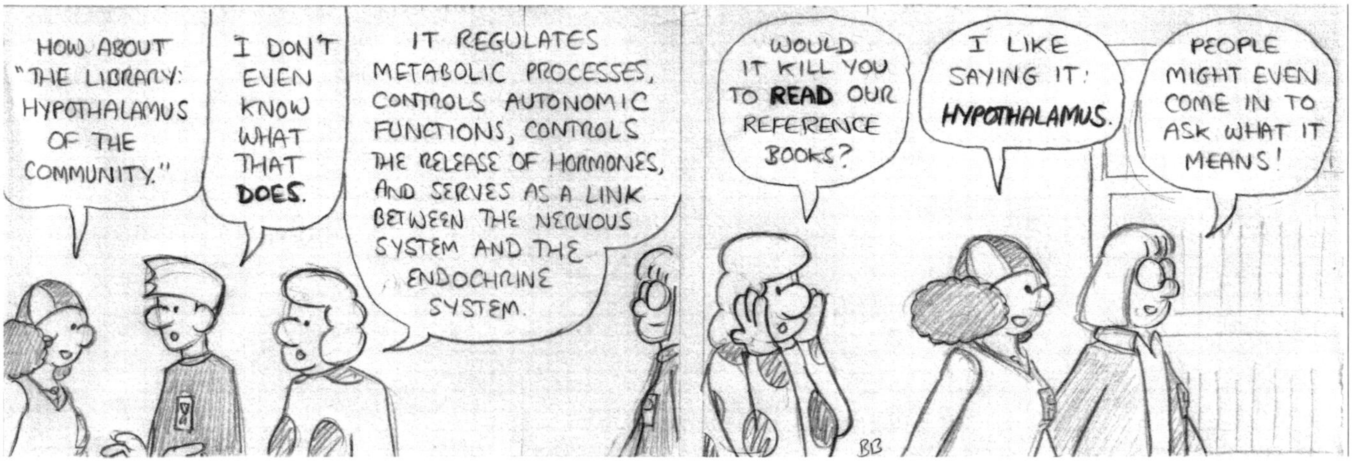
HOW ABOUT "THE LIBRARY: HYPOTHALAMUS OF THE COMMUNITY."
I DON'T EVEN KNOW WHAT THAT **DOES**.
IT REGULATES METABOLIC PROCESSES, CONTROLS AUTONOMIC FUNCTIONS, CONTROLS THE RELEASE OF HORMONES, AND SERVES AS A LINK BETWEEN THE NERVOUS SYSTEM AND THE ENDOCHRINE SYSTEM.
WOULD IT KILL YOU TO **READ** OUR REFERENCE BOOKS?
I LIKE SAYING IT: **HYPOTHALAMUS**.
PEOPLE MIGHT EVEN COME IN TO ASK WHAT IT MEANS!
BB

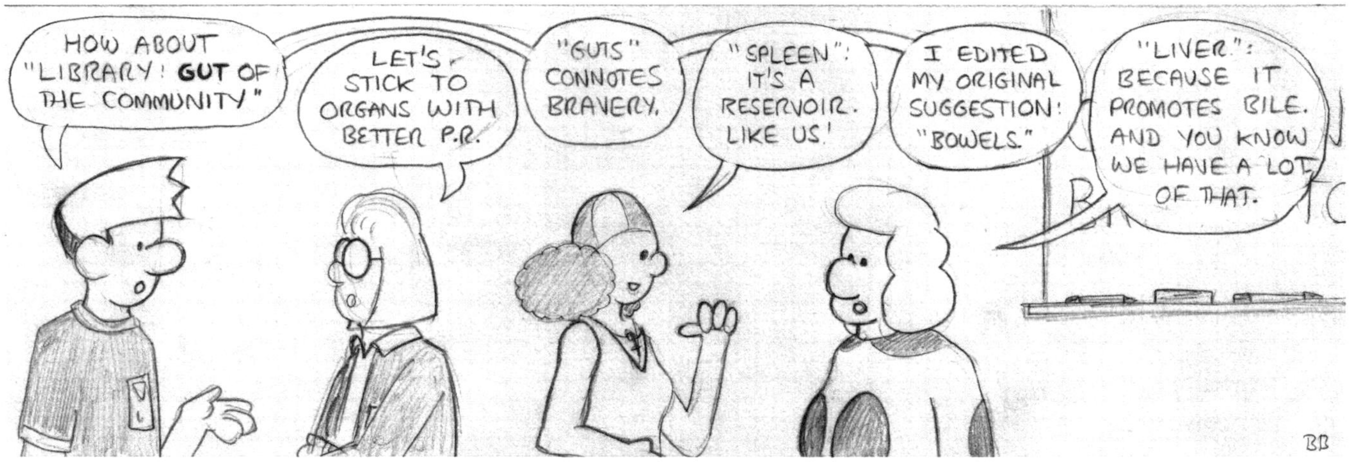
HOW ABOUT "LIBRARY: **GUT** OF THE COMMUNITY"
LET'S STICK TO ORGANS WITH BETTER P.R.
"GUTS" CONNOTES BRAVERY.
"SPLEEN": IT'S A RESERVOIR. LIKE US!
I EDITED MY ORIGINAL SUGGESTION: "BOWELS."
"LIVER": BECAUSE IT PROMOTES BILE. AND YOU KNOW WE HAVE A LOT OF THAT.
BB

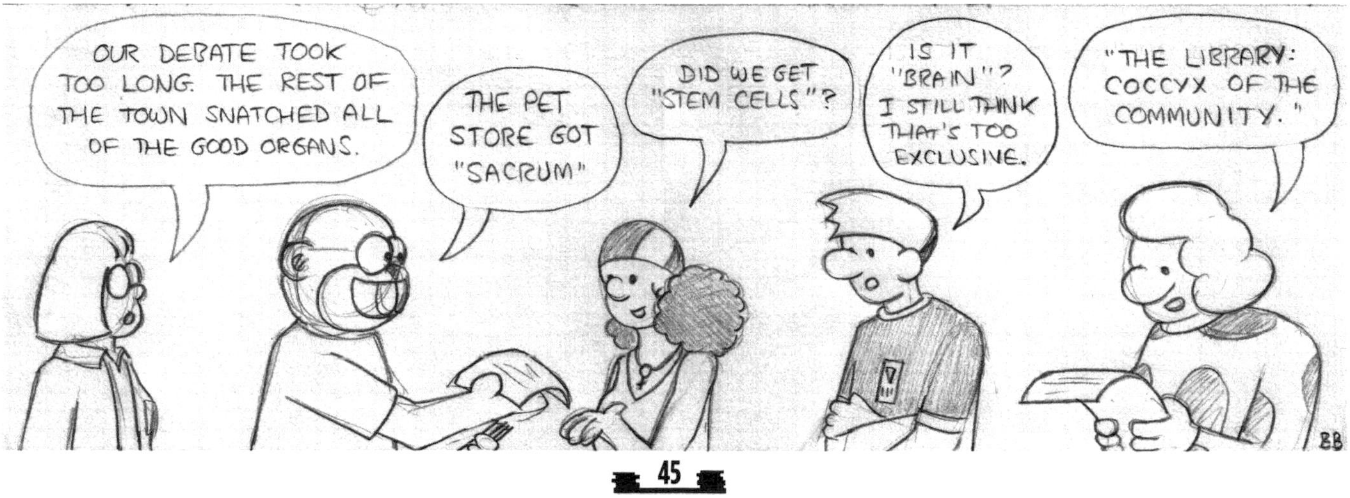
OUR DEBATE TOOK TOO LONG. THE REST OF THE TOWN SNATCHED ALL OF THE GOOD ORGANS.
THE PET STORE GOT "SACRUM"
DID WE GET "STEM CELLS"?
IS IT "BRAIN"? I STILL THINK THAT'S TOO EXCLUSIVE.
"THE LIBRARY: COCCYX OF THE COMMUNITY."
BB

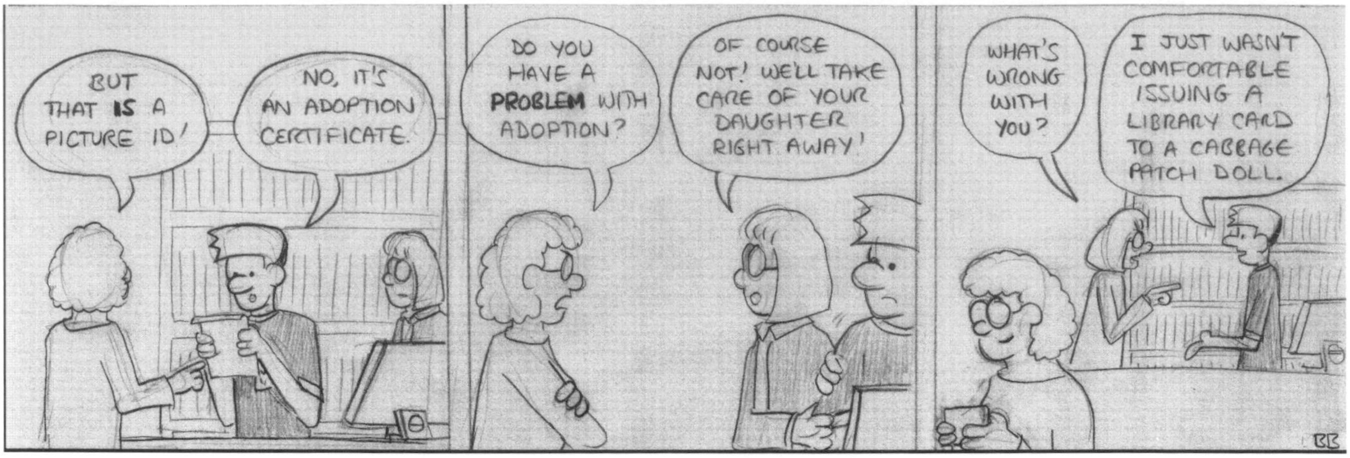
BUT THAT IS A PICTURE ID!
NO, IT'S AN ADOPTION CERTIFICATE.
DO YOU HAVE A PROBLEM WITH ADOPTION?
OF COURSE NOT! WE'LL TAKE CARE OF YOUR DAUGHTER RIGHT AWAY!
WHAT'S WRONG WITH YOU?
I JUST WASN'T COMFORTABLE ISSUING A LIBRARY CARD TO A CABBAGE PATCH DOLL.

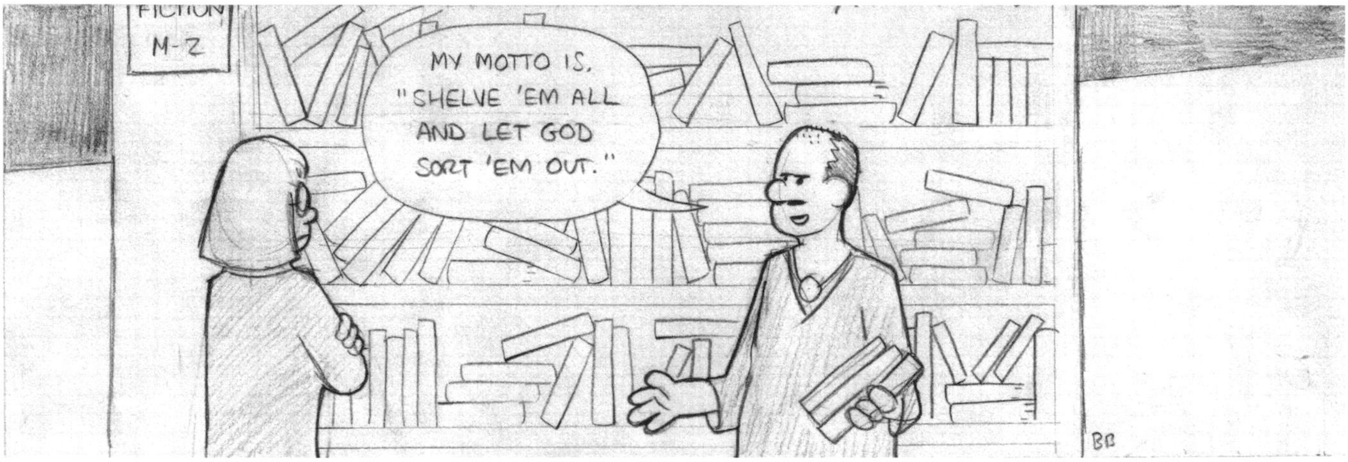
M-Z
MY MOTTO IS, "SHELVE 'EM ALL AND LET GOD SORT 'EM OUT."

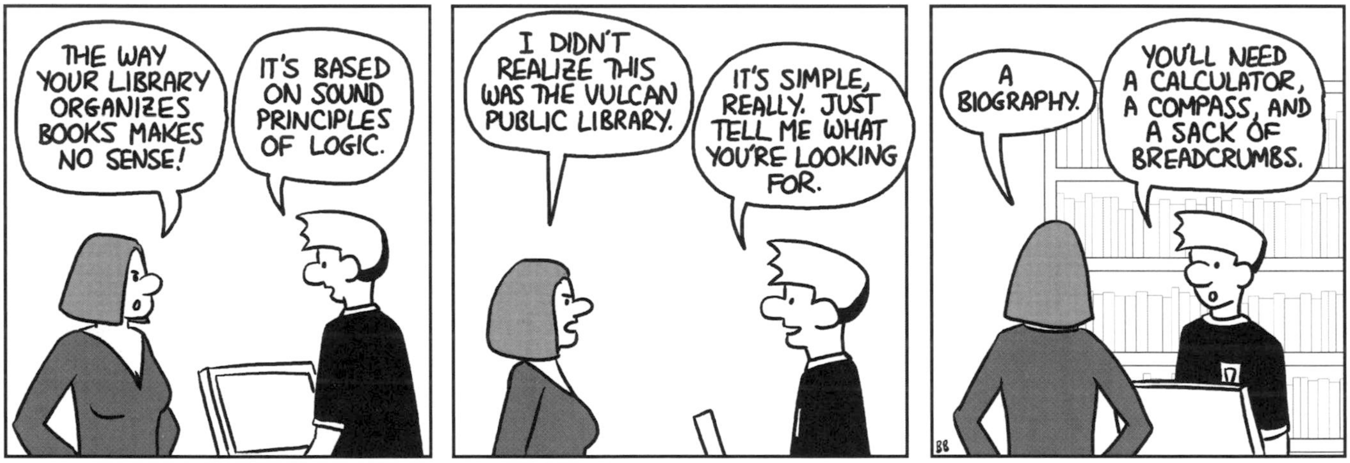
THE WAY YOUR LIBRARY ORGANIZES BOOKS MAKES NO SENSE!
IT'S BASED ON SOUND PRINCIPLES OF LOGIC.
I DIDN'T REALIZE THIS WAS THE VULCAN PUBLIC LIBRARY.
IT'S SIMPLE, REALLY. JUST TELL ME WHAT YOU'RE LOOKING FOR.
A BIOGRAPHY.
YOU'LL NEED A CALCULATOR, A COMPASS, AND A SACK OF BREADCRUMBS.

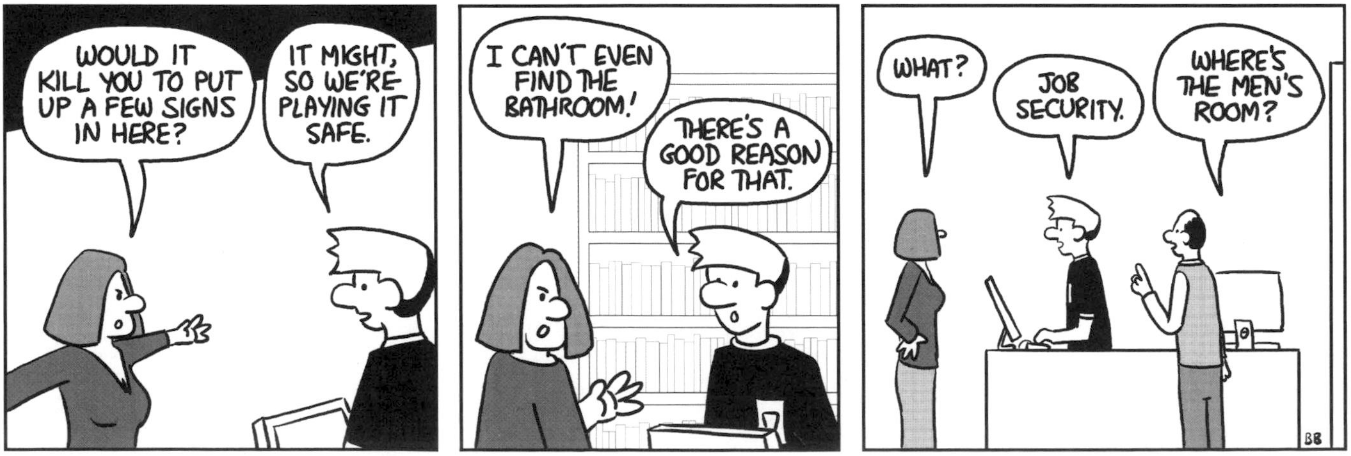
WOULD IT KILL YOU TO PUT UP A FEW SIGNS IN HERE?
IT MIGHT, SO WE'RE PLAYING IT SAFE.
I CAN'T EVEN FIND THE BATHROOM!
THERE'S A GOOD REASON FOR THAT.
WHAT?
JOB SECURITY.
WHERE'S THE MEN'S ROOM?

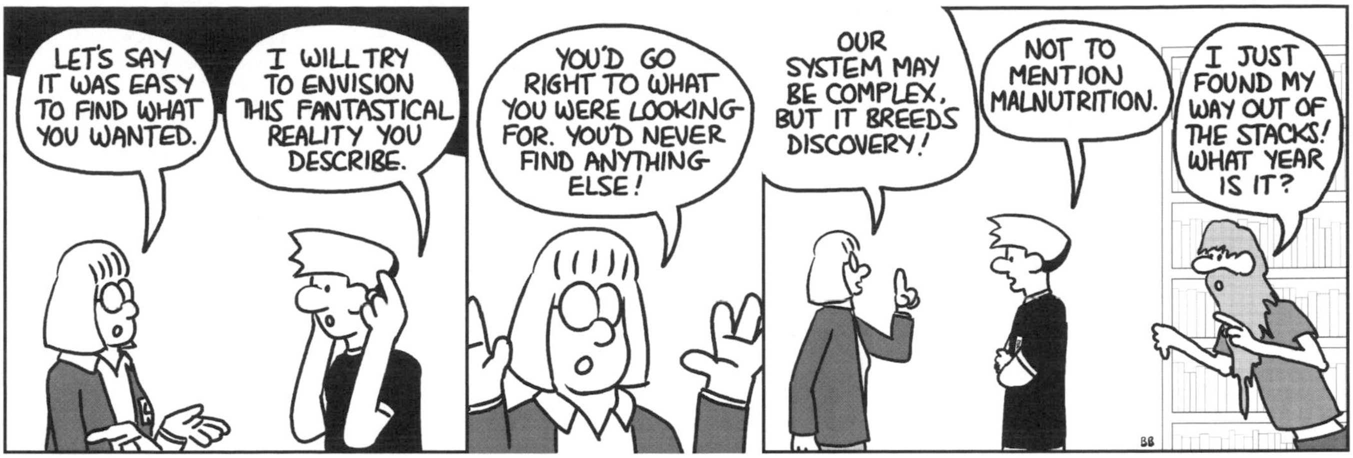
LET'S SAY IT WAS EASY TO FIND WHAT YOU WANTED.
I WILL TRY TO ENVISION THIS FANTASTICAL REALITY YOU DESCRIBE.
YOU'D GO RIGHT TO WHAT YOU WERE LOOKING FOR. YOU'D NEVER FIND ANYTHING ELSE!
OUR SYSTEM MAY BE COMPLEX, BUT IT BREEDS DISCOVERY!
NOT TO MENTION MALNUTRITION.
I JUST FOUND MY WAY OUT OF THE STACKS! WHAT YEAR IS IT?
BB

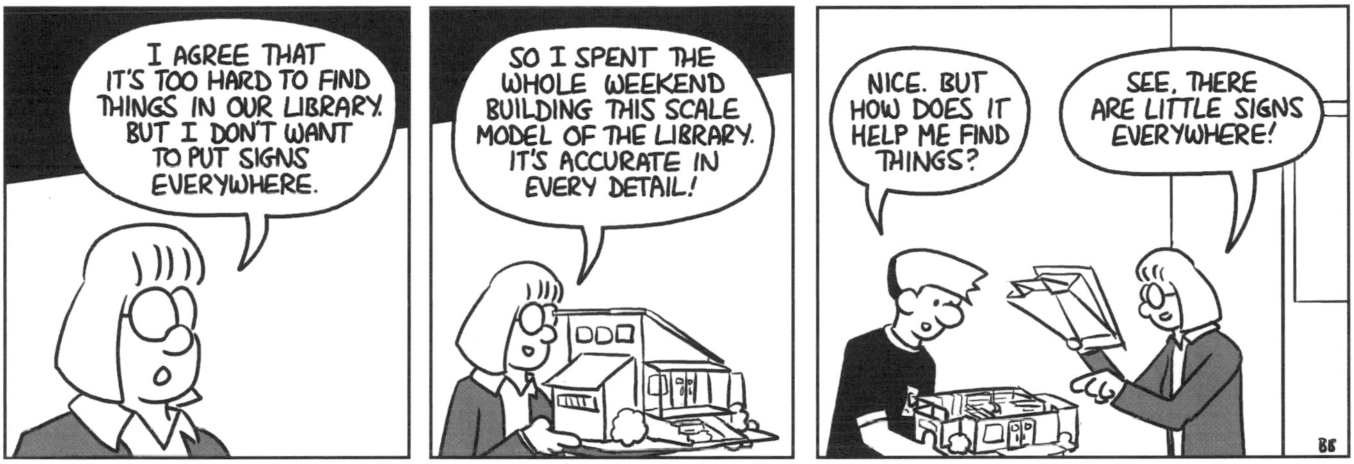
I AGREE THAT IT'S TOO HARD TO FIND THINGS IN OUR LIBRARY. BUT I DON'T WANT TO PUT SIGNS EVERYWHERE.
SO I SPENT THE WHOLE WEEKEND BUILDING THIS SCALE MODEL OF THE LIBRARY. IT'S ACCURATE IN EVERY DETAIL!
NICE. BUT HOW DOES IT HELP ME FIND THINGS?
SEE, THERE ARE LITTLE SIGNS EVERYWHERE!
BB

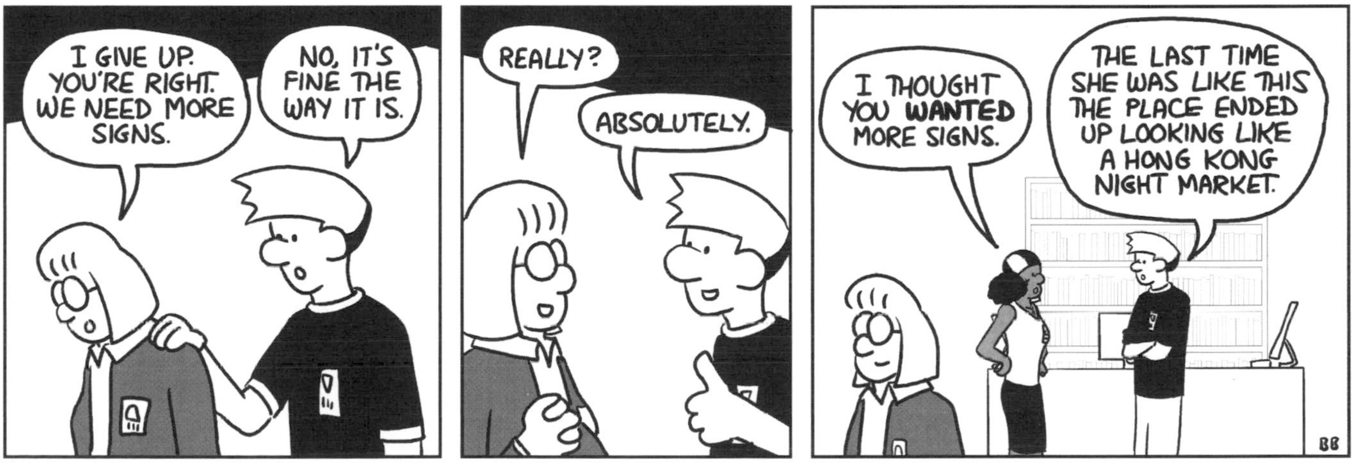
I GIVE UP. YOU'RE RIGHT. WE NEED MORE SIGNS.
NO, IT'S FINE THE WAY IT IS.
REALLY?
ABSOLUTELY.
I THOUGHT YOU **WANTED** MORE SIGNS.
THE LAST TIME SHE WAS LIKE THIS THE PLACE ENDED UP LOOKING LIKE A HONG KONG NIGHT MARKET.
BB

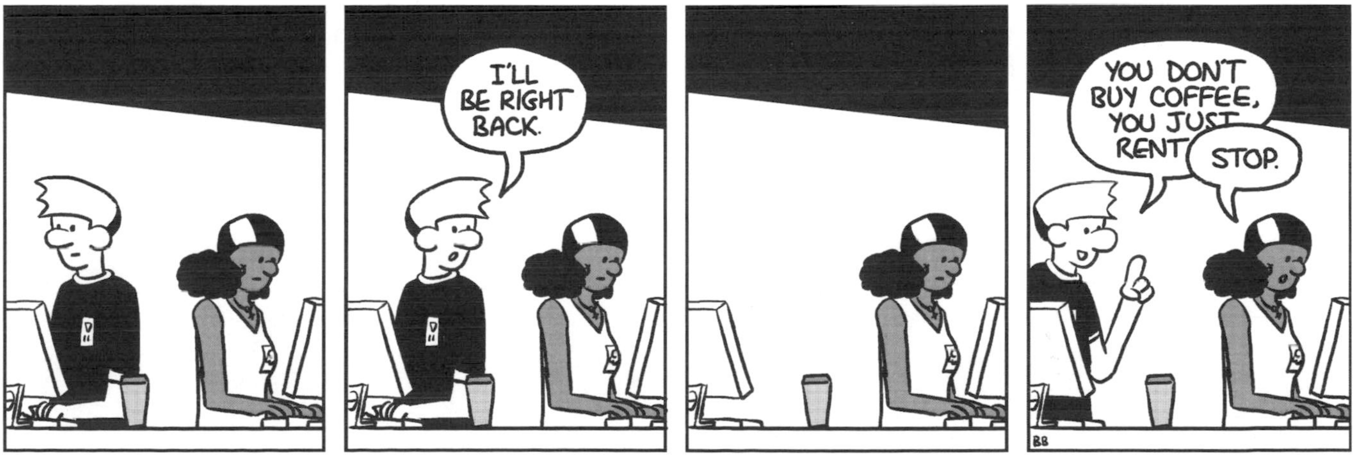
I'LL BE RIGHT BACK.
YOU DON'T BUY COFFEE, YOU JUST RENT
STOP.
BB

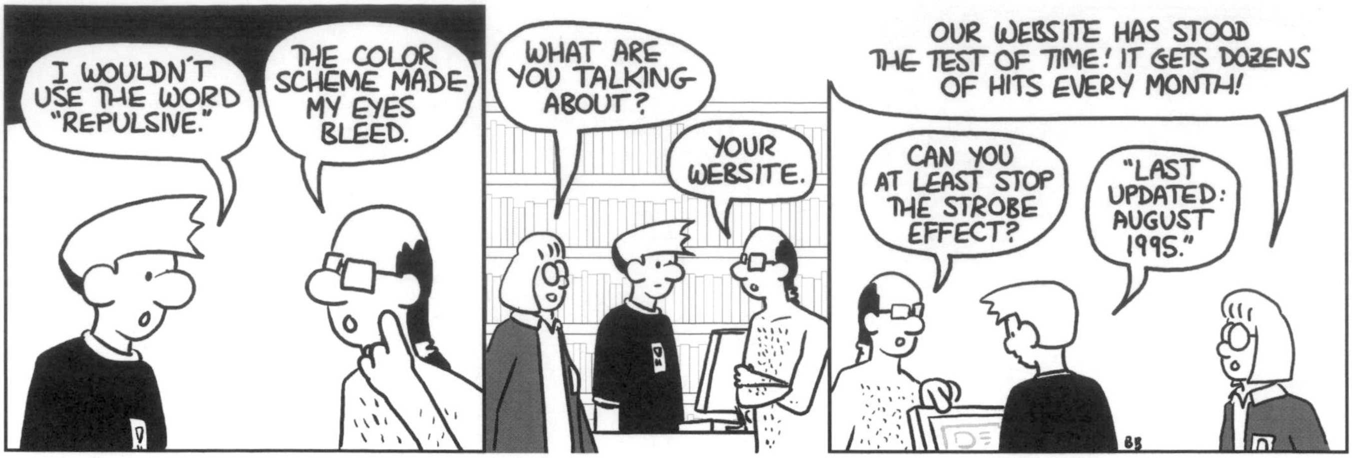
I WOULDN'T USE THE WORD "REPULSIVE."
THE COLOR SCHEME MADE MY EYES BLEED.
WHAT ARE YOU TALKING ABOUT?
YOUR WEBSITE.
OUR WEBSITE HAS STOOD THE TEST OF TIME! IT GETS DOZENS OF HITS EVERY MONTH!
CAN YOU AT LEAST STOP THE STROBE EFFECT?
"LAST UPDATED: AUGUST 1995."

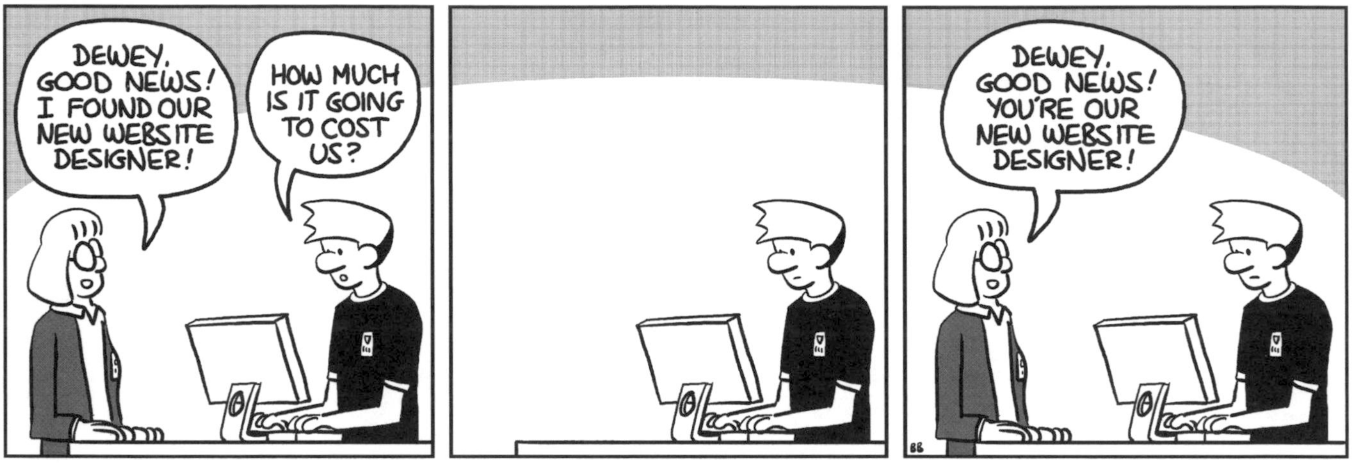
DEWEY. GOOD NEWS! I FOUND OUR NEW WEBSITE DESIGNER!
HOW MUCH IS IT GOING TO COST US?
DEWEY. GOOD NEWS! YOU'RE OUR NEW WEBSITE DESIGNER!

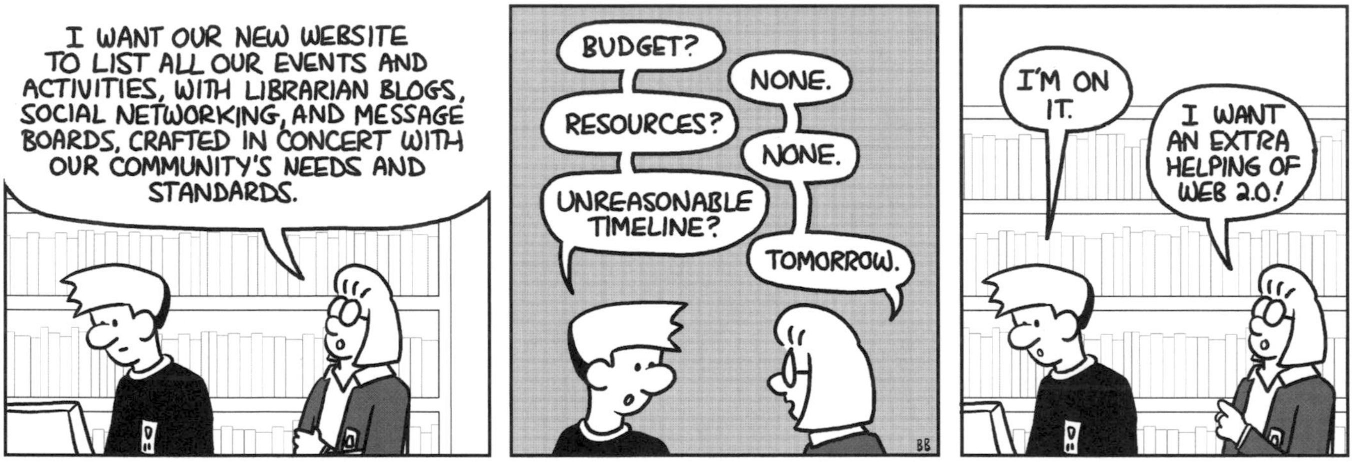
I WANT OUR NEW WEBSITE TO LIST ALL OUR EVENTS AND ACTIVITIES, WITH LIBRARIAN BLOGS, SOCIAL NETWORKING, AND MESSAGE BOARDS, CRAFTED IN CONCERT WITH OUR COMMUNITY'S NEEDS AND STANDARDS.
BUDGET?
NONE.
RESOURCES?
NONE.
UNREASONABLE TIMELINE?
TOMORROW.
I'M ON IT.
I WANT AN EXTRA HELPING OF WEB 2.0!

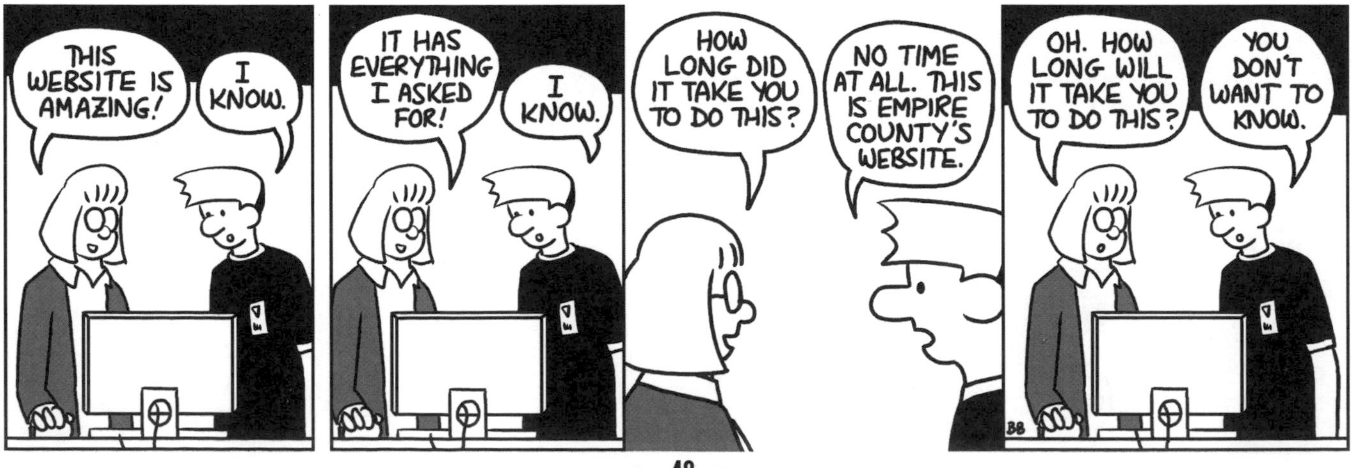
THIS WEBSITE IS AMAZING!
I KNOW.
IT HAS EVERYTHING I ASKED FOR!
I KNOW.
HOW LONG DID IT TAKE YOU TO DO THIS?
NO TIME AT ALL. THIS IS EMPIRE COUNTY'S WEBSITE.
OH. HOW LONG WILL IT TAKE YOU TO DO THIS?
YOU DON'T WANT TO KNOW.

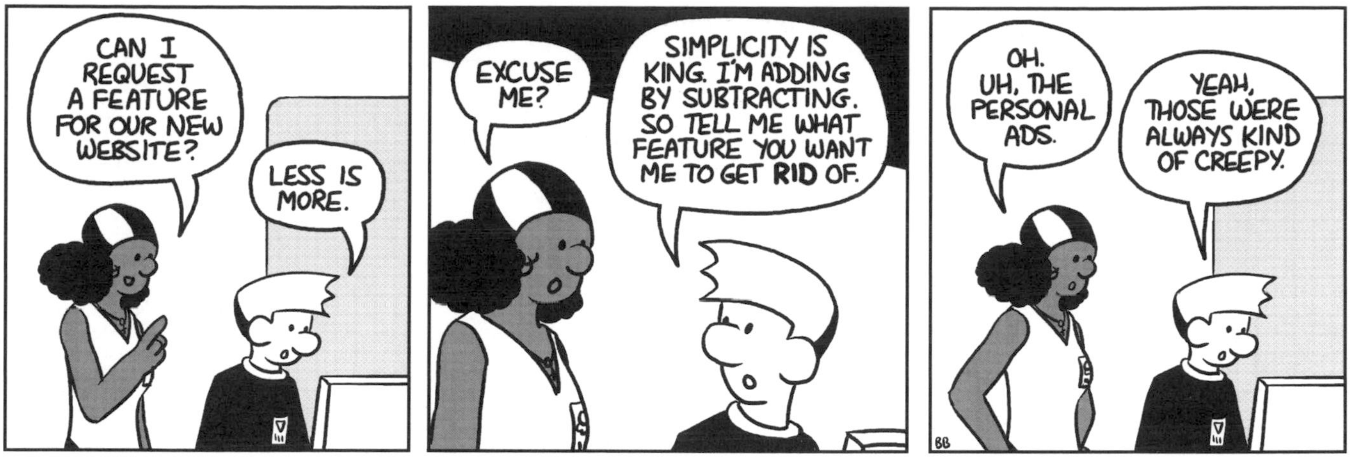
CAN I REQUEST A FEATURE FOR OUR NEW WEBSITE?
LESS IS MORE.
EXCUSE ME?
SIMPLICITY IS KING. I'M ADDING BY SUBTRACTING. SO TELL ME WHAT FEATURE YOU WANT ME TO GET **RID** OF.
OH. UH, THE PERSONAL ADS.
YEAH, THOSE WERE ALWAYS KIND OF CREEPY.
BB

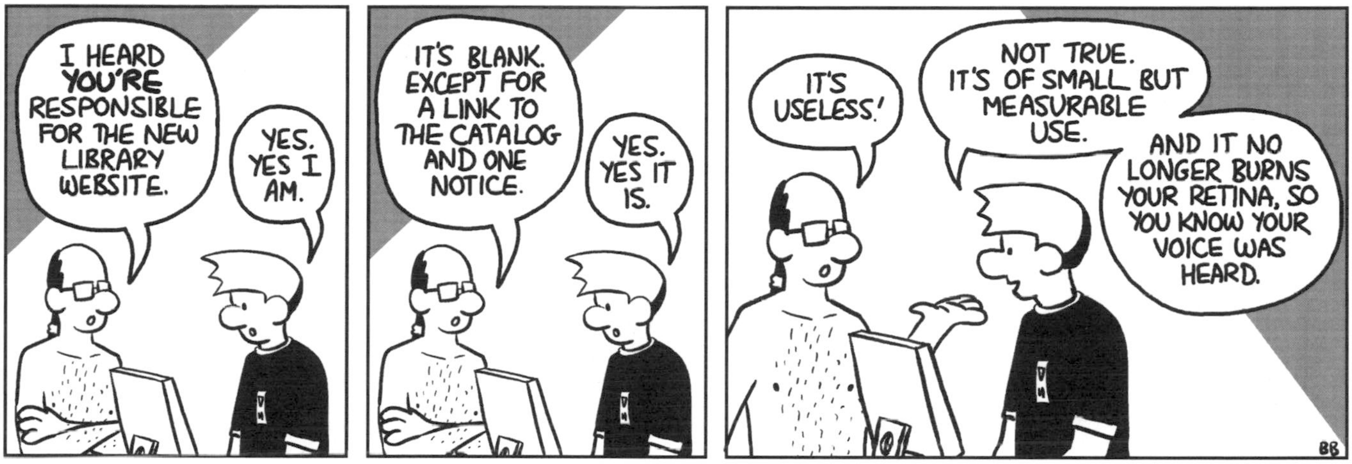
I HEARD **YOU'RE** RESPONSIBLE FOR THE NEW LIBRARY WEBSITE.
YES. YES I AM.
IT'S BLANK. EXCEPT FOR A LINK TO THE CATALOG AND ONE NOTICE.
YES. YES IT IS.
IT'S USELESS!
NOT TRUE. IT'S OF SMALL BUT MEASURABLE USE.
AND IT NO LONGER BURNS YOUR RETINA, SO YOU KNOW YOUR VOICE WAS HEARD.
BB

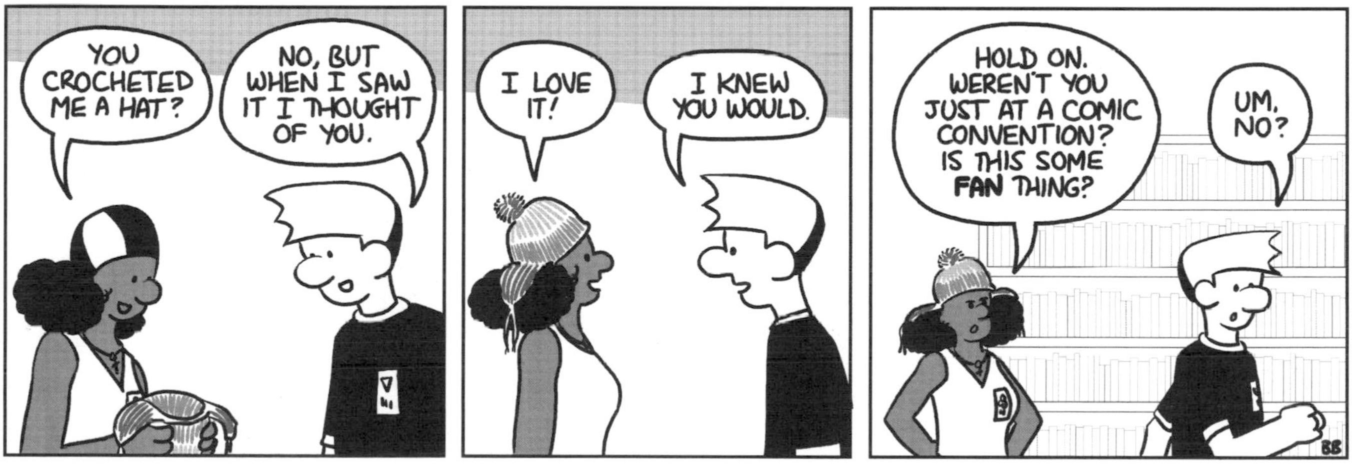
YOU CROCHETED ME A HAT?
NO, BUT WHEN I SAW IT I THOUGHT OF YOU.
I LOVE IT!
I KNEW YOU WOULD.
HOLD ON. WEREN'T YOU JUST AT A COMIC CONVENTION? IS THIS SOME **FAN** THING?
UM, NO?
BB

Dewey's lying. The hat is a reference to the short-lived sci-fi series Firefly *whose fans ("browncoats") are well-mobilized, to say the least.*

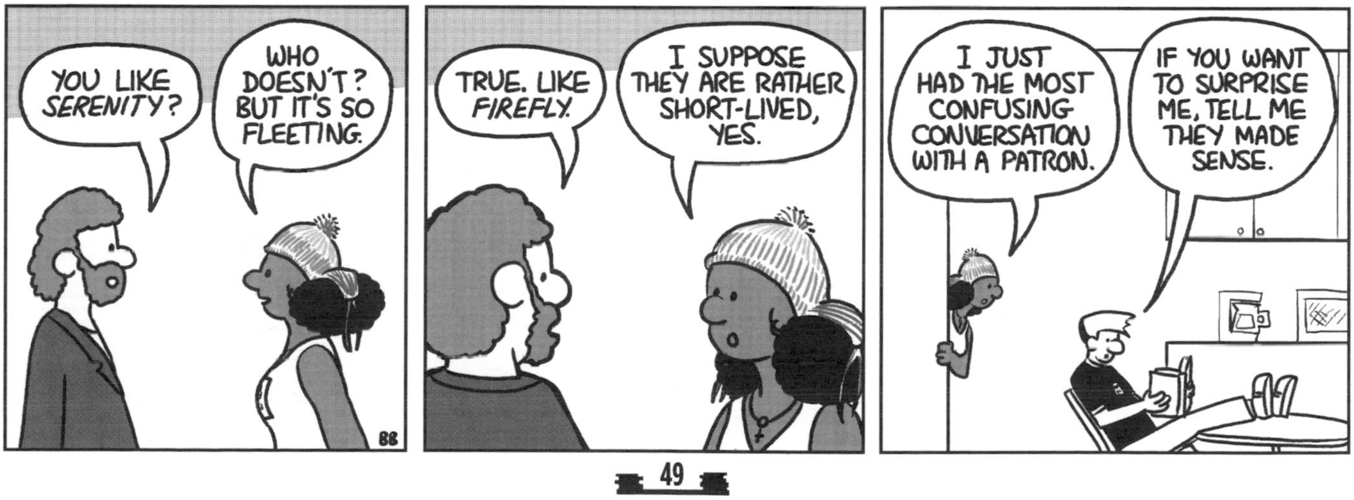
YOU LIKE *SERENITY*?
WHO DOESN'T? BUT IT'S SO FLEETING.
BB
TRUE. LIKE *FIREFLY*.
I SUPPOSE THEY ARE RATHER SHORT-LIVED, YES.
I JUST HAD THE MOST CONFUSING CONVERSATION WITH A PATRON.
IF YOU WANT TO SURPRISE ME, TELL ME THEY MADE SENSE.

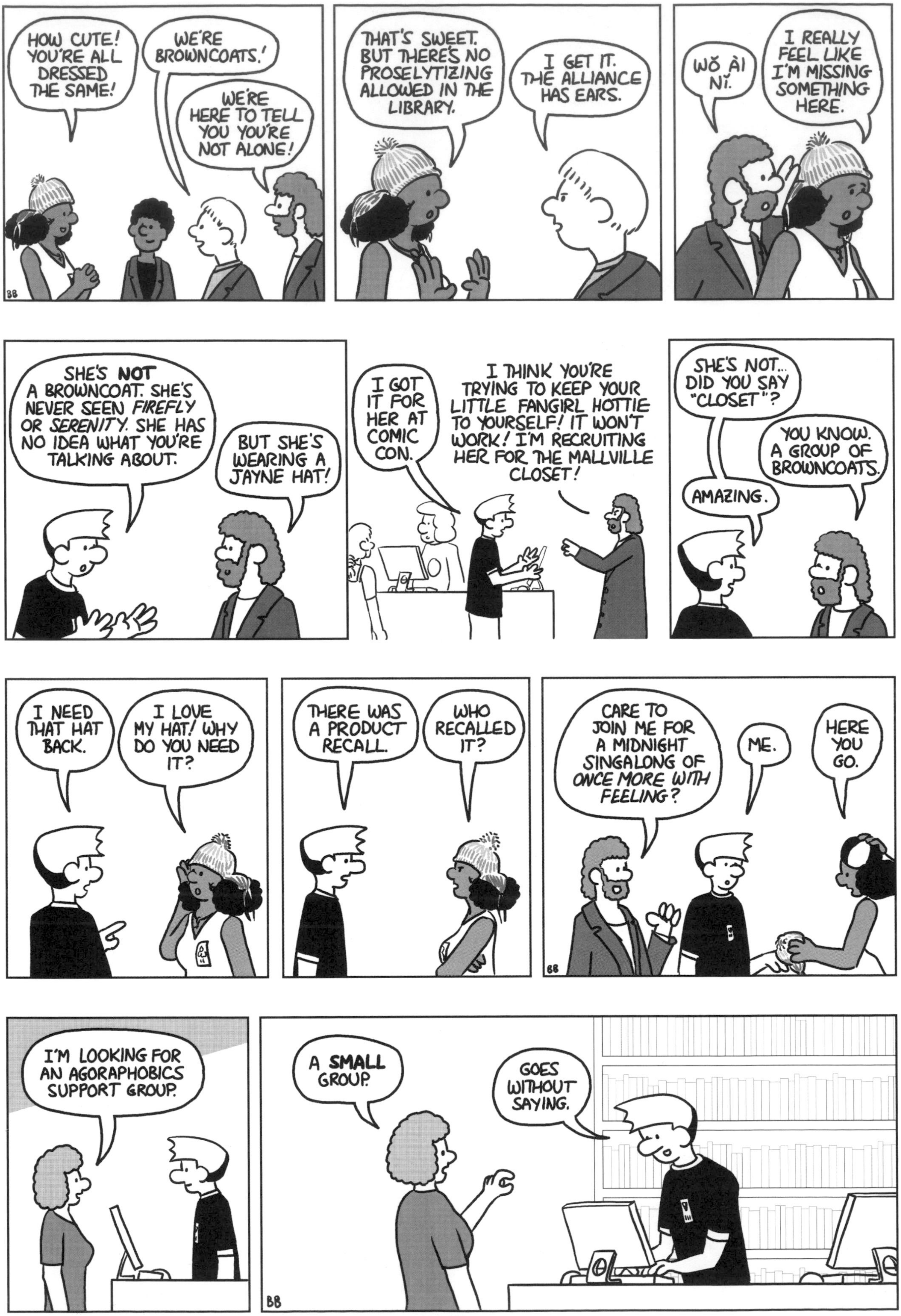

HOW CUTE! YOU'RE ALL DRESSED THE SAME!
WE'RE BROWNCOATS!
WE'RE HERE TO TELL YOU YOU'RE NOT ALONE!
BB
THAT'S SWEET. BUT THERE'S NO PROSELYTIZING ALLOWED IN THE LIBRARY.
I GET IT. THE ALLIANCE HAS EARS.
WǑ ÀI NǏ.
I REALLY FEEL LIKE I'M MISSING SOMETHING HERE.
SHE'S **NOT** A BROWNCOAT. SHE'S NEVER SEEN *FIREFLY* OR *SERENITY*. SHE HAS NO IDEA WHAT YOU'RE TALKING ABOUT.
BUT SHE'S WEARING A JAYNE HAT!
I GOT IT FOR HER AT COMIC CON.
I THINK YOU'RE TRYING TO KEEP YOUR LITTLE FANGIRL HOTTIE TO YOURSELF! IT WON'T WORK! I'M RECRUITING HER FOR THE MALLVILLE CLOSET!
SHE'S NOT... DID YOU SAY "CLOSET"?
YOU KNOW. A GROUP OF BROWNCOATS.
AMAZING.
I NEED THAT HAT BACK.
I LOVE MY HAT! WHY DO YOU NEED IT?
THERE WAS A PRODUCT RECALL.
WHO RECALLED IT?
CARE TO JOIN ME FOR A MIDNIGHT SINGALONG OF *ONCE MORE WITH FEELING*?
ME.
HERE YOU GO.
BB
I'M LOOKING FOR AN AGORAPHOBICS SUPPORT GROUP.
A **SMALL** GROUP.
GOES WITHOUT SAYING.
BB

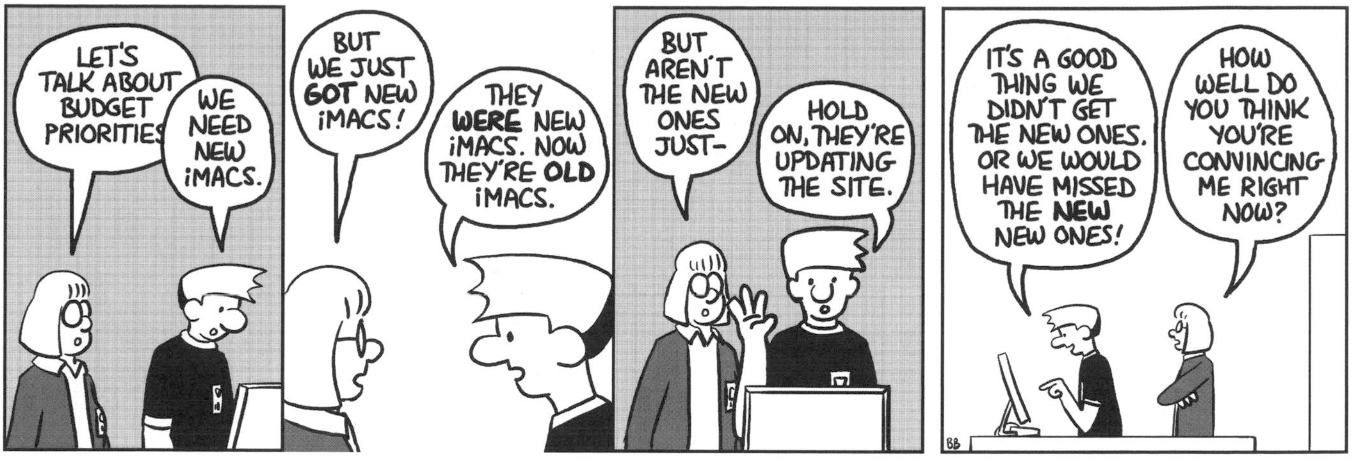
LET'S TALK ABOUT BUDGET PRIORITIES.
WE NEED NEW iMACS.
BUT WE JUST **GOT** NEW iMACS!
THEY **WERE** NEW iMACS. NOW THEY'RE **OLD** iMACS.
BUT AREN'T THE NEW ONES JUST-
HOLD ON, THEY'RE UPDATING THE SITE.
IT'S A GOOD THING WE DIDN'T GET THE NEW ONES. OR WE WOULD HAVE MISSED THE **NEW** NEW ONES!
HOW WELL DO YOU THINK YOU'RE CONVINCING ME RIGHT NOW?
BB

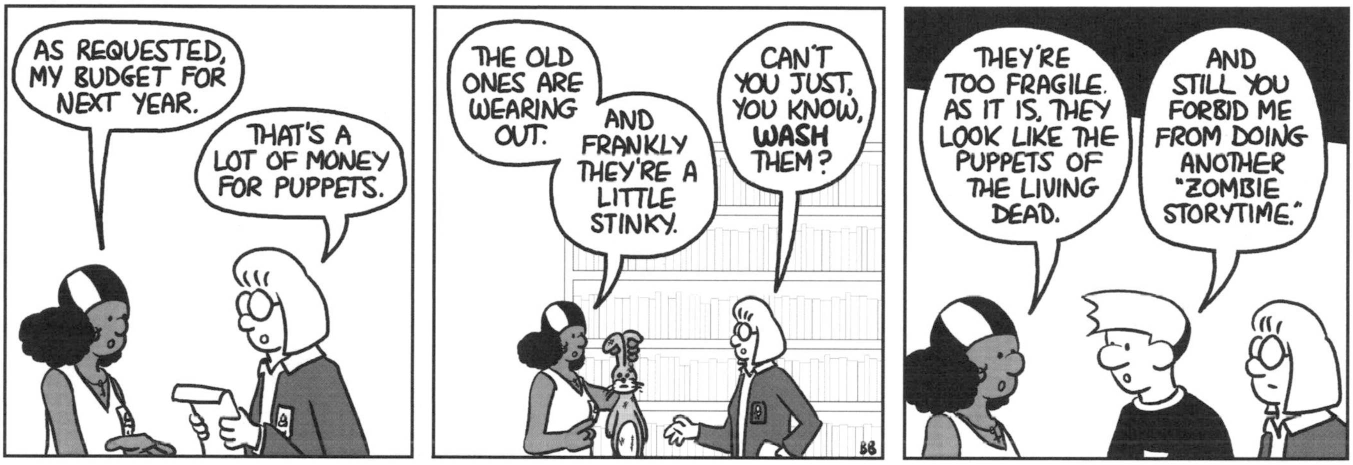
AS REQUESTED, MY BUDGET FOR NEXT YEAR.
THAT'S A LOT OF MONEY FOR PUPPETS.
THE OLD ONES ARE WEARING OUT.
AND FRANKLY THEY'RE A LITTLE STINKY.
CAN'T YOU JUST, YOU KNOW, **WASH** THEM?
THEY'RE TOO FRAGILE. AS IT IS, THEY LOOK LIKE THE PUPPETS OF THE LIVING DEAD.
AND STILL YOU FORBID ME FROM DOING ANOTHER "ZOMBIE STORYTIME."
BB

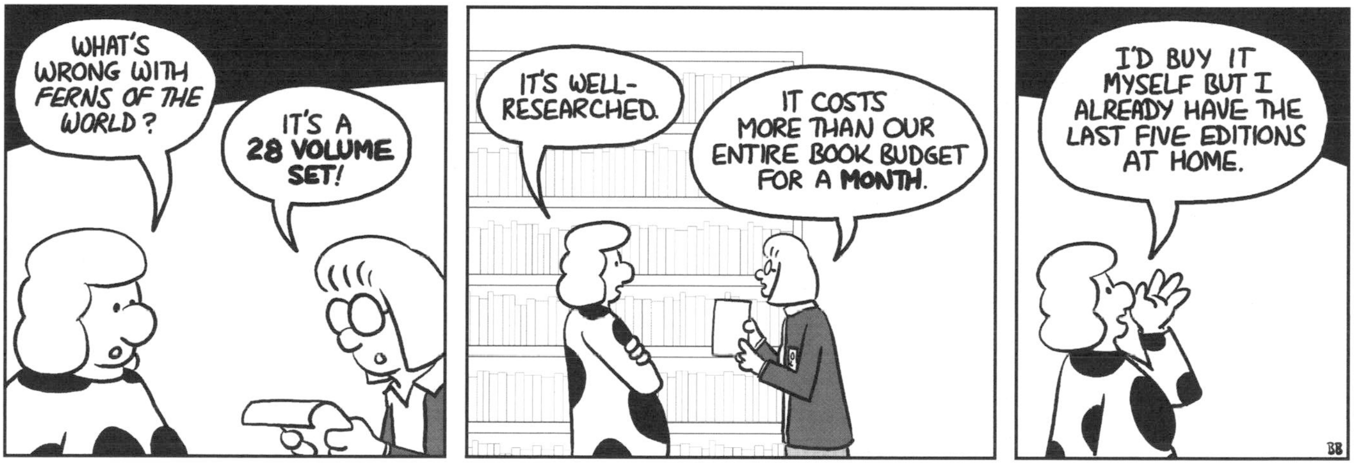
WHAT'S WRONG WITH *FERNS OF THE WORLD*?
IT'S A **28 VOLUME SET**!
IT'S WELL-RESEARCHED.
IT COSTS MORE THAN OUR ENTIRE BOOK BUDGET FOR A **MONTH**.
I'D BUY IT MYSELF BUT I ALREADY HAVE THE LAST FIVE EDITIONS AT HOME.
BB

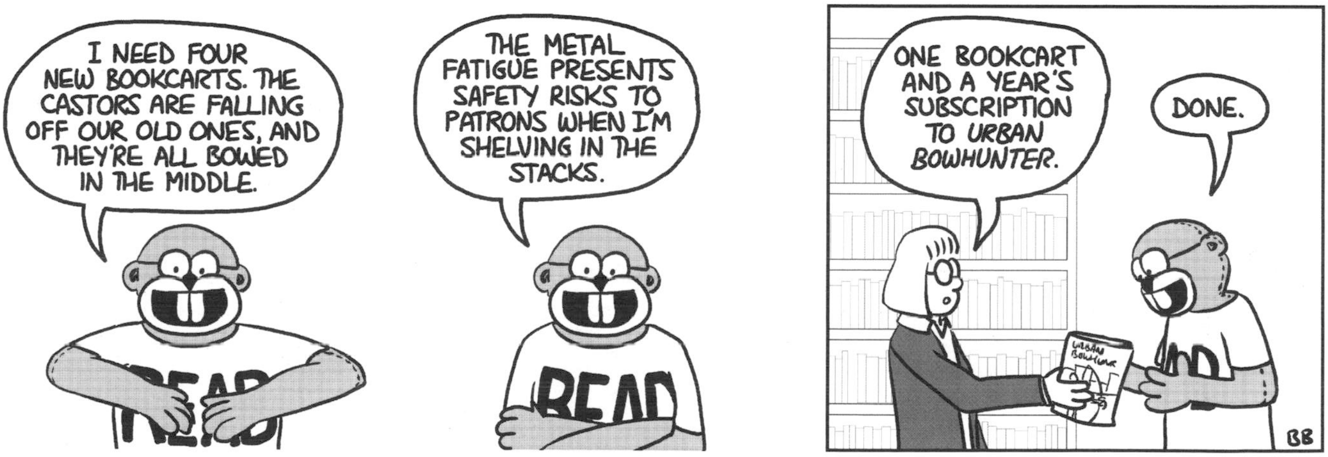
I NEED FOUR NEW BOOKCARTS. THE CASTORS ARE FALLING OFF OUR OLD ONES, AND THEY'RE ALL BOWED IN THE MIDDLE.
THE METAL FATIGUE PRESENTS SAFETY RISKS TO PATRONS WHEN I'M SHELVING IN THE STACKS.
ONE BOOKCART AND A YEAR'S SUBSCRIPTION TO *URBAN BOWHUNTER*.
DONE.
BB

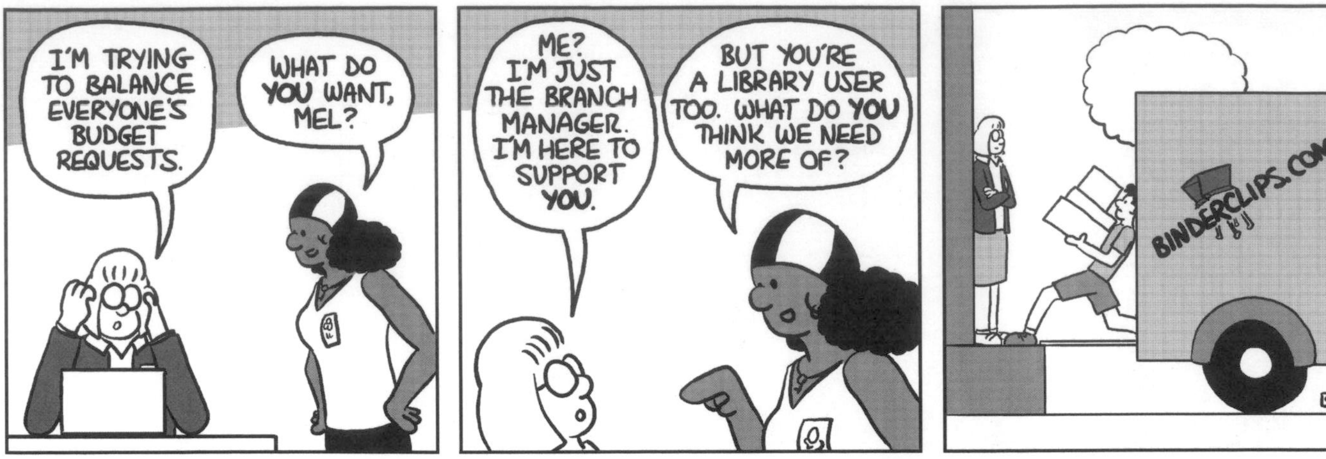
I'M TRYING TO BALANCE EVERYONE'S BUDGET REQUESTS.
WHAT DO YOU WANT, MEL?
ME? I'M JUST THE BRANCH MANAGER. I'M HERE TO SUPPORT YOU.
BUT YOU'RE A LIBRARY USER TOO. WHAT DO YOU THINK WE NEED MORE OF?
BINDERCLIPS.COM
BB

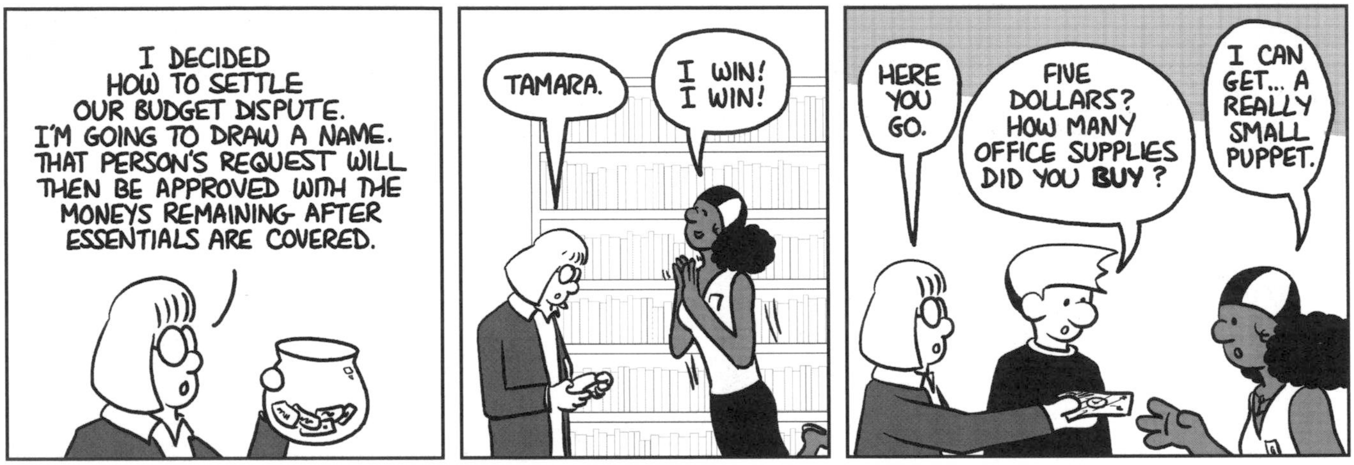
I DECIDED HOW TO SETTLE OUR BUDGET DISPUTE. I'M GOING TO DRAW A NAME. THAT PERSON'S REQUEST WILL THEN BE APPROVED WITH THE MONEYS REMAINING AFTER ESSENTIALS ARE COVERED.
TAMARA.
I WIN! I WIN!
HERE YOU GO.
FIVE DOLLARS? HOW MANY OFFICE SUPPLIES DID YOU BUY?
I CAN GET... A REALLY SMALL PUPPET.

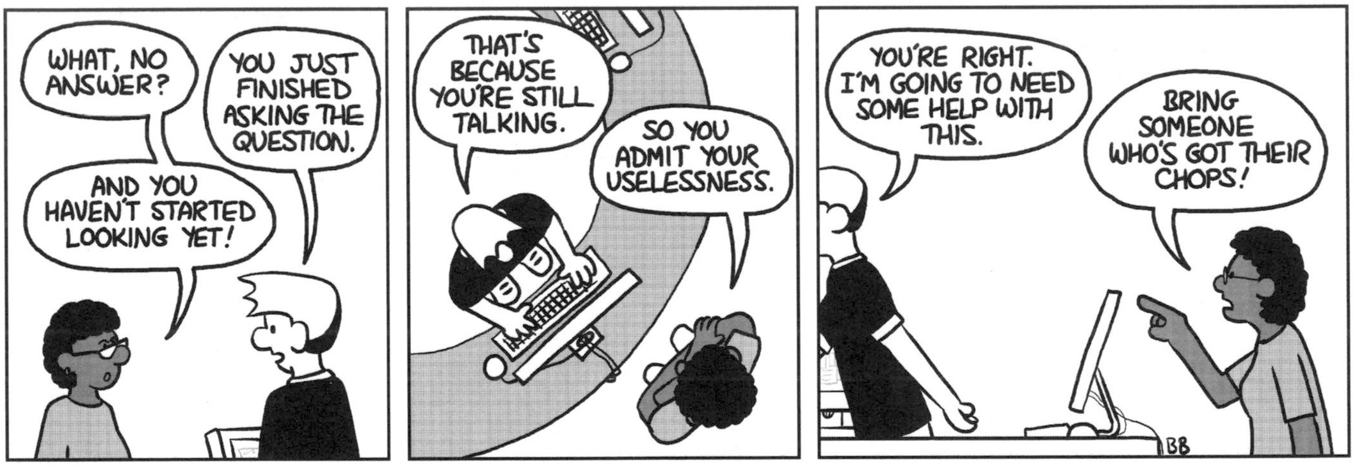
WHAT, NO ANSWER?
YOU JUST FINISHED ASKING THE QUESTION.
AND YOU HAVEN'T STARTED LOOKING YET!
THAT'S BECAUSE YOU'RE STILL TALKING.
SO YOU ADMIT YOUR USELESSNESS.
YOU'RE RIGHT. I'M GOING TO NEED SOME HELP WITH THIS.
BRING SOMEONE WHO'S GOT THEIR CHOPS!
BB

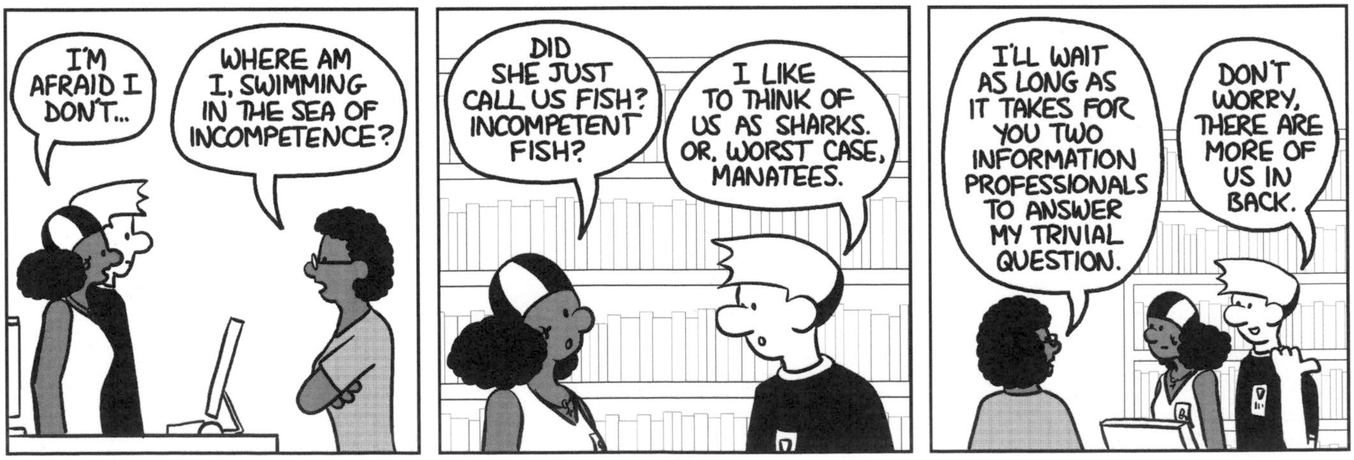
I'M AFRAID I DON'T...
WHERE AM I, SWIMMING IN THE SEA OF INCOMPETENCE?
DID SHE JUST CALL US FISH? INCOMPETENT FISH?
I LIKE TO THINK OF US AS SHARKS. OR, WORST CASE, MANATEES.
I'LL WAIT AS LONG AS IT TAKES FOR YOU TWO INFORMATION PROFESSIONALS TO ANSWER MY TRIVIAL QUESTION.
DON'T WORRY, THERE ARE MORE OF US IN BACK.

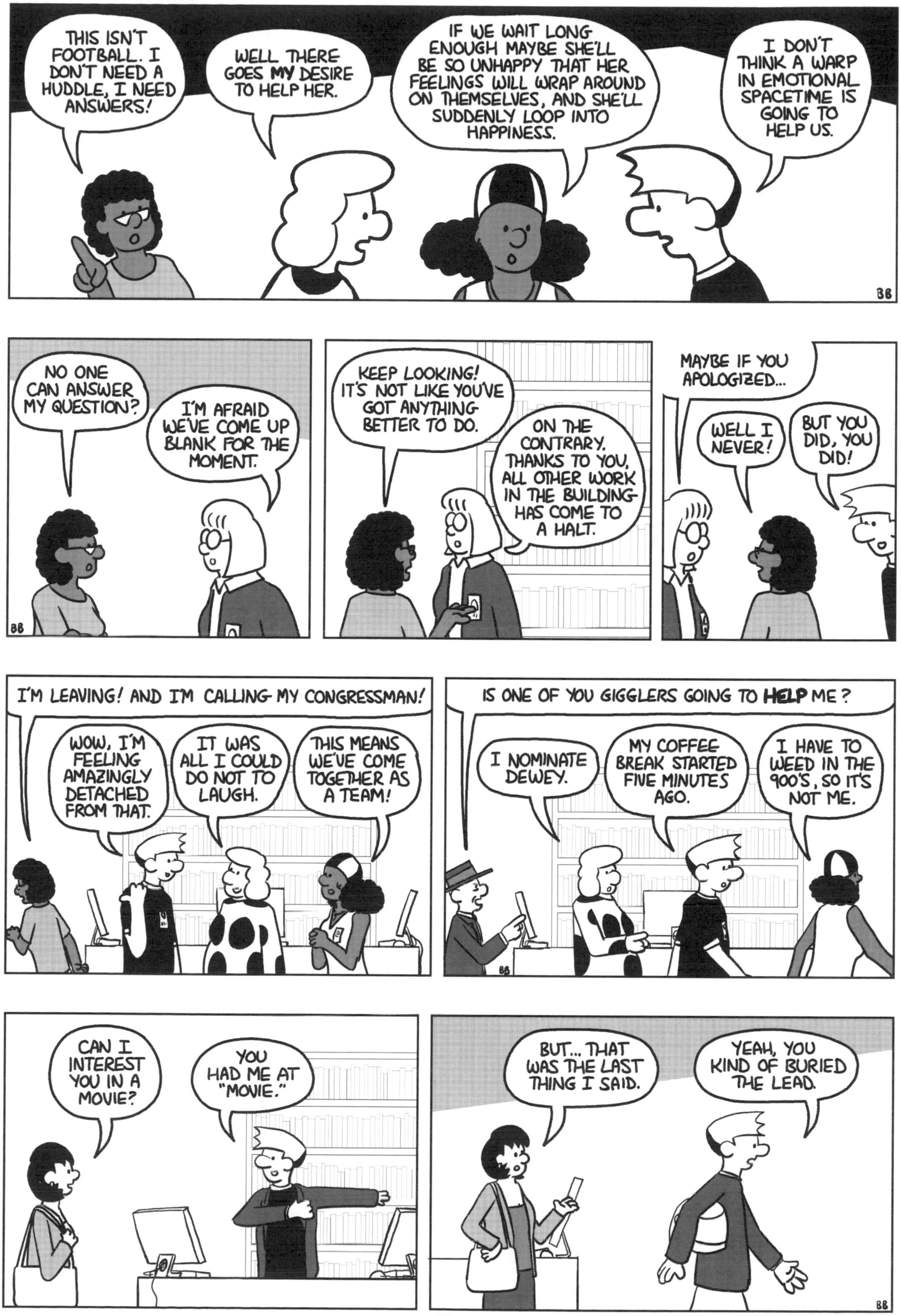
THIS ISN'T FOOTBALL. I DON'T NEED A HUDDLE, I NEED ANSWERS!
WELL THERE GOES MY DESIRE TO HELP HER.
IF WE WAIT LONG ENOUGH MAYBE SHE'LL BE SO UNHAPPY THAT HER FEELINGS WILL WRAP AROUND ON THEMSELVES, AND SHE'LL SUDDENLY LOOP INTO HAPPINESS.
I DON'T THINK A WARP IN EMOTIONAL SPACETIME IS GOING TO HELP US.
BB
NO ONE CAN ANSWER MY QUESTION?
I'M AFRAID WE'VE COME UP BLANK FOR THE MOMENT.
BB
KEEP LOOKING! IT'S NOT LIKE YOU'VE GOT ANYTHING BETTER TO DO.
ON THE CONTRARY. THANKS TO YOU, ALL OTHER WORK IN THE BUILDING HAS COME TO A HALT.
MAYBE IF YOU APOLOGIZED...
WELL I NEVER!
BUT YOU DID, YOU DID!
I'M LEAVING! AND I'M CALLING MY CONGRESSMAN!
WOW, I'M FEELING AMAZINGLY DETACHED FROM THAT.
IT WAS ALL I COULD DO NOT TO LAUGH.
THIS MEANS WE'VE COME TOGETHER AS A TEAM!
IS ONE OF YOU GIGGLERS GOING TO **HELP** ME?
I NOMINATE DEWEY.
MY COFFEE BREAK STARTED FIVE MINUTES AGO.
I HAVE TO WEED IN THE 900'S, SO IT'S NOT ME.
BB
CAN I INTEREST YOU IN A MOVIE?
YOU HAD ME AT "MOVIE."
BUT... THAT WAS THE LAST THING I SAID.
YEAH, YOU KIND OF BURIED THE LEAD.
BB

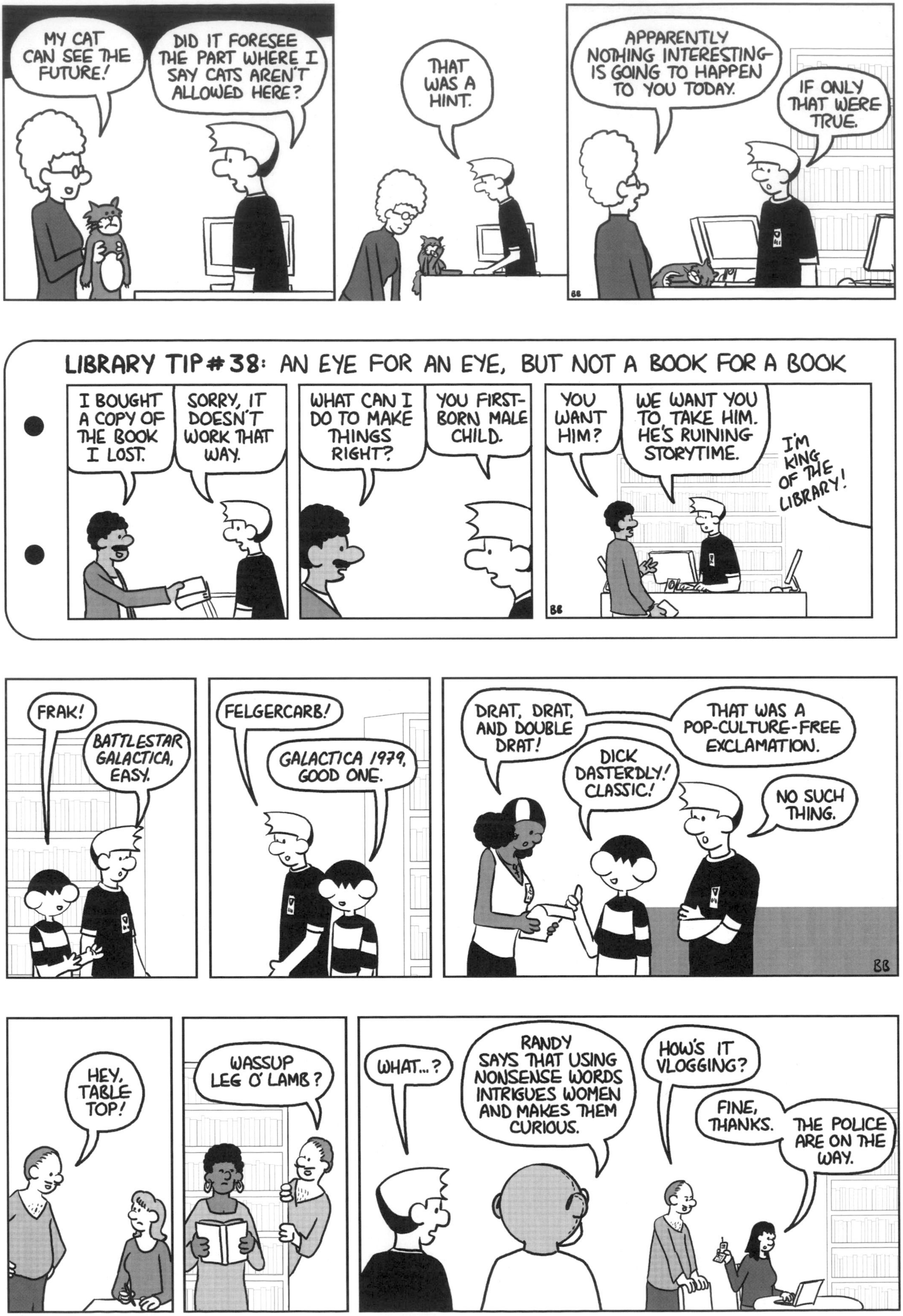
MY CAT CAN SEE THE FUTURE!
DID IT FORESEE THE PART WHERE I SAY CATS AREN'T ALLOWED HERE?
THAT WAS A HINT.
APPARENTLY NOTHING INTERESTING IS GOING TO HAPPEN TO YOU TODAY.
IF ONLY THAT WERE TRUE.
BB
LIBRARY TIP #38: AN EYE FOR AN EYE, BUT NOT A BOOK FOR A BOOK
I BOUGHT A COPY OF THE BOOK I LOST.
SORRY, IT DOESN'T WORK THAT WAY.
WHAT CAN I DO TO MAKE THINGS RIGHT?
YOU FIRST-BORN MALE CHILD.
YOU WANT HIM?
WE WANT YOU TO TAKE HIM. HE'S RUINING STORYTIME.
I'M KING OF THE LIBRARY!
BB
FRAK!
BATTLESTAR GALACTICA, EASY.
FELGERCARB!
GALACTICA 1979, GOOD ONE.
DRAT, DRAT, AND DOUBLE DRAT!
THAT WAS A POP-CULTURE-FREE EXCLAMATION.
DICK DASTERDLY! CLASSIC!
NO SUCH THING.
BB
HEY, TABLE TOP!
WASSUP LEG O' LAMB?
WHAT...?
RANDY SAYS THAT USING NONSENSE WORDS INTRIGUES WOMEN AND MAKES THEM CURIOUS.
HOW'S IT VLOGGING?
FINE, THANKS.
THE POLICE ARE ON THE WAY.

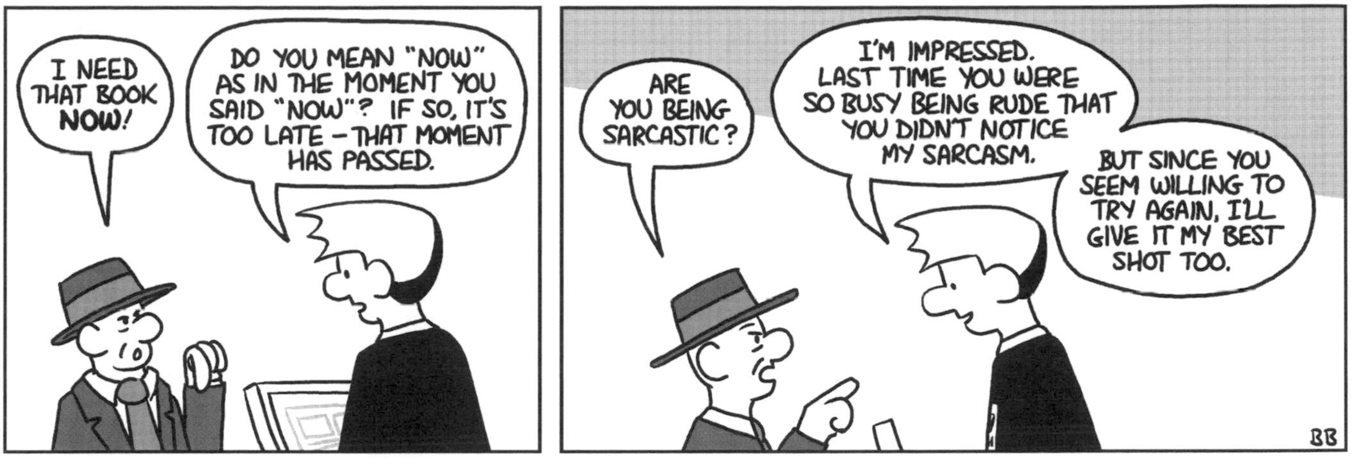
I NEED THAT BOOK **NOW**!
DO YOU MEAN "NOW" AS IN THE MOMENT YOU SAID "NOW"? IF SO, IT'S TOO LATE – THAT MOMENT HAS PASSED.
ARE YOU BEING SARCASTIC?
I'M IMPRESSED. LAST TIME YOU WERE SO BUSY BEING RUDE THAT YOU DIDN'T NOTICE MY SARCASM.
BUT SINCE YOU SEEM WILLING TO TRY AGAIN, I'LL GIVE IT MY BEST SHOT TOO.
BB

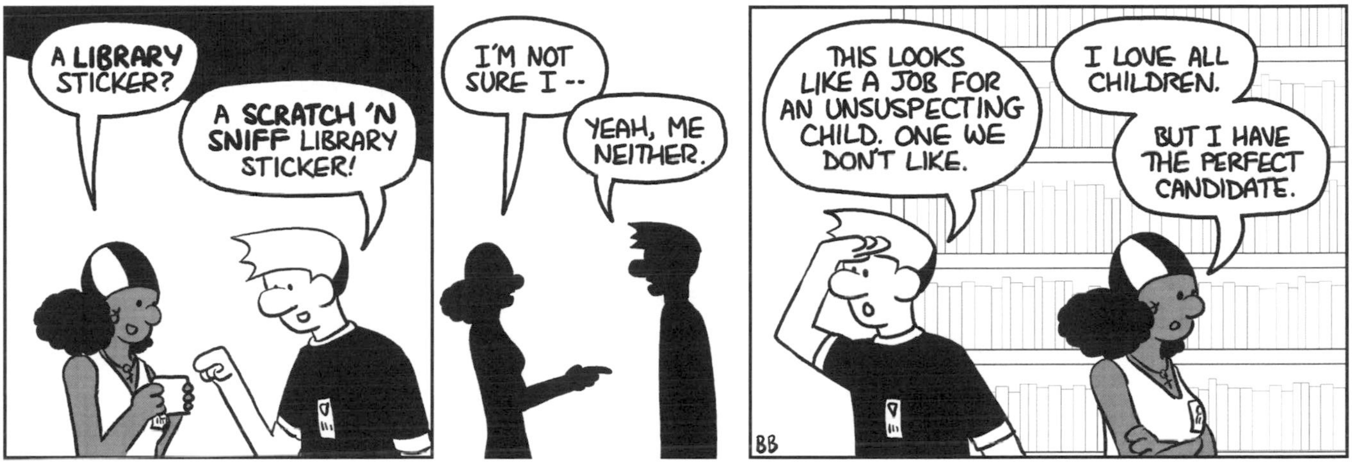
A **LIBRARY** STICKER?
A **SCRATCH 'N SNIFF** LIBRARY STICKER!
I'M NOT SURE I --
YEAH, ME NEITHER.
THIS LOOKS LIKE A JOB FOR AN UNSUSPECTING CHILD. ONE WE DON'T LIKE.
I LOVE ALL CHILDREN.
BUT I HAVE THE PERFECT CANDIDATE.
BB

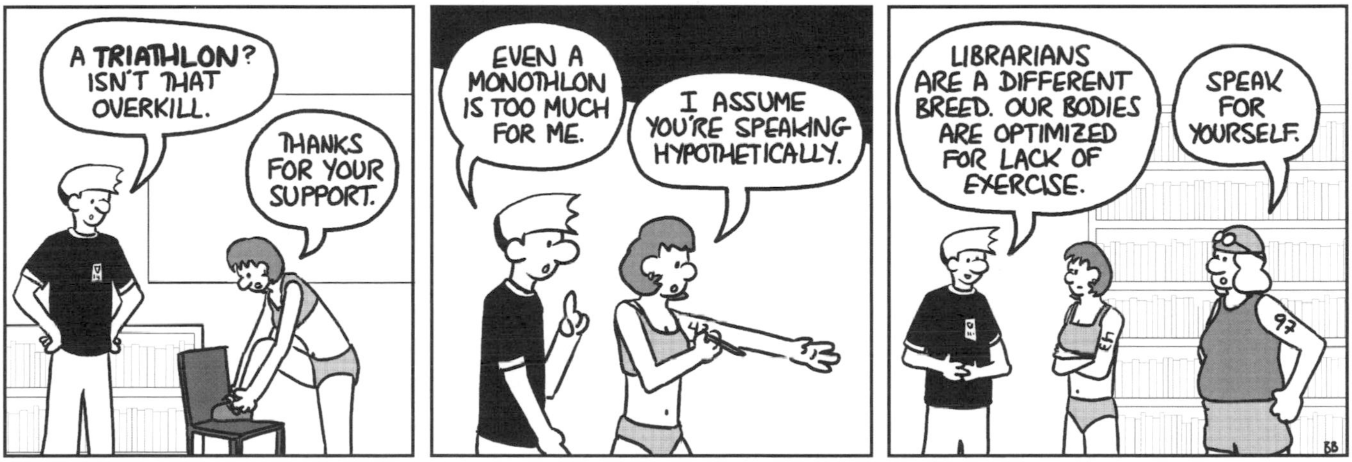
A **TRIATHLON**? ISN'T THAT OVERKILL.
THANKS FOR YOUR SUPPORT.
EVEN A MONOTHLON IS TOO MUCH FOR ME.
I ASSUME YOU'RE SPEAKING HYPOTHETICALLY.
LIBRARIANS ARE A DIFFERENT BREED. OUR BODIES ARE OPTIMIZED FOR LACK OF EXERCISE.
SPEAK FOR YOURSELF.
BB

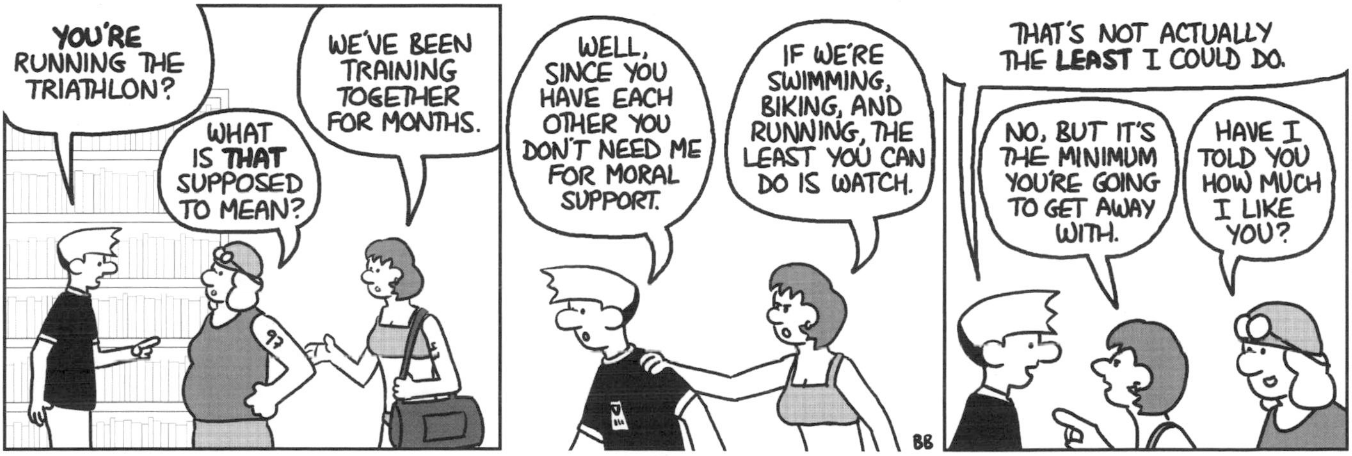
YOU'RE RUNNING THE TRIATHLON?
WHAT IS **THAT** SUPPOSED TO MEAN?
WE'VE BEEN TRAINING TOGETHER FOR MONTHS.
WELL, SINCE YOU HAVE EACH OTHER YOU DON'T NEED ME FOR MORAL SUPPORT.
IF WE'RE SWIMMING, BIKING, AND RUNNING, THE LEAST YOU CAN DO IS WATCH.
THAT'S NOT ACTUALLY THE **LEAST** I COULD DO.
NO, BUT IT'S THE MINIMUM YOU'RE GOING TO GET AWAY WITH.
HAVE I TOLD YOU HOW MUCH I LIKE YOU?
BB

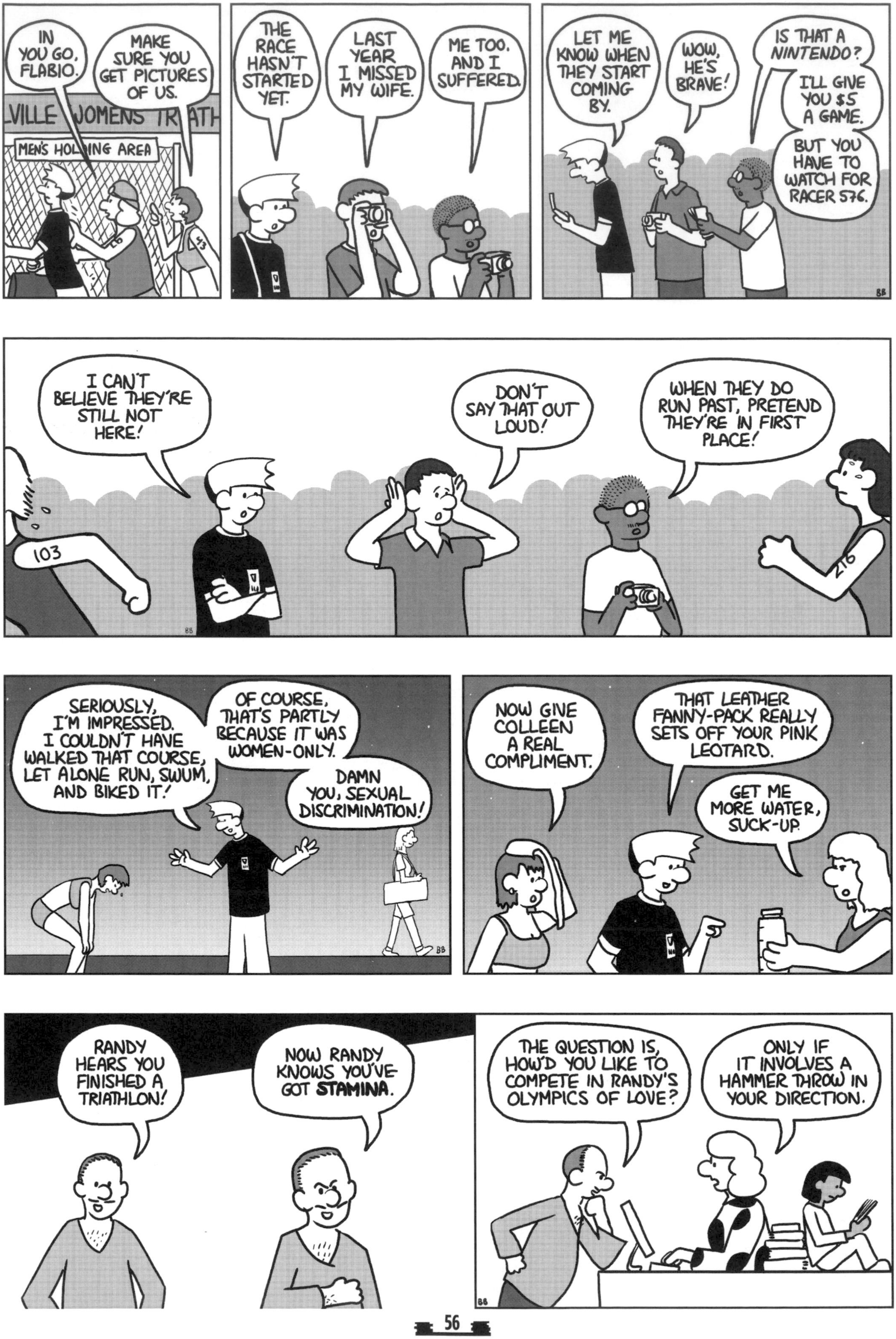
IN YOU GO, FLABIO.
MAKE SURE YOU GET PICTURES OF US.
THE RACE HASN'T STARTED YET.
LAST YEAR I MISSED MY WIFE.
ME TOO. AND I SUFFERED.
LET ME KNOW WHEN THEY START COMING BY.
WOW, HE'S BRAVE!
IS THAT A *NINTENDO?*
I'LL GIVE YOU $5 A GAME.
BUT YOU HAVE TO WATCH FOR RACER 576.
I CAN'T BELIEVE THEY'RE STILL NOT HERE!
DON'T SAY THAT OUT LOUD!
WHEN THEY DO RUN PAST, PRETEND THEY'RE IN FIRST PLACE!
103
216
SERIOUSLY, I'M IMPRESSED. I COULDN'T HAVE WALKED THAT COURSE, LET ALONE RUN, SWUM, AND BIKED IT!
OF COURSE, THAT'S PARTLY BECAUSE IT WAS WOMEN-ONLY.
DAMN YOU, SEXUAL DISCRIMINATION!
NOW GIVE COLLEEN A REAL COMPLIMENT.
THAT LEATHER FANNY-PACK REALLY SETS OFF YOUR PINK LEOTARD.
GET ME MORE WATER, SUCK-UP.
RANDY HEARS YOU FINISHED A TRIATHLON!
NOW RANDY KNOWS YOU'VE GOT **STAMINA**.
THE QUESTION IS, HOW'D YOU LIKE TO COMPETE IN RANDY'S OLYMPICS OF LOVE?
ONLY IF IT INVOLVES A HAMMER THROW IN YOUR DIRECTION.

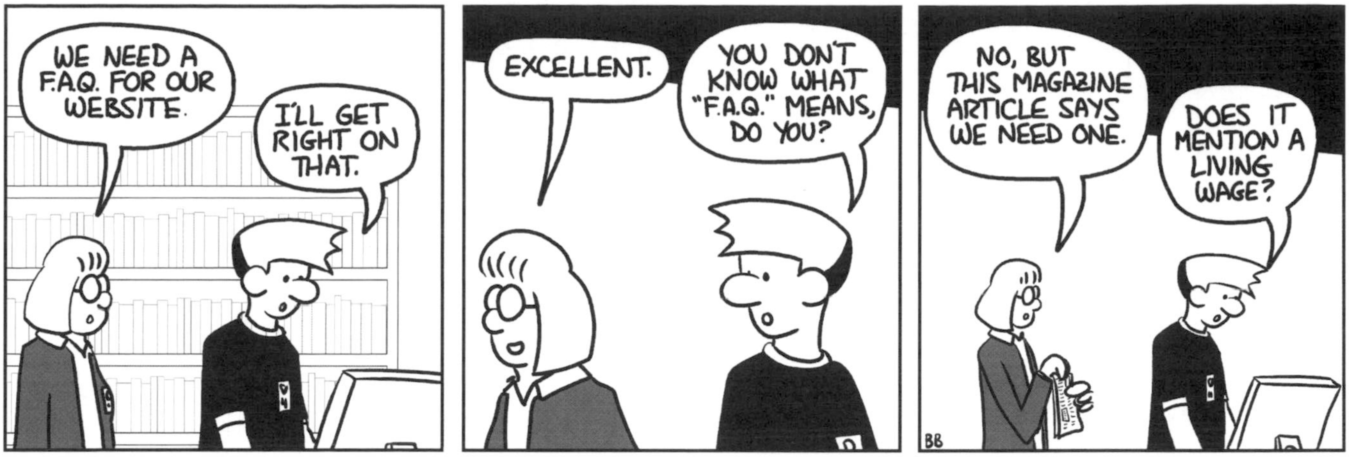
WE NEED A F.A.Q. FOR OUR WEBSITE.
I'LL GET RIGHT ON THAT.
EXCELLENT.
YOU DON'T KNOW WHAT "F.A.Q." MEANS, DO YOU?
NO, BUT THIS MAGAZINE ARTICLE SAYS WE NEED ONE.
DOES IT MENTION A LIVING WAGE?
BB

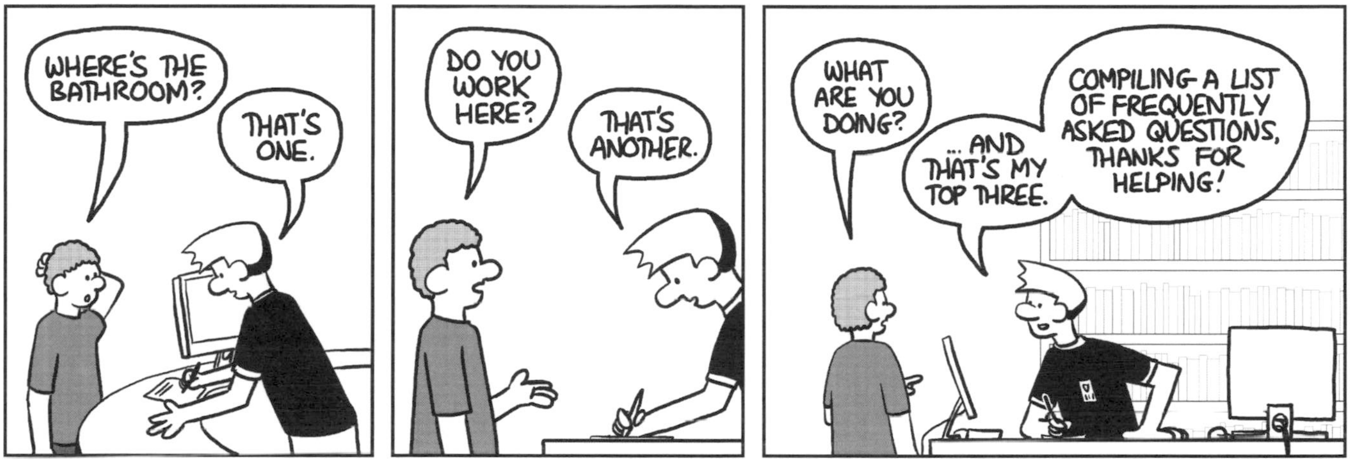
WHERE'S THE BATHROOM?
THAT'S ONE.
DO YOU WORK HERE?
THAT'S ANOTHER.
WHAT ARE YOU DOING?
COMPILING A LIST OF FREQUENTLY ASKED QUESTIONS, THANKS FOR HELPING!
...AND THAT'S MY TOP THREE.

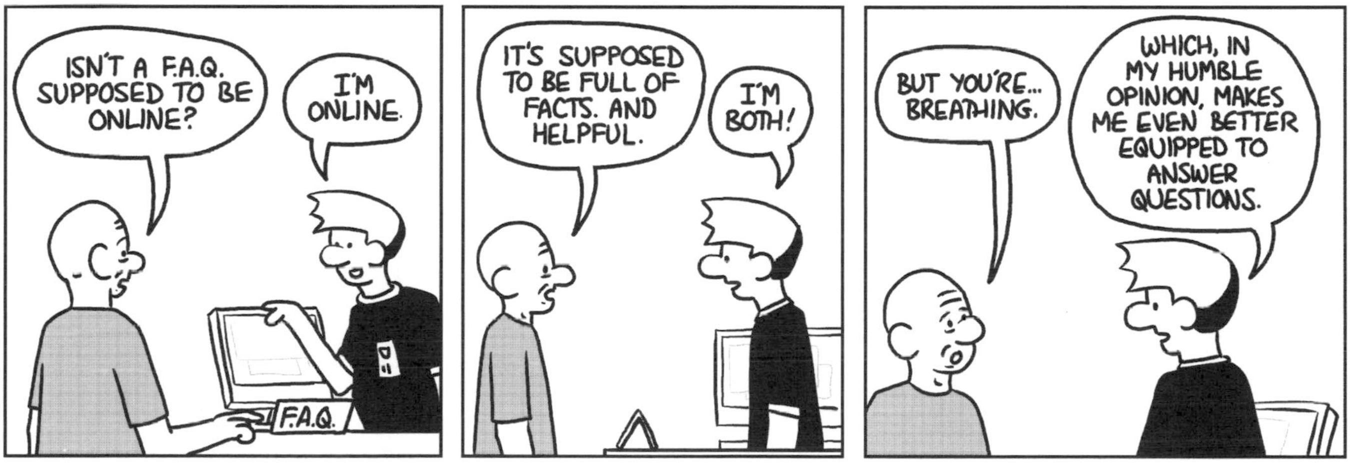
ISN'T A F.A.Q. SUPPOSED TO BE ONLINE?
I'M ONLINE.
F.A.Q.
IT'S SUPPOSED TO BE FULL OF FACTS. AND HELPFUL.
I'M BOTH!
BUT YOU'RE... BREATHING.
WHICH, IN MY HUMBLE OPINION, MAKES ME EVEN BETTER EQUIPPED TO ANSWER QUESTIONS.

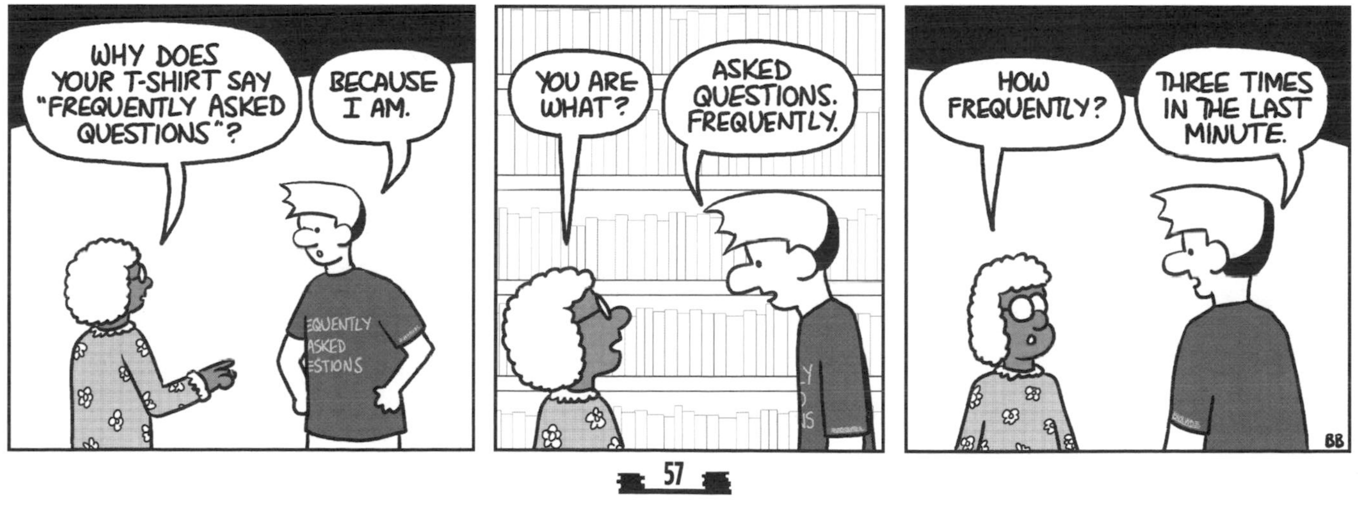
WHY DOES YOUR T-SHIRT SAY "FREQUENTLY ASKED QUESTIONS"?
BECAUSE I AM.
YOU ARE WHAT?
ASKED QUESTIONS. FREQUENTLY.
HOW FREQUENTLY?
THREE TIMES IN THE LAST MINUTE.
BB

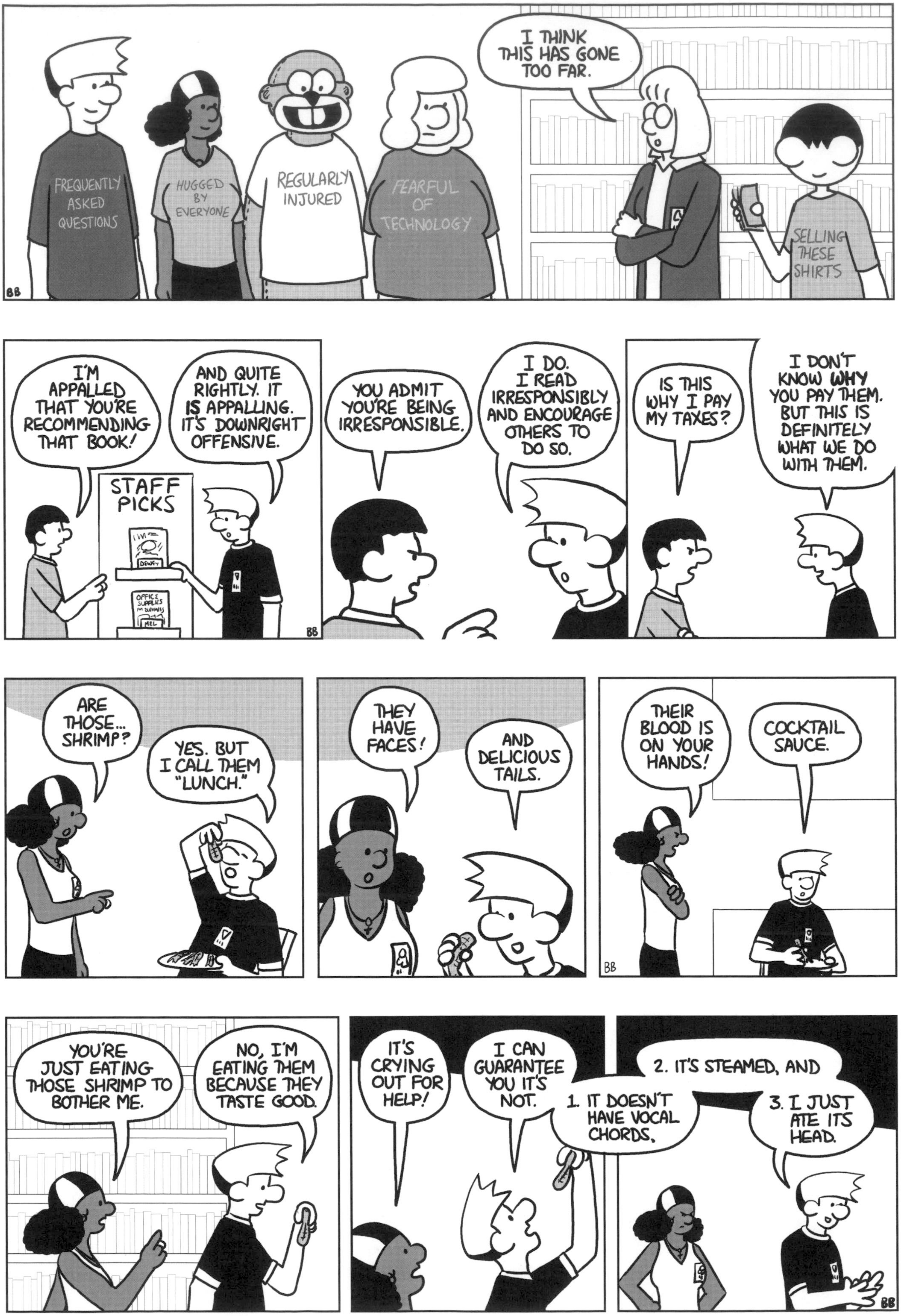
FREQUENTLY ASKED QUESTIONS
HUGGED BY EVERYONE
REGULARLY INJURED
FEARFUL OF TECHNOLOGY
I THINK THIS HAS GONE TOO FAR.
SELLING THESE SHIRTS
BB
I'M APPALLED THAT YOU'RE RECOMMENDING THAT BOOK!
AND QUITE RIGHTLY. IT IS APPALLING. IT'S DOWNRIGHT OFFENSIVE.
STAFF PICKS
DEWEY
MEL
BB
YOU ADMIT YOU'RE BEING IRRESPONSIBLE.
I DO. I READ IRRESPONSIBLY AND ENCOURAGE OTHERS TO DO SO.
IS THIS WHY I PAY MY TAXES?
I DON'T KNOW WHY YOU PAY THEM. BUT THIS IS DEFINITELY WHAT WE DO WITH THEM.
ARE THOSE... SHRIMP?
YES. BUT I CALL THEM "LUNCH."
THEY HAVE FACES!
AND DELICIOUS TAILS.
THEIR BLOOD IS ON YOUR HANDS!
COCKTAIL SAUCE.
BB
YOU'RE JUST EATING THOSE SHRIMP TO BOTHER ME.
NO, I'M EATING THEM BECAUSE THEY TASTE GOOD.
IT'S CRYING OUT FOR HELP!
I CAN GUARANTEE YOU IT'S NOT.
1. IT DOESN'T HAVE VOCAL CHORDS,
2. IT'S STEAMED, AND
3. I JUST ATE ITS HEAD.
BB

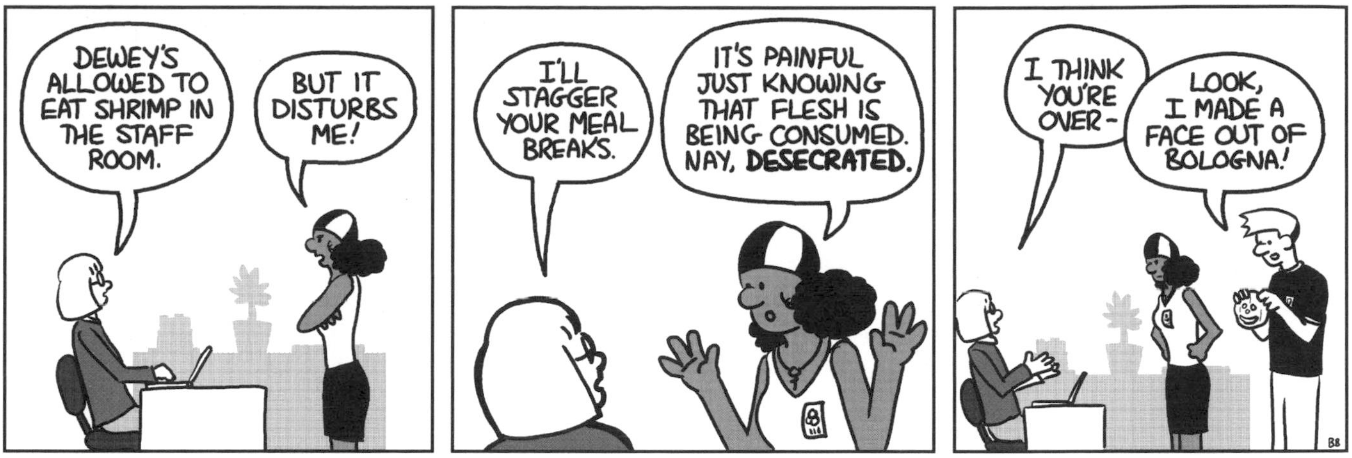
DEWEY'S ALLOWED TO EAT SHRIMP IN THE STAFF ROOM.
BUT IT DISTURBS ME!
I'LL STAGGER YOUR MEAL BREAKS.
IT'S PAINFUL JUST KNOWING THAT FLESH IS BEING CONSUMED. NAY, **DESECRATED**.
I THINK YOU'RE OVER-
LOOK, I MADE A FACE OUT OF BOLOGNA!
BB

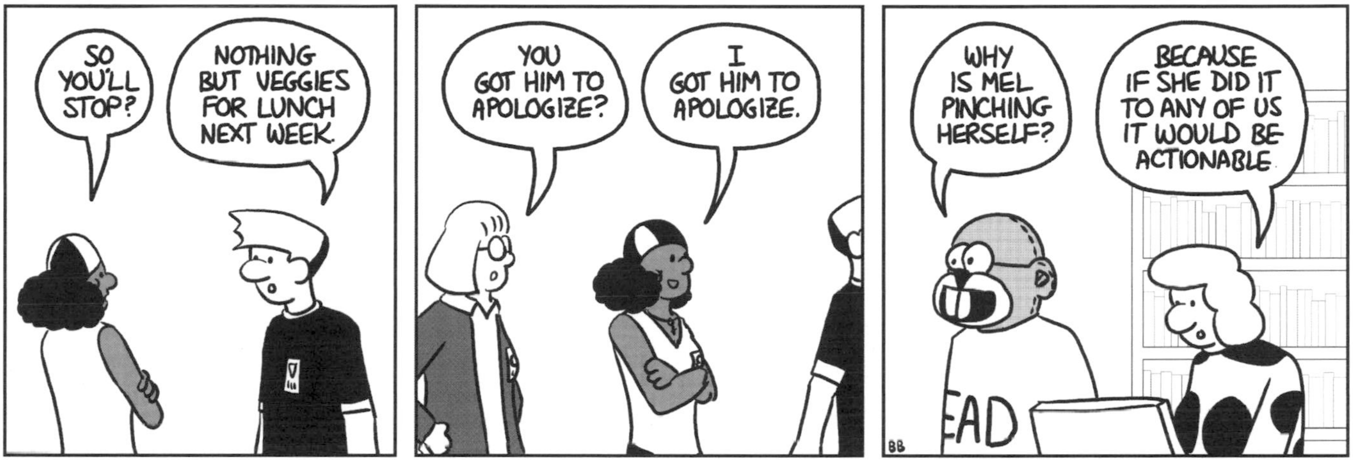
SO YOU'LL STOP?
NOTHING BUT VEGGIES FOR LUNCH NEXT WEEK.
YOU GOT HIM TO APOLOGIZE?
I GOT HIM TO APOLOGIZE.
WHY IS MEL PINCHING HERSELF?
BECAUSE IF SHE DID IT TO ANY OF US IT WOULD BE ACTIONABLE.
EAD
BB

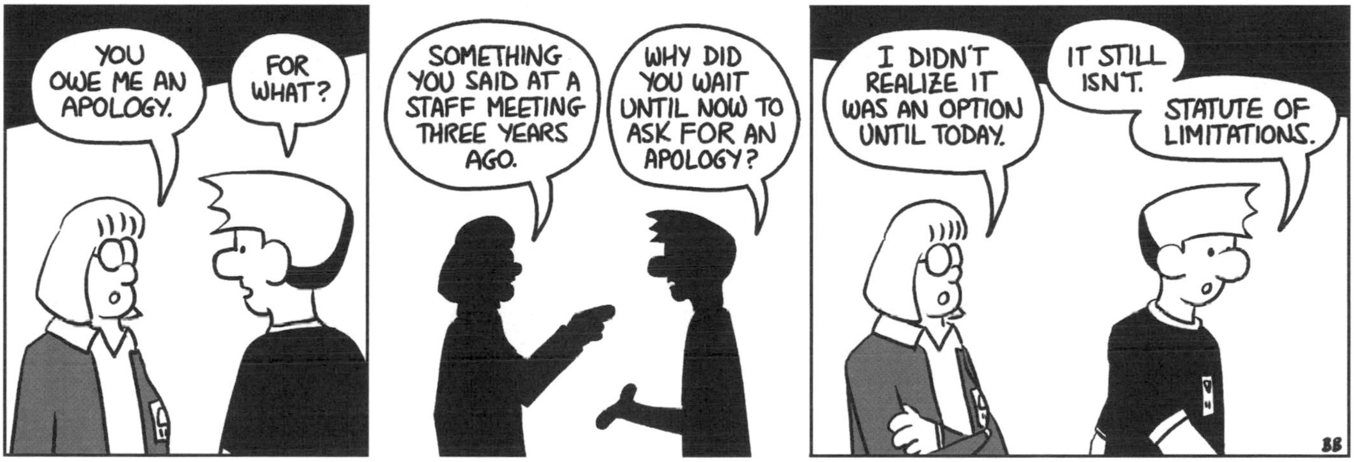
YOU OWE ME AN APOLOGY.
FOR WHAT?
SOMETHING YOU SAID AT A STAFF MEETING THREE YEARS AGO.
WHY DID YOU WAIT UNTIL NOW TO ASK FOR AN APOLOGY?
I DIDN'T REALIZE IT WAS AN OPTION UNTIL TODAY.
IT STILL ISN'T.
STATUTE OF LIMITATIONS.
BB

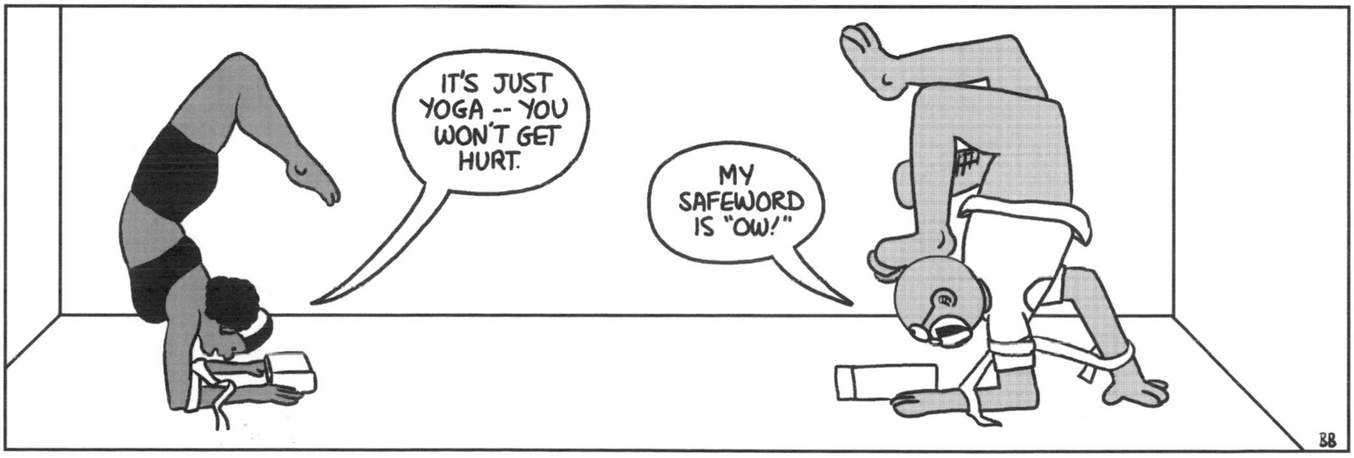
IT'S JUST YOGA -- YOU WON'T GET HURT.
MY SAFEWORD IS "OW!"
BB

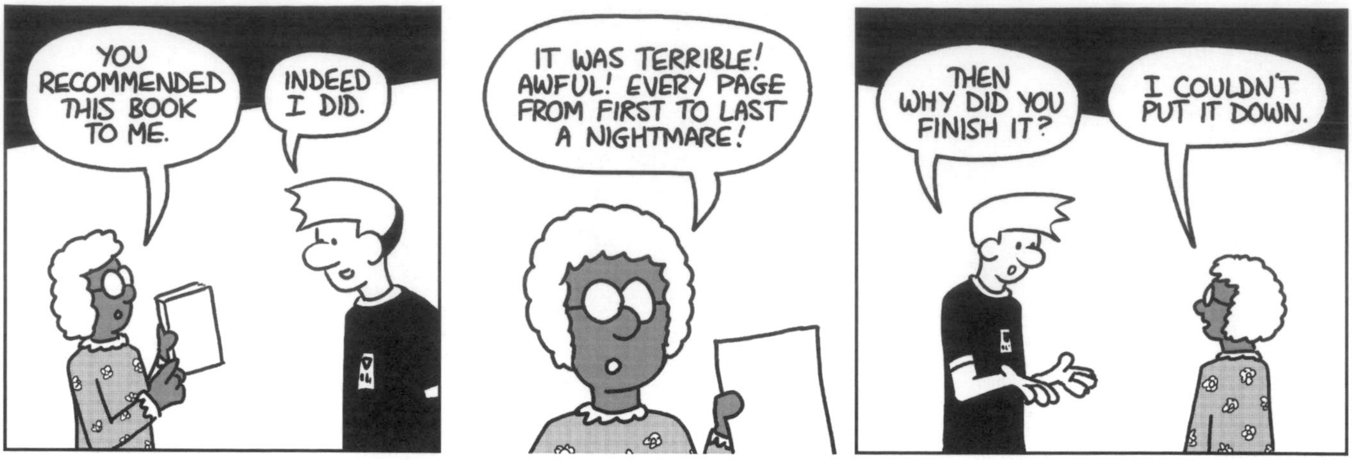
YOU RECOMMENDED THIS BOOK TO ME.
INDEED I DID.
IT WAS TERRIBLE! AWFUL! EVERY PAGE FROM FIRST TO LAST A NIGHTMARE!
THEN WHY DID YOU FINISH IT?
I COULDN'T PUT IT DOWN.

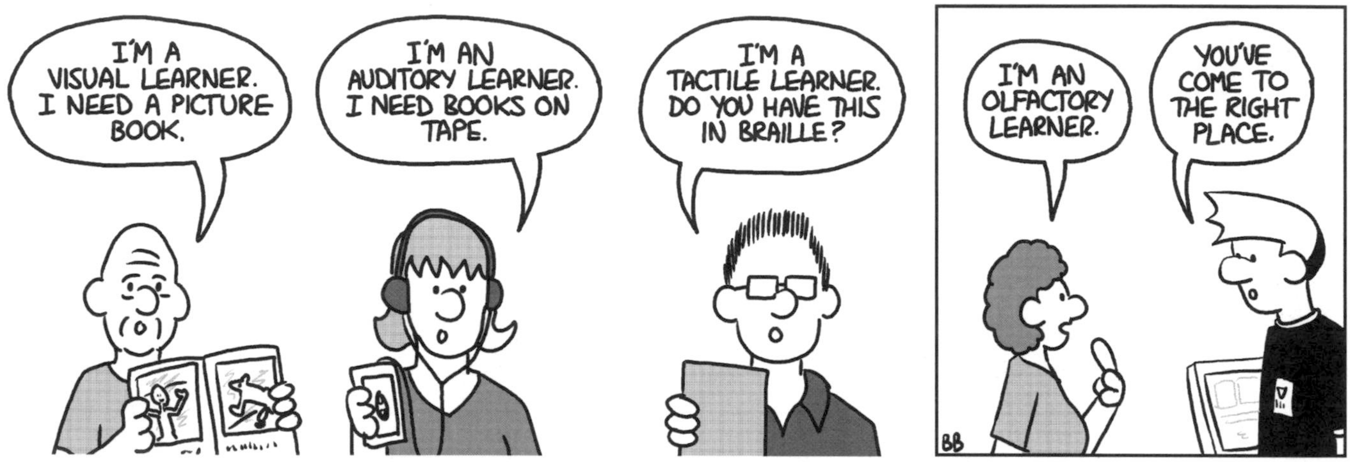
I'M A VISUAL LEARNER. I NEED A PICTURE BOOK.
I'M AN AUDITORY LEARNER. I NEED BOOKS ON TAPE.
I'M A TACTILE LEARNER. DO YOU HAVE THIS IN BRAILLE?
I'M AN OLFACTORY LEARNER.
YOU'VE COME TO THE RIGHT PLACE.
BB

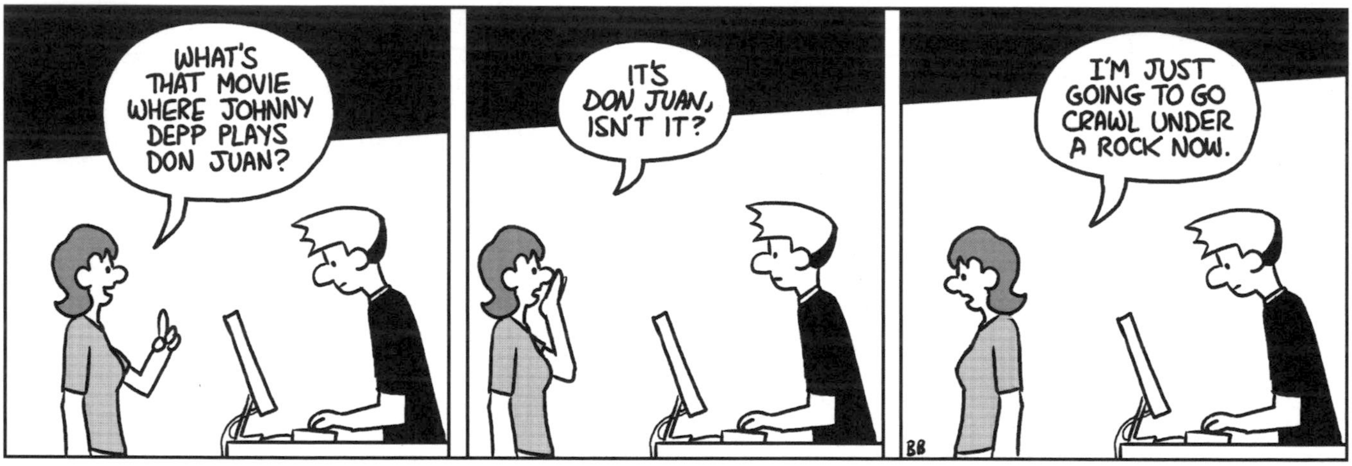
WHAT'S THAT MOVIE WHERE JOHNNY DEPP PLAYS DON JUAN?
IT'S *DON JUAN*, ISN'T IT?
I'M JUST GOING TO GO CRAWL UNDER A ROCK NOW.
BB

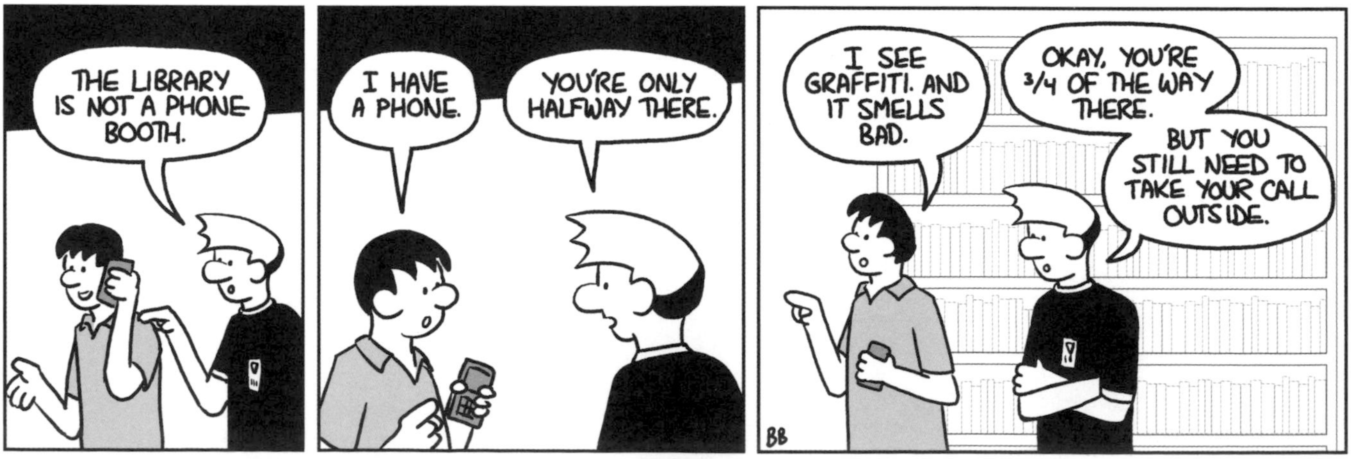
THE LIBRARY IS NOT A PHONE BOOTH.
I HAVE A PHONE.
YOU'RE ONLY HALFWAY THERE.
I SEE GRAFFITI. AND IT SMELLS BAD.
OKAY, YOU'RE 3/4 OF THE WAY THERE.
BUT YOU STILL NEED TO TAKE YOUR CALL OUTSIDE.
BB

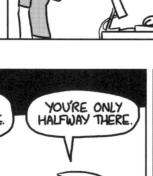

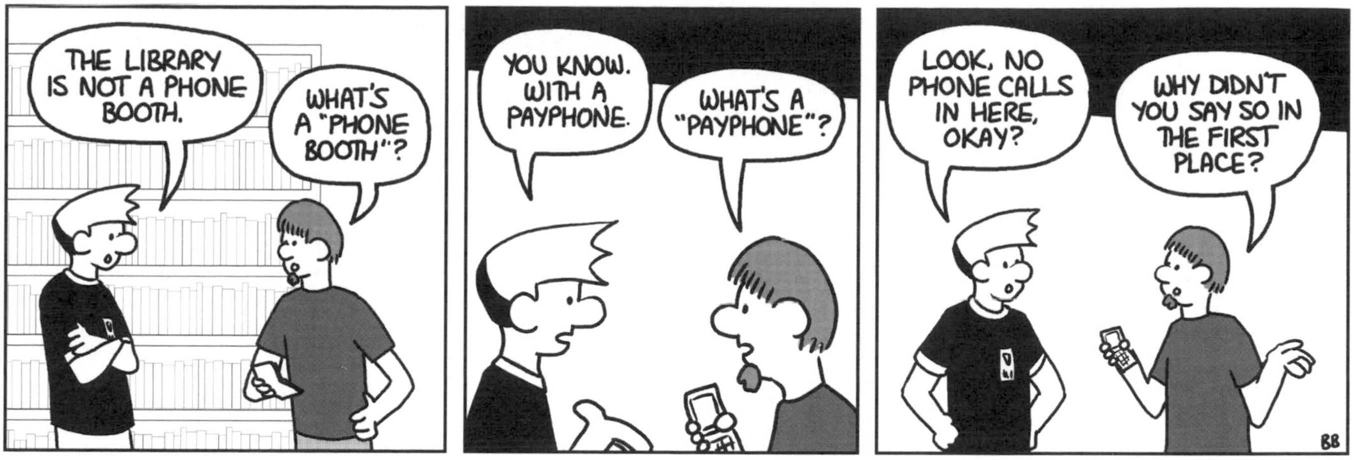
THE LIBRARY IS NOT A PHONE BOOTH.
WHAT'S A "PHONE BOOTH"?
YOU KNOW. WITH A PAYPHONE.
WHAT'S A "PAYPHONE"?
LOOK, NO PHONE CALLS IN HERE, OKAY?
WHY DIDN'T YOU SAY SO IN THE FIRST PLACE?
BB

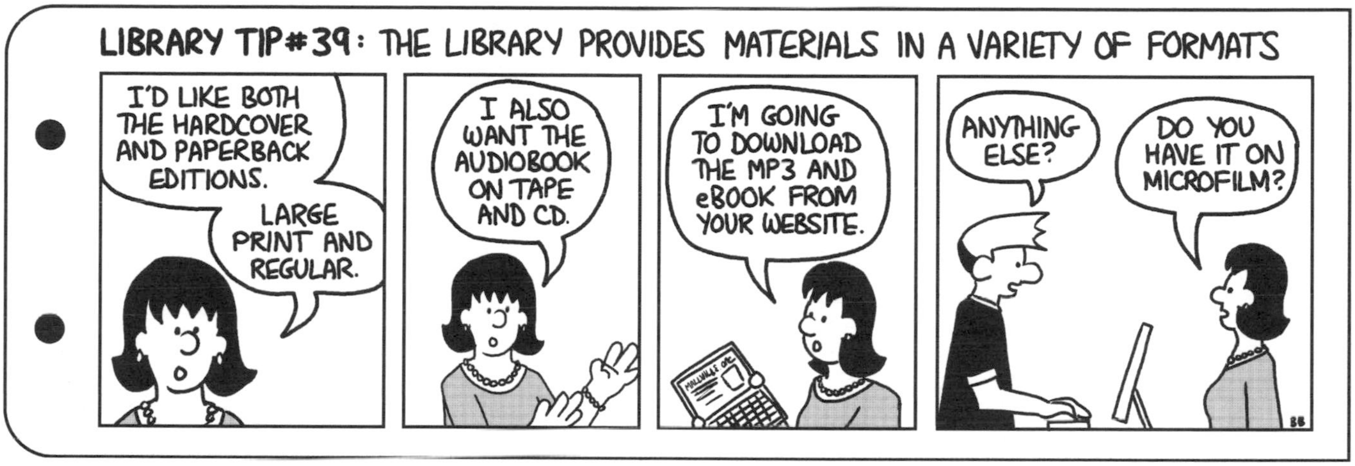
LIBRARY TIP #39: THE LIBRARY PROVIDES MATERIALS IN A VARIETY OF FORMATS
I'D LIKE BOTH THE HARDCOVER AND PAPERBACK EDITIONS.
LARGE PRINT AND REGULAR.
I ALSO WANT THE AUDIOBOOK ON TAPE AND CD.
I'M GOING TO DOWNLOAD THE MP3 AND eBOOK FROM YOUR WEBSITE.
ANYTHING ELSE?
DO YOU HAVE IT ON MICROFILM?
BB

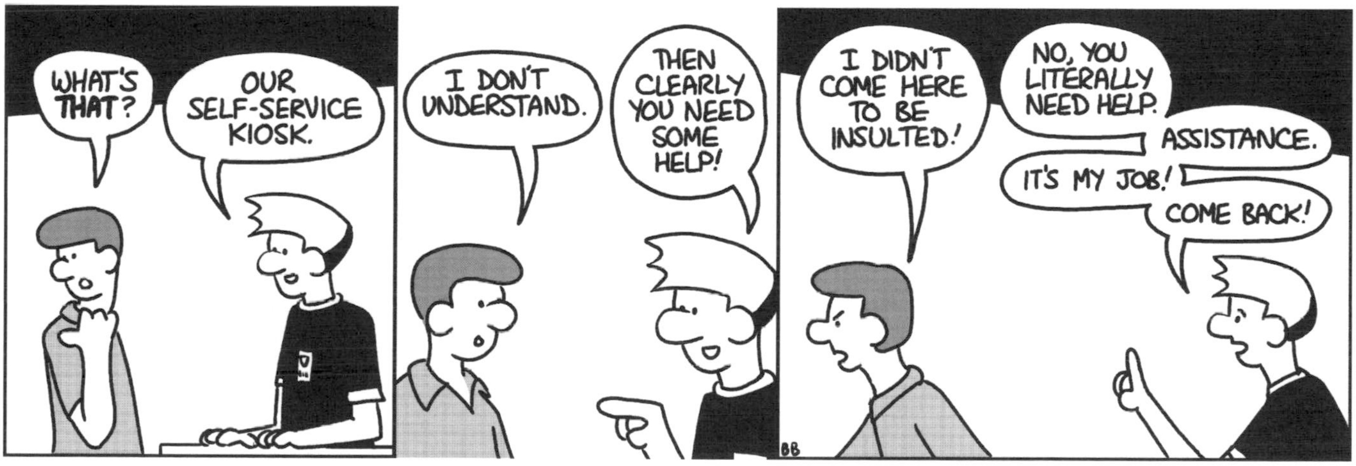
WHAT'S THAT?
OUR SELF-SERVICE KIOSK.
I DON'T UNDERSTAND.
THEN CLEARLY YOU NEED SOME HELP!
I DIDN'T COME HERE TO BE INSULTED!
NO, YOU LITERALLY NEED HELP.
ASSISTANCE.
IT'S MY JOB!
COME BACK!
BB

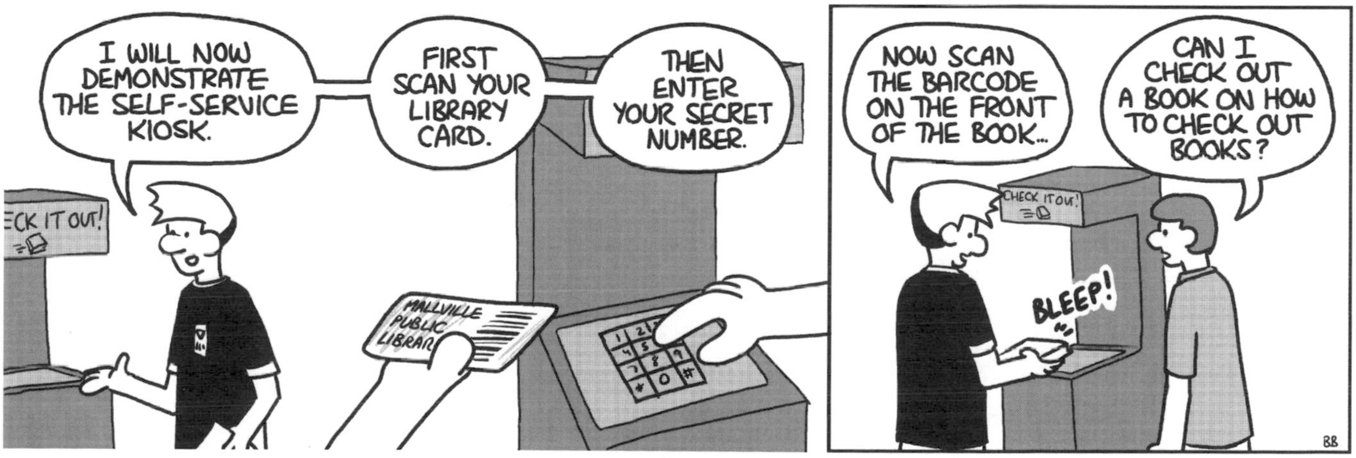
I WILL NOW DEMONSTRATE THE SELF-SERVICE KIOSK.
FIRST SCAN YOUR LIBRARY CARD.
THEN ENTER YOUR SECRET NUMBER.
NOW SCAN THE BARCODE ON THE FRONT OF THE BOOK...
CAN I CHECK OUT A BOOK ON HOW TO CHECK OUT BOOKS?
BLEEP!
BB

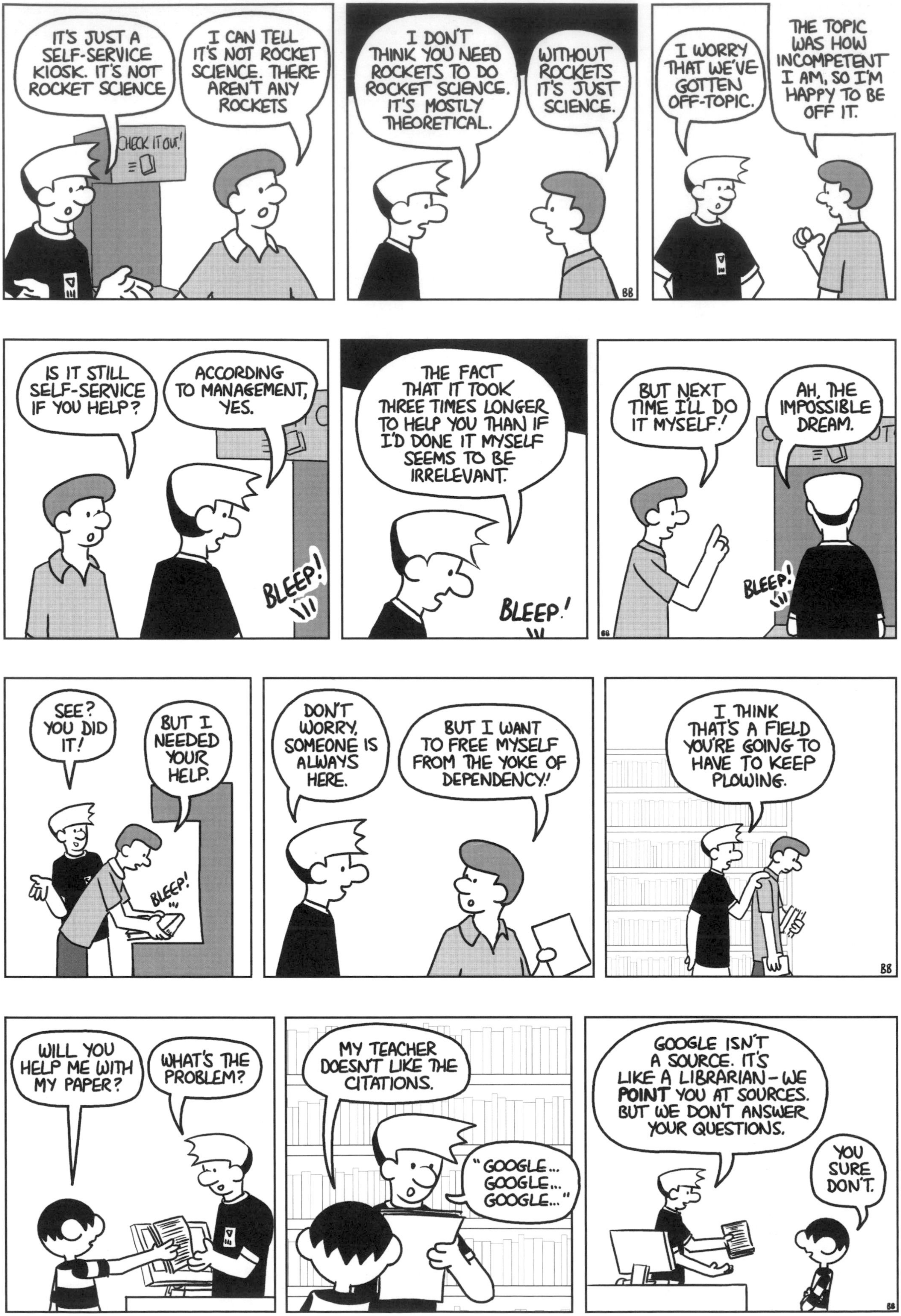
IT'S JUST A SELF-SERVICE KIOSK. IT'S NOT ROCKET SCIENCE
I CAN TELL IT'S NOT ROCKET SCIENCE. THERE AREN'T ANY ROCKETS
CHECK IT OUT!
I DON'T THINK YOU NEED ROCKETS TO DO ROCKET SCIENCE. IT'S MOSTLY THEORETICAL.
WITHOUT ROCKETS IT'S JUST SCIENCE.
I WORRY THAT WE'VE GOTTEN OFF-TOPIC.
THE TOPIC WAS HOW INCOMPETENT I AM, SO I'M HAPPY TO BE OFF IT.
IS IT STILL SELF-SERVICE IF YOU HELP?
ACCORDING TO MANAGEMENT, YES.
BLEEP!
THE FACT THAT IT TOOK THREE TIMES LONGER TO HELP YOU THAN IF I'D DONE IT MYSELF SEEMS TO BE IRRELEVANT.
BLEEP!
BUT NEXT TIME I'LL DO IT MYSELF!
AH, THE IMPOSSIBLE DREAM.
BLEEP!
SEE? YOU DID IT!
BUT I NEEDED YOUR HELP.
BLEEP!
DON'T WORRY, SOMEONE IS ALWAYS HERE.
BUT I WANT TO FREE MYSELF FROM THE YOKE OF DEPENDENCY!
I THINK THAT'S A FIELD YOU'RE GOING TO HAVE TO KEEP PLOWING.
WILL YOU HELP ME WITH MY PAPER?
WHAT'S THE PROBLEM?
MY TEACHER DOESN'T LIKE THE CITATIONS.
"GOOGLE... GOOGLE... GOOGLE..."
GOOGLE ISN'T A SOURCE. IT'S LIKE A LIBRARIAN – WE POINT YOU AT SOURCES. BUT WE DON'T ANSWER YOUR QUESTIONS.
YOU SURE DON'T.

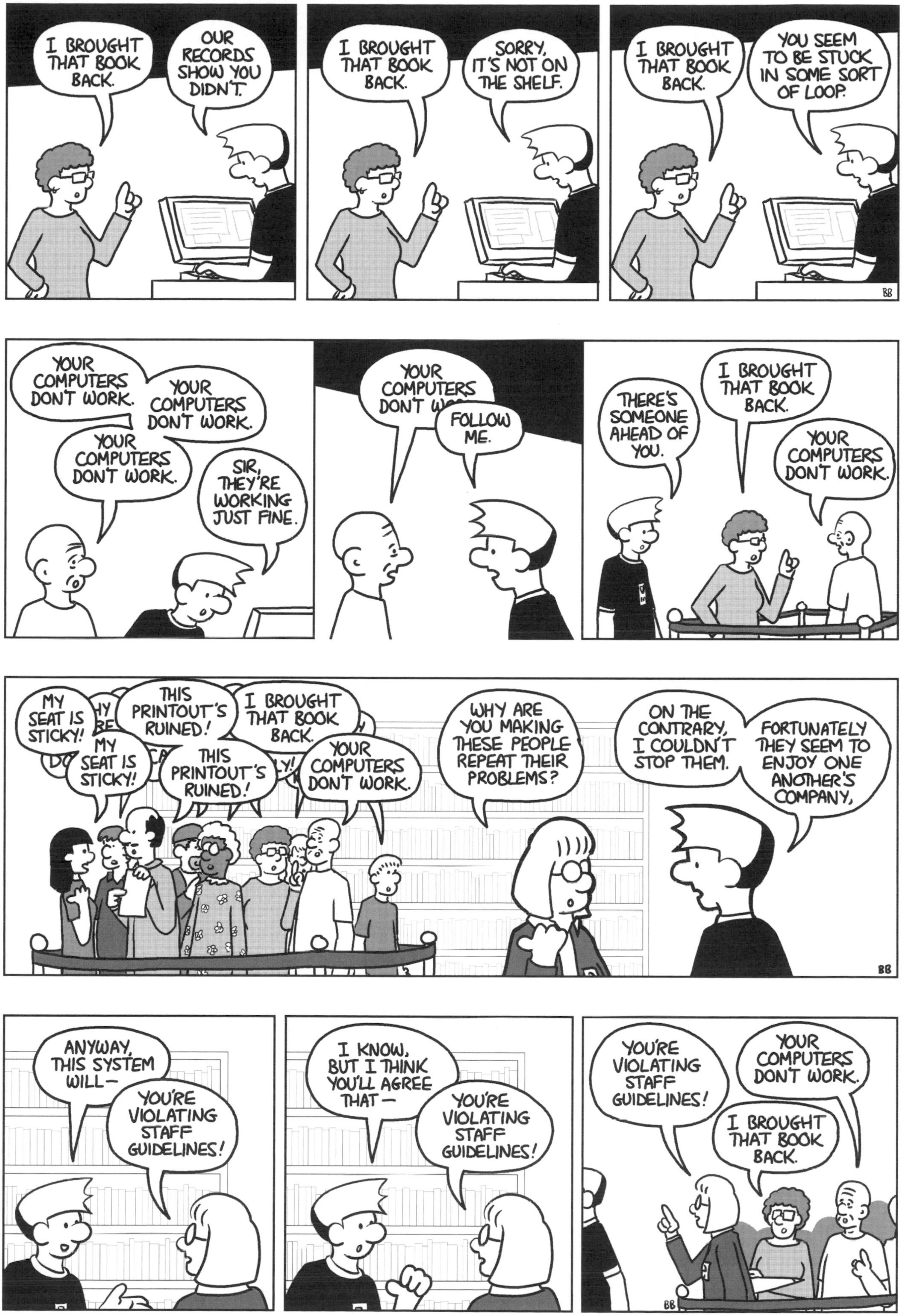

I BROUGHT THAT BOOK BACK.
OUR RECORDS SHOW YOU DIDN'T.
I BROUGHT THAT BOOK BACK.
SORRY, IT'S NOT ON THE SHELF.
I BROUGHT THAT BOOK BACK.
YOU SEEM TO BE STUCK IN SOME SORT OF LOOP.
BB
YOUR COMPUTERS DON'T WORK.
YOUR COMPUTERS DON'T WORK.
YOUR COMPUTERS DON'T WORK.
SIR, THEY'RE WORKING JUST FINE.
FOLLOW ME.
THERE'S SOMEONE AHEAD OF YOU.
I BROUGHT THAT BOOK BACK.
YOUR COMPUTERS DON'T WORK.
MY SEAT IS STICKY!
THIS PRINTOUT'S RUINED!
I BROUGHT THAT BOOK BACK.
MY SEAT IS STICKY!
THIS PRINTOUT'S RUINED!
YOUR COMPUTERS DON'T WORK.
WHY ARE YOU MAKING THESE PEOPLE REPEAT THEIR PROBLEMS?
ON THE CONTRARY, I COULDN'T STOP THEM.
FORTUNATELY THEY SEEM TO ENJOY ONE ANOTHER'S COMPANY,
BB
ANYWAY, THIS SYSTEM WILL—
YOU'RE VIOLATING STAFF GUIDELINES!
I KNOW, BUT I THINK YOU'LL AGREE THAT—
YOU'RE VIOLATING STAFF GUIDELINES!
YOU'RE VIOLATING STAFF GUIDELINES!
YOUR COMPUTERS DON'T WORK.
I BROUGHT THAT BOOK BACK.
BB

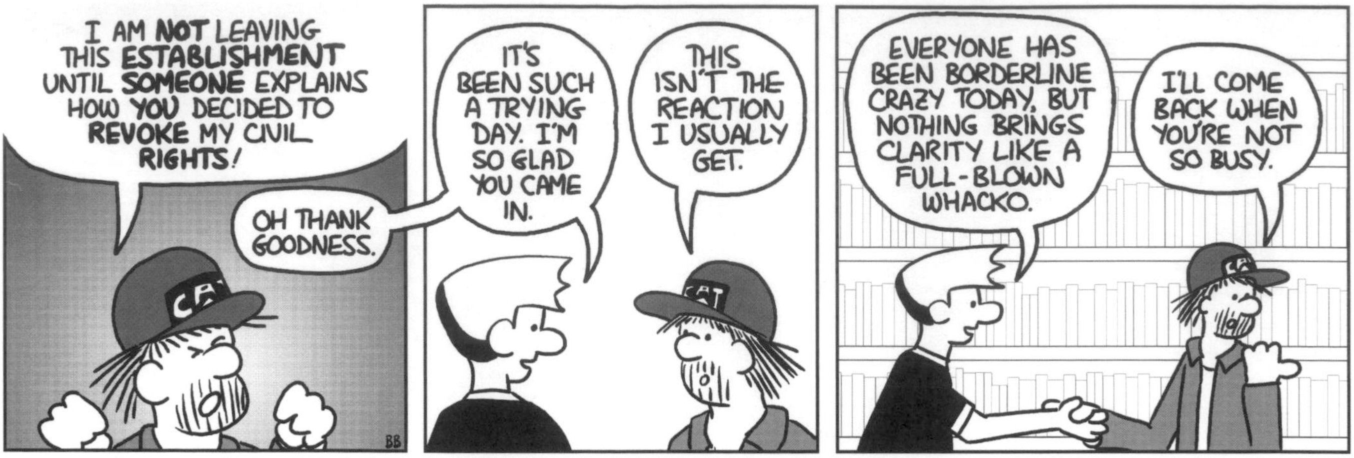
I AM NOT LEAVING THIS ESTABLISHMENT UNTIL SOMEONE EXPLAINS HOW YOU DECIDED TO REVOKE MY CIVIL RIGHTS!
OH THANK GOODNESS.
IT'S BEEN SUCH A TRYING DAY. I'M SO GLAD YOU CAME IN.
THIS ISN'T THE REACTION I USUALLY GET.
EVERYONE HAS BEEN BORDERLINE CRAZY TODAY, BUT NOTHING BRINGS CLARITY LIKE A FULL-BLOWN WHACKO.
I'LL COME BACK WHEN YOU'RE NOT SO BUSY.
BB

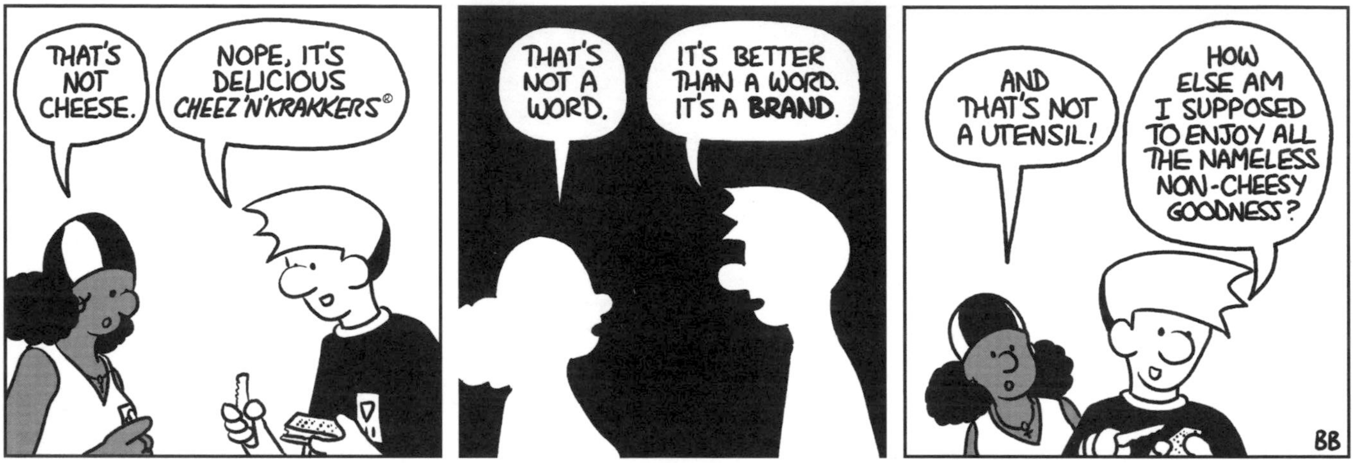
THAT'S NOT CHEESE.
NOPE, IT'S DELICIOUS CHEEZ 'N' KRAKKERS©
THAT'S NOT A WORD.
IT'S BETTER THAN A WORD. IT'S A BRAND.
AND THAT'S NOT A UTENSIL!
HOW ELSE AM I SUPPOSED TO ENJOY ALL THE NAMELESS NON-CHEESY GOODNESS?
BB

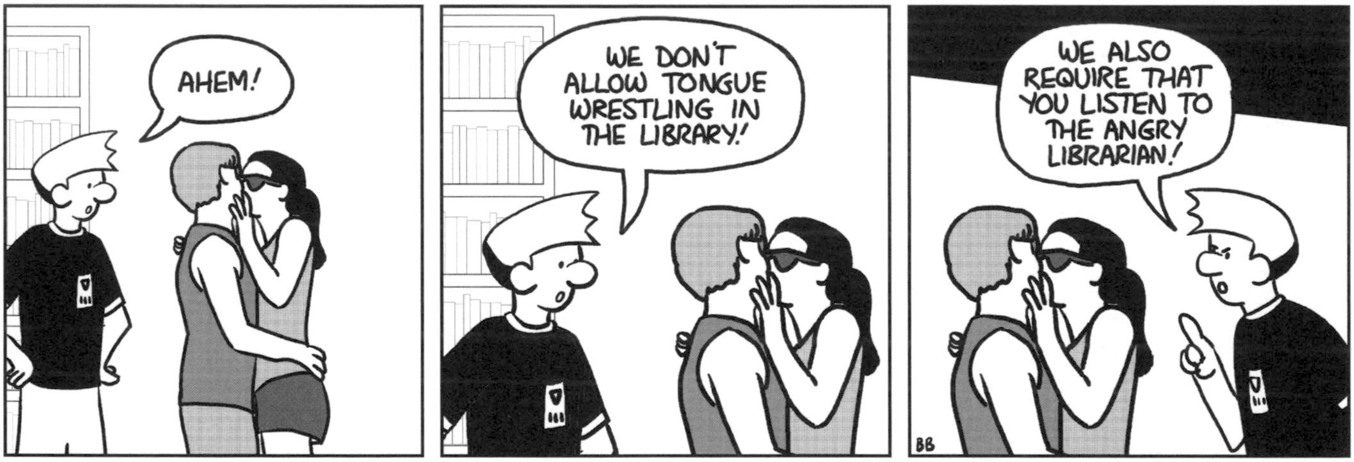
AHEM!
WE DON'T ALLOW TONGUE WRESTLING IN THE LIBRARY!
WE ALSO REQUIRE THAT YOU LISTEN TO THE ANGRY LIBRARIAN!
BB

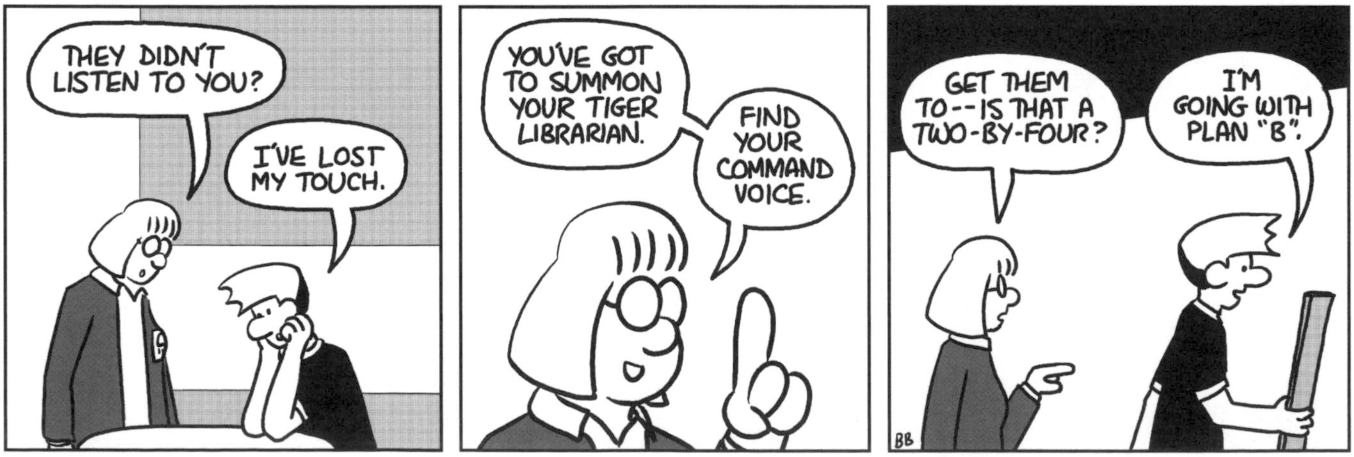
THEY DIDN'T LISTEN TO YOU?
I'VE LOST MY TOUCH.
YOU'VE GOT TO SUMMON YOUR TIGER LIBRARIAN.
FIND YOUR COMMAND VOICE.
GET THEM TO--IS THAT A TWO-BY-FOUR?
I'M GOING WITH PLAN "B".
BB

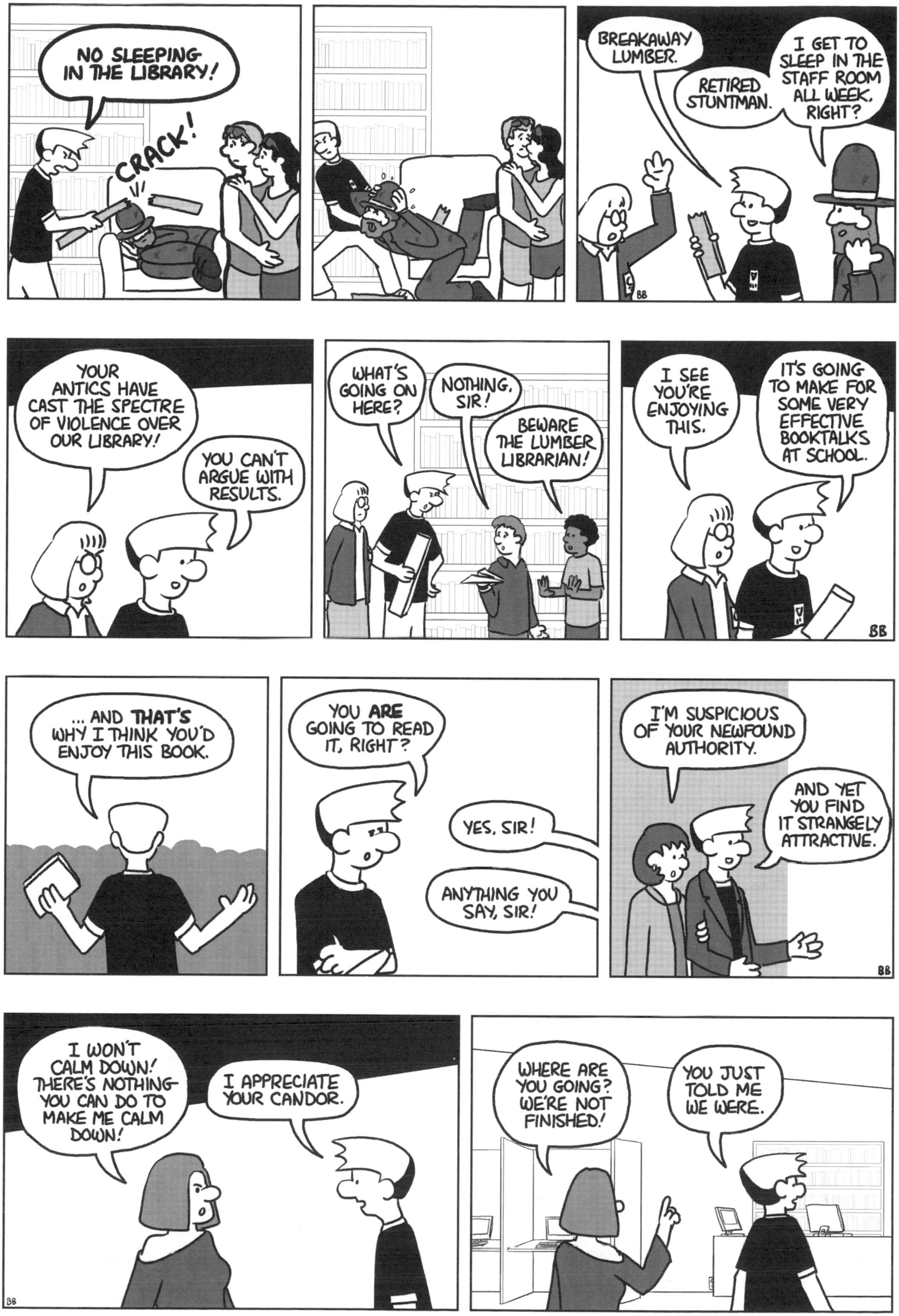
NO SLEEPING IN THE LIBRARY!
CRACK!
BREAKAWAY LUMBER.
RETIRED STUNTMAN.
I GET TO SLEEP IN THE STAFF ROOM ALL WEEK, RIGHT?
BB
YOUR ANTICS HAVE CAST THE SPECTRE OF VIOLENCE OVER OUR LIBRARY!
YOU CAN'T ARGUE WITH RESULTS.
WHAT'S GOING ON HERE?
NOTHING, SIR!
BEWARE THE LUMBER LIBRARIAN!
I SEE YOU'RE ENJOYING THIS.
IT'S GOING TO MAKE FOR SOME VERY EFFECTIVE BOOKTALKS AT SCHOOL.
BB
... AND **THAT'S** WHY I THINK YOU'D ENJOY THIS BOOK.
YOU **ARE** GOING TO READ IT, RIGHT?
YES, SIR!
ANYTHING YOU SAY, SIR!
I'M SUSPICIOUS OF YOUR NEWFOUND AUTHORITY.
AND YET YOU FIND IT STRANGELY ATTRACTIVE.
BB
I WON'T CALM DOWN! THERE'S NOTHING YOU CAN DO TO MAKE ME CALM DOWN!
I APPRECIATE YOUR CANDOR.
BB
WHERE ARE YOU GOING? WE'RE NOT FINISHED!
YOU JUST TOLD ME WE WERE.

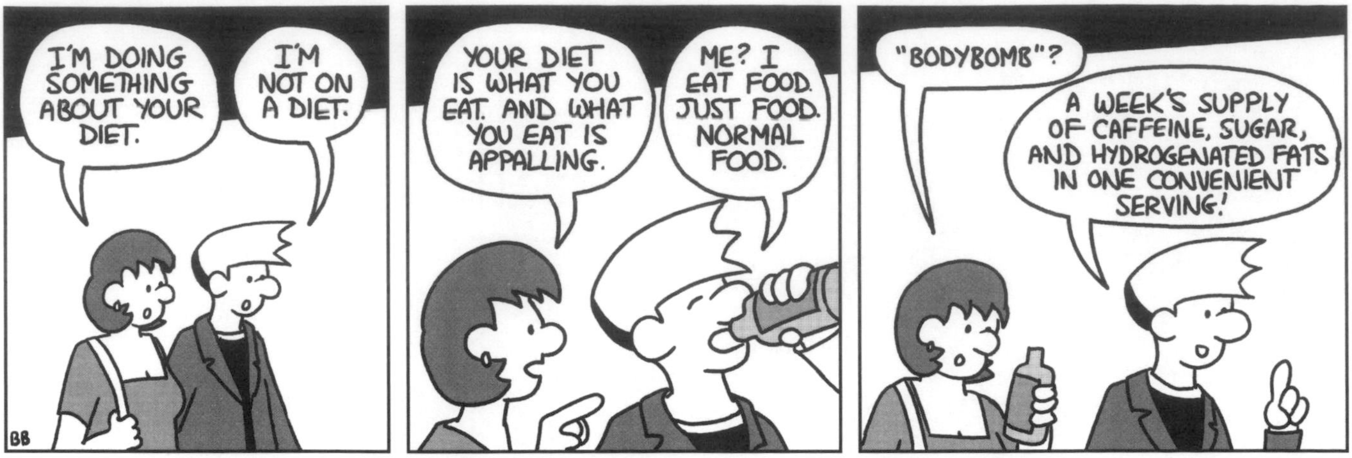
BB
I'M DOING SOMETHING ABOUT YOUR DIET.
I'M NOT ON A DIET.
YOUR DIET IS WHAT YOU EAT. AND WHAT YOU EAT IS APPALLING.
ME? I EAT FOOD. JUST FOOD. NORMAL FOOD.
"BODYBOMB"?
A WEEK'S SUPPLY OF CAFFEINE, SUGAR, AND HYDROGENATED FATS IN ONE CONVENIENT SERVING!

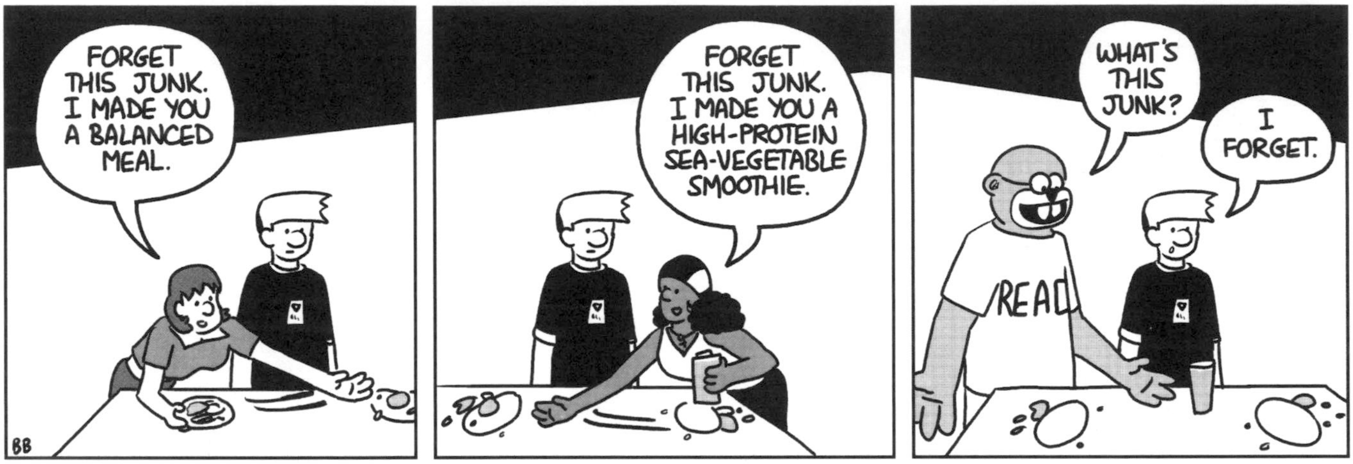
FORGET THIS JUNK. I MADE YOU A BALANCED MEAL.
BB
FORGET THIS JUNK. I MADE YOU A HIGH-PROTEIN SEA-VEGETABLE SMOOTHIE.
WHAT'S THIS JUNK?
I FORGET.
READ

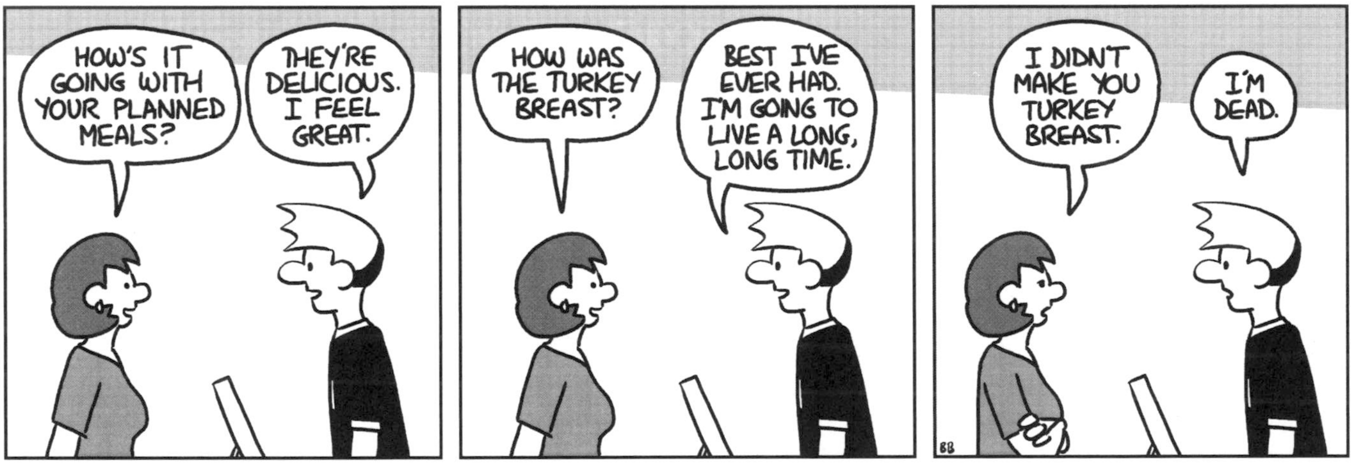
HOW'S IT GOING WITH YOUR PLANNED MEALS?
THEY'RE DELICIOUS. I FEEL GREAT.
HOW WAS THE TURKEY BREAST?
BEST I'VE EVER HAD. I'M GOING TO LIVE A LONG, LONG TIME.
I DIDN'T MAKE YOU TURKEY BREAST.
I'M DEAD.
BB

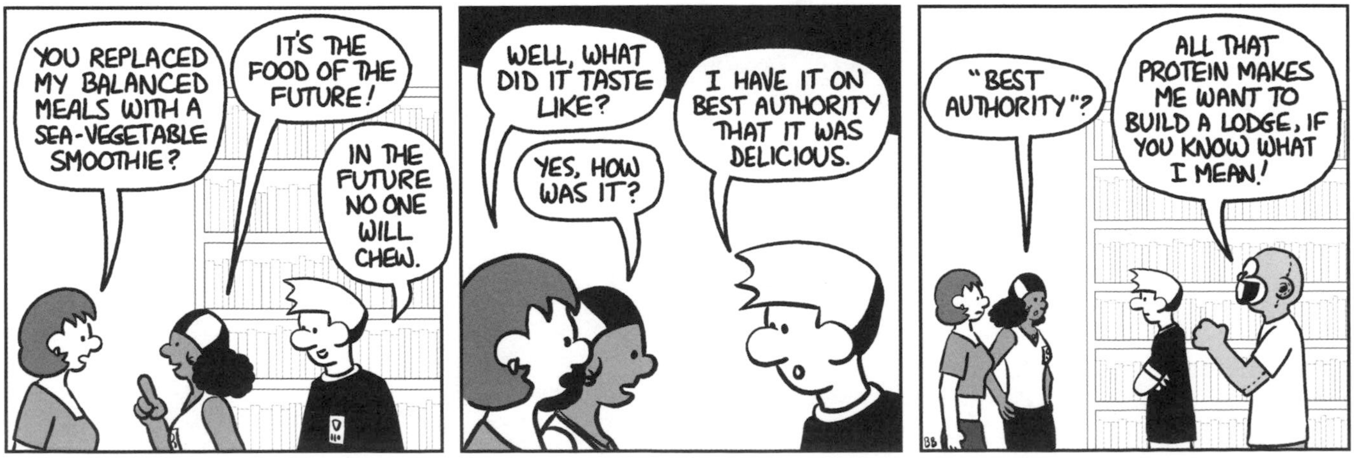
YOU REPLACED MY BALANCED MEALS WITH A SEA-VEGETABLE SMOOTHIE?
IT'S THE FOOD OF THE FUTURE!
IN THE FUTURE NO ONE WILL CHEW.
WELL, WHAT DID IT TASTE LIKE?
YES, HOW WAS IT?
I HAVE IT ON BEST AUTHORITY THAT IT WAS DELICIOUS.
"BEST AUTHORITY"?
ALL THAT PROTEIN MAKES ME WANT TO BUILD A LODGE, IF YOU KNOW WHAT I MEAN!
BB

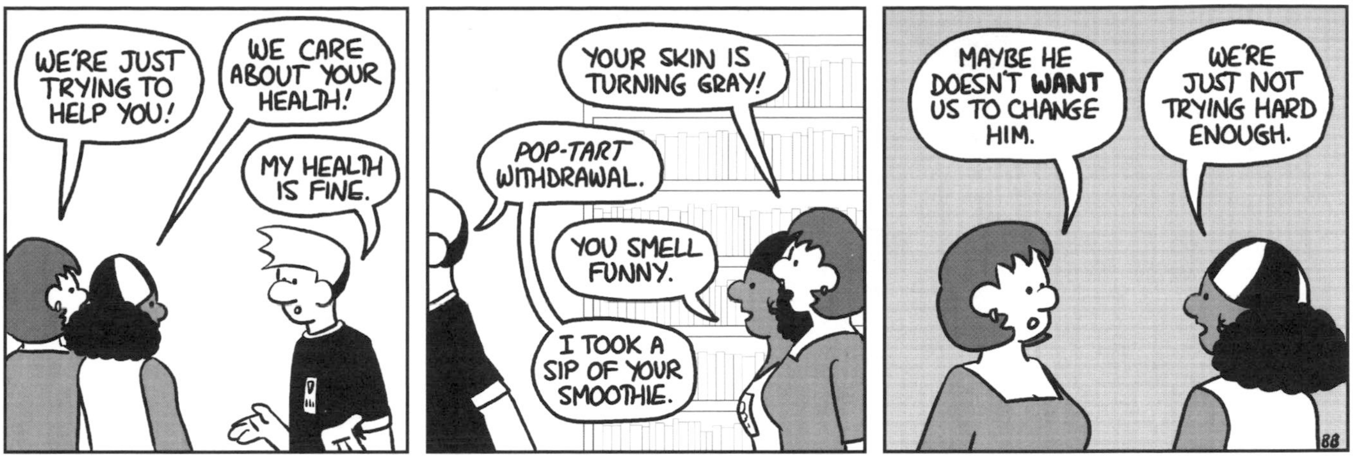
WE'RE JUST TRYING TO HELP YOU!
WE CARE ABOUT YOUR HEALTH!
MY HEALTH IS FINE.
YOUR SKIN IS TURNING GRAY!
POP-TART WITHDRAWAL.
YOU SMELL FUNNY.
I TOOK A SIP OF YOUR SMOOTHIE.
MAYBE HE DOESN'T WANT US TO CHANGE HIM.
WE'RE JUST NOT TRYING HARD ENOUGH.
BB

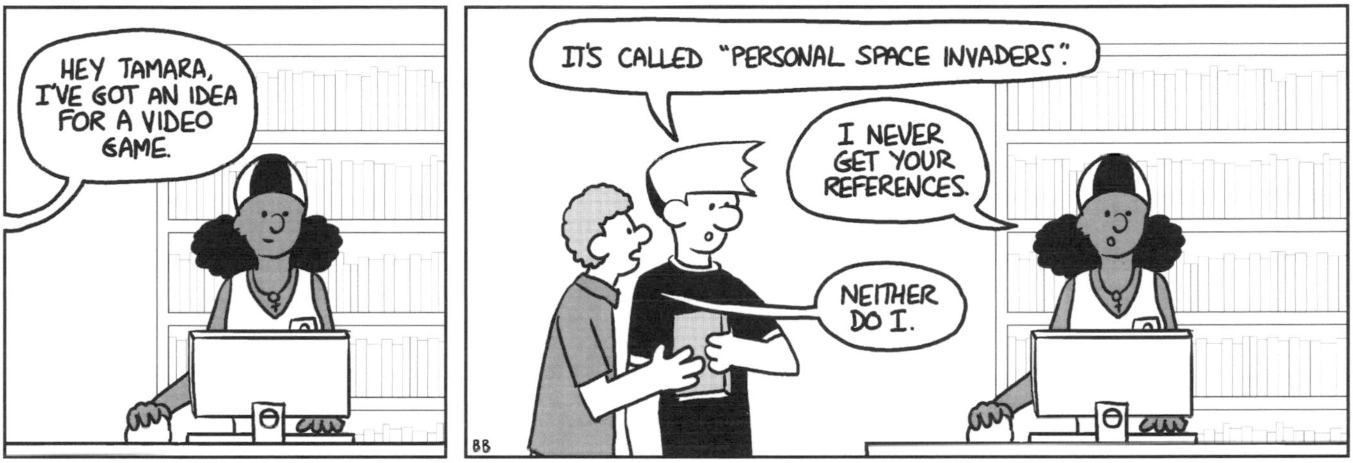
HEY TAMARA, I'VE GOT AN IDEA FOR A VIDEO GAME.
IT'S CALLED "PERSONAL SPACE INVADERS."
I NEVER GET YOUR REFERENCES.
NEITHER DO I.
BB

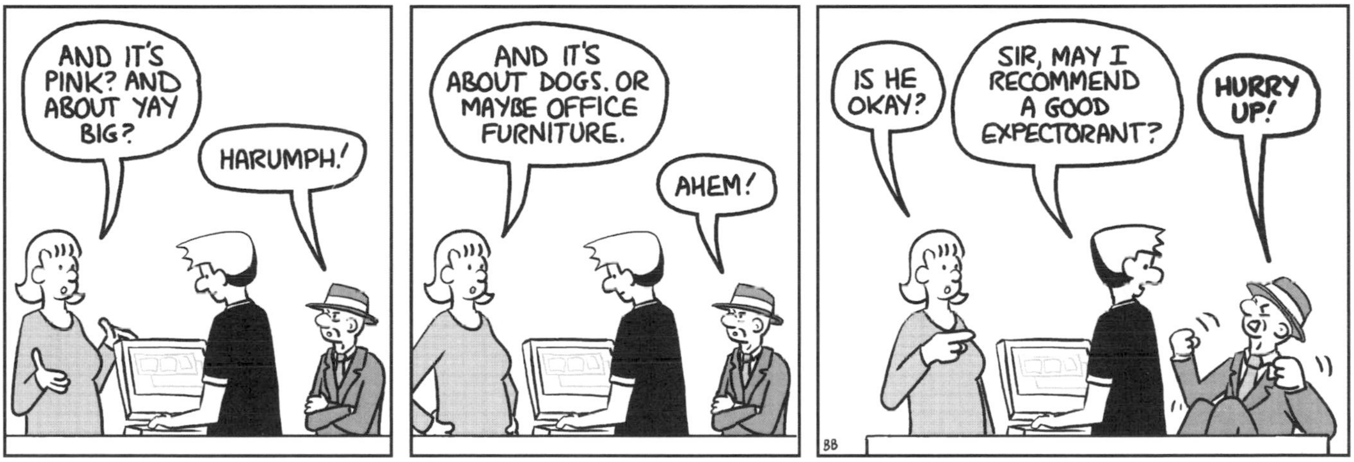
AND IT'S PINK? AND ABOUT YAY BIG?
HARUMPH!
AND IT'S ABOUT DOGS. OR MAYBE OFFICE FURNITURE.
AHEM!
IS HE OKAY?
SIR, MAY I RECOMMEND A GOOD EXPECTORANT?
HURRY UP!
BB

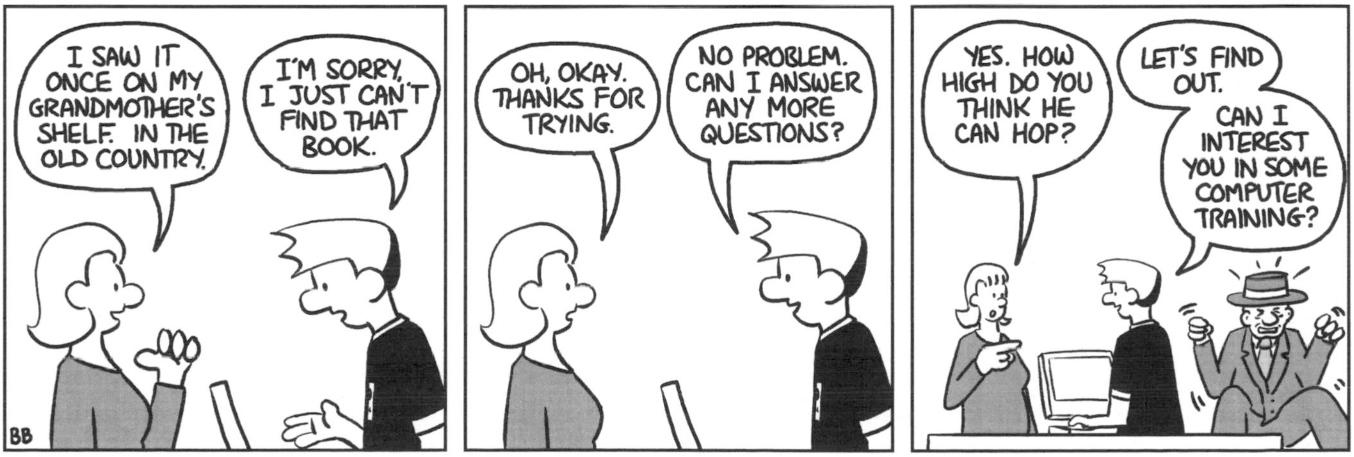
I SAW IT ONCE ON MY GRANDMOTHER'S SHELF. IN THE OLD COUNTRY.
I'M SORRY, I JUST CAN'T FIND THAT BOOK.
OH, OKAY. THANKS FOR TRYING.
NO PROBLEM. CAN I ANSWER ANY MORE QUESTIONS?
YES. HOW HIGH DO YOU THINK HE CAN HOP?
LET'S FIND OUT.
CAN I INTEREST YOU IN SOME COMPUTER TRAINING?
BB

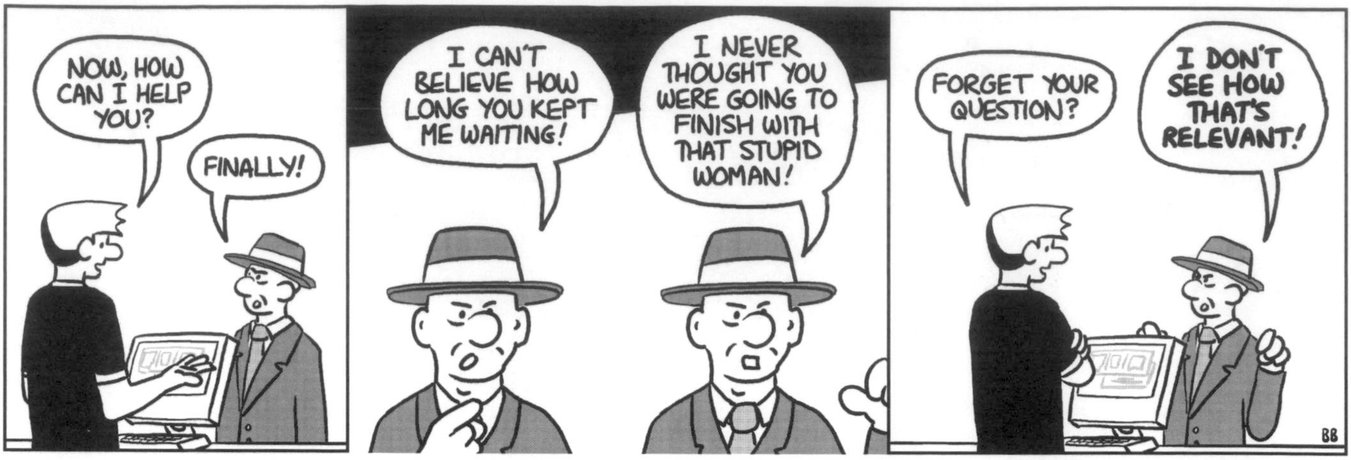
NOW, HOW CAN I HELP YOU?
FINALLY!
I CAN'T BELIEVE HOW LONG YOU KEPT ME WAITING!
I NEVER THOUGHT YOU WERE GOING TO FINISH WITH THAT STUPID WOMAN!
FORGET YOUR QUESTION?
I DON'T SEE HOW THAT'S RELEVANT!

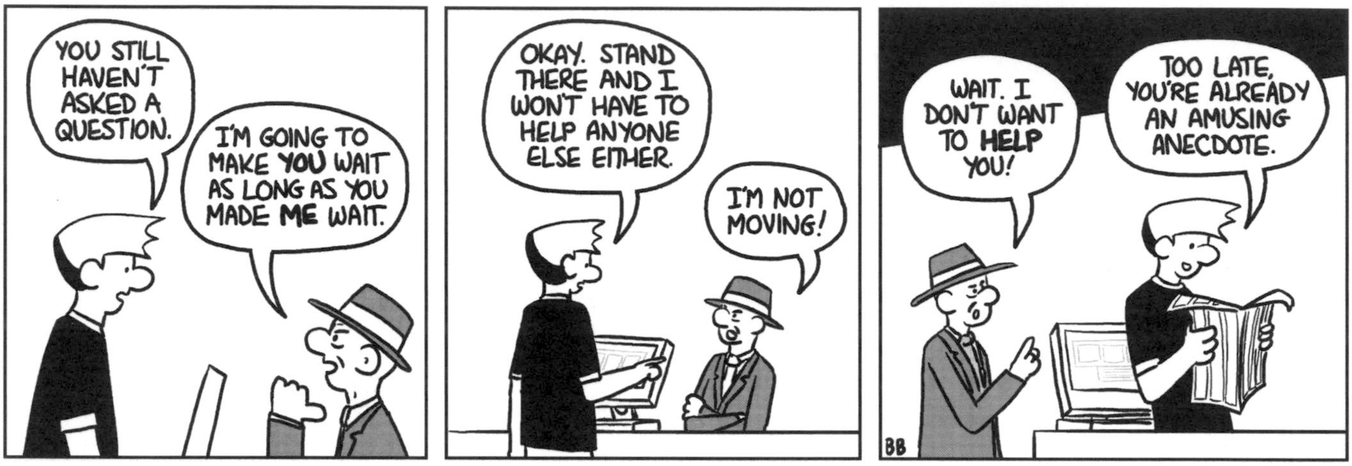
YOU STILL HAVEN'T ASKED A QUESTION.
I'M GOING TO MAKE YOU WAIT AS LONG AS YOU MADE ME WAIT.
OKAY. STAND THERE AND I WON'T HAVE TO HELP ANYONE ELSE EITHER.
I'M NOT MOVING!
WAIT. I DON'T WANT TO HELP YOU!
TOO LATE, YOU'RE ALREADY AN AMUSING ANECDOTE.

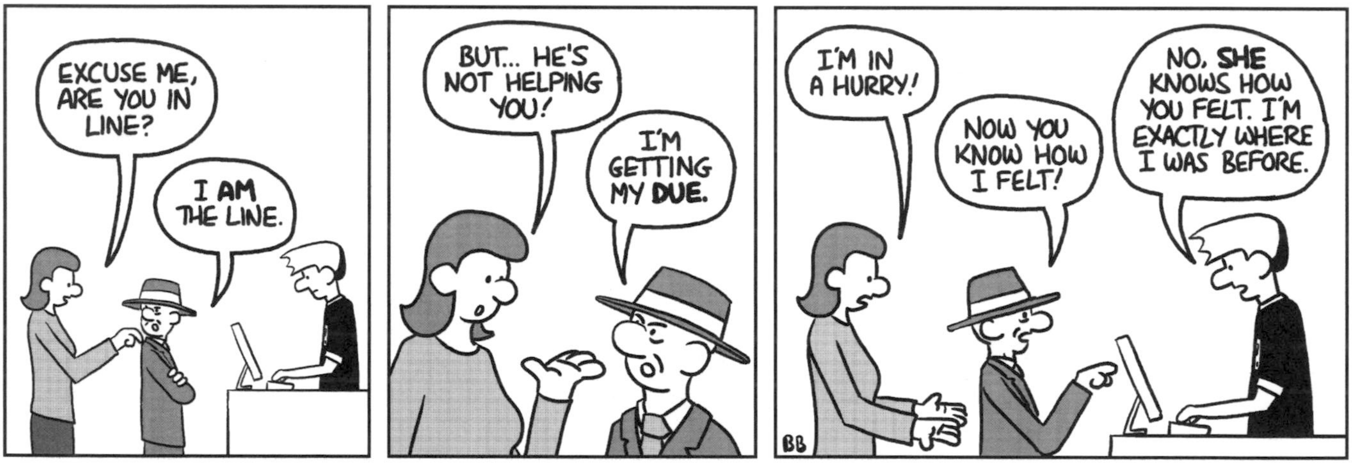
EXCUSE ME, ARE YOU IN LINE?
I AM THE LINE.
BUT... HE'S NOT HELPING YOU!
I'M GETTING MY DUE.
I'M IN A HURRY!
NOW YOU KNOW HOW I FELT!
NO, SHE KNOWS HOW YOU FELT. I'M EXACTLY WHERE I WAS BEFORE.

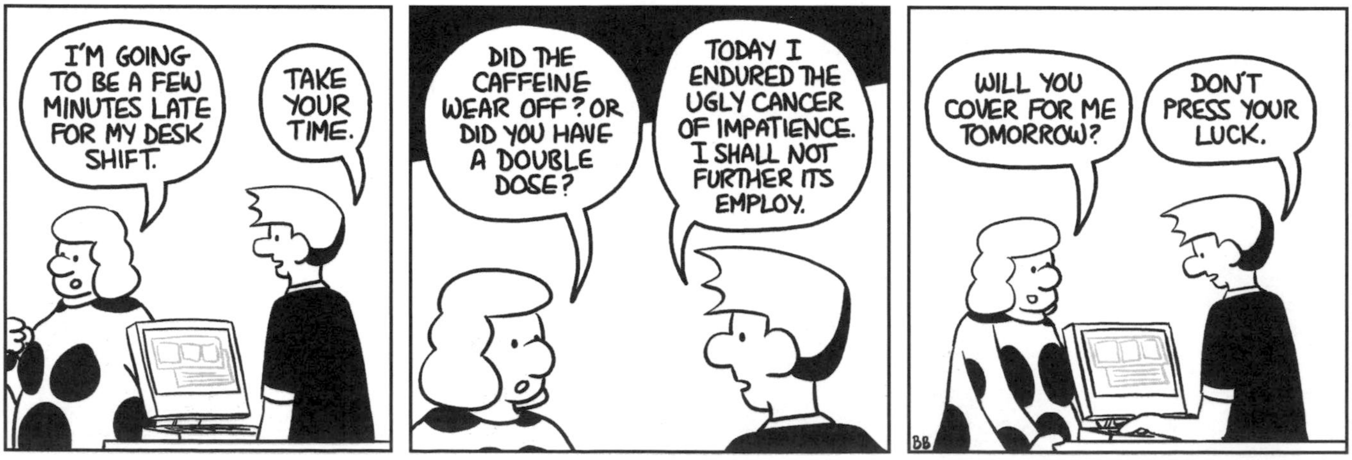
I'M GOING TO BE A FEW MINUTES LATE FOR MY DESK SHIFT.
TAKE YOUR TIME.
DID THE CAFFEINE WEAR OFF? OR DID YOU HAVE A DOUBLE DOSE?
TODAY I ENDURED THE UGLY CANCER OF IMPATIENCE. I SHALL NOT FURTHER ITS EMPLOY.
WILL YOU COVER FOR ME TOMORROW?
DON'T PRESS YOUR LUCK.

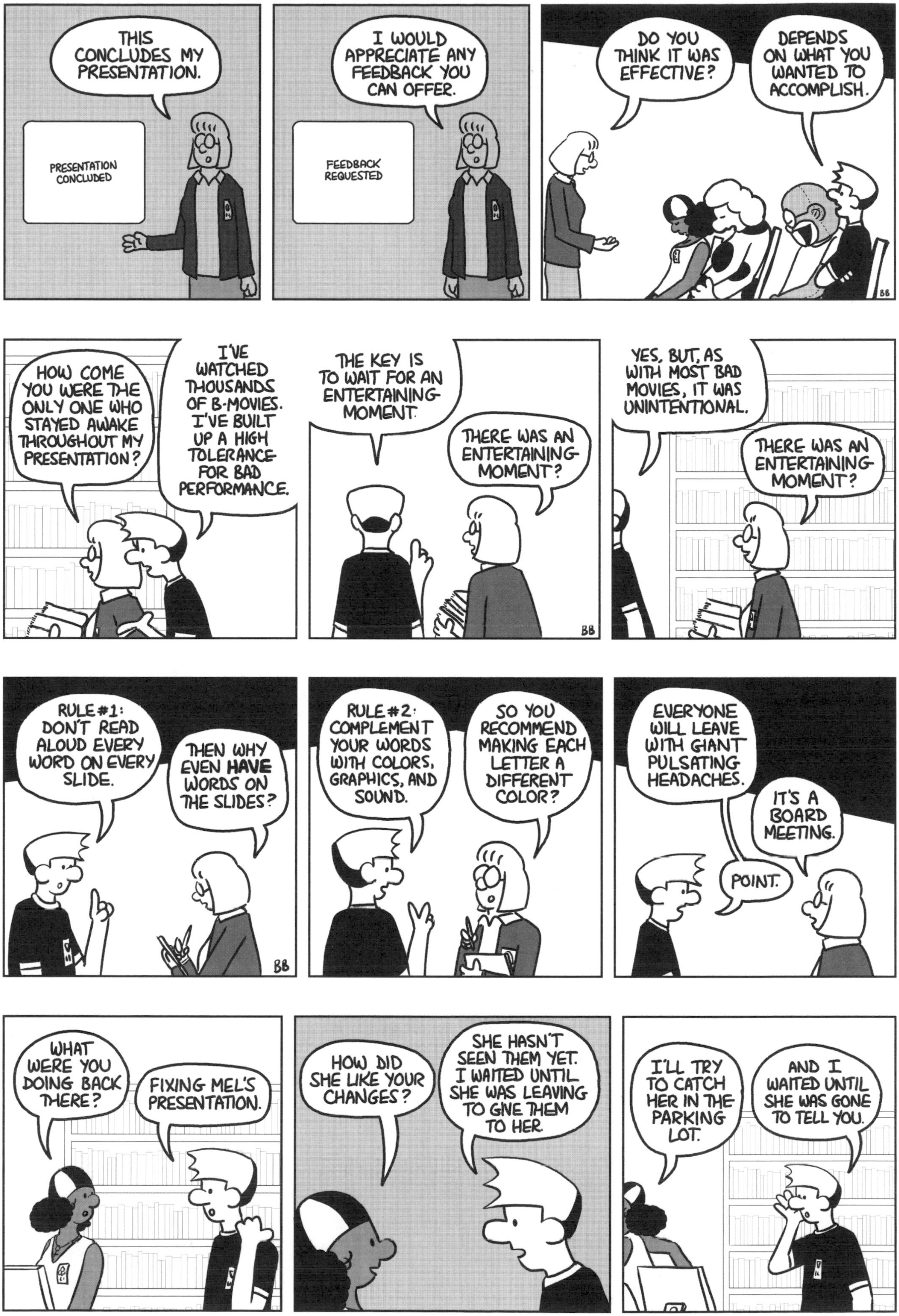
THIS CONCLUDES MY PRESENTATION.
PRESENTATION CONCLUDED
I WOULD APPRECIATE ANY FEEDBACK YOU CAN OFFER.
FEEDBACK REQUESTED
DO YOU THINK IT WAS EFFECTIVE?
DEPENDS ON WHAT YOU WANTED TO ACCOMPLISH.
BB
HOW COME YOU WERE THE ONLY ONE WHO STAYED AWAKE THROUGHOUT MY PRESENTATION?
I'VE WATCHED THOUSANDS OF B-MOVIES. I'VE BUILT UP A HIGH TOLERANCE FOR BAD PERFORMANCE.
THE KEY IS TO WAIT FOR AN ENTERTAINING MOMENT.
THERE WAS AN ENTERTAINING MOMENT?
YES, BUT, AS WITH MOST BAD MOVIES, IT WAS UNINTENTIONAL.
THERE WAS AN ENTERTAINING MOMENT?
BB
RULE #1: DON'T READ ALOUD EVERY WORD ON EVERY SLIDE.
THEN WHY EVEN **HAVE** WORDS ON THE SLIDES?
BB
RULE #2: COMPLEMENT YOUR WORDS WITH COLORS, GRAPHICS, AND SOUND.
SO YOU RECOMMEND MAKING EACH LETTER A DIFFERENT COLOR?
EVERYONE WILL LEAVE WITH GIANT PULSATING HEADACHES.
IT'S A BOARD MEETING.
POINT.
WHAT WERE YOU DOING BACK THERE?
FIXING MEL'S PRESENTATION.
HOW DID SHE LIKE YOUR CHANGES?
SHE HASN'T SEEN THEM YET. I WAITED UNTIL SHE WAS LEAVING TO GIVE THEM TO HER.
I'LL TRY TO CATCH HER IN THE PARKING LOT.
AND I WAITED UNTIL SHE WAS GONE TO TELL YOU.

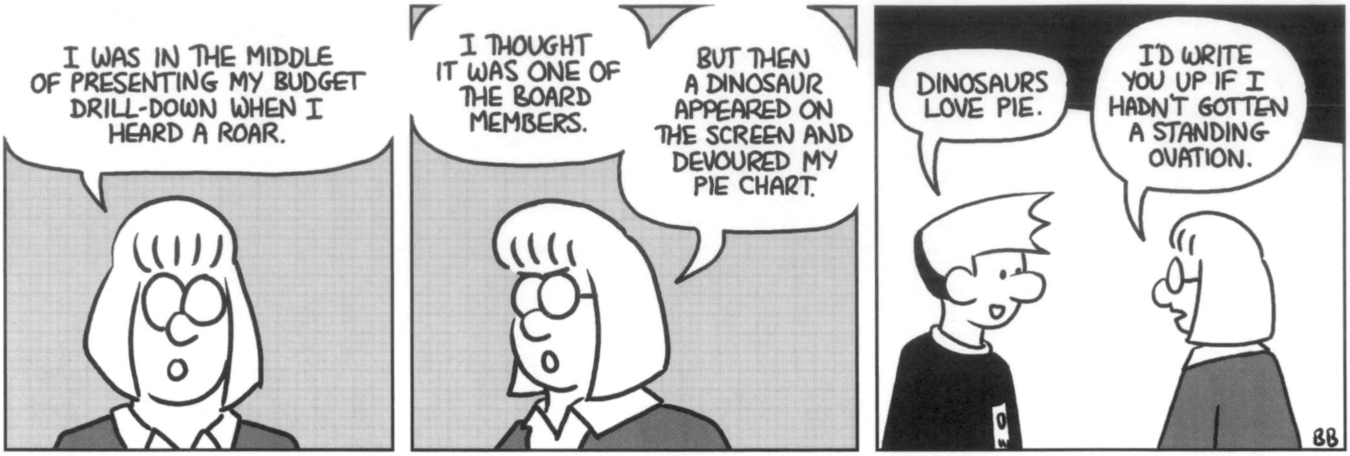
I WAS IN THE MIDDLE OF PRESENTING MY BUDGET DRILL-DOWN WHEN I HEARD A ROAR.
I THOUGHT IT WAS ONE OF THE BOARD MEMBERS.
BUT THEN A DINOSAUR APPEARED ON THE SCREEN AND DEVOURED MY PIE CHART.
DINOSAURS LOVE PIE.
I'D WRITE YOU UP IF I HADN'T GOTTEN A STANDING OVATION.
BB

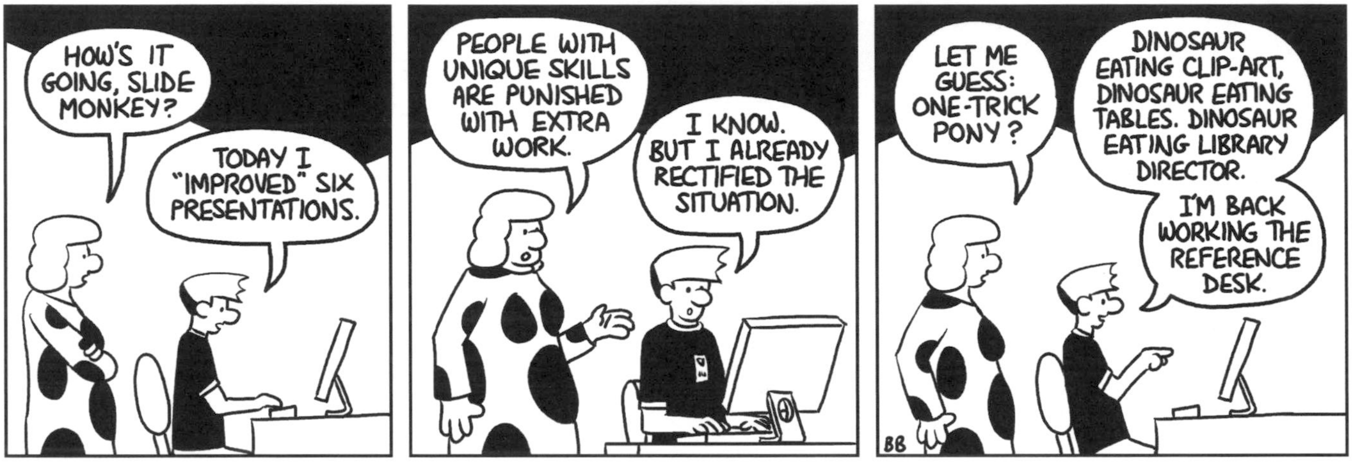
HOW'S IT GOING, SLIDE MONKEY?
TODAY I "IMPROVED" SIX PRESENTATIONS.
PEOPLE WITH UNIQUE SKILLS ARE PUNISHED WITH EXTRA WORK.
I KNOW. BUT I ALREADY RECTIFIED THE SITUATION.
LET ME GUESS: ONE-TRICK PONY?
DINOSAUR EATING CLIP-ART, DINOSAUR EATING TABLES. DINOSAUR EATING LIBRARY DIRECTOR.
I'M BACK WORKING THE REFERENCE DESK.
BB

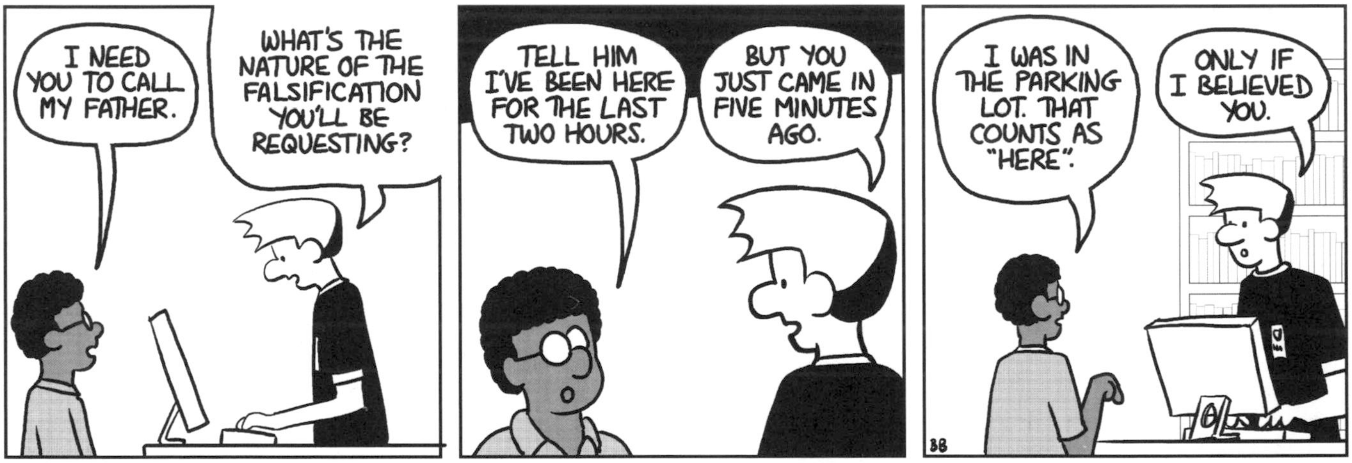
I NEED YOU TO CALL MY FATHER.
WHAT'S THE NATURE OF THE FALSIFICATION YOU'LL BE REQUESTING?
TELL HIM I'VE BEEN HERE FOR THE LAST TWO HOURS.
BUT YOU JUST CAME IN FIVE MINUTES AGO.
I WAS IN THE PARKING LOT. THAT COUNTS AS "HERE".
ONLY IF I BELIEVED YOU.
BB

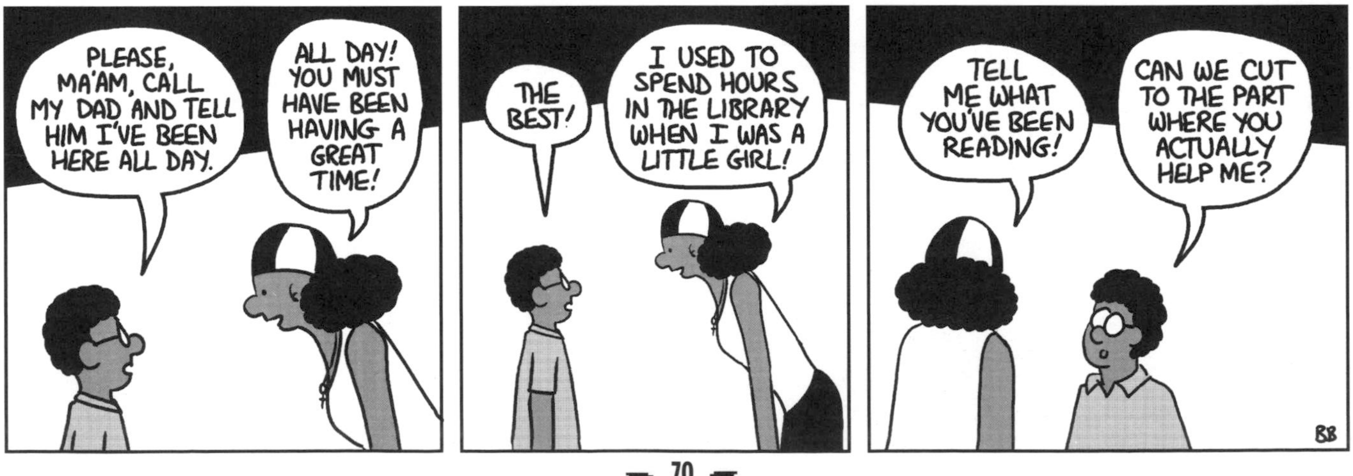
PLEASE, MA'AM, CALL MY DAD AND TELL HIM I'VE BEEN HERE ALL DAY.
ALL DAY! YOU MUST HAVE BEEN HAVING A GREAT TIME!
THE BEST!
I USED TO SPEND HOURS IN THE LIBRARY WHEN I WAS A LITTLE GIRL!
TELL ME WHAT YOU'VE BEEN READING!
CAN WE CUT TO THE PART WHERE YOU ACTUALLY HELP ME?
BB

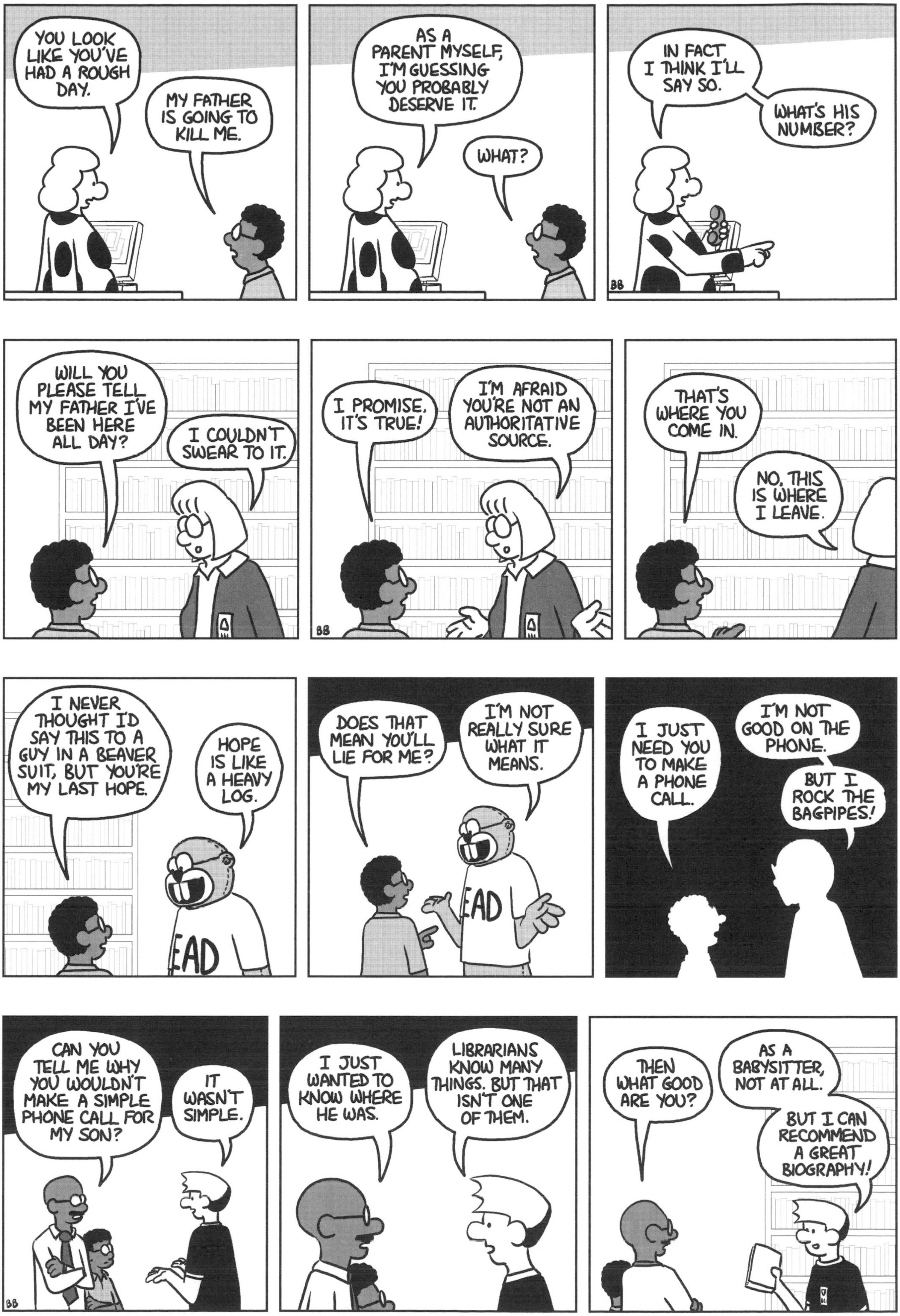
YOU LOOK LIKE YOU'VE HAD A ROUGH DAY.
MY FATHER IS GOING TO KILL ME.
AS A PARENT MYSELF, I'M GUESSING YOU PROBABLY DESERVE IT.
WHAT?
IN FACT, I THINK I'LL SAY SO.
WHAT'S HIS NUMBER?
BB
WILL YOU PLEASE TELL MY FATHER I'VE BEEN HERE ALL DAY?
I COULDN'T SWEAR TO IT.
I PROMISE, IT'S TRUE!
I'M AFRAID YOU'RE NOT AN AUTHORITATIVE SOURCE.
BB
THAT'S WHERE YOU COME IN.
NO, THIS IS WHERE I LEAVE.
I NEVER THOUGHT I'D SAY THIS TO A GUY IN A BEAVER SUIT, BUT YOU'RE MY LAST HOPE.
HOPE IS LIKE A HEAVY LOG.
EAD
DOES THAT MEAN YOU'LL LIE FOR ME?
I'M NOT REALLY SURE WHAT IT MEANS.
EAD
I JUST NEED YOU TO MAKE A PHONE CALL.
I'M NOT GOOD ON THE PHONE.
BUT I ROCK THE BAGPIPES!
CAN YOU TELL ME WHY YOU WOULDN'T MAKE A SIMPLE PHONE CALL FOR MY SON?
IT WASN'T SIMPLE.
BB
I JUST WANTED TO KNOW WHERE HE WAS.
LIBRARIANS KNOW MANY THINGS. BUT THAT ISN'T ONE OF THEM.
THEN WHAT GOOD ARE YOU?
AS A BABYSITTER, NOT AT ALL.
BUT I CAN RECOMMEND A GREAT BIOGRAPHY!

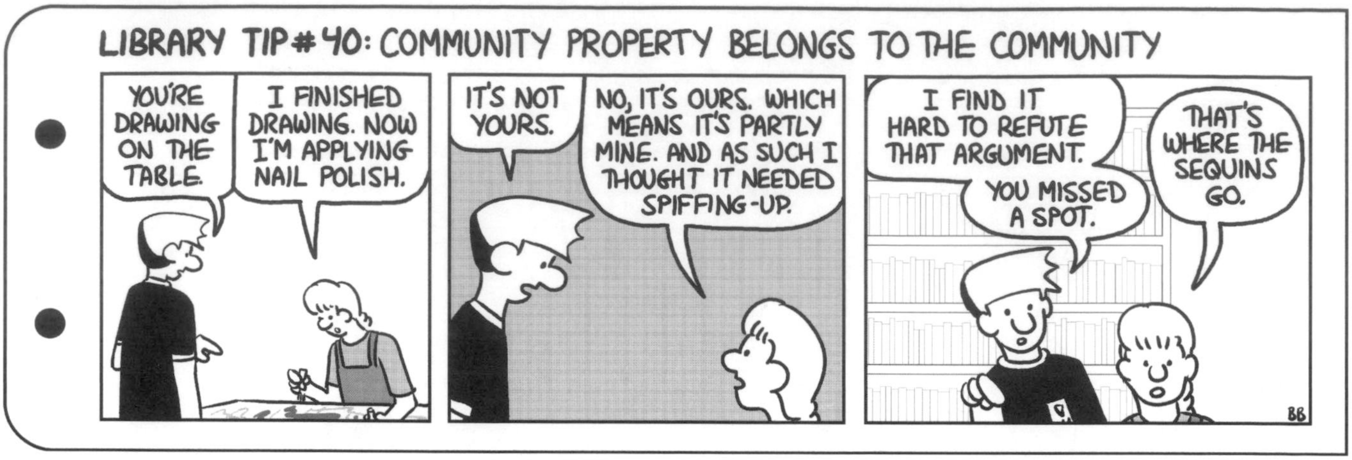
LIBRARY TIP #40: COMMUNITY PROPERTY BELONGS TO THE COMMUNITY
YOU'RE DRAWING ON THE TABLE.
I FINISHED DRAWING. NOW I'M APPLYING NAIL POLISH.
IT'S NOT YOURS.
NO, IT'S OURS. WHICH MEANS IT'S PARTLY MINE. AND AS SUCH I THOUGHT IT NEEDED SPIFFING-UP.
I FIND IT HARD TO REFUTE THAT ARGUMENT.
YOU MISSED A SPOT.
THAT'S WHERE THE SEQUINS GO.
BB

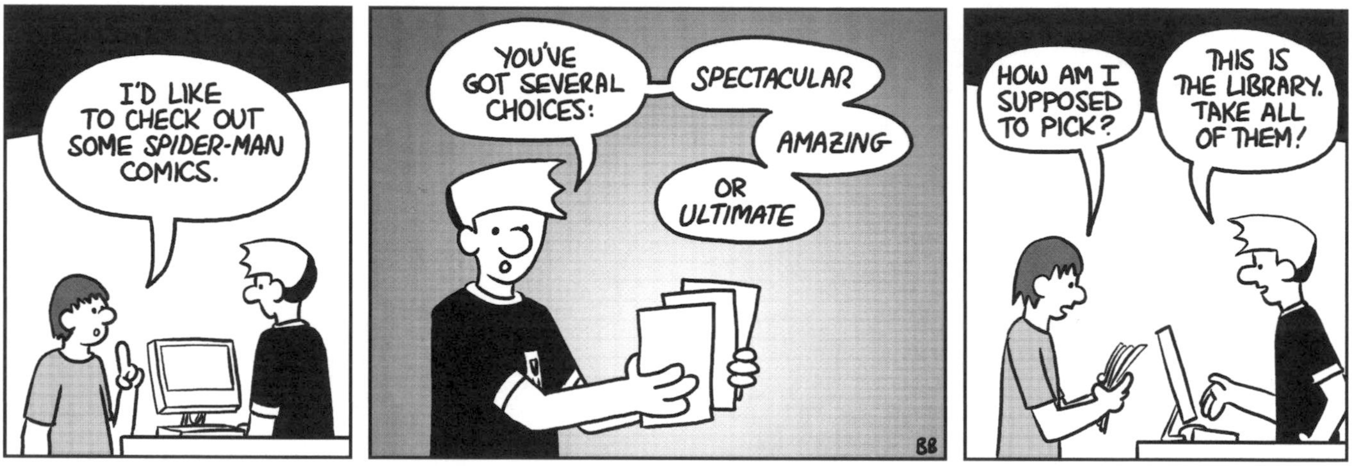
I'D LIKE TO CHECK OUT SOME SPIDER-MAN COMICS.
YOU'VE GOT SEVERAL CHOICES:
SPECTACULAR
AMAZING
OR ULTIMATE
BB
HOW AM I SUPPOSED TO PICK?
THIS IS THE LIBRARY. TAKE ALL OF THEM!

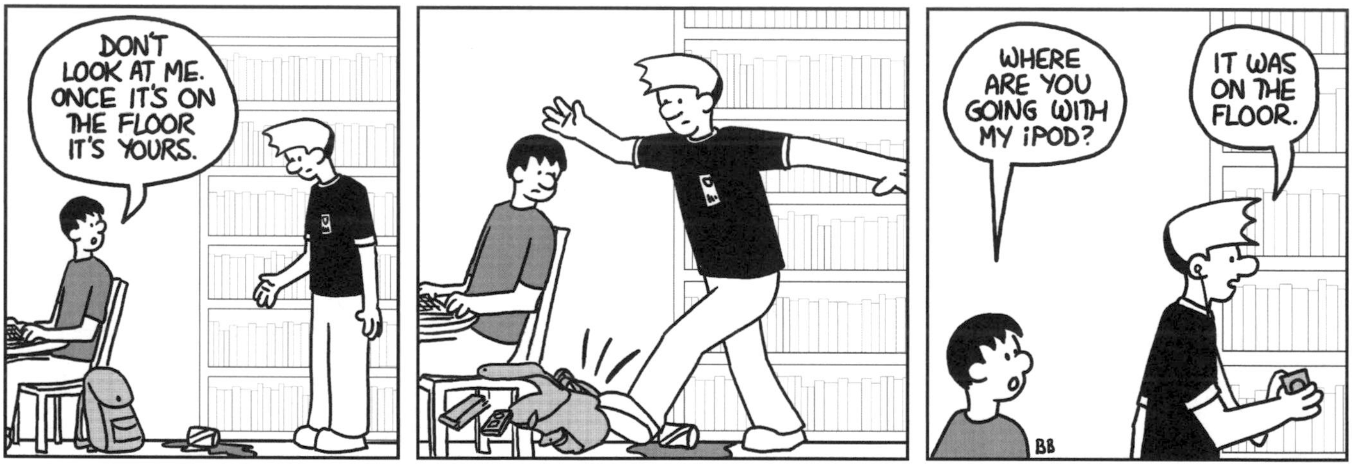
DON'T LOOK AT ME. ONCE IT'S ON THE FLOOR IT'S YOURS.
WHERE ARE YOU GOING WITH MY iPOD?
IT WAS ON THE FLOOR.
BB

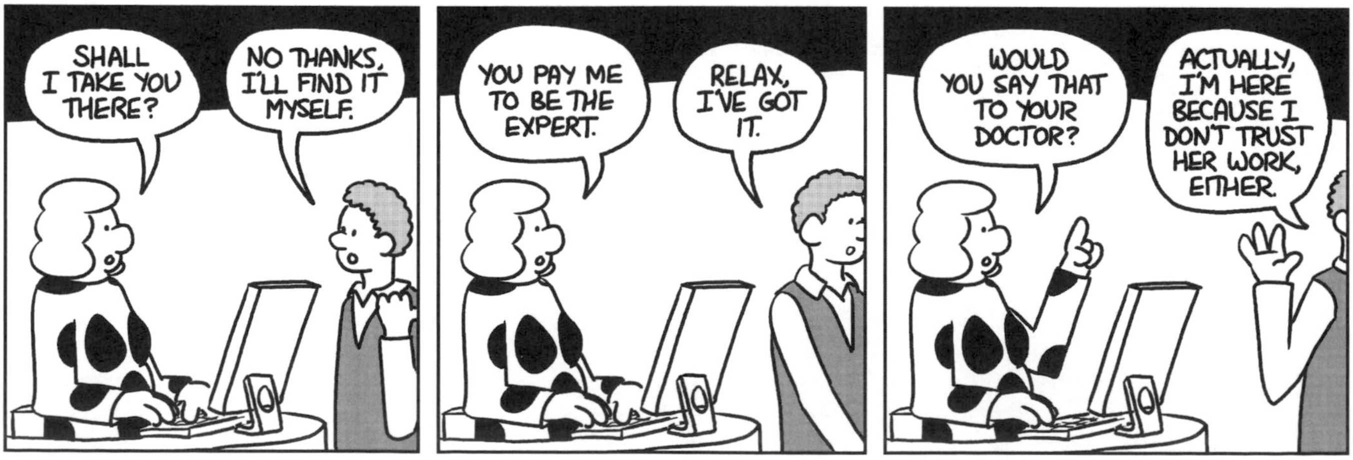
SHALL I TAKE YOU THERE?
NO THANKS, I'LL FIND IT MYSELF.
YOU PAY ME TO BE THE EXPERT.
RELAX, I'VE GOT IT.
WOULD YOU SAY THAT TO YOUR DOCTOR?
ACTUALLY, I'M HERE BECAUSE I DON'T TRUST HER WORK, EITHER.

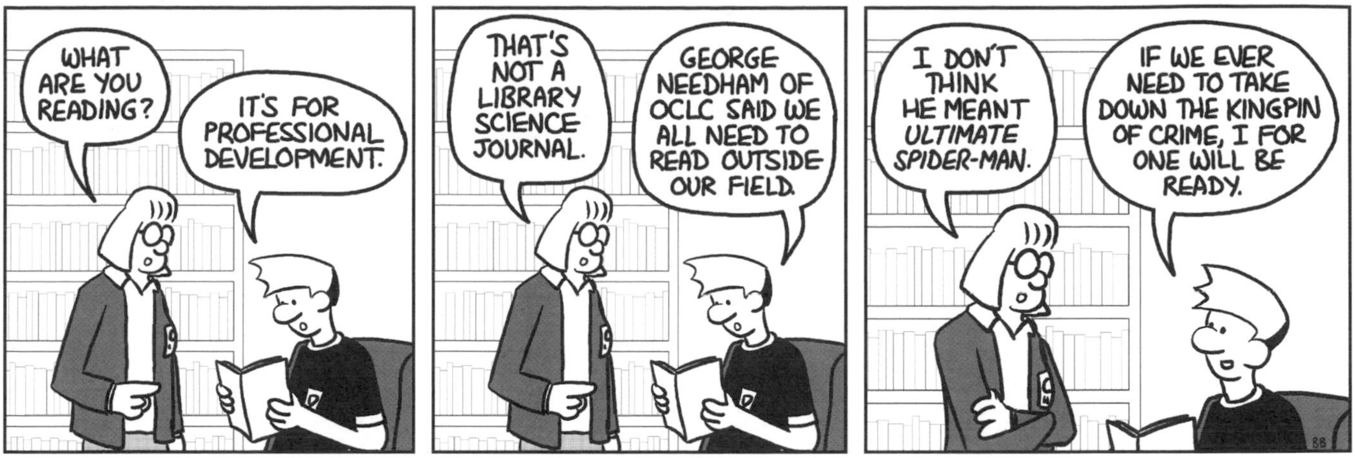
WHAT ARE YOU READING?
IT'S FOR PROFESSIONAL DEVELOPMENT.
THAT'S NOT A LIBRARY SCIENCE JOURNAL.
GEORGE NEEDHAM OF OCLC SAID WE ALL NEED TO READ OUTSIDE OUR FIELD.
I DON'T THINK HE MEANT *ULTIMATE SPIDER-MAN.*
IF WE EVER NEED TO TAKE DOWN THE KINGPIN OF CRIME, I FOR ONE WILL BE READY.
BB

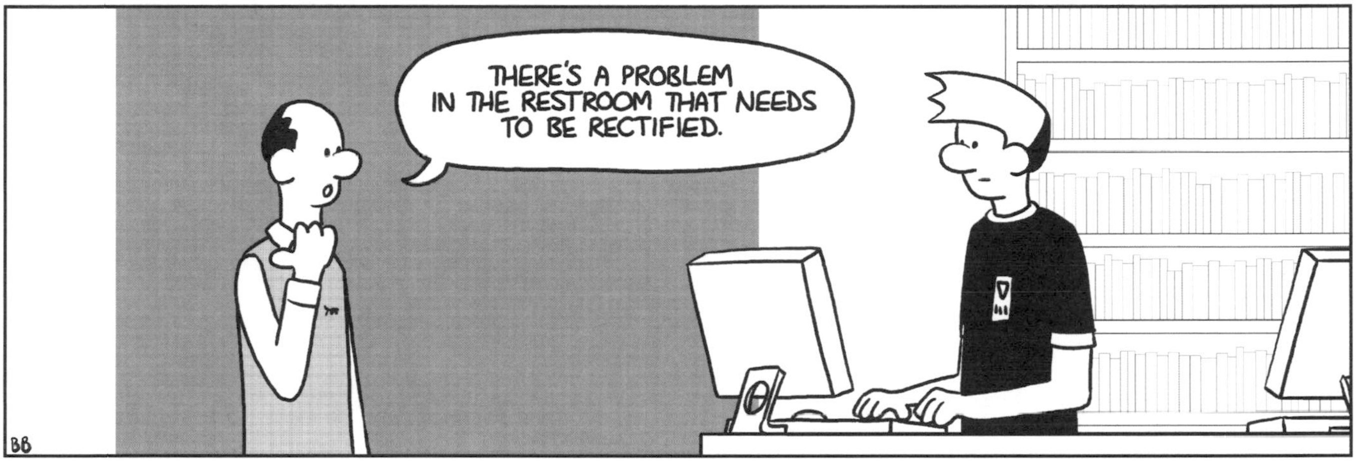
THERE'S A PROBLEM IN THE RESTROOM THAT NEEDS TO BE RECTIFIED.
BB

Every year on Gene's birthday Bill draws a strip about bathrooms. It's the gift that keeps on giving.

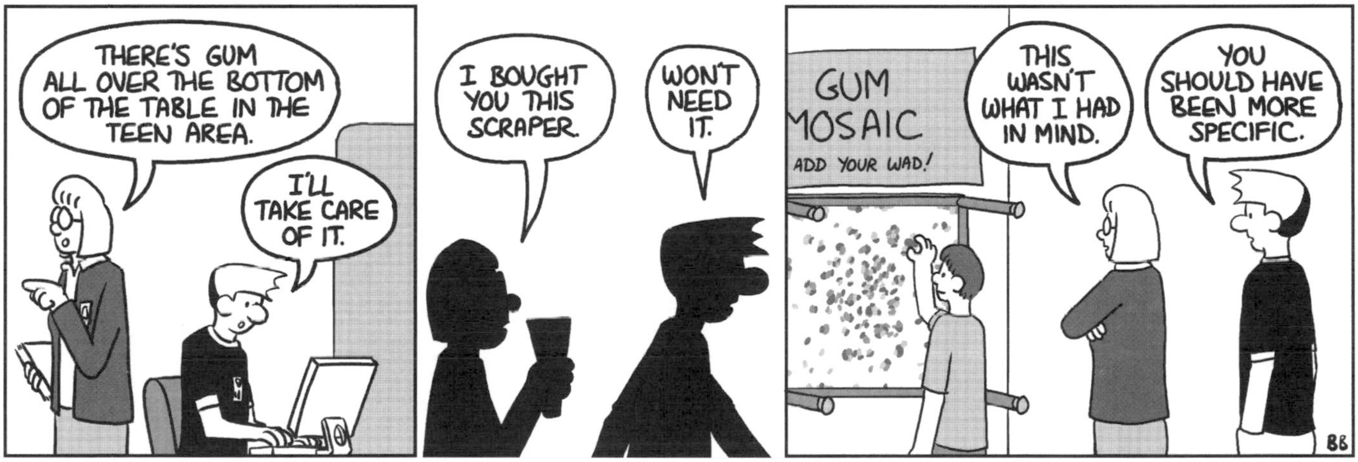
THERE'S GUM ALL OVER THE BOTTOM OF THE TABLE IN THE TEEN AREA.
I'LL TAKE CARE OF IT.
I BOUGHT YOU THIS SCRAPER.
WON'T NEED IT.
GUM MOSAIC
ADD YOUR WAD!
THIS WASN'T WHAT I HAD IN MIND.
YOU SHOULD HAVE BEEN MORE SPECIFIC.
BB

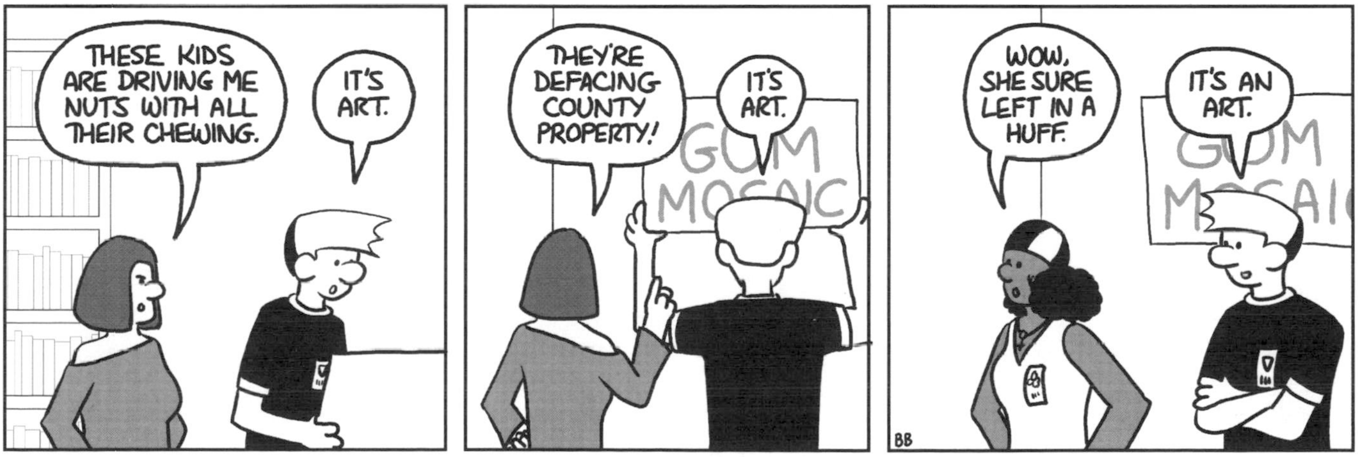
THESE KIDS ARE DRIVING ME NUTS WITH ALL THEIR CHEWING.
IT'S ART.
THEY'RE DEFACING COUNTY PROPERTY!
IT'S ART.
GUM MOSAIC
WOW, SHE SURE LEFT IN A HUFF.
IT'S AN ART.
BB

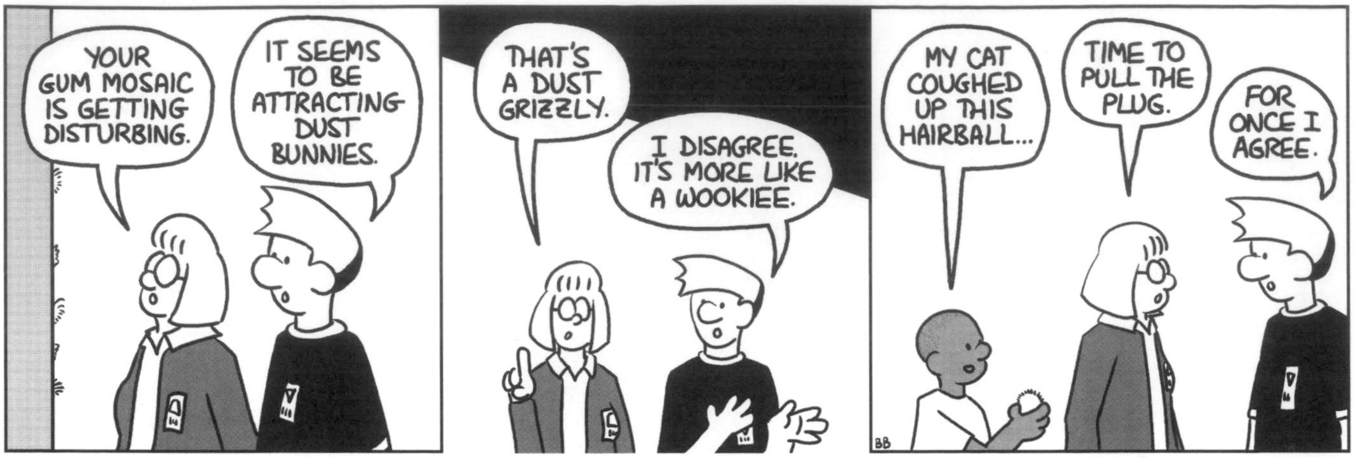
YOUR GUM MOSAIC IS GETTING DISTURBING.
IT SEEMS TO BE ATTRACTING DUST BUNNIES.
THAT'S A DUST GRIZZLY.
I DISAGREE. IT'S MORE LIKE A WOOKIEE.
MY CAT COUGHED UP THIS HAIRBALL...
TIME TO PULL THE PLUG.
FOR ONCE I AGREE.
BB

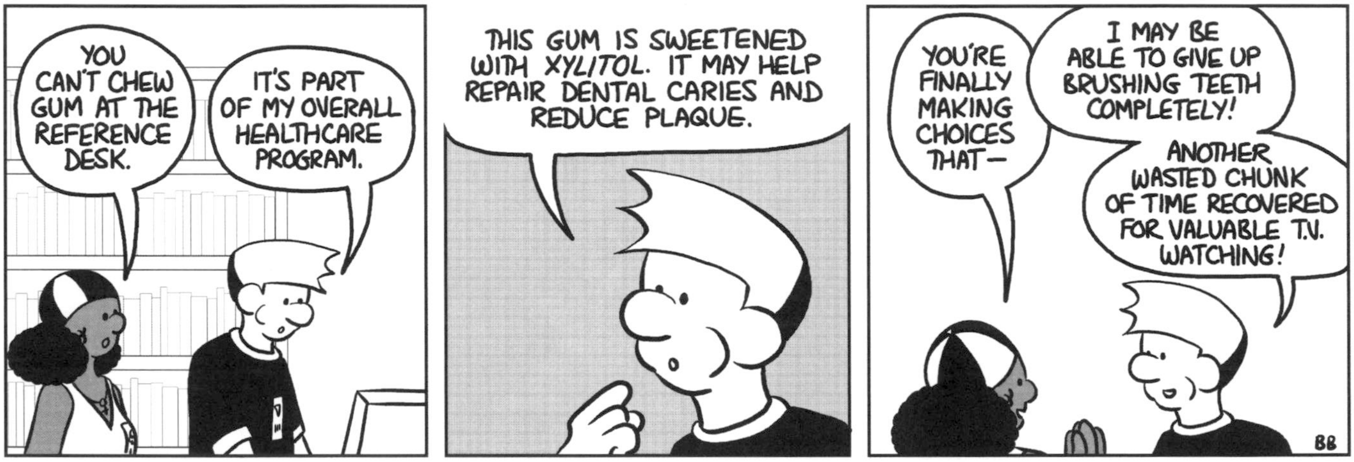
YOU CAN'T CHEW GUM AT THE REFERENCE DESK.
IT'S PART OF MY OVERALL HEALTHCARE PROGRAM.
THIS GUM IS SWEETENED WITH *XYLITOL*. IT MAY HELP REPAIR DENTAL CARIES AND REDUCE PLAQUE.
YOU'RE FINALLY MAKING CHOICES THAT—
I MAY BE ABLE TO GIVE UP BRUSHING TEETH COMPLETELY!
ANOTHER WASTED CHUNK OF TIME RECOVERED FOR VALUABLE T.V. WATCHING!
BB

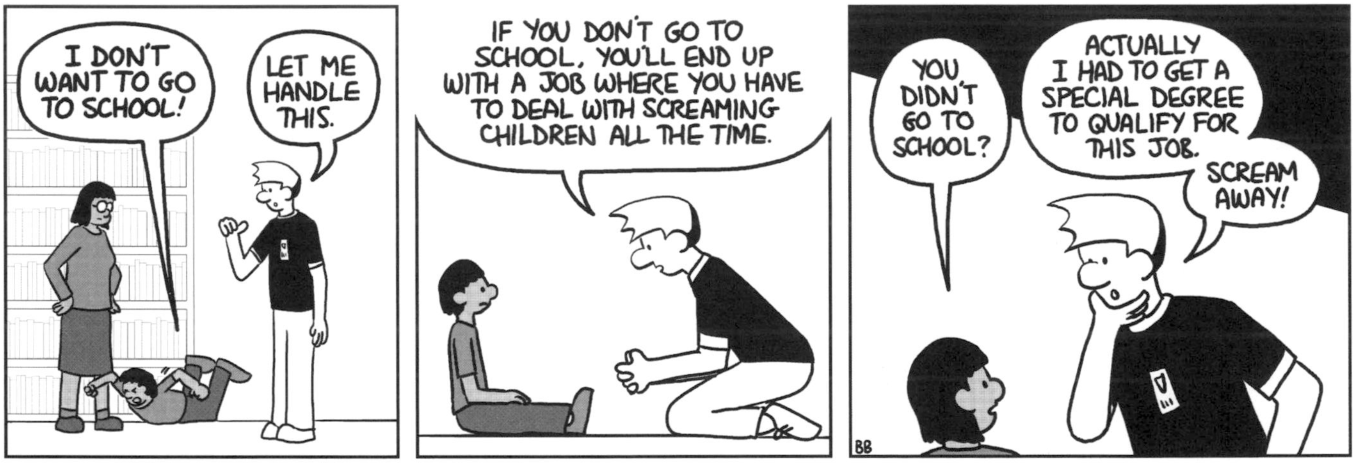
I DON'T WANT TO GO TO SCHOOL!
LET ME HANDLE THIS.
IF YOU DON'T GO TO SCHOOL, YOU'LL END UP WITH A JOB WHERE YOU HAVE TO DEAL WITH SCREAMING CHILDREN ALL THE TIME.
YOU DIDN'T GO TO SCHOOL?
ACTUALLY I HAD TO GET A SPECIAL DEGREE TO QUALIFY FOR THIS JOB.
SCREAM AWAY!
BB

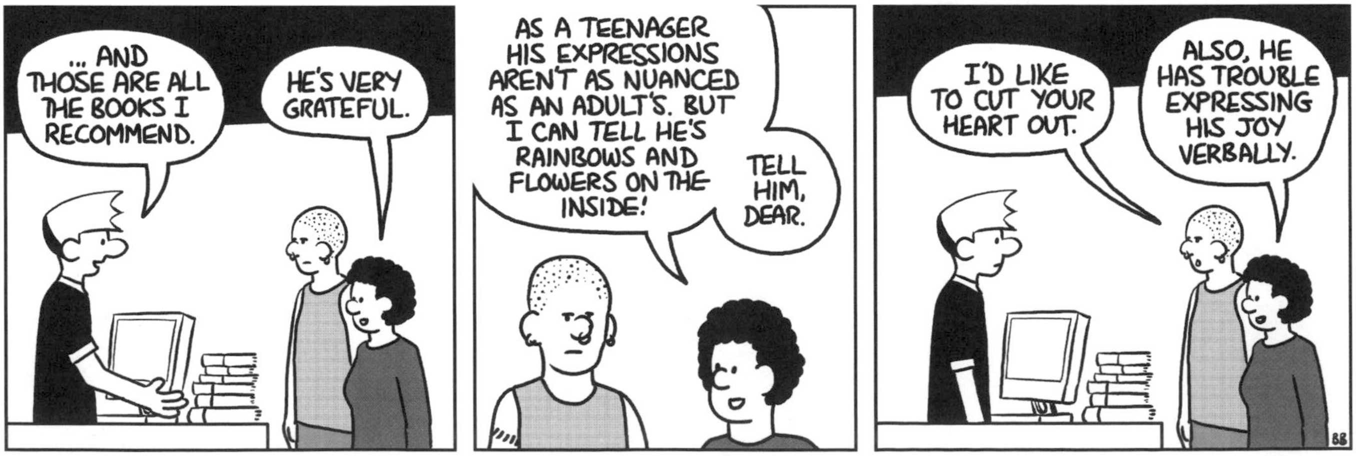
... AND THOSE ARE ALL THE BOOKS I RECOMMEND.
HE'S VERY GRATEFUL.
AS A TEENAGER HIS EXPRESSIONS AREN'T AS NUANCED AS AN ADULT'S. BUT I CAN TELL HE'S RAINBOWS AND FLOWERS ON THE INSIDE!
TELL HIM, DEAR.
I'D LIKE TO CUT YOUR HEART OUT.
ALSO, HE HAS TROUBLE EXPRESSING HIS JOY VERBALLY.
BB

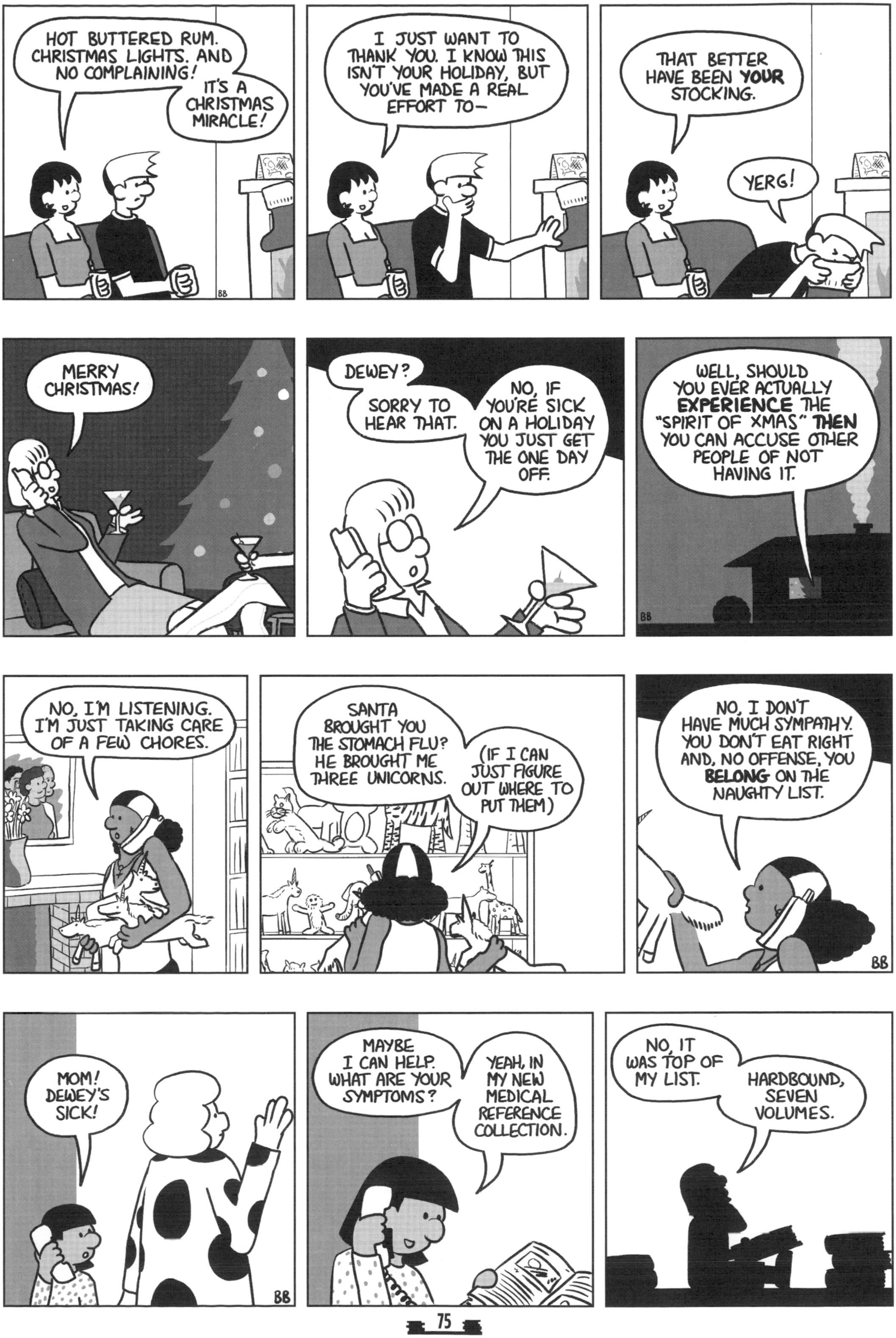
HOT BUTTERED RUM. CHRISTMAS LIGHTS. AND NO COMPLAINING!
IT'S A CHRISTMAS MIRACLE!
BB
I JUST WANT TO THANK YOU. I KNOW THIS ISN'T YOUR HOLIDAY, BUT YOU'VE MADE A REAL EFFORT TO—
THAT BETTER HAVE BEEN **YOUR** STOCKING.
YERG!
MERRY CHRISTMAS!
DEWEY?
SORRY TO HEAR THAT.
NO, IF YOU'RE SICK ON A HOLIDAY YOU JUST GET THE ONE DAY OFF.
WELL, SHOULD YOU EVER ACTUALLY **EXPERIENCE** THE "SPIRIT OF XMAS" **THEN** YOU CAN ACCUSE OTHER PEOPLE OF NOT HAVING IT.
BB
NO, I'M LISTENING. I'M JUST TAKING CARE OF A FEW CHORES.
SANTA BROUGHT YOU THE STOMACH FLU? HE BROUGHT ME THREE UNICORNS.
(IF I CAN JUST FIGURE OUT WHERE TO PUT THEM)
NO, I DON'T HAVE MUCH SYMPATHY. YOU DON'T EAT RIGHT AND, NO OFFENSE, YOU **BELONG** ON THE NAUGHTY LIST.
BB
MOM! DEWEY'S SICK!
BB
MAYBE I CAN HELP. WHAT ARE YOUR SYMPTOMS?
YEAH, IN MY NEW MEDICAL REFERENCE COLLECTION.
NO, IT WAS TOP OF MY LIST.
HARDBOUND, SEVEN VOLUMES.

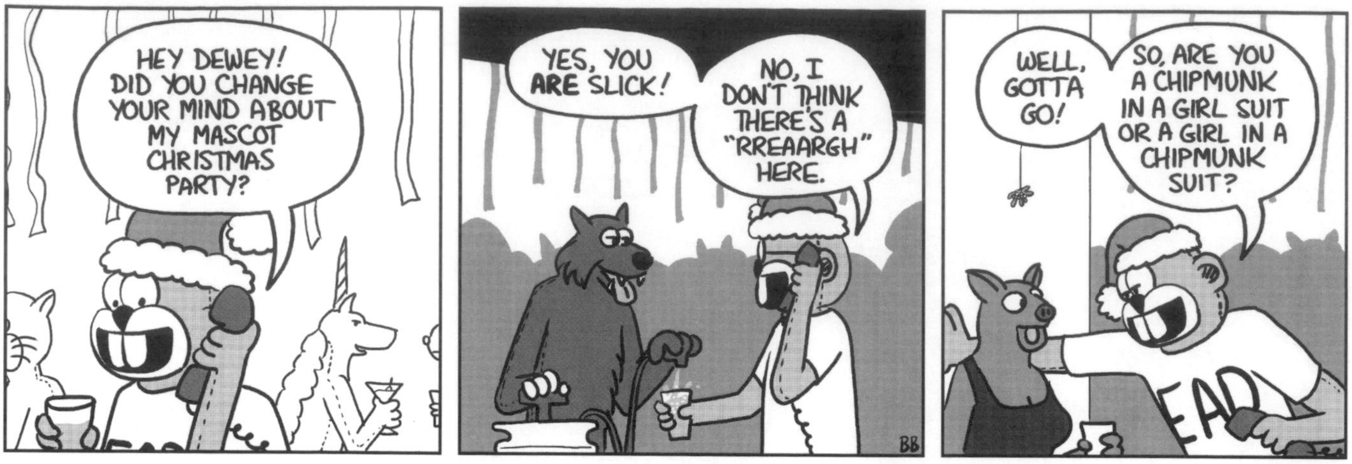
HEY DEWEY! DID YOU CHANGE YOUR MIND ABOUT MY MASCOT CHRISTMAS PARTY?
YES, YOU **ARE** SLICK!
NO, I DON'T THINK THERE'S A "RREAARGH" HERE.
WELL, GOTTA GO!
SO, ARE YOU A CHIPMUNK IN A GIRL SUIT OR A GIRL IN A CHIPMUNK SUIT?
BB

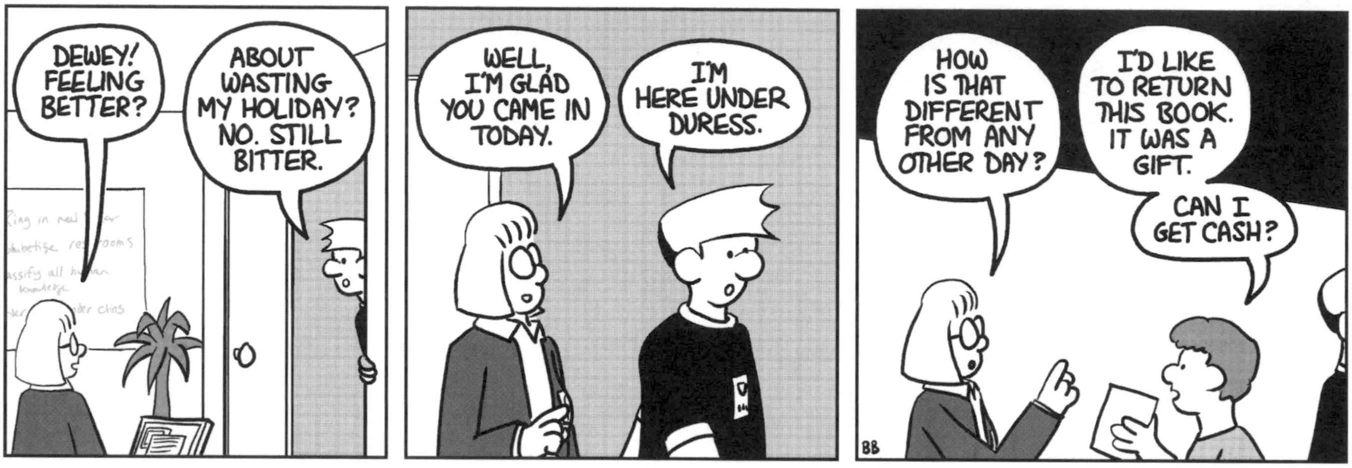
DEWEY! FEELING BETTER?
ABOUT WASTING MY HOLIDAY? NO. STILL BITTER.
WELL, I'M GLAD YOU CAME IN TODAY.
I'M HERE UNDER DURESS.
HOW IS THAT DIFFERENT FROM ANY OTHER DAY?
I'D LIKE TO RETURN THIS BOOK. IT WAS A GIFT.
CAN I GET CASH?
BB

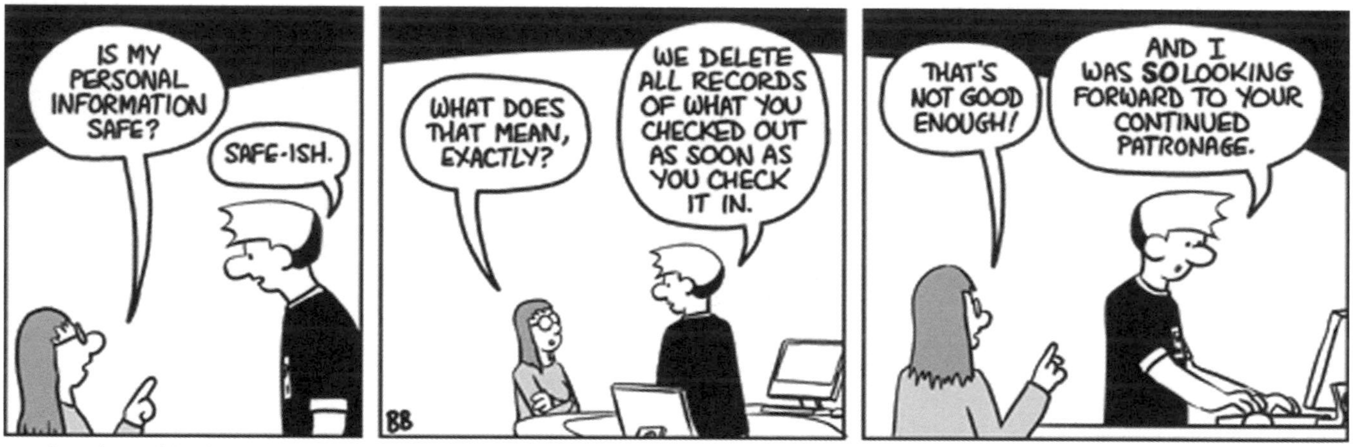
IS MY PERSONAL INFORMATION SAFE?
SAFE-ISH.
WHAT DOES THAT MEAN, EXACTLY?
WE DELETE ALL RECORDS OF WHAT YOU CHECKED OUT AS SOON AS YOU CHECK IT IN.
BB
THAT'S NOT GOOD ENOUGH!
AND I WAS **SO** LOOKING FORWARD TO YOUR CONTINUED PATRONAGE.

Once in a while there's a computer disaster and we lose the original art to a strip, left only with the lo-res web version. Like this one.

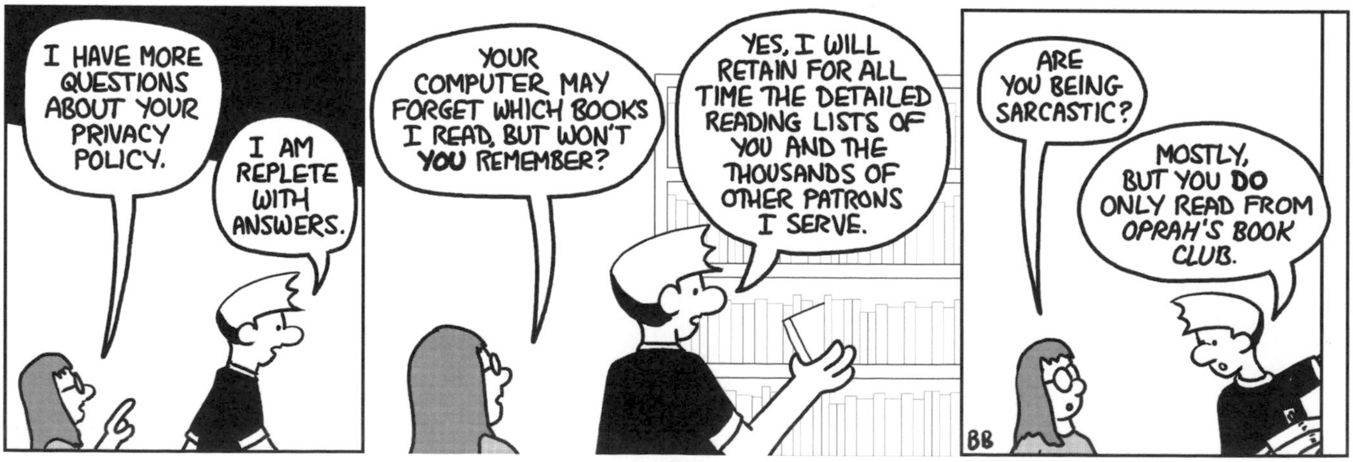
I HAVE MORE QUESTIONS ABOUT YOUR PRIVACY POLICY.
I AM REPLETE WITH ANSWERS.
YOUR COMPUTER MAY FORGET WHICH BOOKS I READ, BUT WON'T **YOU** REMEMBER?
YES, I WILL RETAIN FOR ALL TIME THE DETAILED READING LISTS OF YOU AND THE THOUSANDS OF OTHER PATRONS I SERVE.
ARE YOU BEING SARCASTIC?
MOSTLY, BUT YOU **DO** ONLY READ FROM *OPRAH'S BOOK CLUB*.
BB

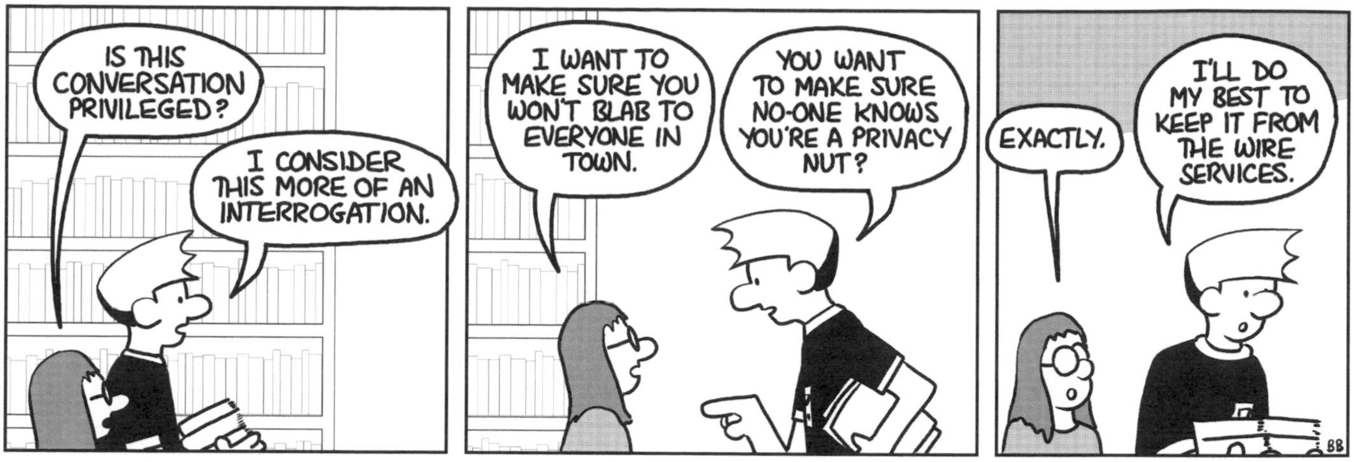
IS THIS CONVERSATION PRIVILEGED?
I CONSIDER THIS MORE OF AN INTERROGATION.
I WANT TO MAKE SURE YOU WON'T BLAB TO EVERYONE IN TOWN.
YOU WANT TO MAKE SURE NO-ONE KNOWS YOU'RE A PRIVACY NUT?
EXACTLY.
I'LL DO MY BEST TO KEEP IT FROM THE WIRE SERVICES.
BB

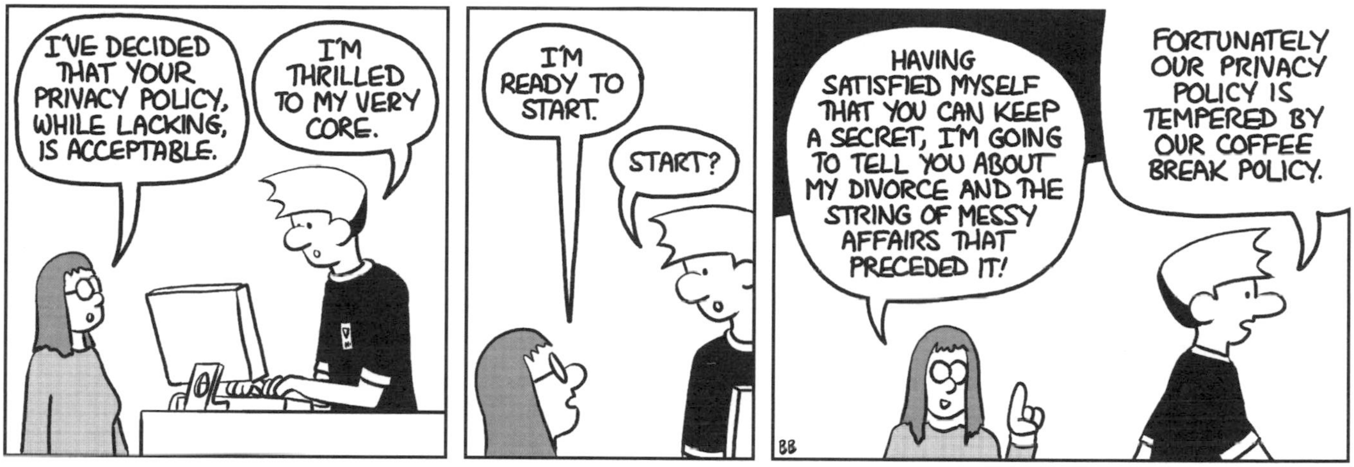
I'VE DECIDED THAT YOUR PRIVACY POLICY, WHILE LACKING, IS ACCEPTABLE.
I'M THRILLED TO MY VERY CORE.
I'M READY TO START.
START?
HAVING SATISFIED MYSELF THAT YOU CAN KEEP A SECRET, I'M GOING TO TELL YOU ABOUT MY DIVORCE AND THE STRING OF MESSY AFFAIRS THAT PRECEDED IT!
FORTUNATELY OUR PRIVACY POLICY IS TEMPERED BY OUR COFFEE BREAK POLICY.
BB

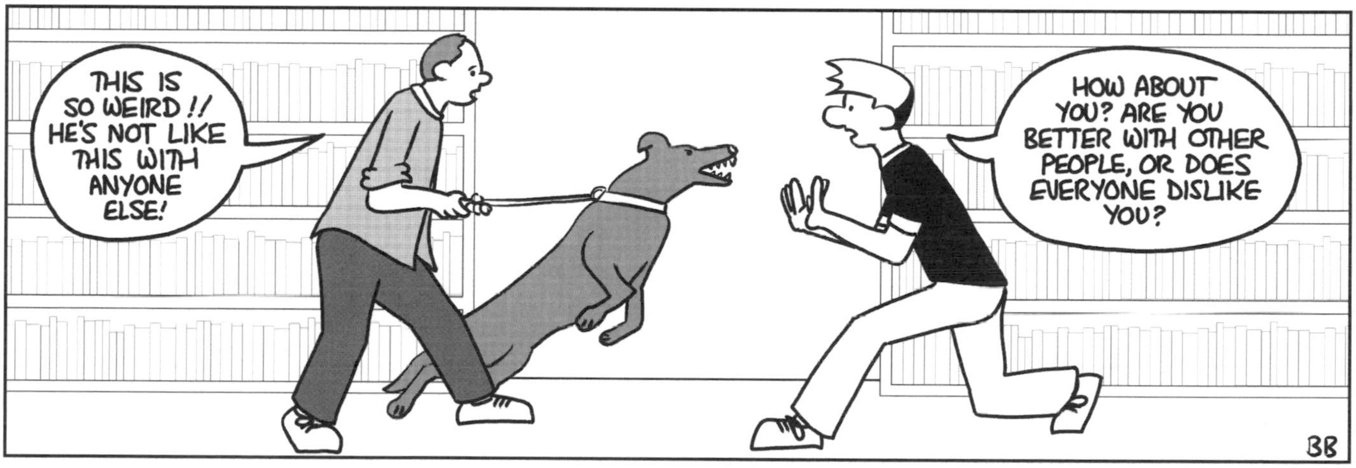
THIS IS SO WEIRD!! HE'S NOT LIKE THIS WITH ANYONE ELSE!
HOW ABOUT YOU? ARE YOU BETTER WITH OTHER PEOPLE, OR DOES EVERYONE DISLIKE YOU?
BB

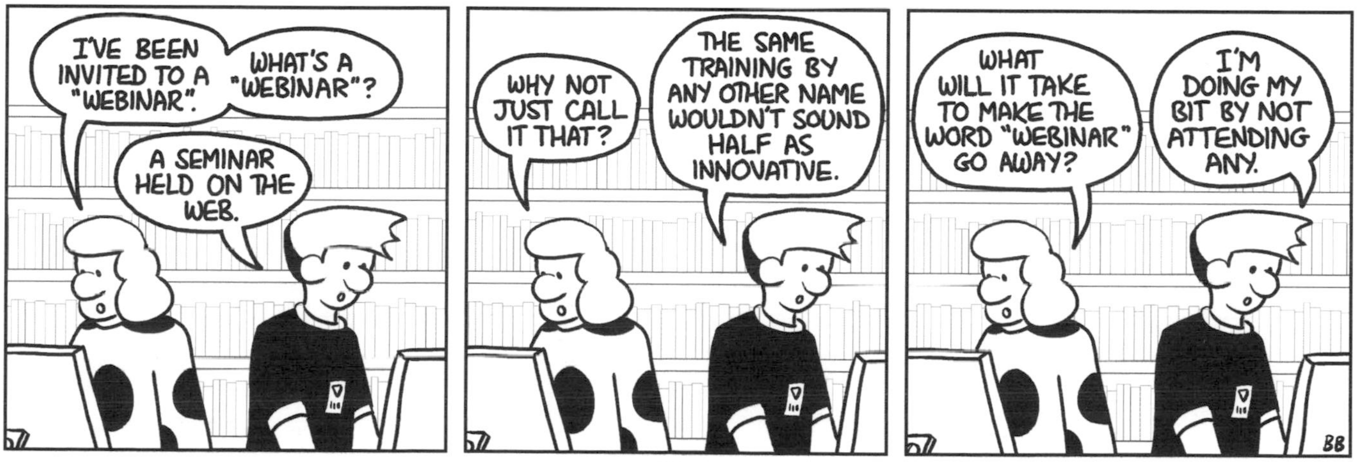
I'VE BEEN INVITED TO A "WEBINAR".
WHAT'S A "WEBINAR"?
A SEMINAR HELD ON THE WEB.
WHY NOT JUST CALL IT THAT?
THE SAME TRAINING BY ANY OTHER NAME WOULDN'T SOUND HALF AS INNOVATIVE.
WHAT WILL IT TAKE TO MAKE THE WORD "WEBINAR" GO AWAY?
I'M DOING MY BIT BY NOT ATTENDING ANY.
BB

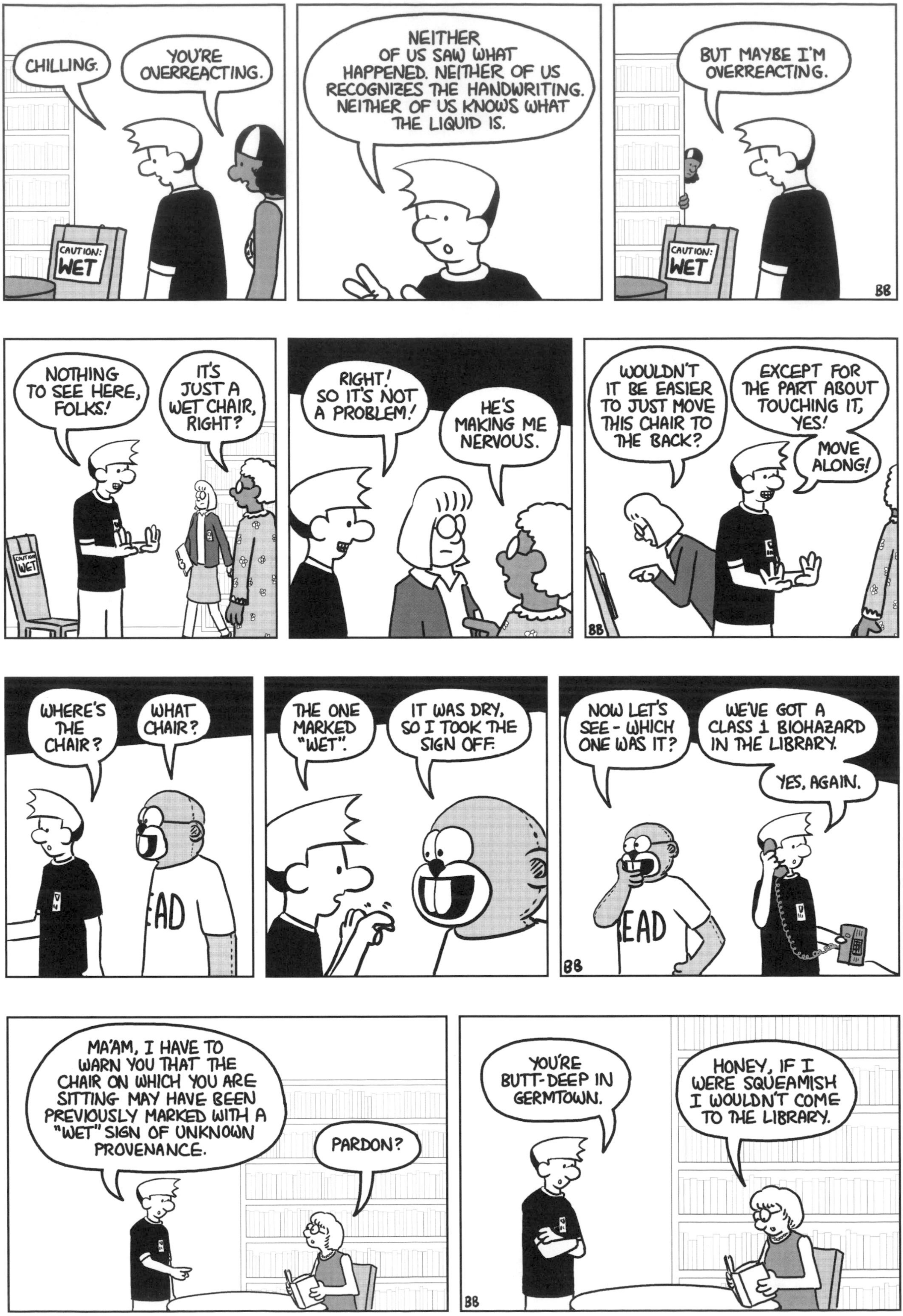
CHILLING.
YOU'RE OVERREACTING.
CAUTION: WET
NEITHER OF US SAW WHAT HAPPENED. NEITHER OF US RECOGNIZES THE HANDWRITING. NEITHER OF US KNOWS WHAT THE LIQUID IS.
BUT MAYBE I'M OVERREACTING.
CAUTION: WET
BB
NOTHING TO SEE HERE, FOLKS!
IT'S JUST A WET CHAIR, RIGHT?
CAUTION WET
RIGHT! SO IT'S NOT A PROBLEM!
HE'S MAKING ME NERVOUS.
WOULDN'T IT BE EASIER TO JUST MOVE THIS CHAIR TO THE BACK?
EXCEPT FOR THE PART ABOUT TOUCHING IT, YES!
MOVE ALONG!
BB
WHERE'S THE CHAIR?
WHAT CHAIR?
THE ONE MARKED "WET".
IT WAS DRY, SO I TOOK THE SIGN OFF.
NOW LET'S SEE - WHICH ONE WAS IT?
WE'VE GOT A CLASS 1 BIOHAZARD IN THE LIBRARY.
YES, AGAIN.
BB
MA'AM, I HAVE TO WARN YOU THAT THE CHAIR ON WHICH YOU ARE SITTING MAY HAVE BEEN PREVIOUSLY MARKED WITH A "WET" SIGN OF UNKNOWN PROVENANCE.
PARDON?
YOU'RE BUTT-DEEP IN GERMTOWN.
HONEY, IF I WERE SQUEAMISH I WOULDN'T COME TO THE LIBRARY.
BB

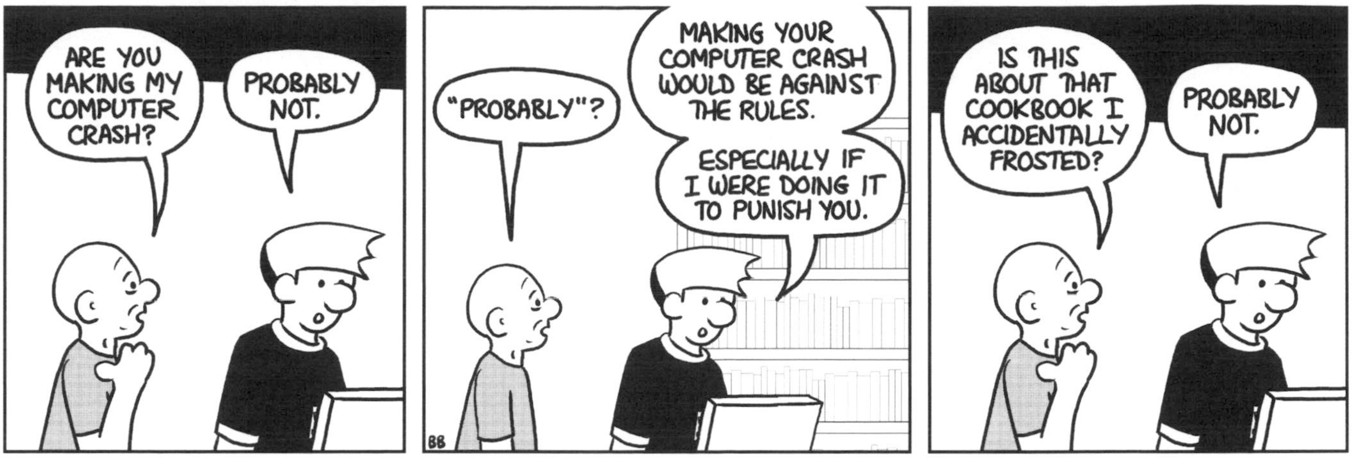
ARE YOU MAKING MY COMPUTER CRASH?
PROBABLY NOT.
"PROBABLY"?
MAKING YOUR COMPUTER CRASH WOULD BE AGAINST THE RULES.
ESPECIALLY IF I WERE DOING IT TO PUNISH YOU.
IS THIS ABOUT THAT COOKBOOK I ACCIDENTALLY FROSTED?
PROBABLY NOT.
BB

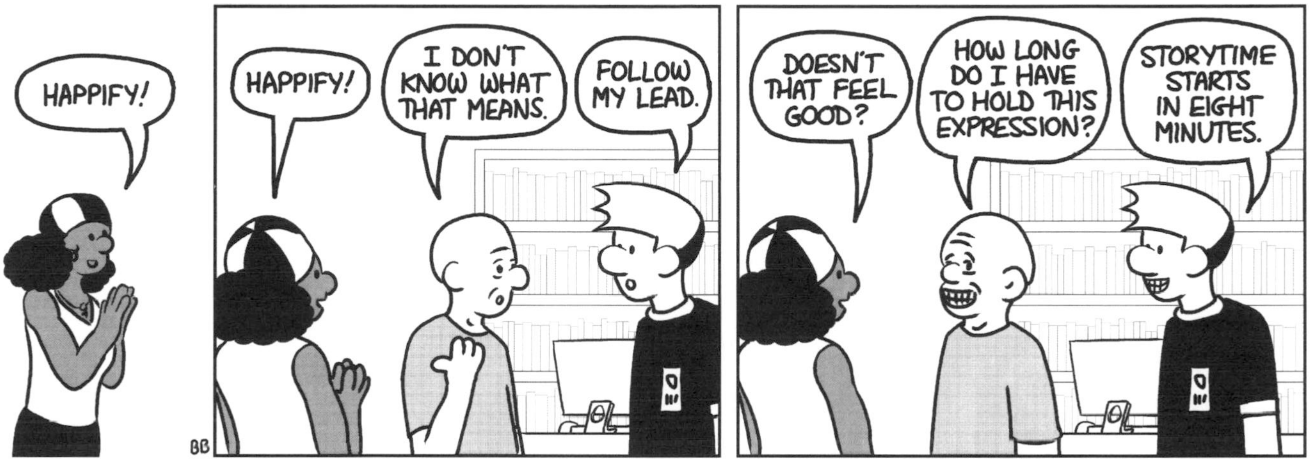
HAPPIFY!
HAPPIFY!
I DON'T KNOW WHAT THAT MEANS.
FOLLOW MY LEAD.
DOESN'T THAT FEEL GOOD?
HOW LONG DO I HAVE TO HOLD THIS EXPRESSION?
STORYTIME STARTS IN EIGHT MINUTES.
BB

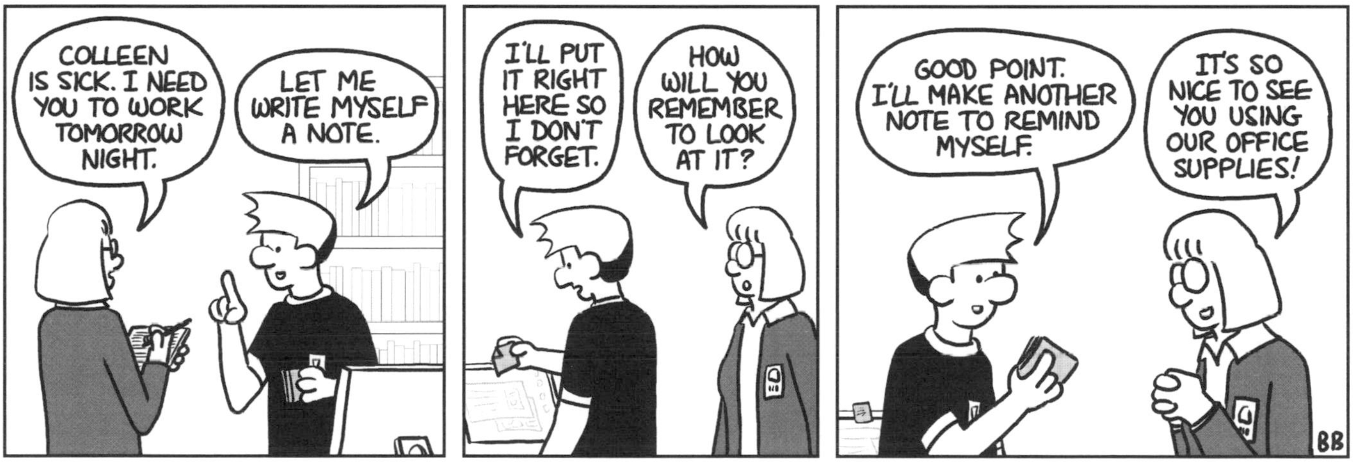
COLLEEN IS SICK. I NEED YOU TO WORK TOMORROW NIGHT.
LET ME WRITE MYSELF A NOTE.
I'LL PUT IT RIGHT HERE SO I DON'T FORGET.
HOW WILL YOU REMEMBER TO LOOK AT IT?
GOOD POINT. I'LL MAKE ANOTHER NOTE TO REMIND MYSELF.
IT'S SO NICE TO SEE YOU USING OUR OFFICE SUPPLIES!
BB

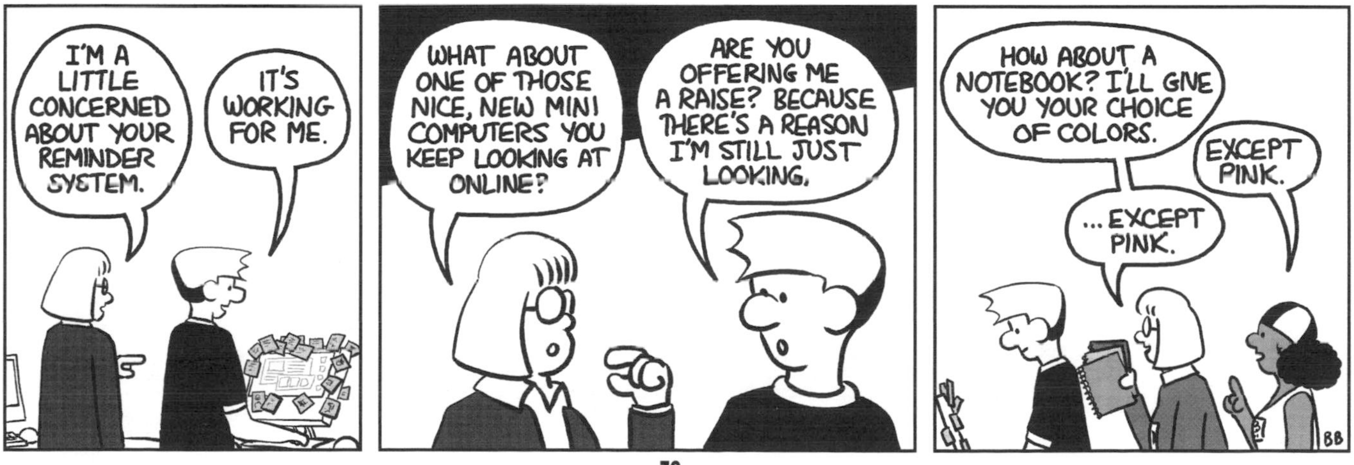
I'M A LITTLE CONCERNED ABOUT YOUR REMINDER SYSTEM.
IT'S WORKING FOR ME.
WHAT ABOUT ONE OF THOSE NICE, NEW MINI COMPUTERS YOU KEEP LOOKING AT ONLINE?
ARE YOU OFFERING ME A RAISE? BECAUSE THERE'S A REASON I'M STILL JUST LOOKING.
HOW ABOUT A NOTEBOOK? I'LL GIVE YOU YOUR CHOICE OF COLORS.
...EXCEPT PINK.
EXCEPT PINK.
BB

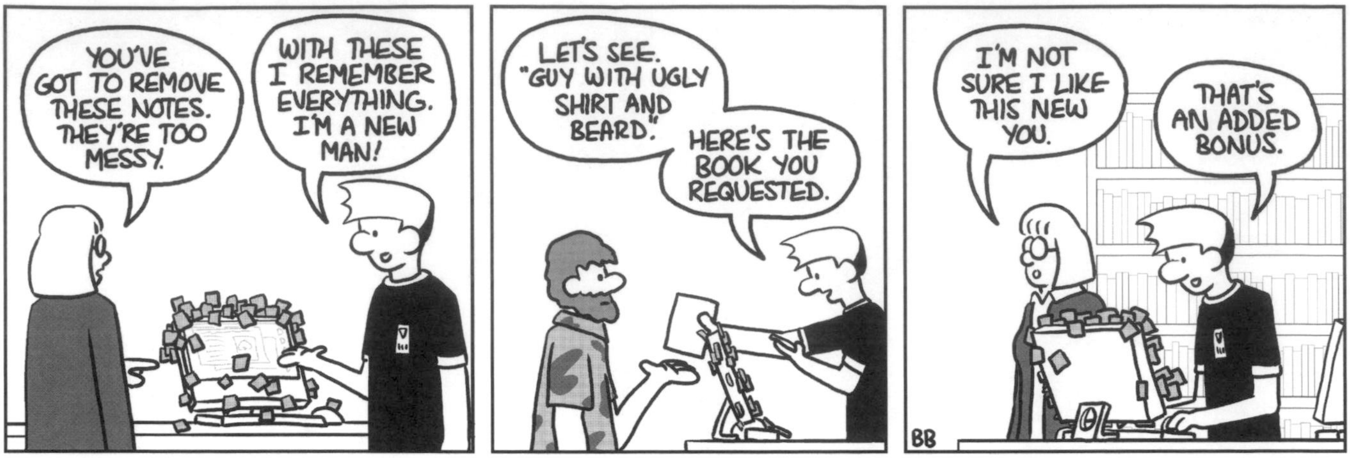
YOU'VE GOT TO REMOVE THESE NOTES. THEY'RE TOO MESSY.
WITH THESE I REMEMBER EVERYTHING. I'M A NEW MAN!
LET'S SEE. "GUY WITH UGLY SHIRT AND BEARD."
HERE'S THE BOOK YOU REQUESTED.
I'M NOT SURE I LIKE THIS NEW YOU.
THAT'S AN ADDED BONUS.
BB

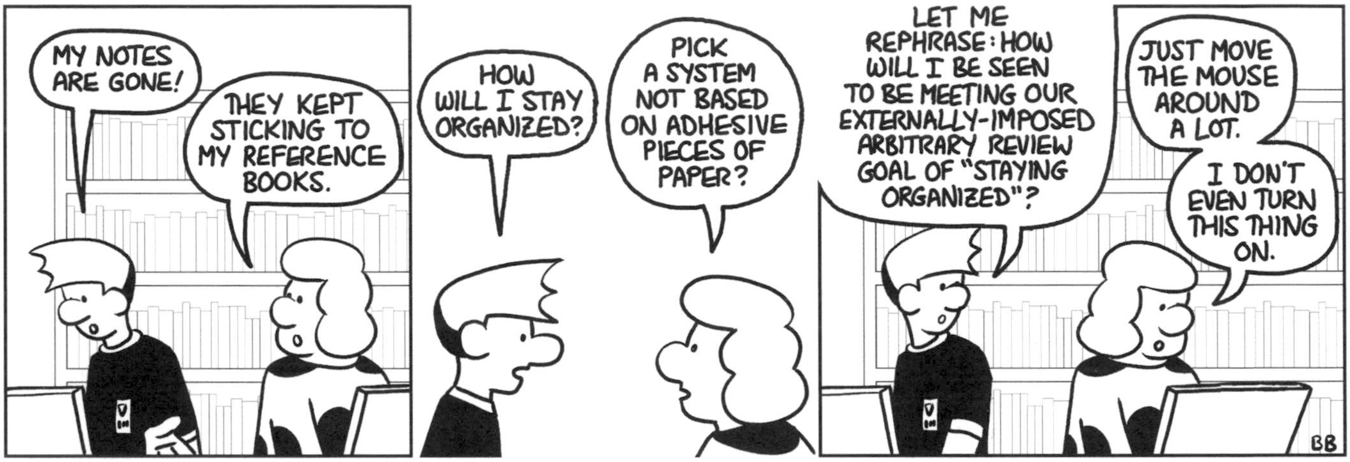
MY NOTES ARE GONE!
THEY KEPT STICKING TO MY REFERENCE BOOKS.
HOW WILL I STAY ORGANIZED?
PICK A SYSTEM NOT BASED ON ADHESIVE PIECES OF PAPER?
LET ME REPHRASE: HOW WILL I BE SEEN TO BE MEETING OUR EXTERNALLY-IMPOSED ARBITRARY REVIEW GOAL OF "STAYING ORGANIZED"?
JUST MOVE THE MOUSE AROUND A LOT.
I DON'T EVEN TURN THIS THING ON.
BB

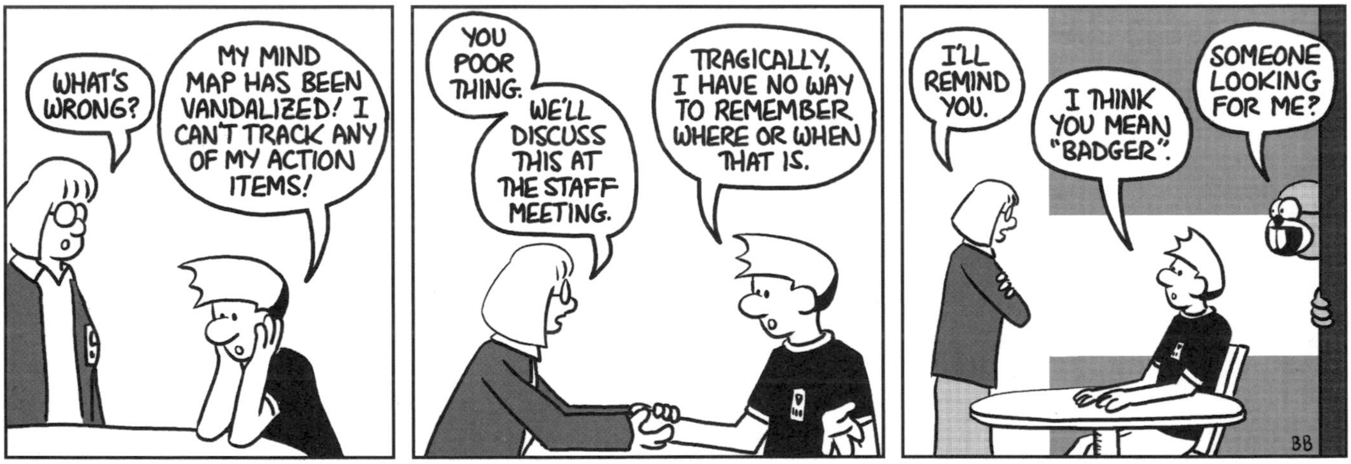
WHAT'S WRONG?
MY MIND MAP HAS BEEN VANDALIZED! I CAN'T TRACK ANY OF MY ACTION ITEMS!
YOU POOR THING.
WE'LL DISCUSS THIS AT THE STAFF MEETING.
TRAGICALLY, I HAVE NO WAY TO REMEMBER WHERE OR WHEN THAT IS.
I'LL REMIND YOU.
I THINK YOU MEAN "BADGER".
SOMEONE LOOKING FOR ME?
BB

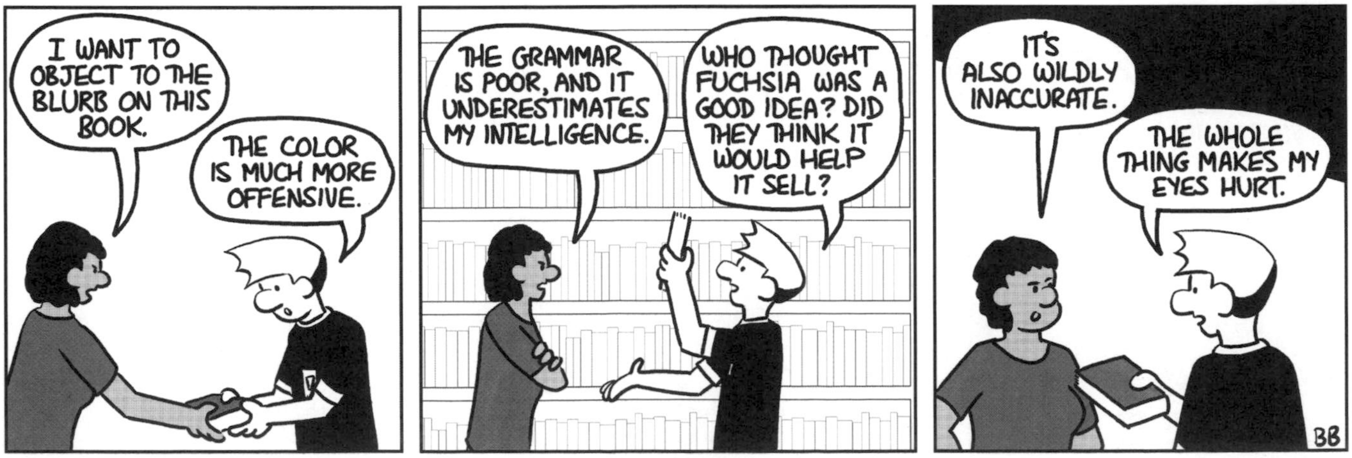
I WANT TO OBJECT TO THE BLURB ON THIS BOOK.
THE COLOR IS MUCH MORE OFFENSIVE.
THE GRAMMAR IS POOR, AND IT UNDERESTIMATES MY INTELLIGENCE.
WHO THOUGHT FUCHSIA WAS A GOOD IDEA? DID THEY THINK IT WOULD HELP IT SELL?
IT'S ALSO WILDLY INACCURATE.
THE WHOLE THING MAKES MY EYES HURT.
BB

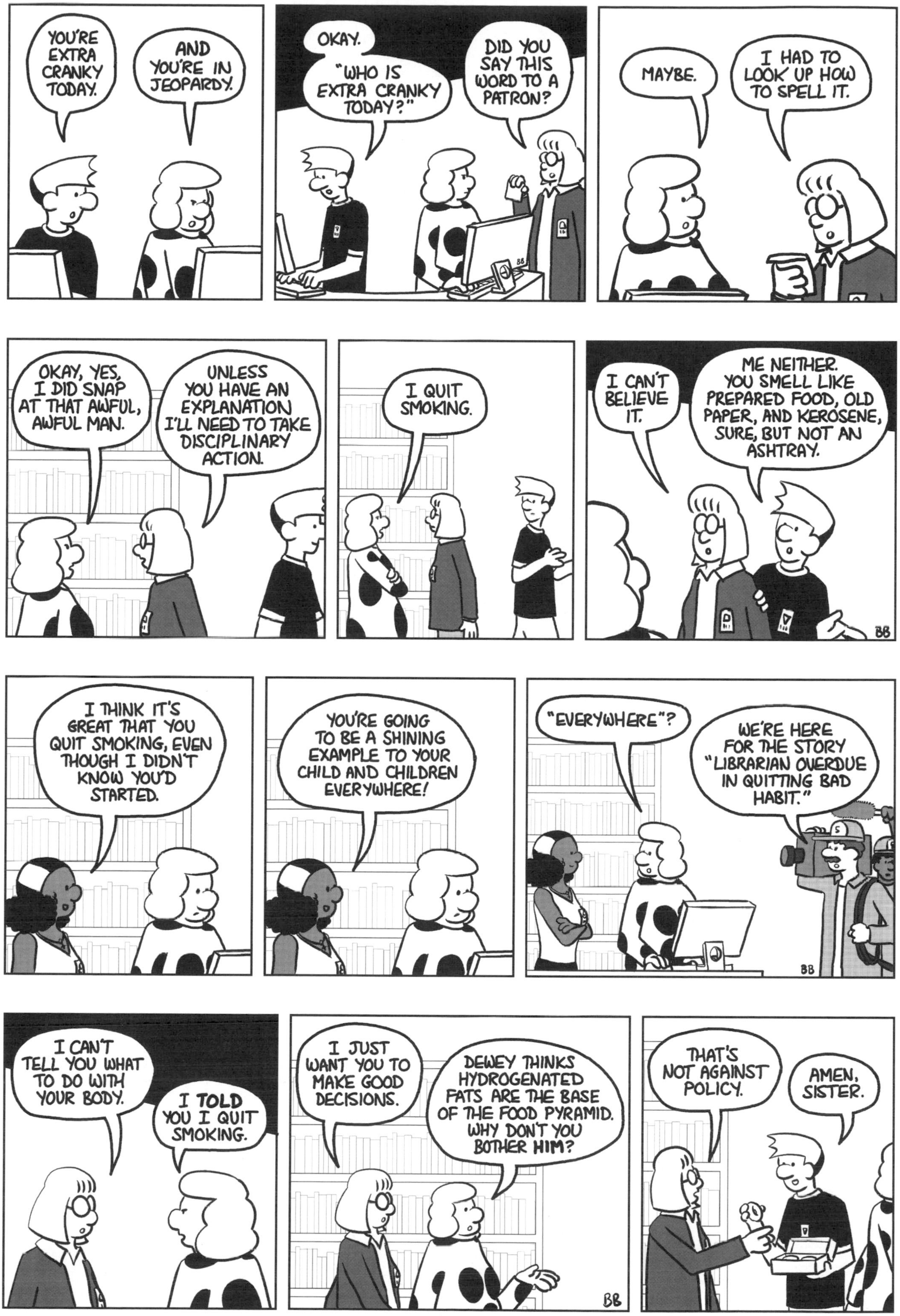
YOU'RE EXTRA CRANKY TODAY.
AND YOU'RE IN JEOPARDY.
OKAY.
"WHO IS EXTRA CRANKY TODAY?"
DID YOU SAY THIS WORD TO A PATRON?
MAYBE.
I HAD TO LOOK UP HOW TO SPELL IT.
OKAY, YES, I DID SNAP AT THAT AWFUL, AWFUL MAN.
UNLESS YOU HAVE AN EXPLANATION I'LL NEED TO TAKE DISCIPLINARY ACTION.
I QUIT SMOKING.
I CAN'T BELIEVE IT.
ME NEITHER. YOU SMELL LIKE PREPARED FOOD, OLD PAPER, AND KEROSENE, SURE, BUT NOT AN ASHTRAY.
BB
I THINK IT'S GREAT THAT YOU QUIT SMOKING, EVEN THOUGH I DIDN'T KNOW YOU'D STARTED.
YOU'RE GOING TO BE A SHINING EXAMPLE TO YOUR CHILD AND CHILDREN EVERYWHERE!
"EVERYWHERE"?
WE'RE HERE FOR THE STORY "LIBRARIAN OVERDUE IN QUITTING BAD HABIT."
BB
I CAN'T TELL YOU WHAT TO DO WITH YOUR BODY.
I **TOLD** YOU I QUIT SMOKING.
I JUST WANT YOU TO MAKE GOOD DECISIONS.
DEWEY THINKS HYDROGENATED FATS ARE THE BASE OF THE FOOD PYRAMID. WHY DON'T YOU BOTHER **HIM**?
BB
THAT'S NOT AGAINST POLICY.
AMEN, SISTER.

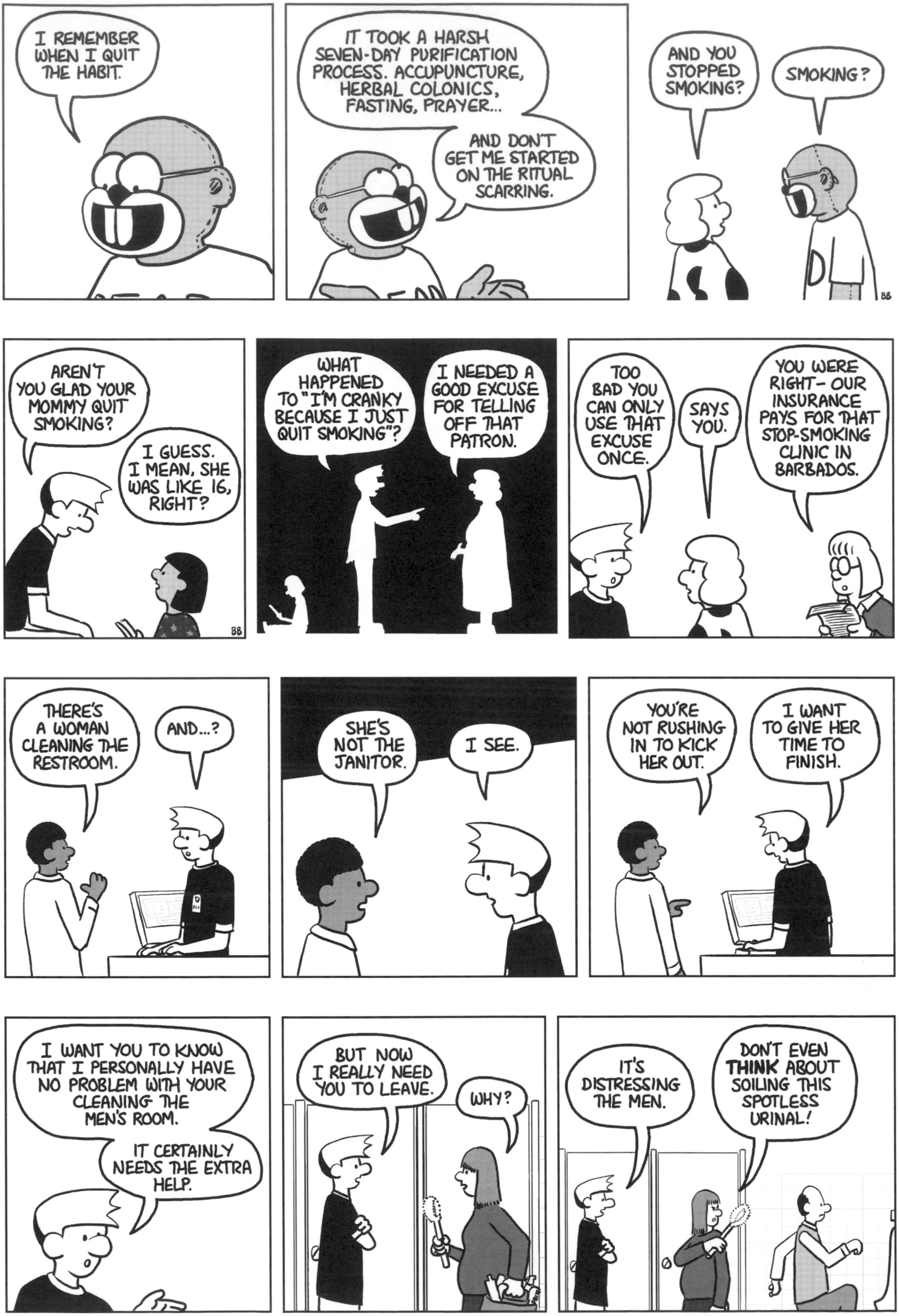

I REMEMBER WHEN I QUIT THE HABIT.
IT TOOK A HARSH SEVEN-DAY PURIFICATION PROCESS. ACCUPUNCTURE, HERBAL COLONICS, FASTING, PRAYER...
AND DON'T GET ME STARTED ON THE RITUAL SCARRING.
AND YOU STOPPED SMOKING?
SMOKING?
BB
AREN'T YOU GLAD YOUR MOMMY QUIT SMOKING?
I GUESS. I MEAN, SHE WAS LIKE 16, RIGHT?
BB
WHAT HAPPENED TO "I'M CRANKY BECAUSE I JUST QUIT SMOKING"?
I NEEDED A GOOD EXCUSE FOR TELLING OFF THAT PATRON.
TOO BAD YOU CAN ONLY USE THAT EXCUSE ONCE.
SAYS YOU.
YOU WERE RIGHT– OUR INSURANCE PAYS FOR THAT STOP-SMOKING CLINIC IN BARBADOS.
THERE'S A WOMAN CLEANING THE RESTROOM.
AND...?
SHE'S NOT THE JANITOR.
I SEE.
YOU'RE NOT RUSHING IN TO KICK HER OUT.
I WANT TO GIVE HER TIME TO FINISH.
I WANT YOU TO KNOW THAT I PERSONALLY HAVE NO PROBLEM WITH YOUR CLEANING THE MEN'S ROOM.
IT CERTAINLY NEEDS THE EXTRA HELP.
BUT NOW I REALLY NEED YOU TO LEAVE.
WHY?
IT'S DISTRESSING THE MEN.
DON'T EVEN THINK ABOUT SOILING THIS SPOTLESS URINAL!

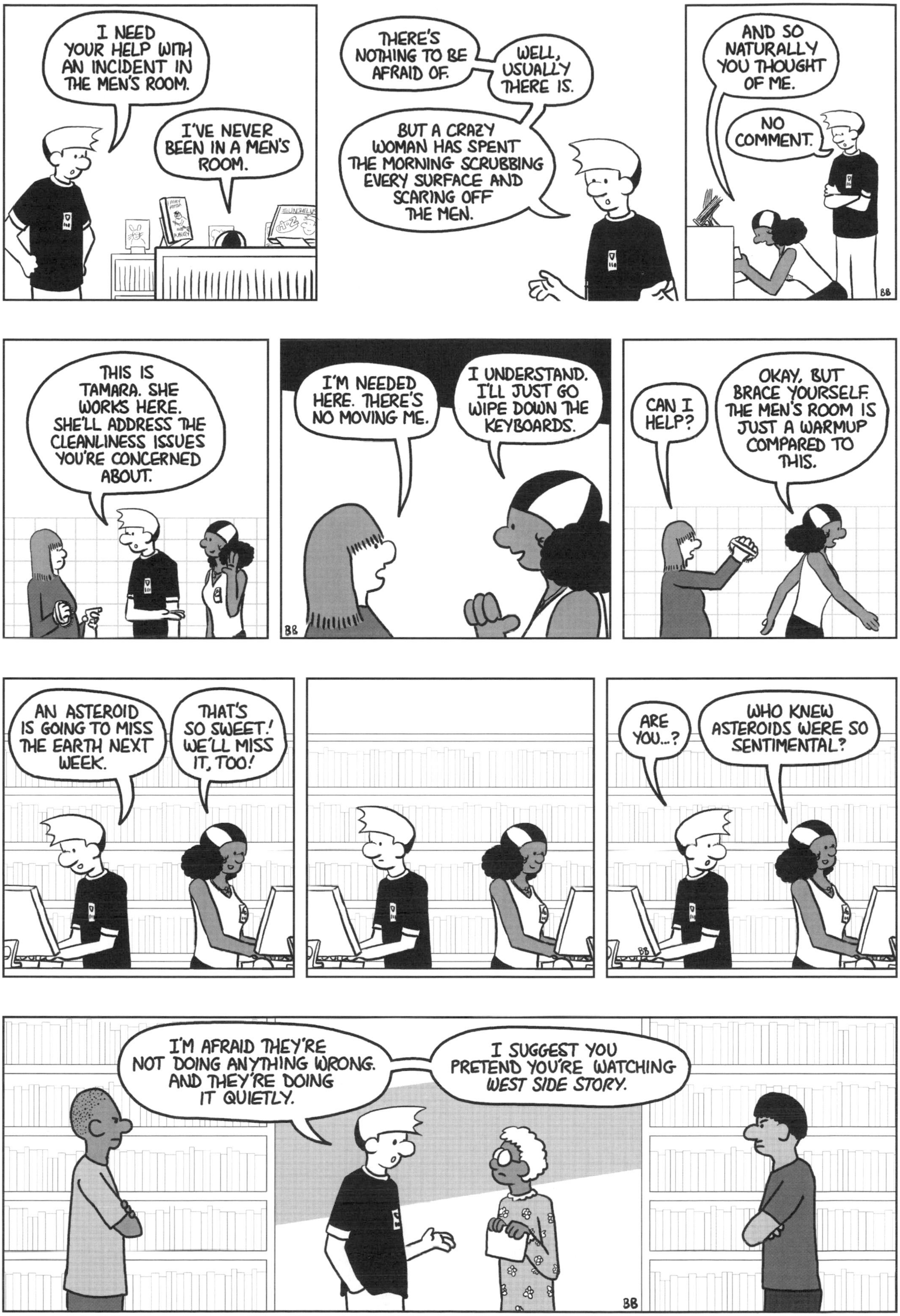
I NEED YOUR HELP WITH AN INCIDENT IN THE MEN'S ROOM.
I'VE NEVER BEEN IN A MEN'S ROOM.
THERE'S NOTHING TO BE AFRAID OF.
WELL, USUALLY THERE IS.
BUT A CRAZY WOMAN HAS SPENT THE MORNING SCRUBBING EVERY SURFACE AND SCARING OFF THE MEN.
AND SO NATURALLY YOU THOUGHT OF ME.
NO COMMENT.
THIS IS TAMARA. SHE WORKS HERE. SHE'LL ADDRESS THE CLEANLINESS ISSUES YOU'RE CONCERNED ABOUT.
I'M NEEDED HERE. THERE'S NO MOVING ME.
I UNDERSTAND. I'LL JUST GO WIPE DOWN THE KEYBOARDS.
CAN I HELP?
OKAY, BUT BRACE YOURSELF. THE MEN'S ROOM IS JUST A WARMUP COMPARED TO THIS.
AN ASTEROID IS GOING TO MISS THE EARTH NEXT WEEK.
THAT'S SO SWEET! WE'LL MISS IT, TOO!
ARE YOU...?
WHO KNEW ASTEROIDS WERE SO SENTIMENTAL?
I'M AFRAID THEY'RE NOT DOING ANYTHING WRONG. AND THEY'RE DOING IT QUIETLY.
I SUGGEST YOU PRETEND YOU'RE WATCHING *WEST SIDE STORY*.

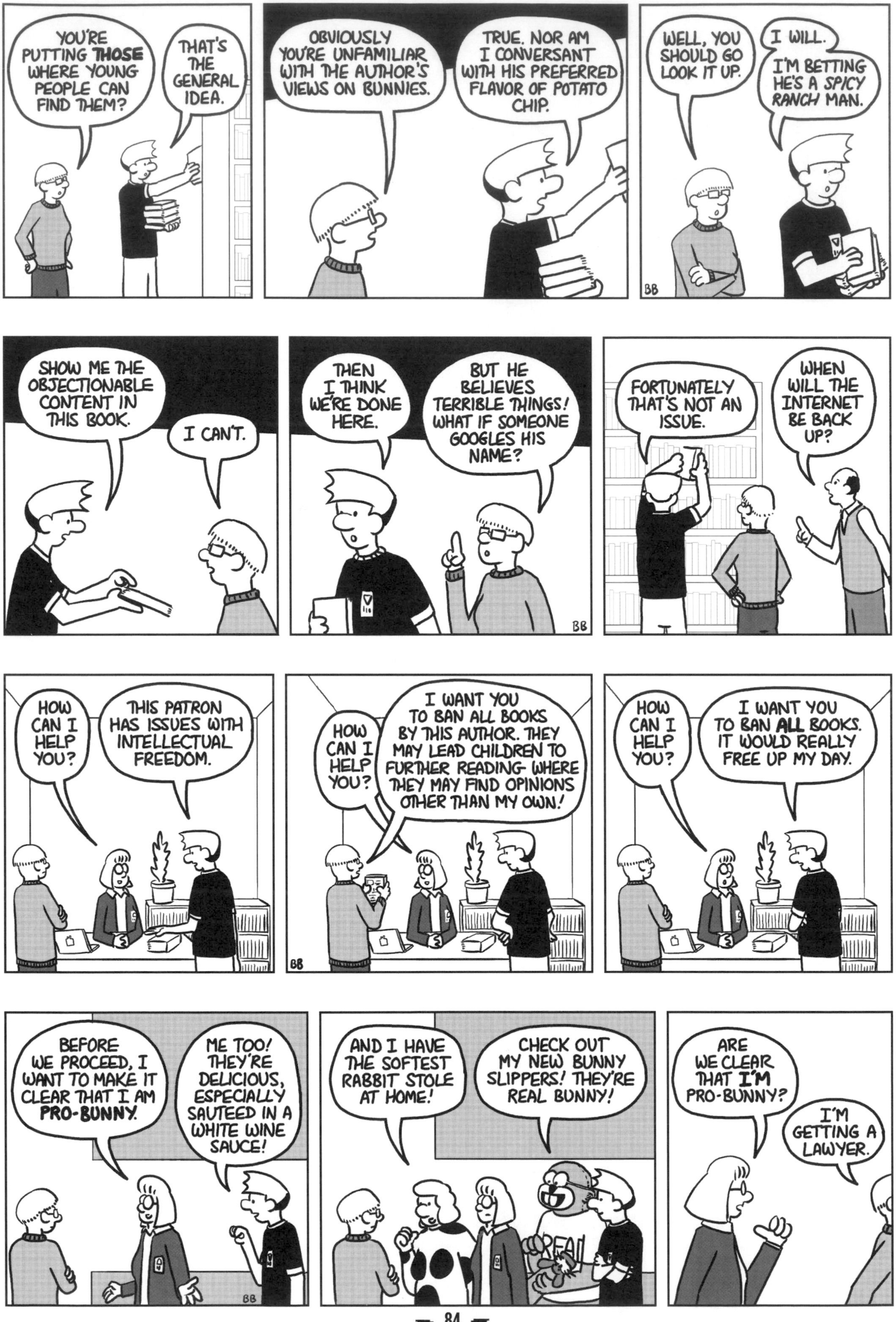
YOU'RE PUTTING THOSE WHERE YOUNG PEOPLE CAN FIND THEM?
THAT'S THE GENERAL IDEA.
OBVIOUSLY YOU'RE UNFAMILIAR WITH THE AUTHOR'S VIEWS ON BUNNIES.
TRUE. NOR AM I CONVERSANT WITH HIS PREFERRED FLAVOR OF POTATO CHIP.
WELL, YOU SHOULD GO LOOK IT UP.
I WILL.
I'M BETTING HE'S A SPICY RANCH MAN.
BB
SHOW ME THE OBJECTIONABLE CONTENT IN THIS BOOK.
I CAN'T.
THEN I THINK WE'RE DONE HERE.
BUT HE BELIEVES TERRIBLE THINGS! WHAT IF SOMEONE GOOGLES HIS NAME?
BB
FORTUNATELY THAT'S NOT AN ISSUE.
WHEN WILL THE INTERNET BE BACK UP?
HOW CAN I HELP YOU?
THIS PATRON HAS ISSUES WITH INTELLECTUAL FREEDOM.
HOW CAN I HELP YOU?
I WANT YOU TO BAN ALL BOOKS BY THIS AUTHOR. THEY MAY LEAD CHILDREN TO FURTHER READING WHERE THEY MAY FIND OPINIONS OTHER THAN MY OWN!
BB
HOW CAN I HELP YOU?
I WANT YOU TO BAN ALL BOOKS. IT WOULD REALLY FREE UP MY DAY.
BEFORE WE PROCEED, I WANT TO MAKE IT CLEAR THAT I AM PRO-BUNNY.
ME TOO! THEY'RE DELICIOUS, ESPECIALLY SAUTEED IN A WHITE WINE SAUCE!
BB
AND I HAVE THE SOFTEST RABBIT STOLE AT HOME!
CHECK OUT MY NEW BUNNY SLIPPERS! THEY'RE REAL BUNNY!
REAL
ARE WE CLEAR THAT I'M PRO-BUNNY?
I'M GETTING A LAWYER.

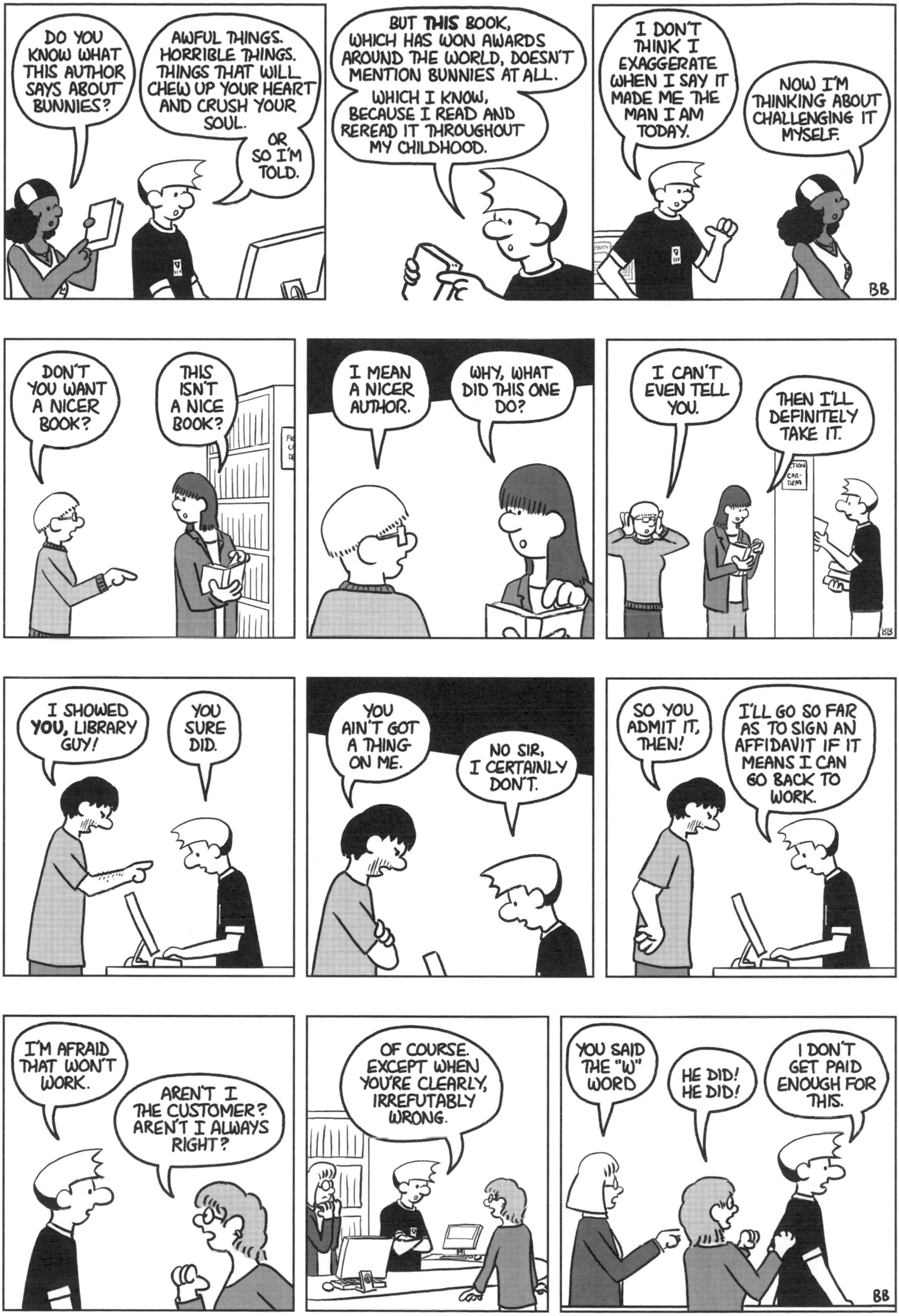
DO YOU KNOW WHAT THIS AUTHOR SAYS ABOUT BUNNIES?
AWFUL THINGS. HORRIBLE THINGS. THINGS THAT WILL CHEW UP YOUR HEART AND CRUSH YOUR SOUL.
OR SO I'M TOLD.
BUT **THIS** BOOK, WHICH HAS WON AWARDS AROUND THE WORLD, DOESN'T MENTION BUNNIES AT ALL.
WHICH I KNOW, BECAUSE I READ AND REREAD IT THROUGHOUT MY CHILDHOOD.
I DON'T THINK I EXAGGERATE WHEN I SAY IT MADE ME THE MAN I AM TODAY.
NOW I'M THINKING ABOUT CHALLENGING IT MYSELF.
BB
DON'T YOU WANT A NICER BOOK?
THIS ISN'T A NICE BOOK?
I MEAN A NICER AUTHOR.
WHY, WHAT DID THIS ONE DO?
I CAN'T EVEN TELL YOU.
THEN I'LL DEFINITELY TAKE IT.
BB
I SHOWED **YOU**, LIBRARY GUY!
YOU SURE DID.
YOU AIN'T GOT A THING ON ME.
NO SIR, I CERTAINLY DON'T.
SO YOU ADMIT IT, THEN!
I'LL GO SO FAR AS TO SIGN AN AFFIDAVIT IF IT MEANS I CAN GO BACK TO WORK.
I'M AFRAID THAT WON'T WORK.
AREN'T I THE CUSTOMER? AREN'T I ALWAYS RIGHT?
OF COURSE. EXCEPT WHEN YOU'RE CLEARLY, IRREFUTABLY WRONG.
YOU SAID THE "W" WORD
HE DID! HE DID!
I DON'T GET PAID ENOUGH FOR THIS.
BB

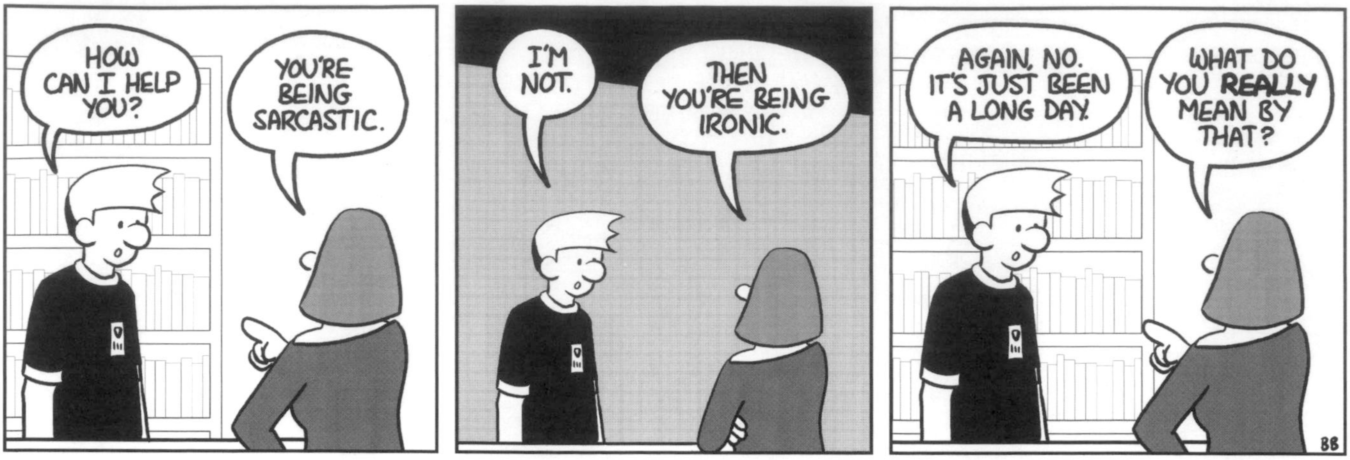
HOW CAN I HELP YOU?
YOU'RE BEING SARCASTIC.
I'M NOT.
THEN YOU'RE BEING IRONIC.
AGAIN, NO. IT'S JUST BEEN A LONG DAY.
WHAT DO YOU **REALLY** MEAN BY THAT?
BB

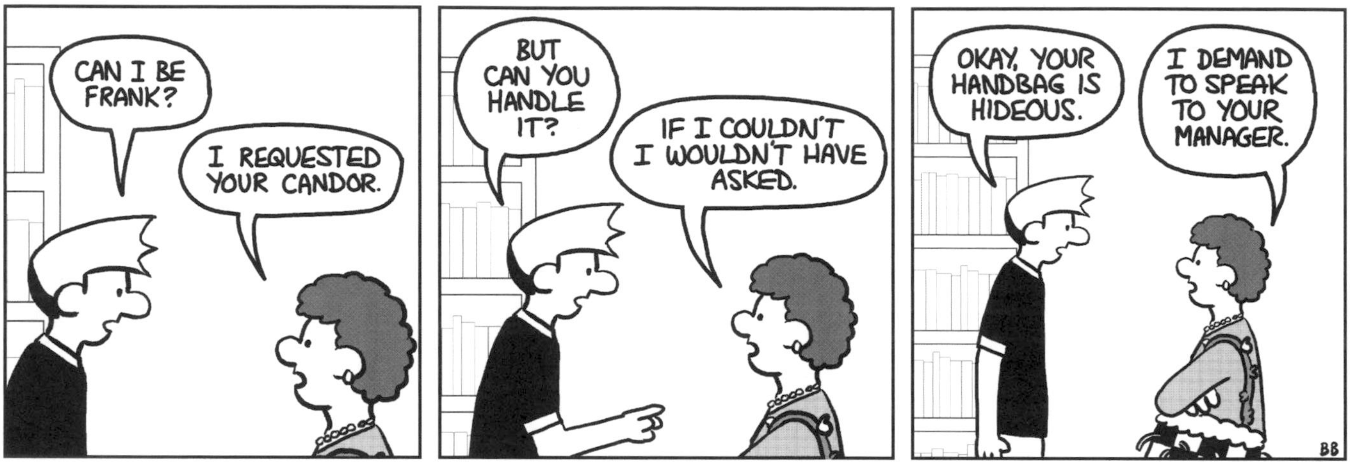
CAN I BE FRANK?
I REQUESTED YOUR CANDOR.
BUT CAN YOU HANDLE IT?
IF I COULDN'T I WOULDN'T HAVE ASKED.
OKAY, YOUR HANDBAG IS HIDEOUS.
I DEMAND TO SPEAK TO YOUR MANAGER.
BB

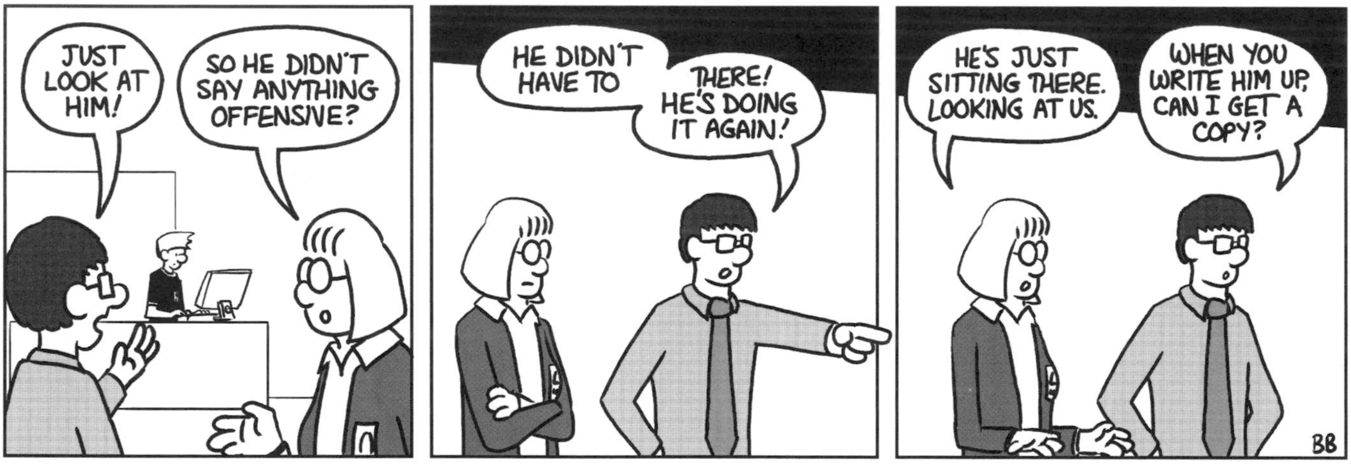
JUST LOOK AT HIM!
SO HE DIDN'T SAY ANYTHING OFFENSIVE?
HE DIDN'T HAVE TO
THERE! HE'S DOING IT AGAIN!
HE'S JUST SITTING THERE. LOOKING AT US.
WHEN YOU WRITE HIM UP, CAN I GET A COPY?
BB

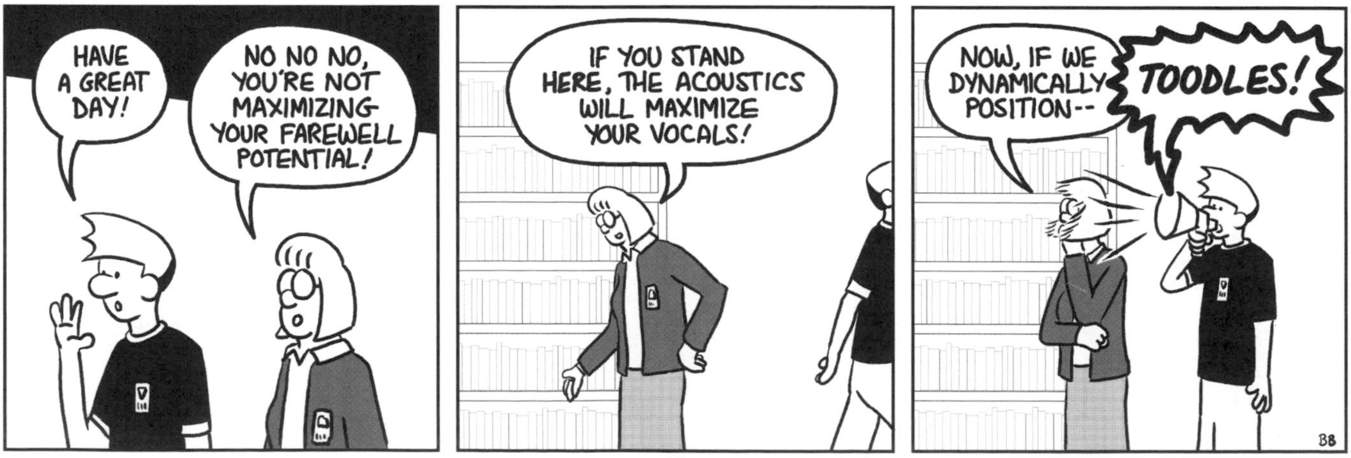
HAVE A GREAT DAY!
NO NO NO, YOU'RE NOT MAXIMIZING YOUR FAREWELL POTENTIAL!
IF YOU STAND HERE, THE ACOUSTICS WILL MAXIMIZE YOUR VOCALS!
NOW, IF WE DYNAMICALLY POSITION--
TOODLES!
BB

Every year we produce a series of Conference Tips *for the American Library Association conferences. They are featured every day in the conference newspaper, and are read by three groups of people:*

1. *Regular* Unshelved *fans who appreciate seeing Dewey's perspective on trade shows.*
2. *Folks (vendors and attendees) who read them, visit our booth, and become regular* Unshelved *fans.*
3. *People who really, really don't think we're funny.*

The latter are, of course, the most awesome of all. They walk by our booth studiously avoiding our gazes. If we hand them a flyer they hand it back. If we try talking to them they look away. They don't have smile lines on their faces because they have never smiled. *Yes, these are the people who don't believe their profession is humorous. "Librarianship is a mission," they might say if we could successfully engage them in conversation, "a calling", they might add. "I don't appreciate it being made fun of."*

And so this small section of the book is dedicated to you, the Librarian Who Takes His- or Herself Way Too Seriously. Library conferences wouldn't be the same without you.

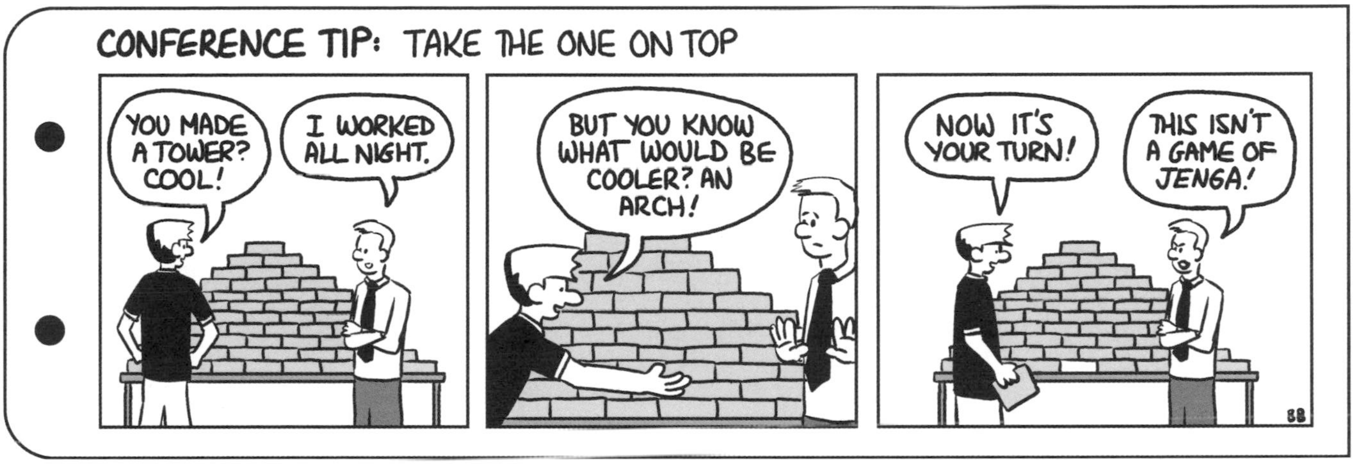
CONFERENCE TIP: TAKE THE ONE ON TOP
YOU MADE A TOWER? COOL!
I WORKED ALL NIGHT.
BUT YOU KNOW WHAT WOULD BE COOLER? AN ARCH!
NOW IT'S YOUR TURN!
THIS ISN'T A GAME OF JENGA!
BB

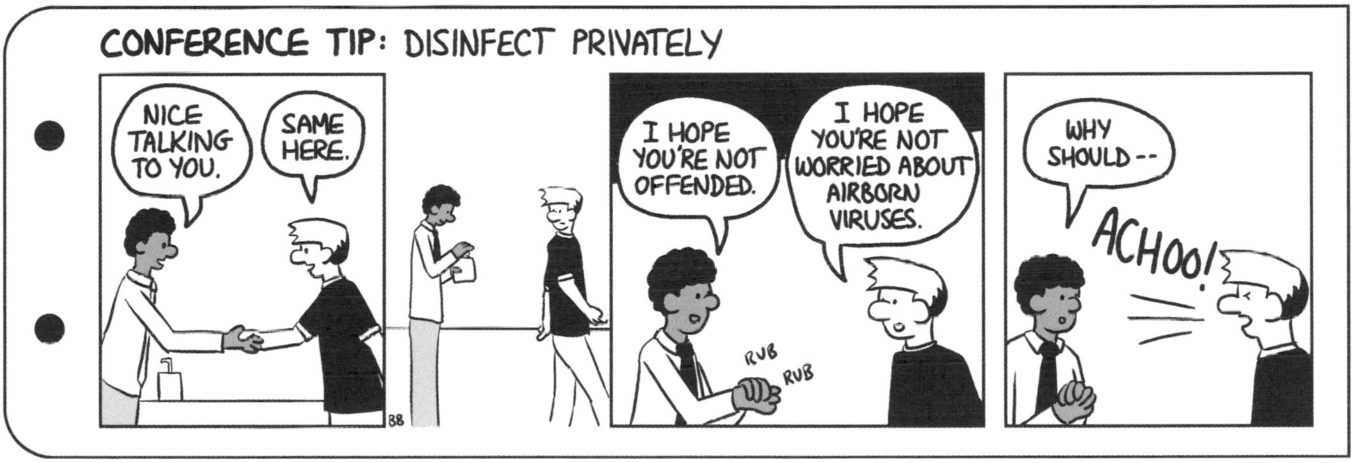
CONFERENCE TIP: DISINFECT PRIVATELY
NICE TALKING TO YOU.
SAME HERE.
BB
I HOPE YOU'RE NOT OFFENDED.
I HOPE YOU'RE NOT WORRIED ABOUT AIRBORN VIRUSES.
RUB
RUB
WHY SHOULD --
ACHOO!

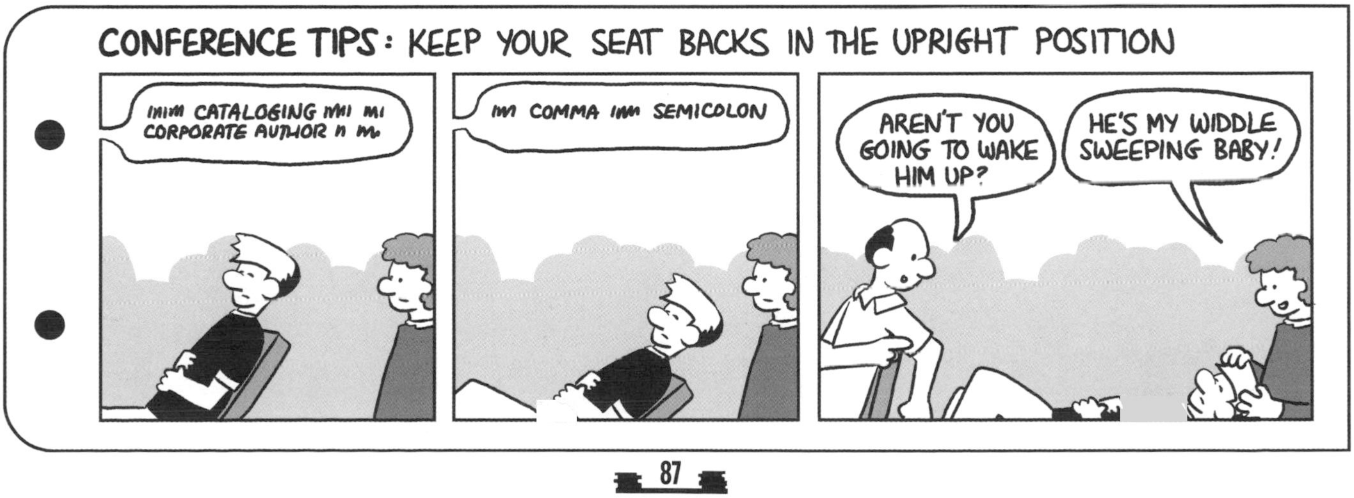
CONFERENCE TIPS: KEEP YOUR SEAT BACKS IN THE UPRIGHT POSITION
CATALOGING
CORPORATE AUTHOR
COMMA
SEMICOLON
AREN'T YOU GOING TO WAKE HIM UP?
HE'S MY WIDDLE SWEEPING BABY!

CONFERENCE TIP: SEEK UNMOTIVATED SALESPEOPLE

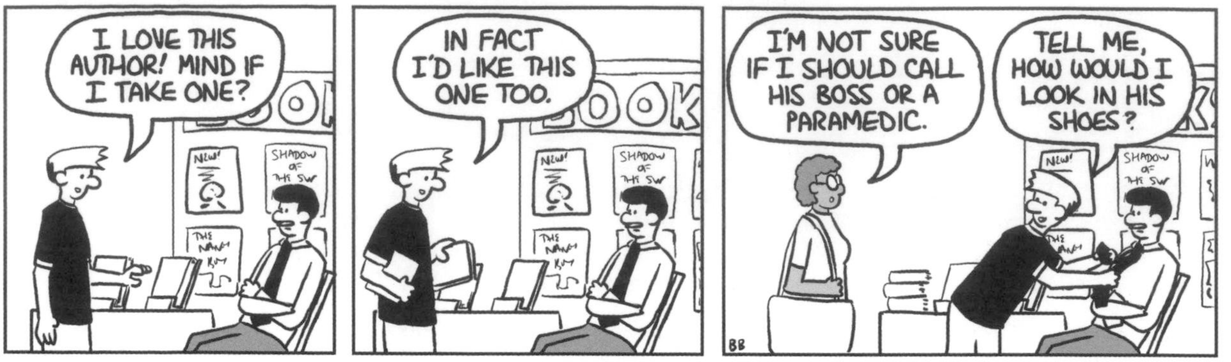
I LOVE THIS AUTHOR! MIND IF I TAKE ONE?
IN FACT I'D LIKE THIS ONE TOO.
I'M NOT SURE IF I SHOULD CALL HIS BOSS OR A PARAMEDIC.
TELL ME, HOW WOULD I LOOK IN HIS SHOES?

CONFERENCE TIP: NO WHEELED LUGGAGE IN THE EXHIBIT HALL

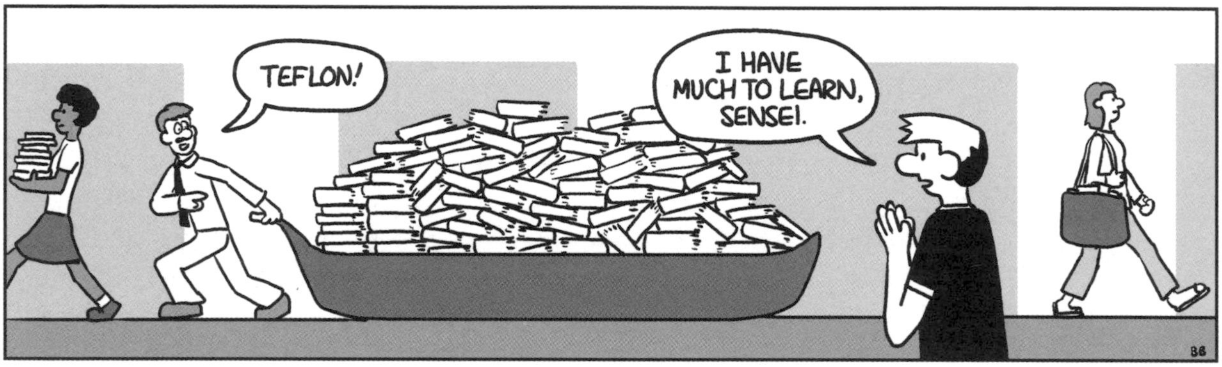
TEFLON!
I HAVE MUCH TO LEARN, SENSEI.

CONFERENCE TIP: ENJOY THE VENDORS

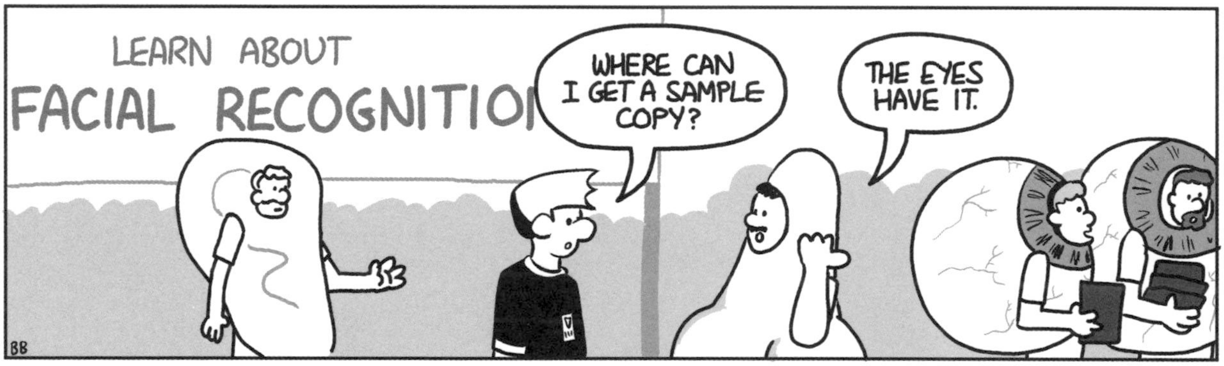
LEARN ABOUT
FACIAL RECOGNITIO
WHERE CAN I GET A SAMPLE COPY?
THE EYES HAVE IT.

CONFERENCE TIP: DON'T COUNT YOUR BOOKS BEFORE THEY'RE READ

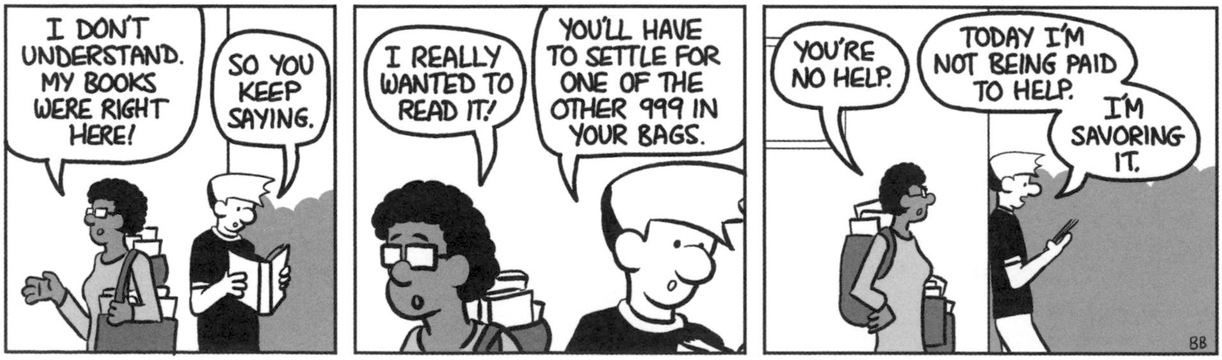
I DON'T UNDERSTAND. MY BOOKS WERE RIGHT HERE!
SO YOU KEEP SAYING.
I REALLY WANTED TO READ IT!
YOU'LL HAVE TO SETTLE FOR ONE OF THE OTHER 999 IN YOUR BAGS.
YOU'RE NO HELP.
TODAY I'M NOT BEING PAID TO HELP.
I'M SAVORING IT.

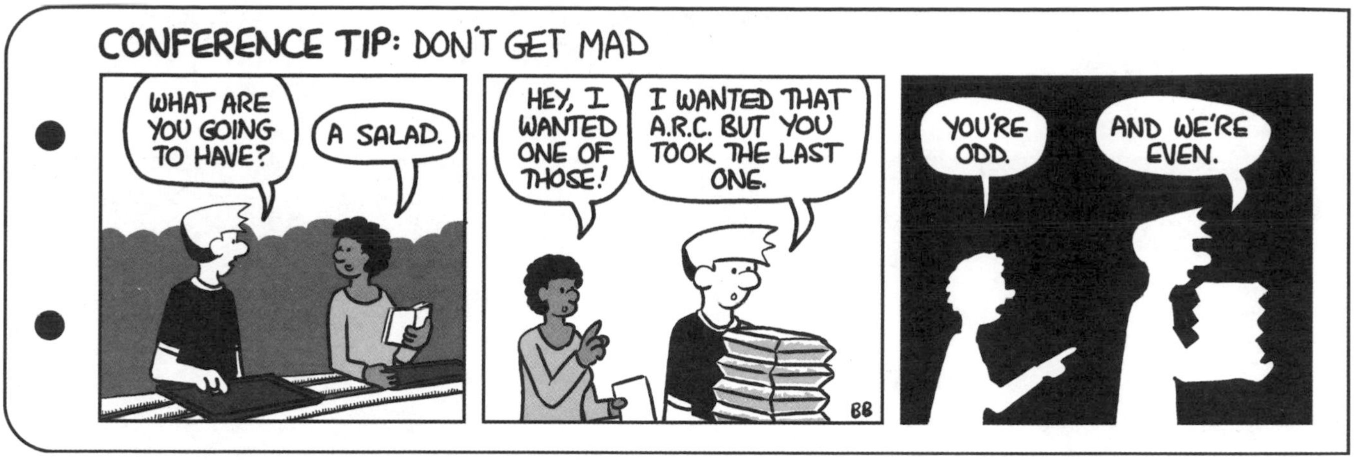
CONFERENCE TIP: DON'T GET MAD
WHAT ARE YOU GOING TO HAVE?
A SALAD.
HEY, I WANTED ONE OF THOSE!
I WANTED THAT A.R.C. BUT YOU TOOK THE LAST ONE.
YOU'RE ODD.
AND WE'RE EVEN.
BB

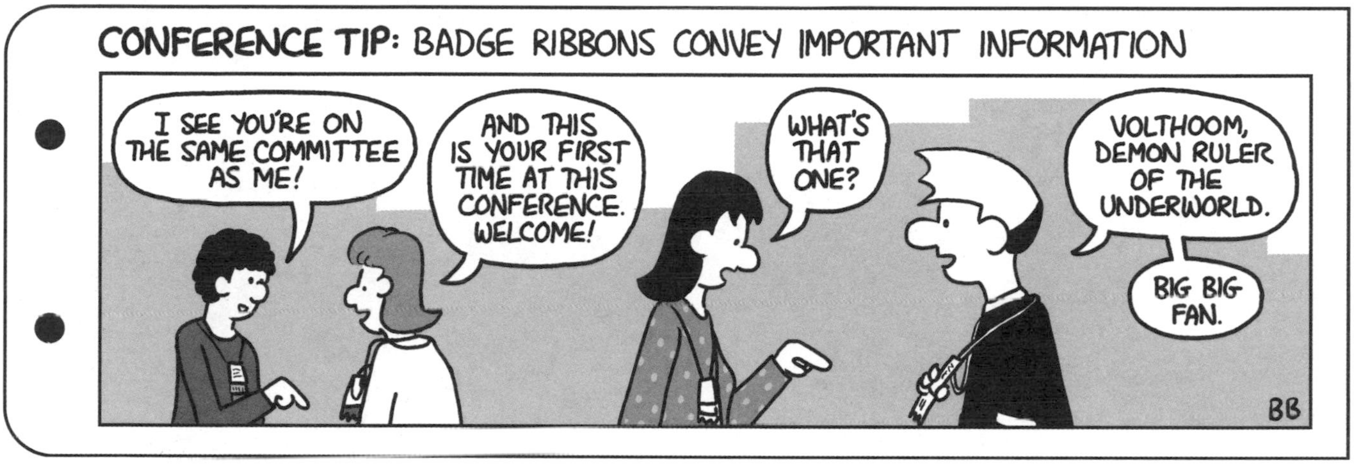
CONFERENCE TIP: BADGE RIBBONS CONVEY IMPORTANT INFORMATION
I SEE YOU'RE ON THE SAME COMMITTEE AS ME!
AND THIS IS YOUR FIRST TIME AT THIS CONFERENCE. WELCOME!
WHAT'S THAT ONE?
VOLTHOOM, DEMON RULER OF THE UNDERWORLD.
BIG BIG FAN.
BB

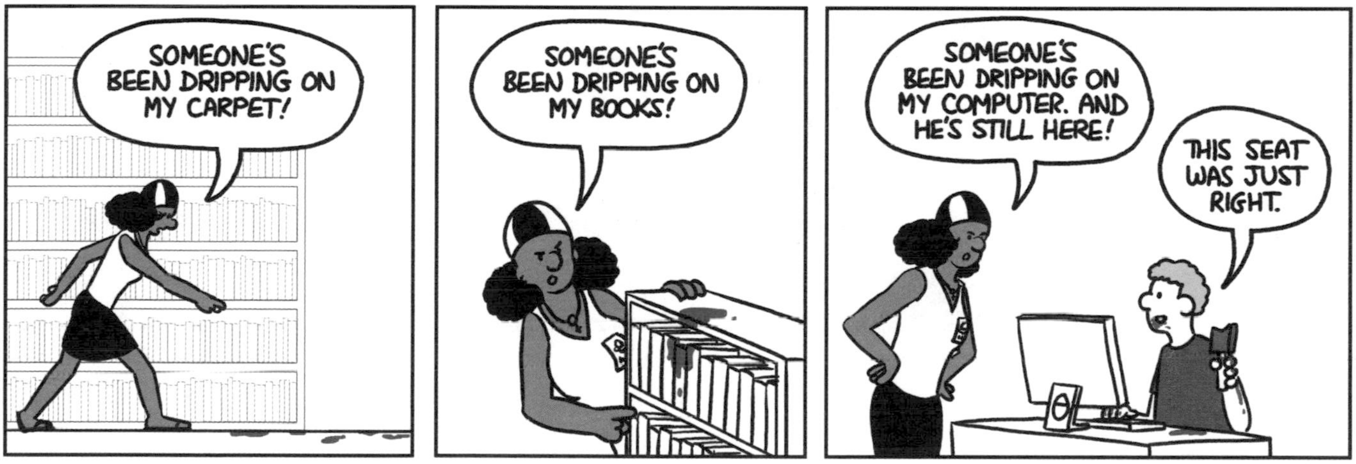
SOMEONE'S BEEN DRIPPING ON MY CARPET!
SOMEONE'S BEEN DRIPPING ON MY BOOKS!
SOMEONE'S BEEN DRIPPING ON MY COMPUTER. AND HE'S STILL HERE!
THIS SEAT WAS JUST RIGHT.

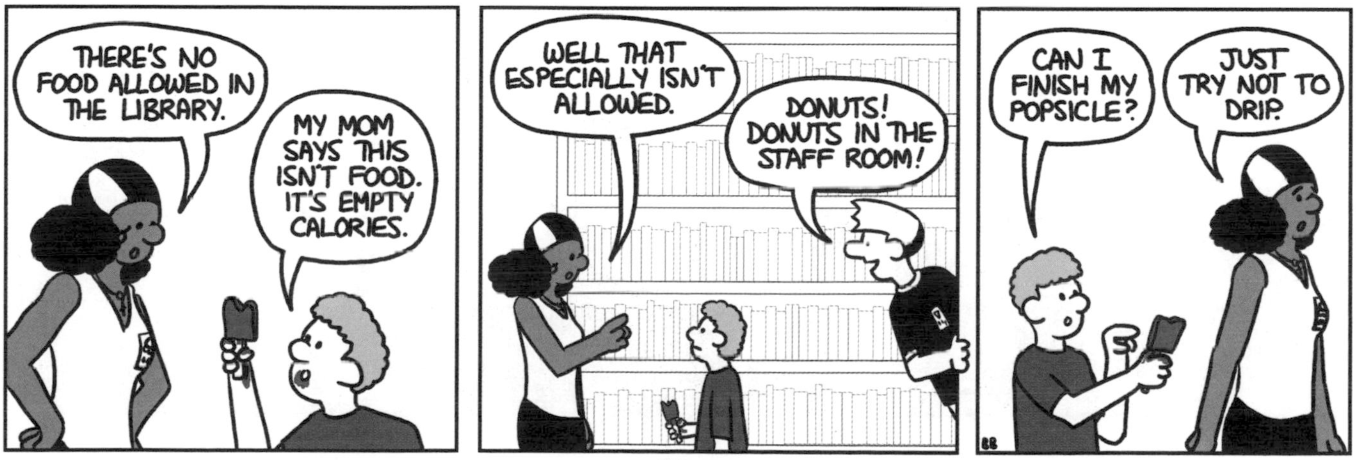
THERE'S NO FOOD ALLOWED IN THE LIBRARY.
MY MOM SAYS THIS ISN'T FOOD. IT'S EMPTY CALORIES.
WELL THAT ESPECIALLY ISN'T ALLOWED.
DONUTS! DONUTS IN THE STAFF ROOM!
CAN I FINISH MY POPSICLE?
JUST TRY NOT TO DRIP.
BB

The Unshelved® Book Club presents

The Shadow of the Wind

by Carlos Ruiz Zafón

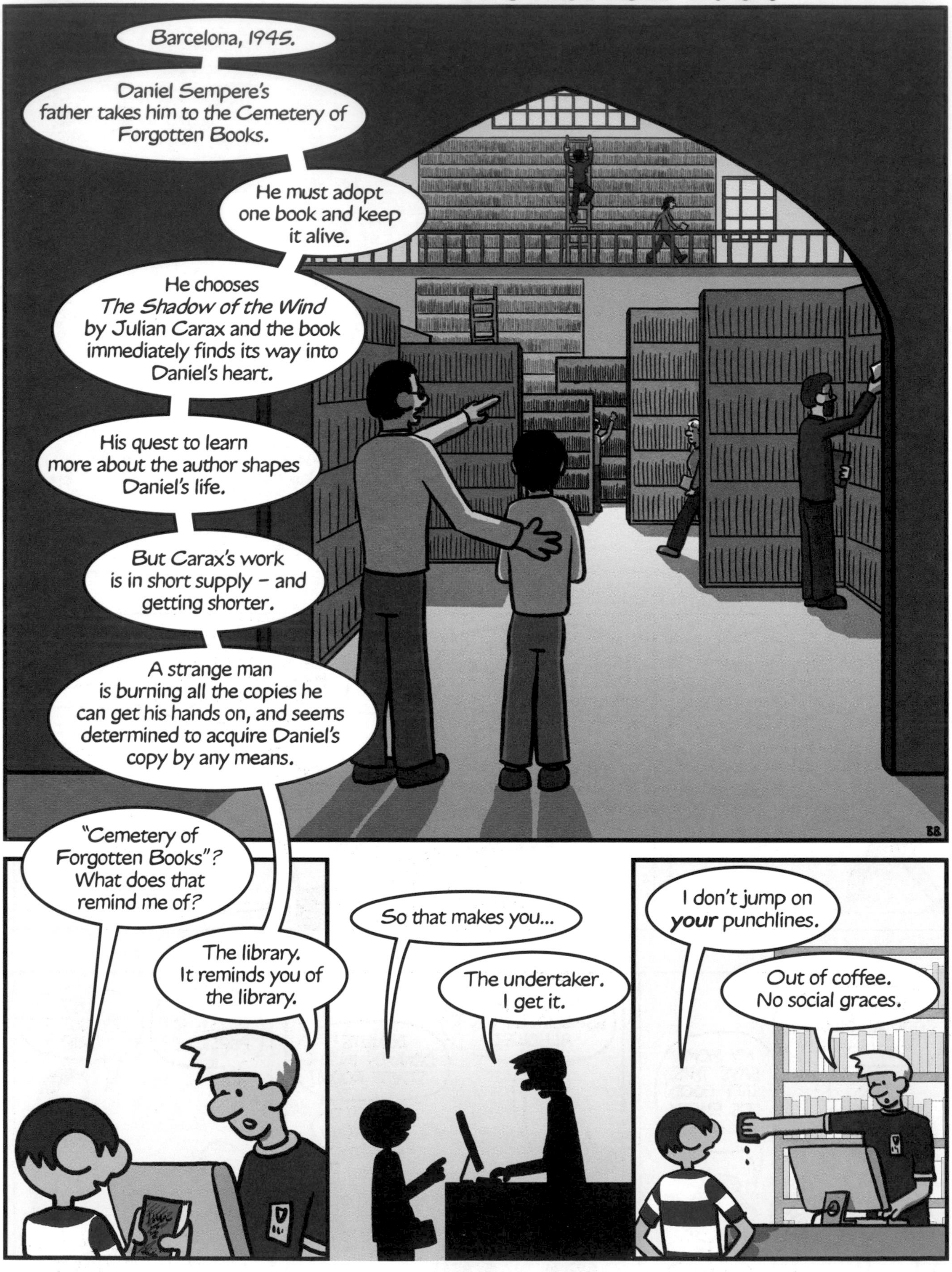

Barcelona, 1945.
Daniel Sempere's father takes him to the Cemetery of Forgotten Books.
He must adopt one book and keep it alive.
He chooses *The Shadow of the Wind* by Julian Carax and the book immediately finds its way into Daniel's heart.
His quest to learn more about the author shapes Daniel's life.
But Carax's work is in short supply – and getting shorter.
A strange man is burning all the copies he can get his hands on, and seems determined to acquire Daniel's copy by any means.
BB
"Cemetery of Forgotten Books"? What does that remind me of?
The library. It reminds you of the library.
So that makes you...
The undertaker. I get it.
I don't jump on **your** punchlines.
Out of coffee. No social graces.

THE Unshelved® BOOK CLUB PRESENTS

SPLIT SCREEN

BY BRENT HARTINGER

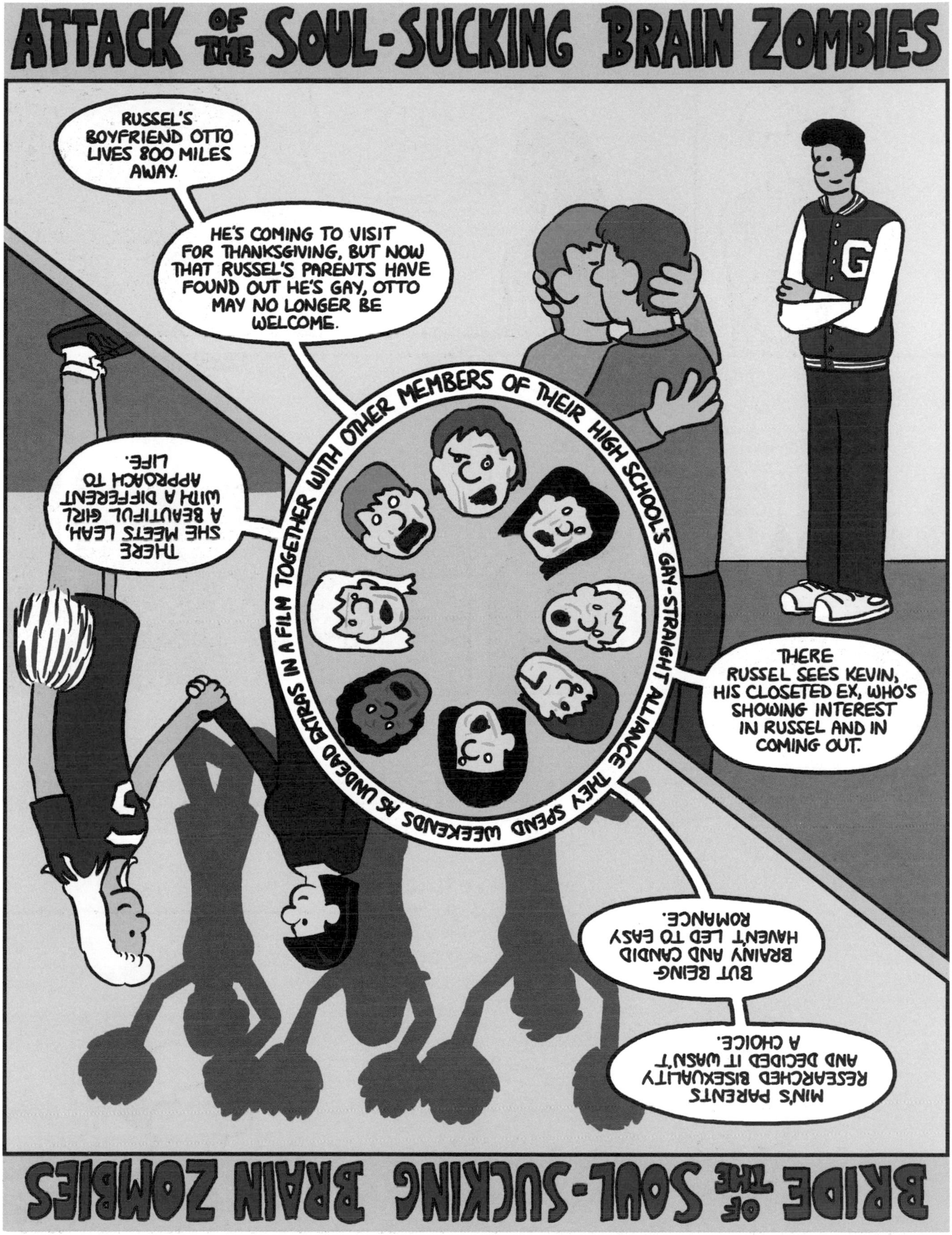

ATTACK OF THE SOUL-SUCKING BRAIN ZOMBIES
RUSSEL'S BOYFRIEND OTTO LIVES 800 MILES AWAY.
HE'S COMING TO VISIT FOR THANKSGIVING, BUT NOW THAT RUSSEL'S PARENTS HAVE FOUND OUT HE'S GAY, OTTO MAY NO LONGER BE WELCOME.
THEY SPEND WEEKENDS AS UNDEAD EXTRAS IN A FILM TOGETHER WITH OTHER MEMBERS OF THEIR HIGH SCHOOL'S GAY-STRAIGHT ALLIANCE.
THERE RUSSEL SEES KEVIN, HIS CLOSETED EX, WHO'S SHOWING INTEREST IN RUSSEL AND IN COMING OUT.
G
THERE SHE MEETS LEAH, A BEAUTIFUL GIRL WITH A DIFFERENT APPROACH TO LIFE.
MIN'S PARENTS RESEARCHED BISEXUALITY AND DECIDED IT WASN'T A CHOICE.
BUT BEING BRAINY AND CANDID HAVEN'T LED TO EASY ROMANCE.
BRIDE OF THE SOUL-SUCKING BRAIN ZOMBIES

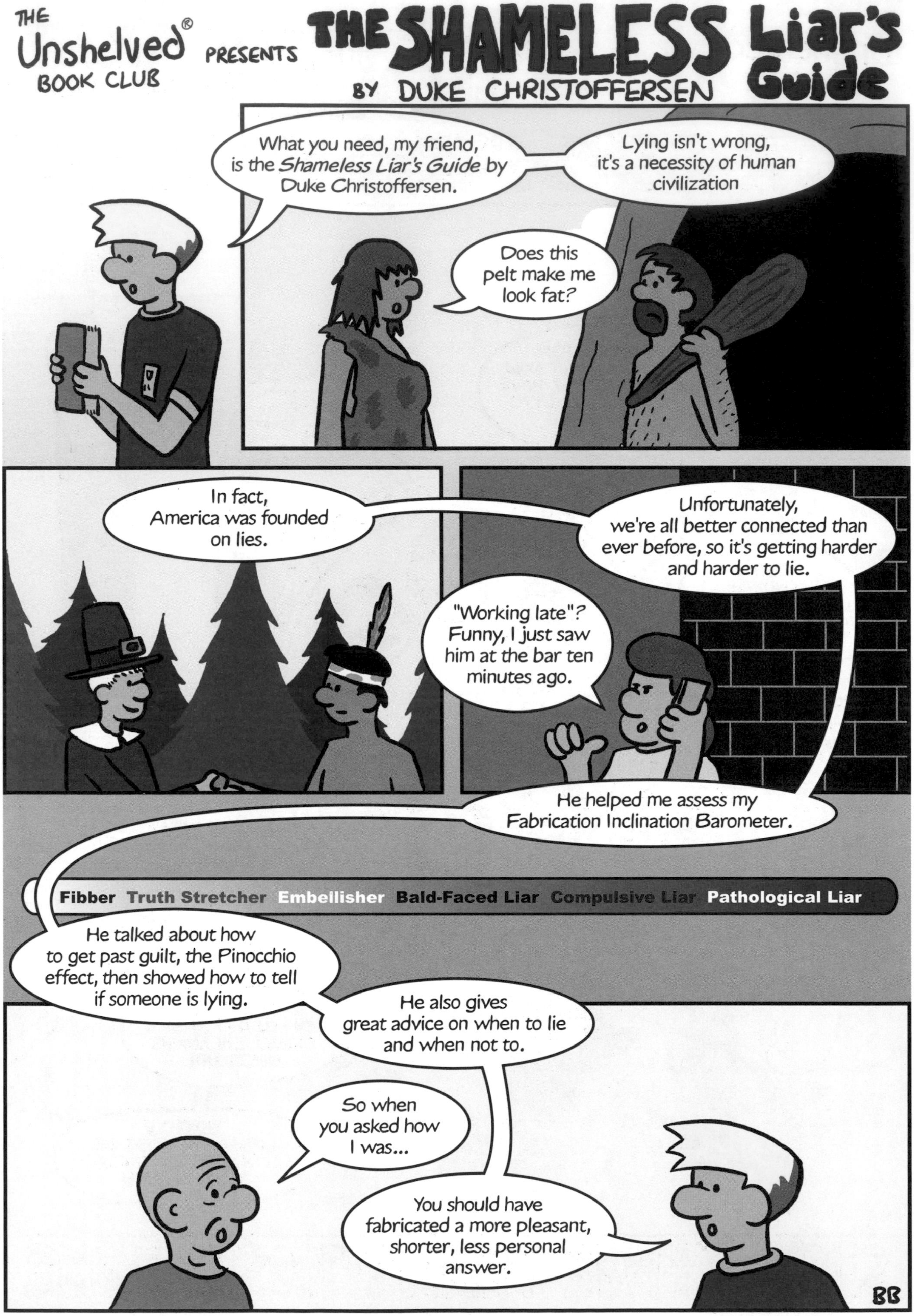
THE Unshelved® BOOK CLUB PRESENTS
THE SHAMELESS Liar's Guide
BY DUKE CHRISTOFFERSEN
What you need, my friend, is the *Shameless Liar's Guide* by Duke Christoffersen.
Lying isn't wrong, it's a necessity of human civilization
Does this pelt make me look fat?
In fact, America was founded on lies.
Unfortunately, we're all better connected than ever before, so it's getting harder and harder to lie.
"Working late"? Funny, I just saw him at the bar ten minutes ago.
He helped me assess my Fabrication Inclination Barometer.
Fibber Truth Stretcher Embellisher Bald-Faced Liar Compulsive Liar Pathological Liar
He talked about how to get past guilt, the Pinocchio effect, then showed how to tell if someone is lying.
He also gives great advice on when to lie and when not to.
So when you asked how I was...
You should have fabricated a more pleasant, shorter, less personal answer.
BB

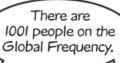

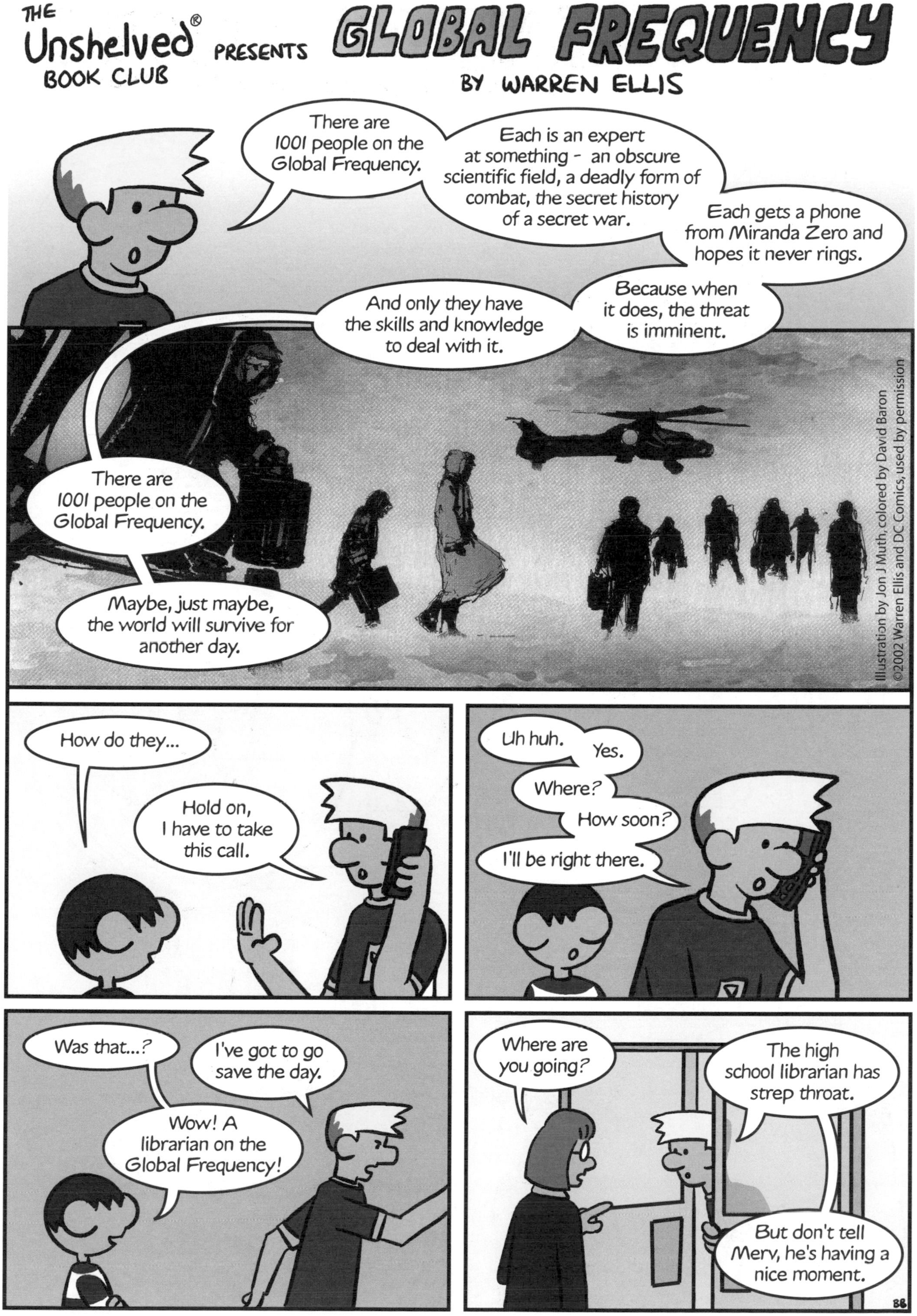

THE Unshelved® BOOK CLUB PRESENTS
GLOBAL FREQUENCY
BY WARREN ELLIS
There are 1001 people on the Global Frequency.
Each is an expert at something - an obscure scientific field, a deadly form of combat, the secret history of a secret war.
Each gets a phone from Miranda Zero and hopes it never rings.
Because when it does, the threat is imminent.
And only they have the skills and knowledge to deal with it.
There are 1001 people on the Global Frequency.
Maybe, just maybe, the world will survive for another day.
Illustration by Jon J Muth, colored by David Baron
©2002 Warren Ellis and DC Comics, used by permission
How do they...
Hold on, I have to take this call.
Uh huh.
Yes.
Where?
How soon?
I'll be right there.
Was that...?
I've got to go save the day.
Wow! A librarian on the Global Frequency!
Where are you going?
The high school librarian has strep throat.
But don't tell Merv, he's having a nice moment.

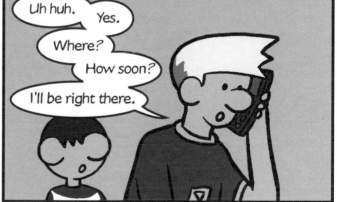

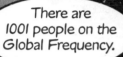

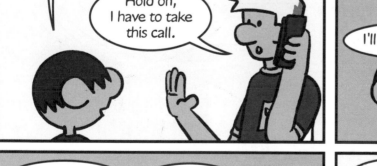

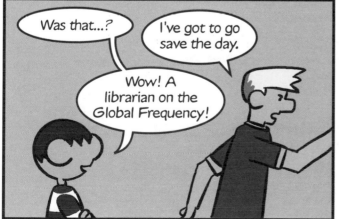

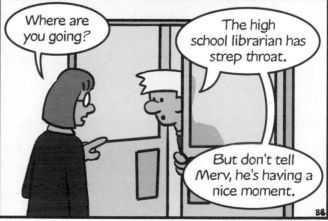

THE Unshelved® BOOK CLUB PRESENTS

TOILETS OF THE WORLD

BY MORNA E GREGORY & SIAN JAMES

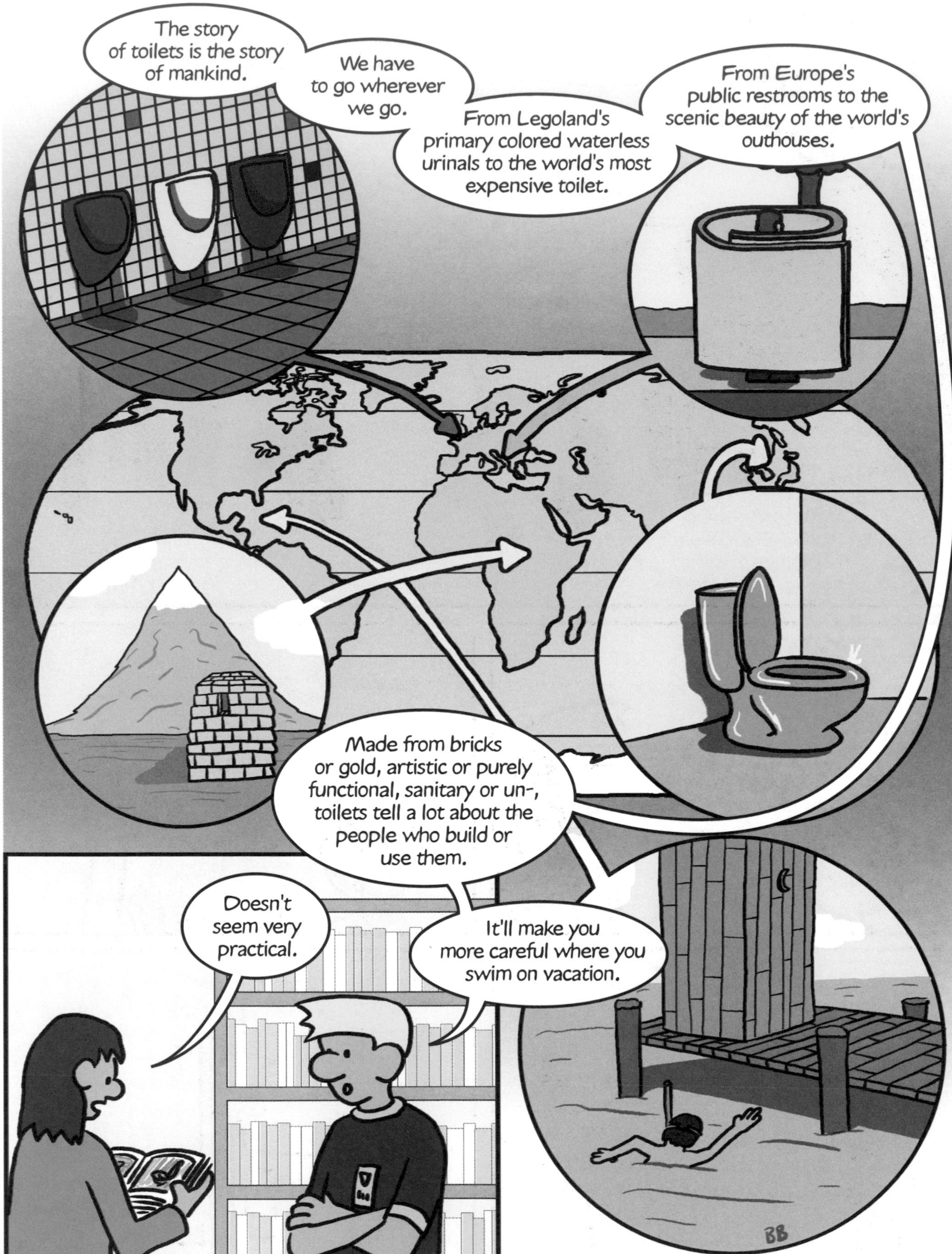

The story of toilets is the story of mankind.
We have to go wherever we go.
From Legoland's primary colored waterless urinals to the world's most expensive toilet.
From Europe's public restrooms to the scenic beauty of the world's outhouses.
Made from bricks or gold, artistic or purely functional, sanitary or un-, toilets tell a lot about the people who build or use them.
Doesn't seem very practical.
It'll make you more careful where you swim on vacation.
BB

THE Unshelved® BOOK CLUB PRESENTS

BRINGING DOWN THE HOUSE

BY BEN MEZRICH

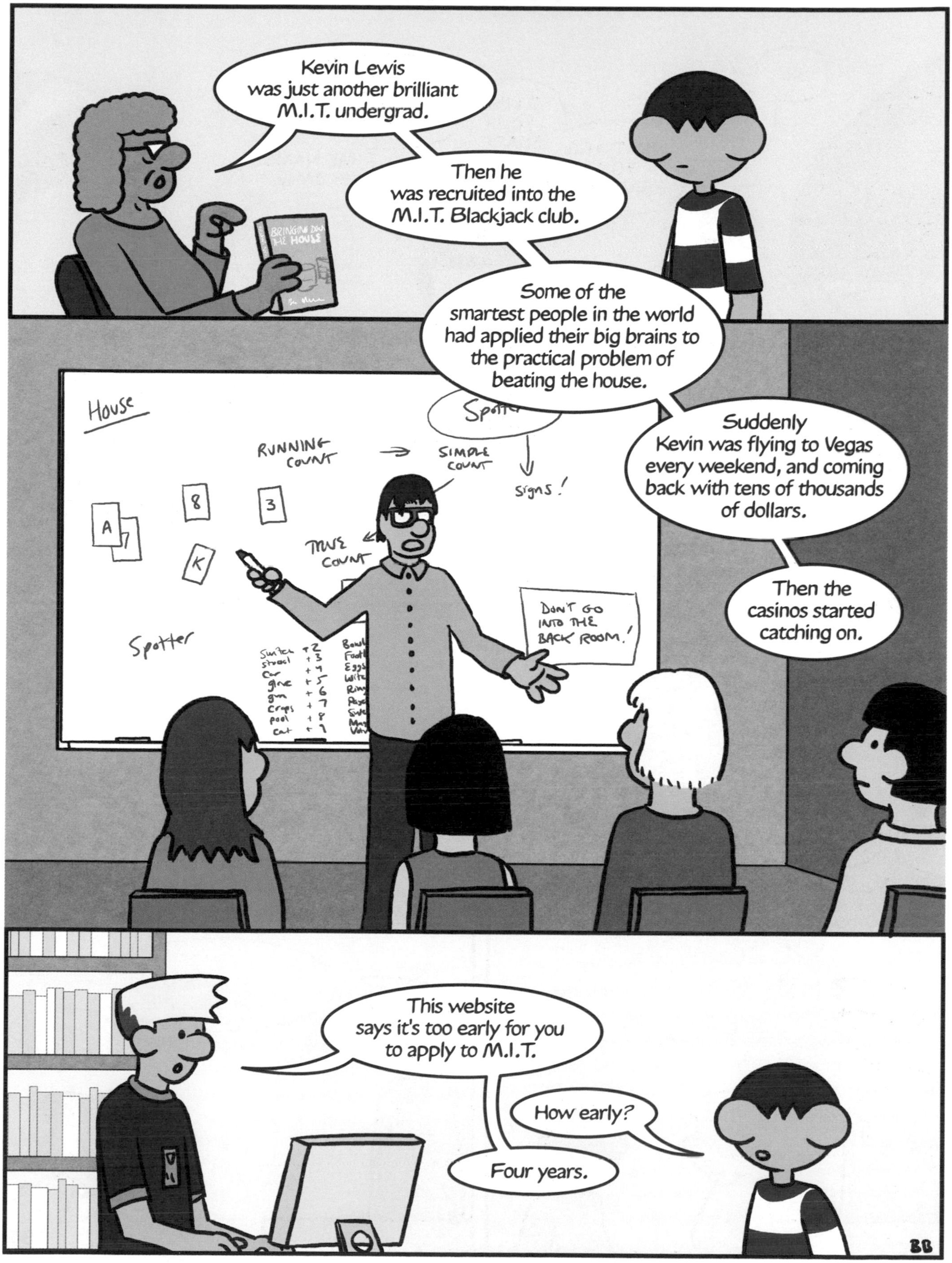

Kevin Lewis was just another brilliant M.I.T. undergrad.
Then he was recruited into the M.I.T. Blackjack club.
Some of the smartest people in the world had applied their big brains to the practical problem of beating the house.
Suddenly Kevin was flying to Vegas every weekend, and coming back with tens of thousands of dollars.
Then the casinos started catching on.
House
RUNNING COUNT
SIMPLE COUNT
Signs!
TRUE COUNT
Spotter
DON'T GO INTO THE BACK ROOM!
This website says it's too early for you to apply to M.I.T.
How early?
Four years.

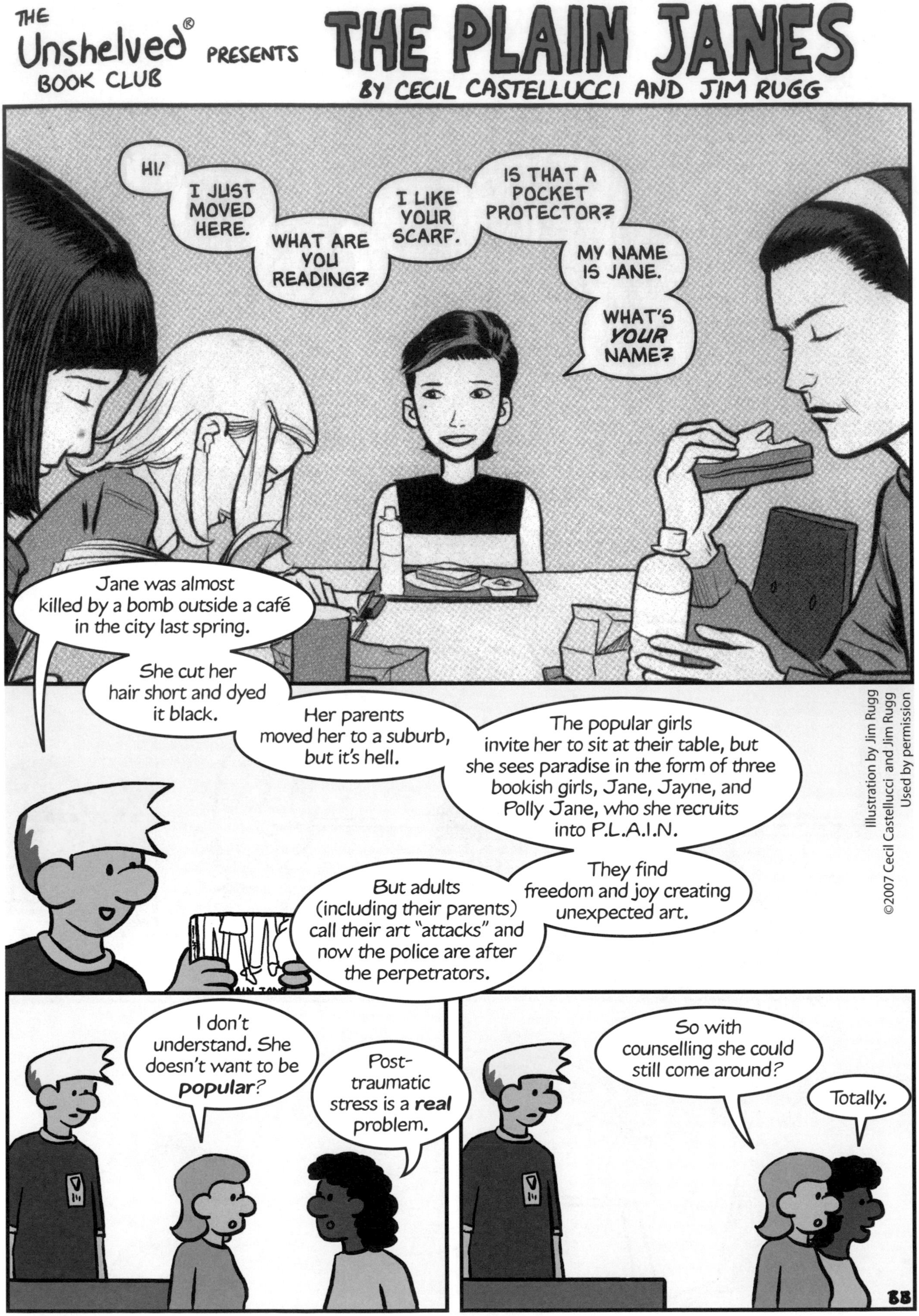

THE Unshelved® BOOK CLUB PRESENTS
THE PLAIN JANES
BY CECIL CASTELLUCCI AND JIM RUGG
HI!
I JUST MOVED HERE.
WHAT ARE YOU READING?
I LIKE YOUR SCARF.
IS THAT A POCKET PROTECTOR?
MY NAME IS JANE.
WHAT'S YOUR NAME?
Jane was almost killed by a bomb outside a café in the city last spring.
She cut her hair short and dyed it black.
Her parents moved her to a suburb, but it's hell.
The popular girls invite her to sit at their table, but she sees paradise in the form of three bookish girls, Jane, Jayne, and Polly Jane, who she recruits into P.L.A.I.N.
They find freedom and joy creating unexpected art.
But adults (including their parents) call their art "attacks" and now the police are after the perpetrators.
Illustration by Jim Rugg
©2007 Cecil Castellucci and Jim Rugg
Used by permission
I don't understand. She doesn't want to be popular?
Post-traumatic stress is a real problem.
So with counselling she could still come around?
Totally.
BB

THE Unshelved® BOOK CLUB PRESENTS

THE POP-UP BOOK

STEP-BY STEP INSTRUCTIONS FOR CREATING OVER 100 ORIGINAL PAPER PROJECTS

BY PAUL JACKSON

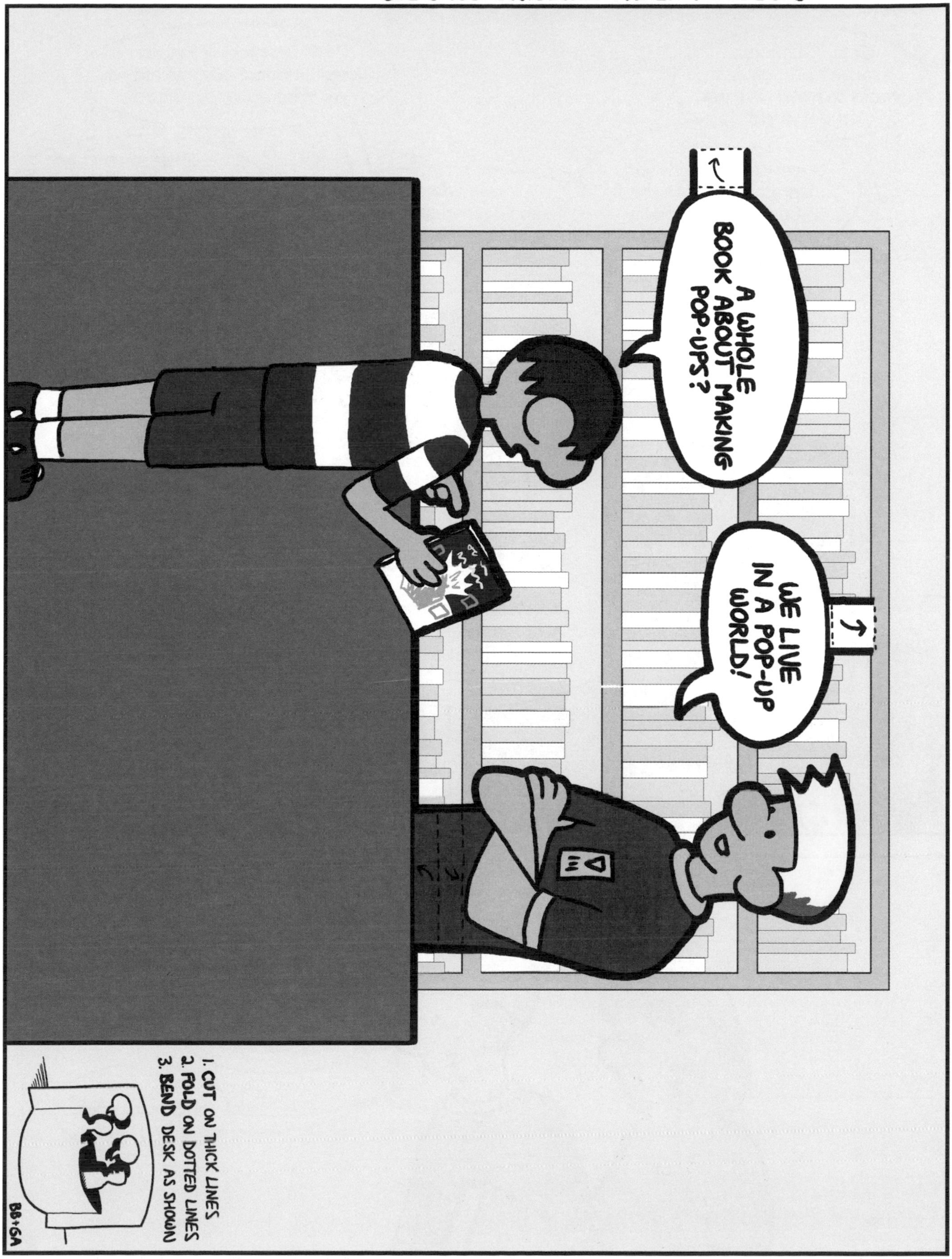

A WHOLE BOOK ABOUT MAKING POP-UPS?
WE LIVE IN A POP-UP WORLD!
1. CUT ON THICK LINES
2. FOLD ON DOTTED LINES
3. BEND DESK AS SHOWN
BB+GA

THE Unshelved® BOOK CLUB PRESENTS

An Abundance of Katherines

BY JOHN GREEN

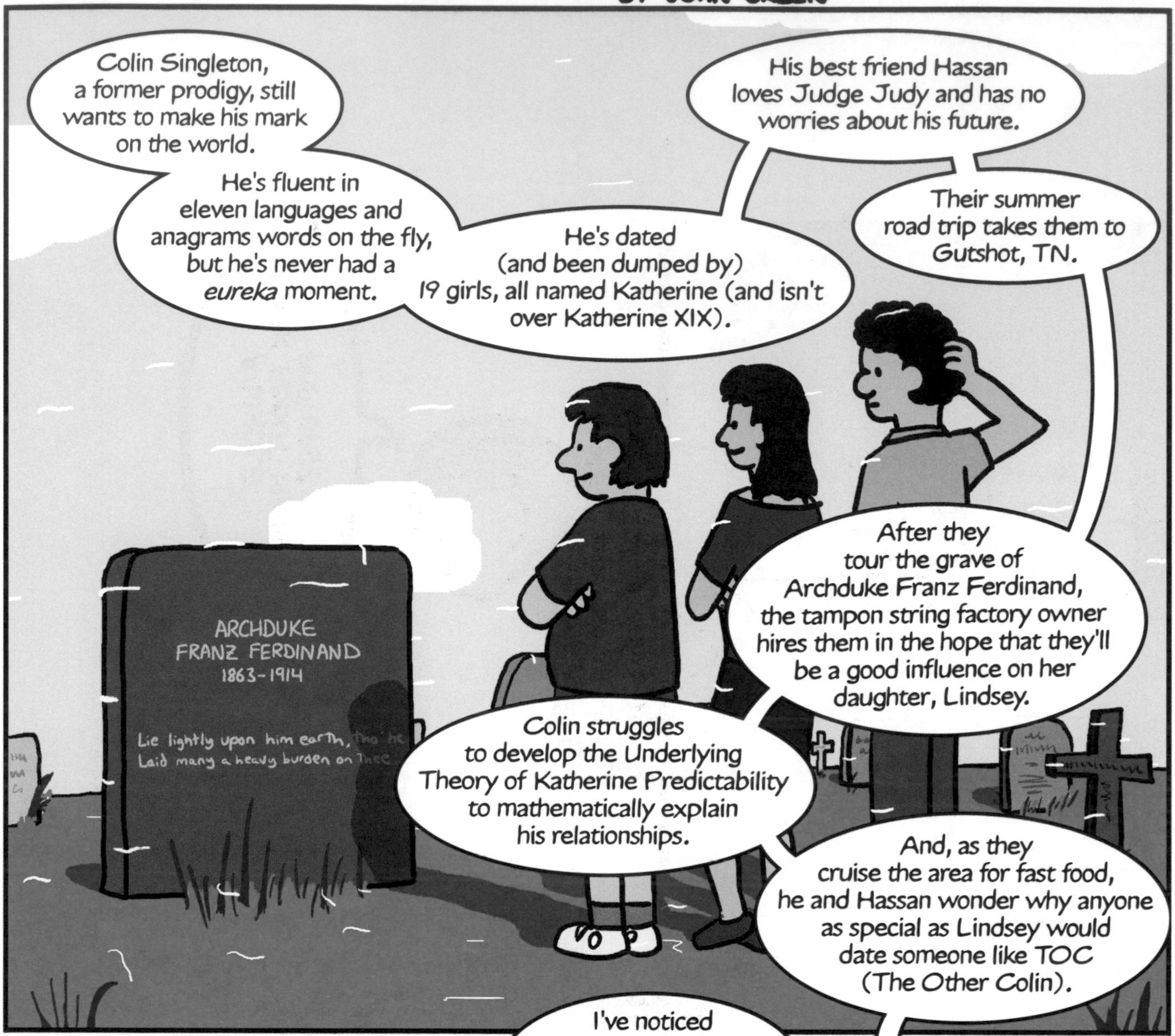
Colin Singleton, a former prodigy, still wants to make his mark on the world.
He's fluent in eleven languages and anagrams words on the fly, but he's never had a *eureka* moment.
He's dated (and been dumped by) 19 girls, all named Katherine (and isn't over Katherine XIX).
His best friend Hassan loves Judge Judy and has no worries about his future.
Their summer road trip takes them to Gutshot, TN.
ARCHDUKE FRANZ FERDINAND 1863-1914
Lie lightly upon him earth, tho' he Laid many a heavy burden on thee
After they tour the grave of Archduke Franz Ferdinand, the tampon string factory owner hires them in the hope that they'll be a good influence on her daughter, Lindsey.
Colin struggles to develop the Underlying Theory of Katherine Predictability to mathematically explain his relationships.
And, as they cruise the area for fast food, he and Hassan wonder why anyone as special as Lindsey would date someone like TOC (The Other Colin).

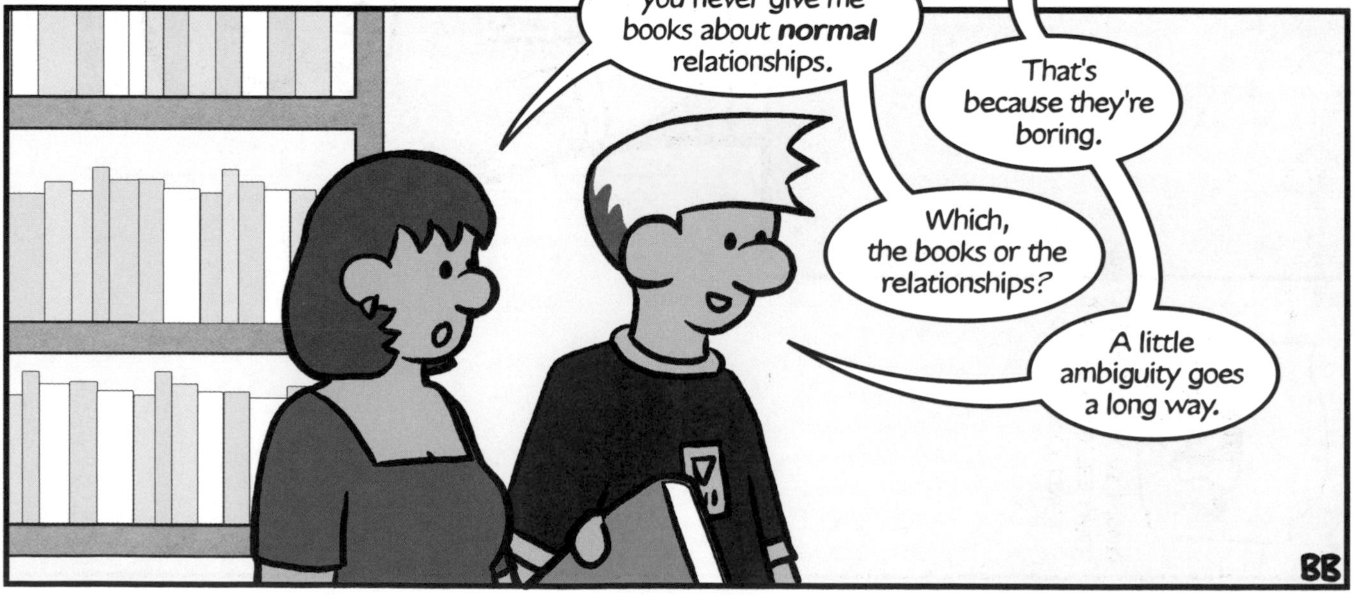
I've noticed you never give me books about **normal** relationships.
That's because they're boring.
Which, the books or the relationships?
A little ambiguity goes a long way.
BB

THE Unshelved® BOOK CLUB PRESENTS

MONKEY PORTRAITS

BY JILL GREENBERG

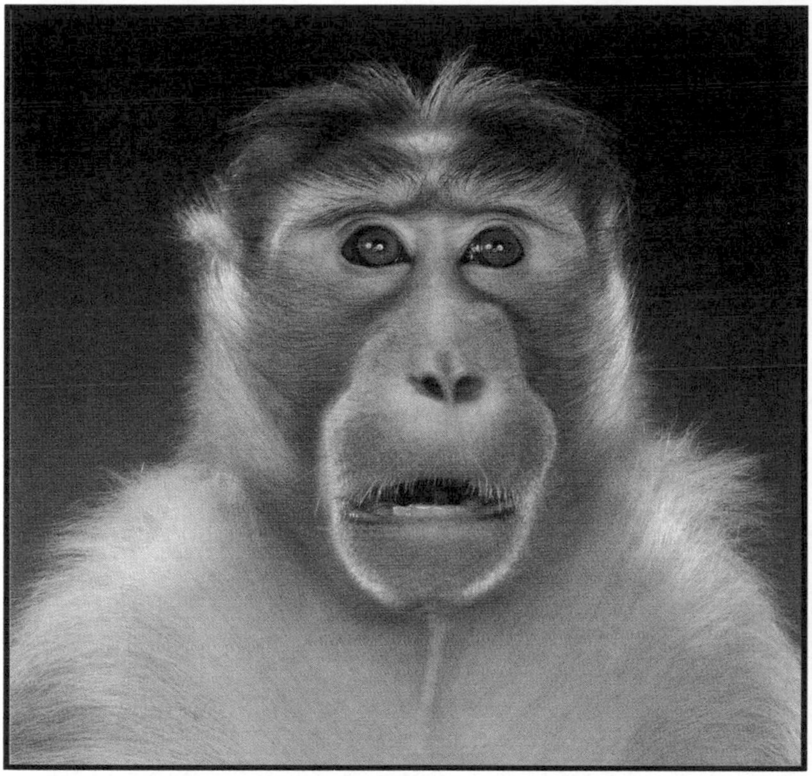

ABU, GOLDEN RHESUS MACAQUE

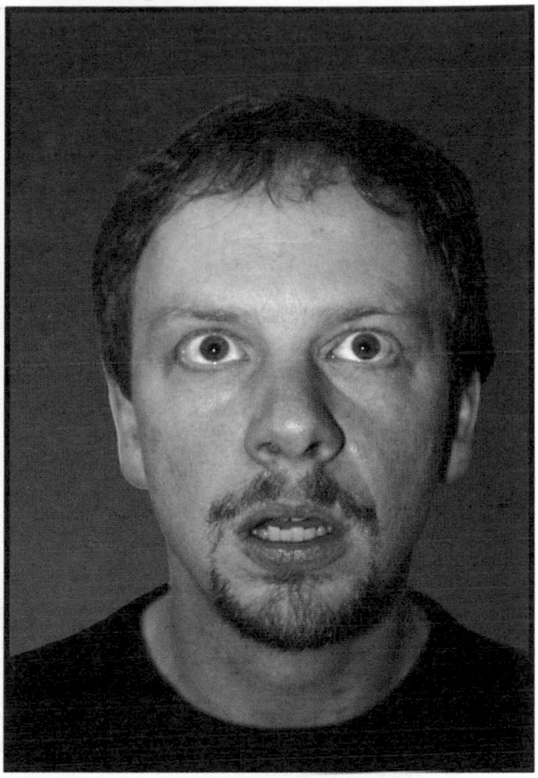

BILL, CARTOONIST

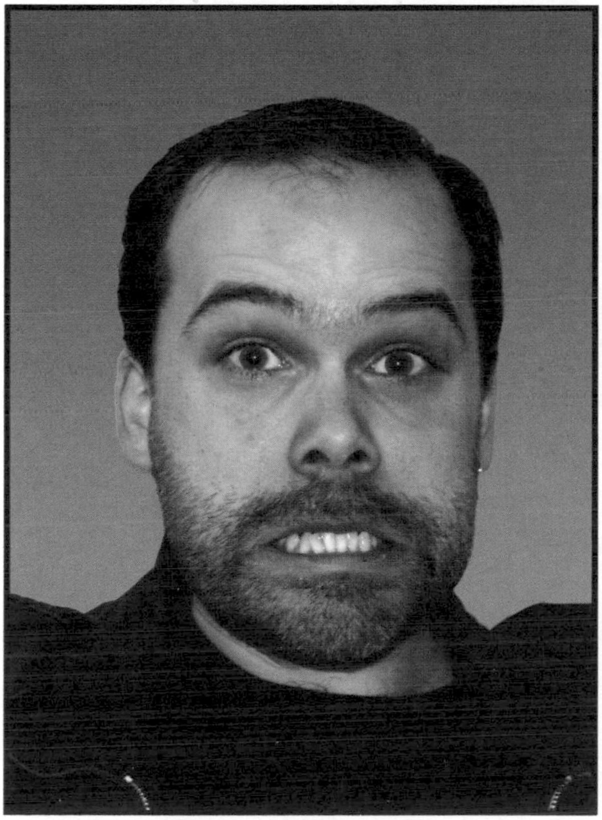

GENE, LIBRARIAN

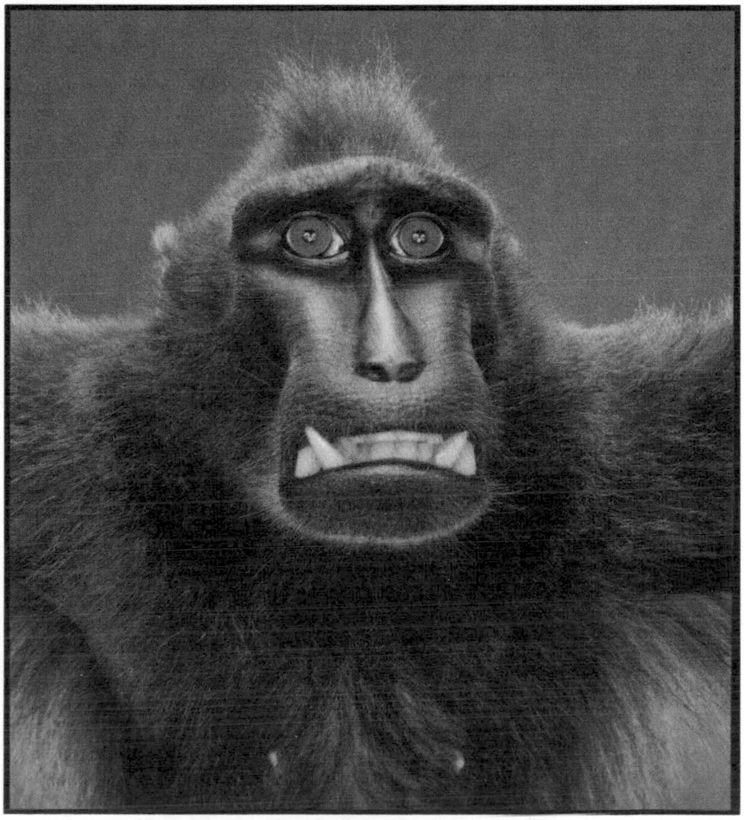

JOSH, CELEBESE MACAQUE

The Unshelved® Book Club presents In the Company of Ogres by A. Lee Martinez

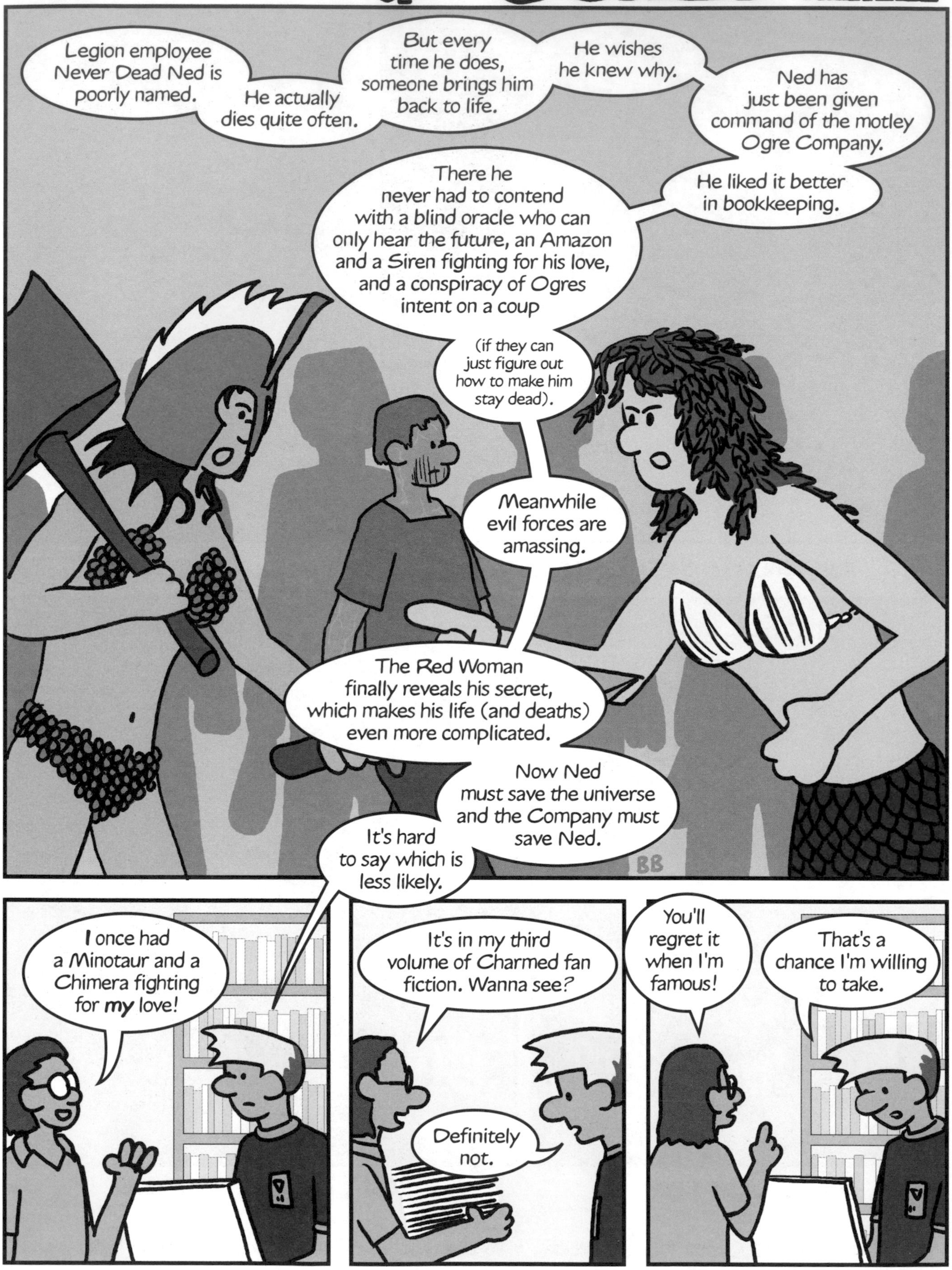

Legion employee Never Dead Ned is poorly named.
He actually dies quite often.
But every time he does, someone brings him back to life.
He wishes he knew why.
Ned has just been given command of the motley Ogre Company.
He liked it better in bookkeeping.
There he never had to contend with a blind oracle who can only hear the future, an Amazon and a Siren fighting for his love, and a conspiracy of Ogres intent on a coup
(if they can just figure out how to make him stay dead).
Meanwhile evil forces are amassing.
The Red Woman finally reveals his secret, which makes his life (and deaths) even more complicated.
Now Ned must save the universe and the Company must save Ned.
It's hard to say which is less likely.
BB
I once had a Minotaur and a Chimera fighting for my love!
It's in my third volume of Charmed fan fiction. Wanna see?
Definitely not.
You'll regret it when I'm famous!
That's a chance I'm willing to take.

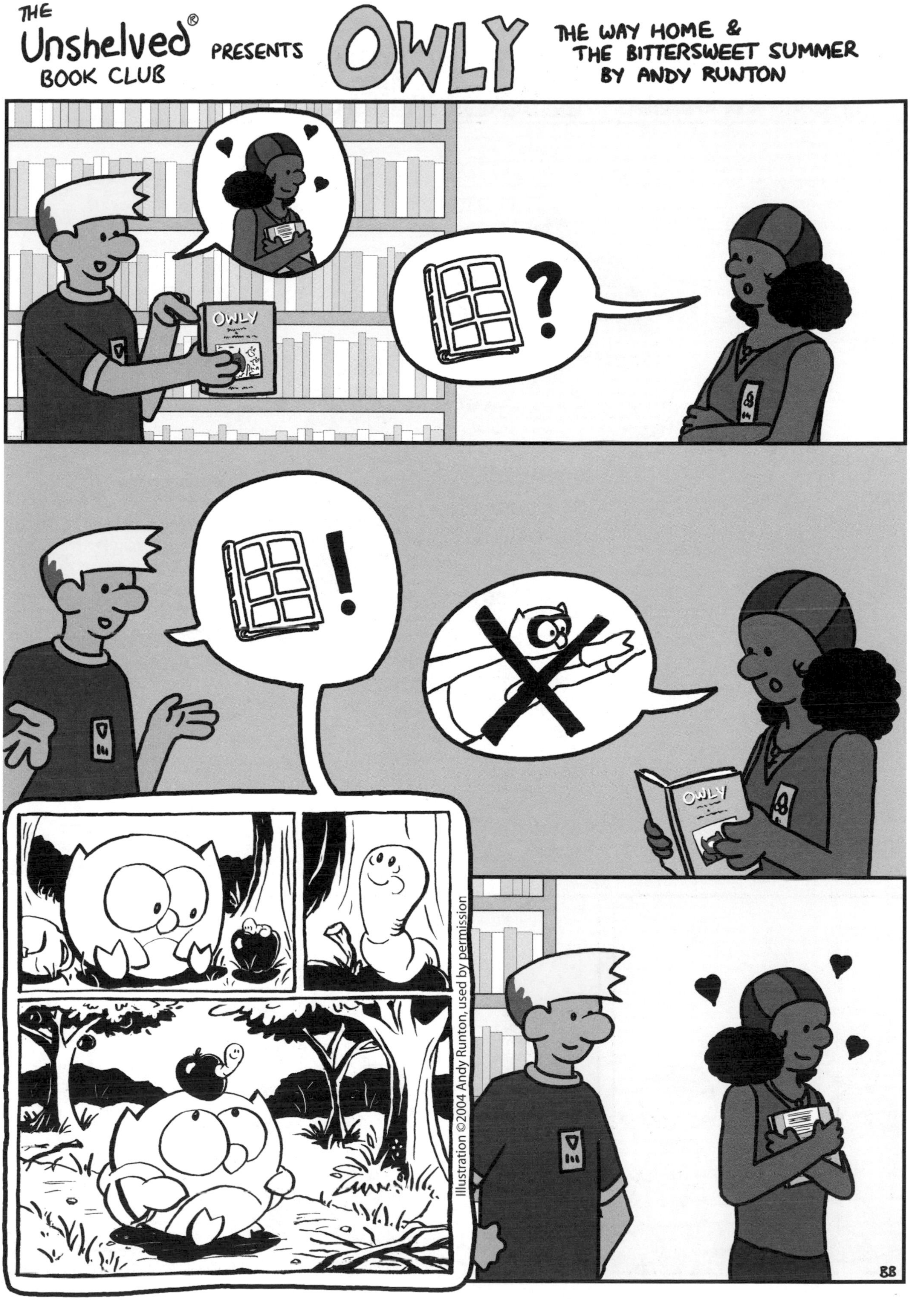
THE Unshelved® BOOK CLUB PRESENTS OWLY
THE WAY HOME & THE BITTERSWEET SUMMER BY ANDY RUNTON
?
!
Illustration ©2004 Andy Runton, used by permission
BB

MORTAL ENGINES BY PHILIP REEVE

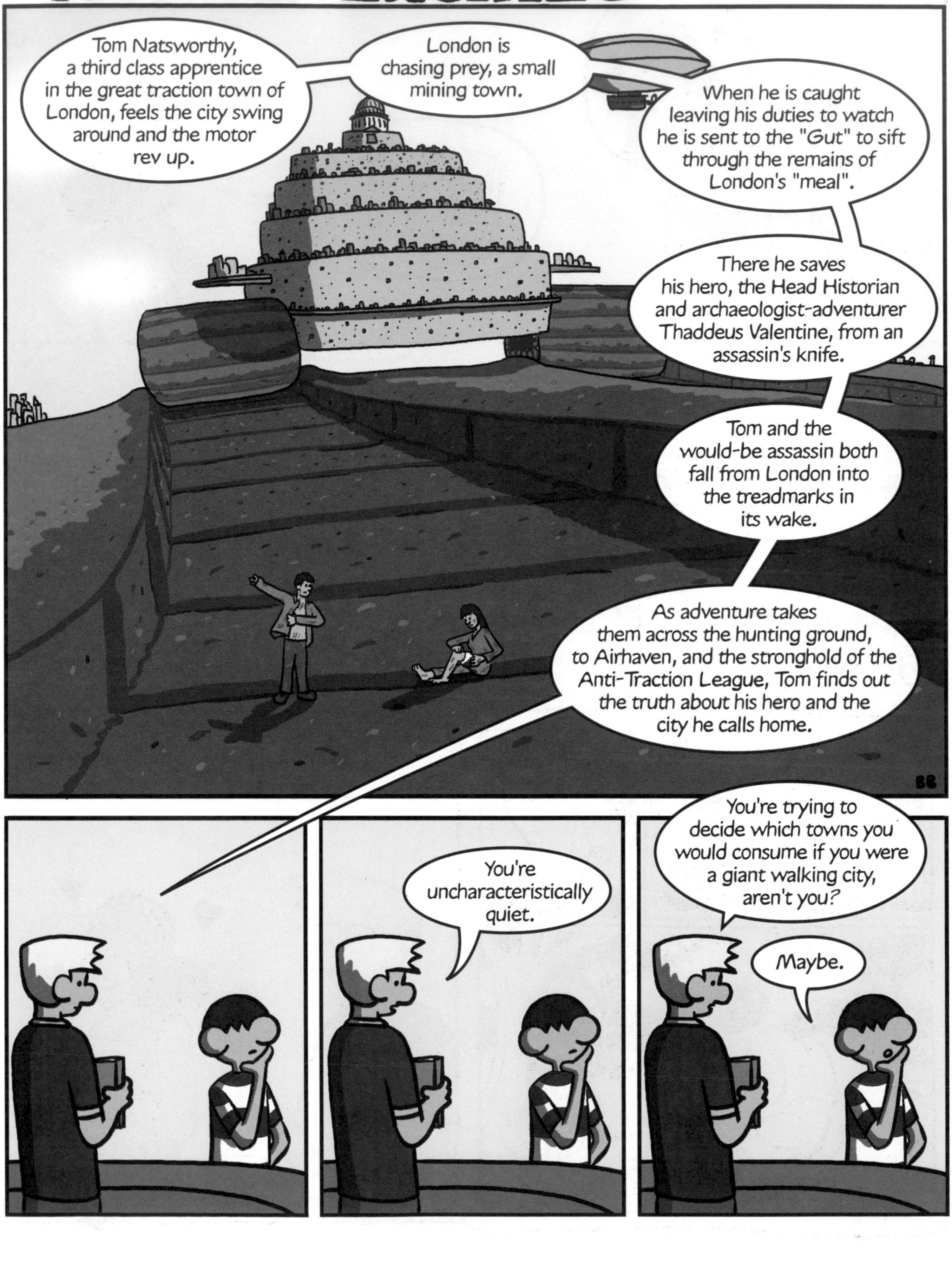
Tom Natsworthy, a third class apprentice in the great traction town of London, feels the city swing around and the motor rev up.
London is chasing prey, a small mining town.
When he is caught leaving his duties to watch he is sent to the "Gut" to sift through the remains of London's "meal".
There he saves his hero, the Head Historian and archaeologist-adventurer Thaddeus Valentine, from an assassin's knife.
Tom and the would-be assassin both fall from London into the treadmarks in its wake.
As adventure takes them across the hunting ground, to Airhaven, and the stronghold of the Anti-Traction League, Tom finds out the truth about his hero and the city he calls home.
BB
You're uncharacteristically quiet.
You're trying to decide which towns you would consume if you were a giant walking city, aren't you?
Maybe.

SUMMER MOONSHINE BY P.G. WODEHOUSE

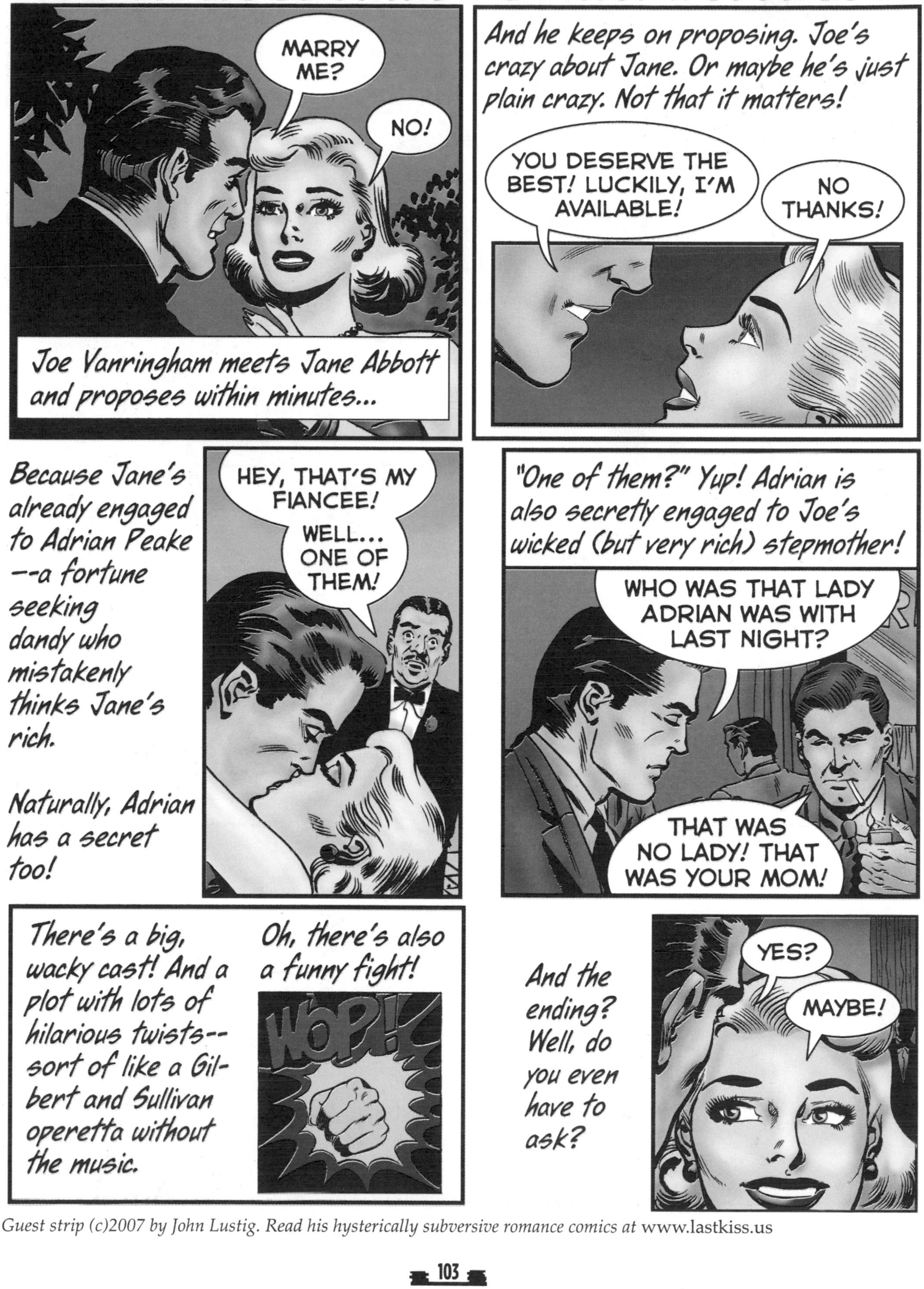
MARRY ME?
NO!
Joe Vanringham meets Jane Abbott and proposes within minutes...
And he keeps on proposing. Joe's crazy about Jane. Or maybe he's just plain crazy. Not that it matters!
YOU DESERVE THE BEST! LUCKILY, I'M AVAILABLE!
NO THANKS!
Because Jane's already engaged to Adrian Peake --a fortune seeking dandy who mistakenly thinks Jane's rich.
Naturally, Adrian has a secret too!
HEY, THAT'S MY FIANCEE!
WELL... ONE OF THEM!
"One of them?" Yup! Adrian is also secretly engaged to Joe's wicked (but very rich) stepmother!
WHO WAS THAT LADY ADRIAN WAS WITH LAST NIGHT?
THAT WAS NO LADY! THAT WAS YOUR MOM!
There's a big, wacky cast! And a plot with lots of hilarious twists--sort of like a Gil-bert and Sullivan operetta without the music.
Oh, there's also a funny fight!
WOP!!
And the ending? Well, do you even have to ask?
YES?
MAYBE!

Guest strip (c)2007 by John Lustig. Read his hysterically subversive romance comics at www.lastkiss.us

THE PICTURE OF DORIAN GRAY

BY OSCAR WILDE

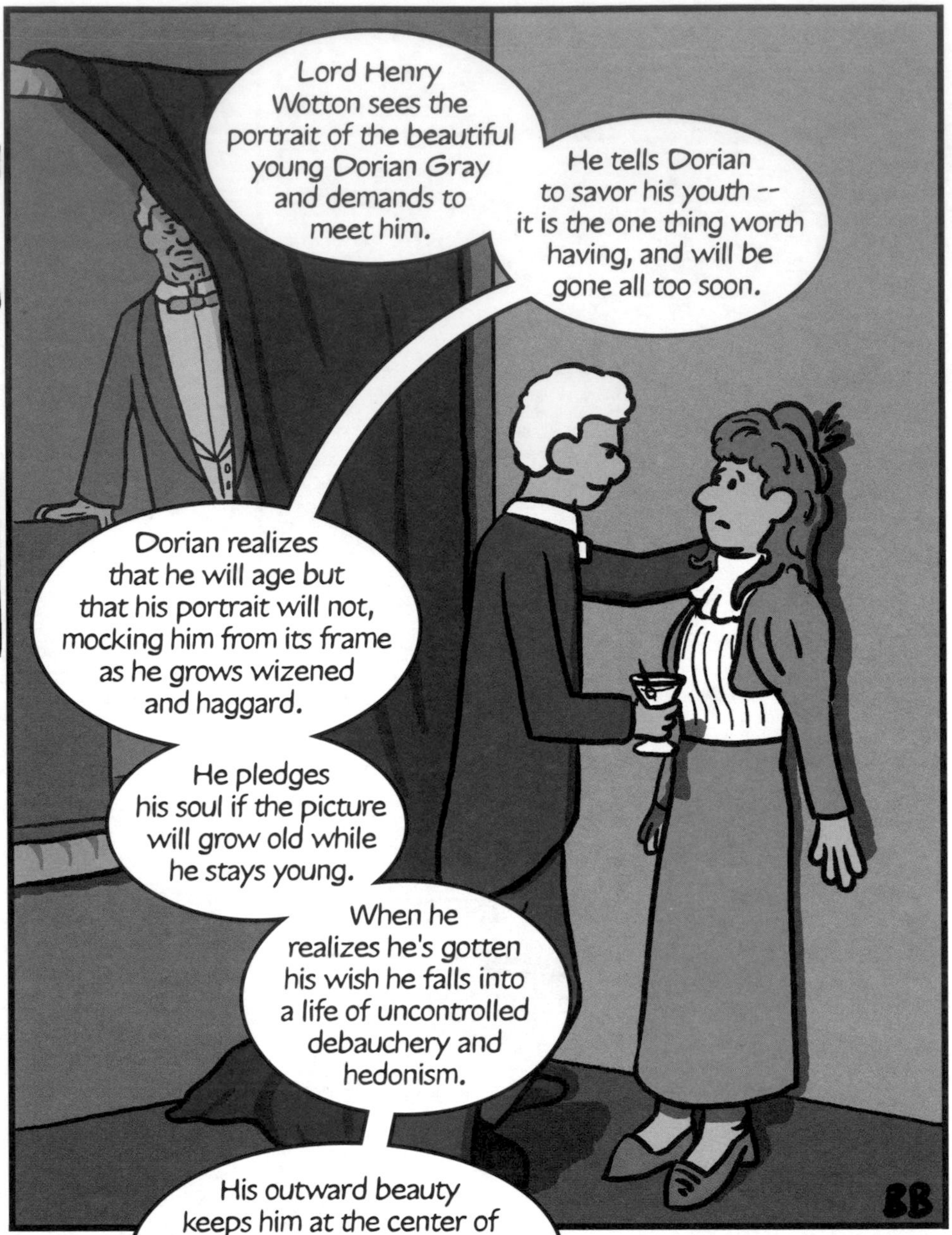
Lord Henry Wotton sees the portrait of the beautiful young Dorian Gray and demands to meet him.
He tells Dorian to savor his youth -- it is the one thing worth having, and will be gone all too soon.
Dorian realizes that he will age but that his portrait will not, mocking him from its frame as he grows wizened and haggard.
He pledges his soul if the picture will grow old while he stays young.
When he realizes he's gotten his wish he falls into a life of uncontrolled debauchery and hedonism.
His outward beauty keeps him at the center of London society despite the stories told about him and the lives he has ruined.
BB

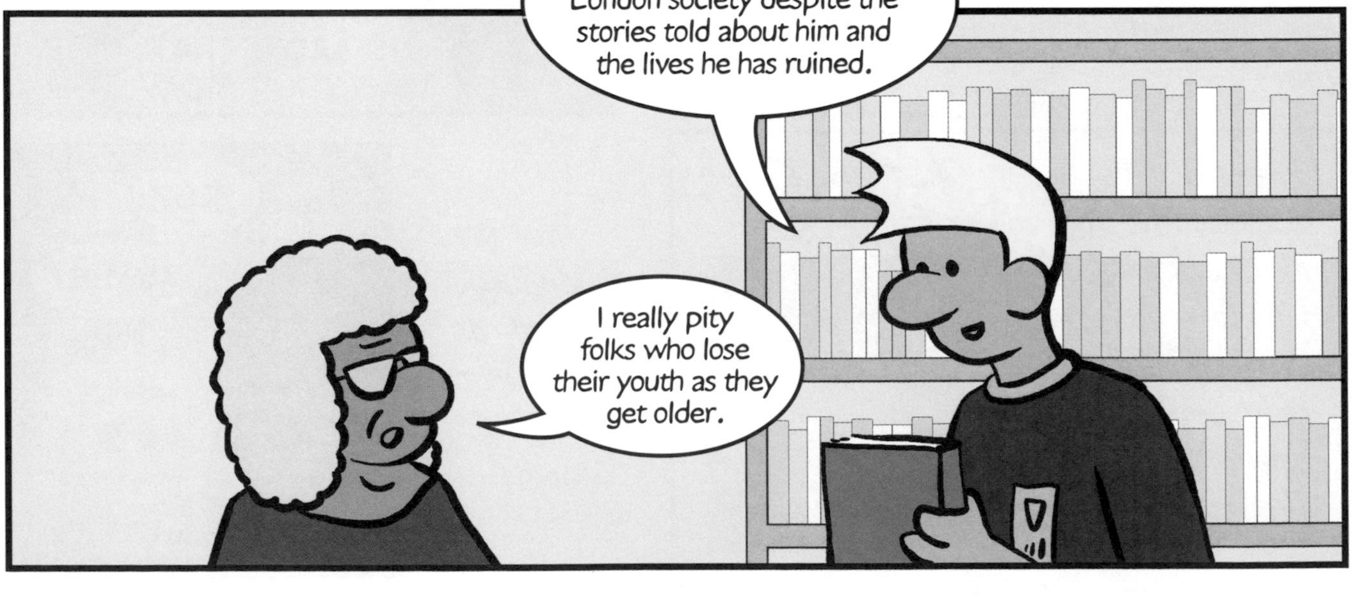
I really pity folks who lose their youth as they get older.

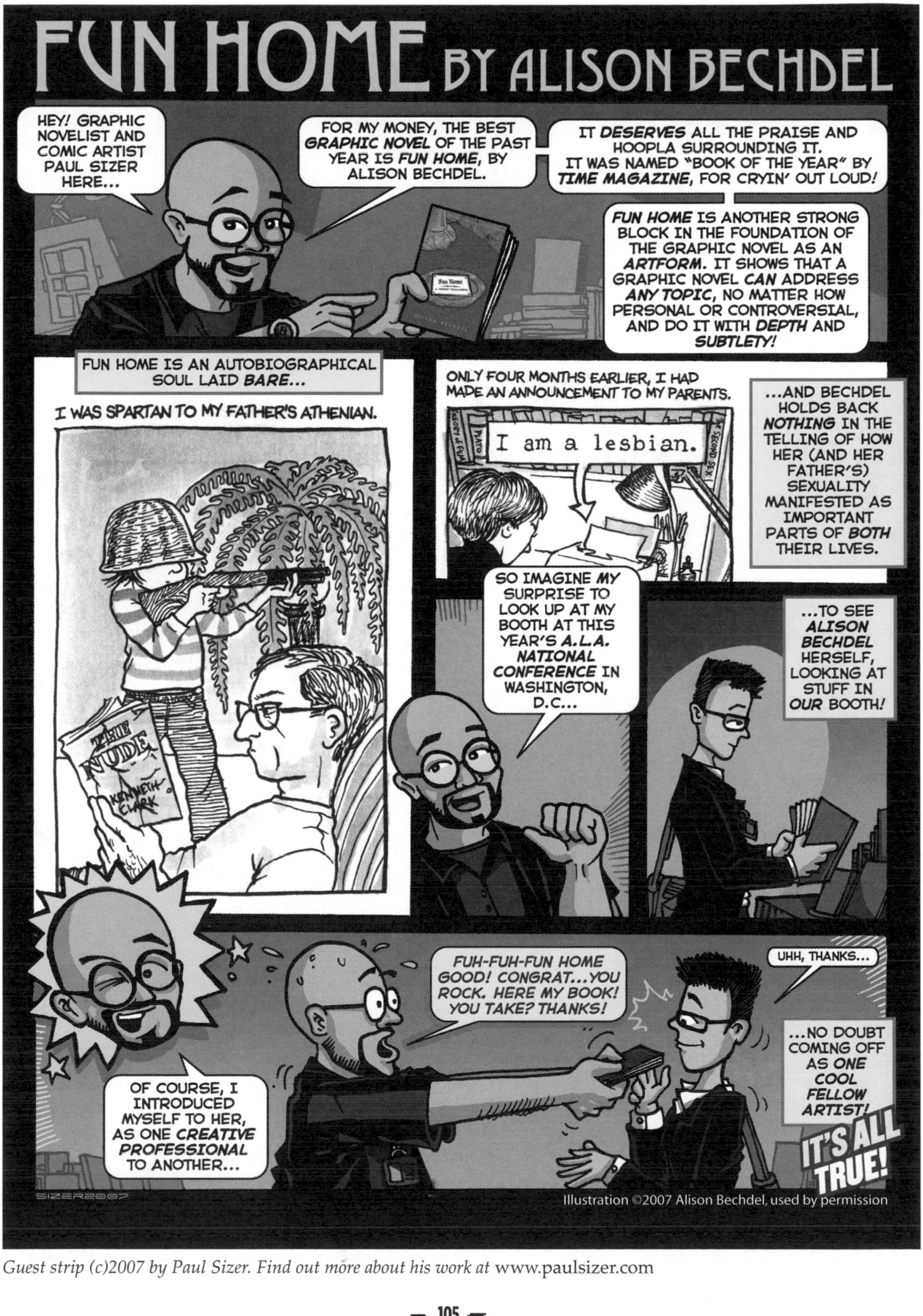
FUN HOME BY ALISON BECHDEL
HEY! GRAPHIC NOVELIST AND COMIC ARTIST PAUL SIZER HERE...
FOR MY MONEY, THE BEST GRAPHIC NOVEL OF THE PAST YEAR IS FUN HOME, BY ALISON BECHDEL.
IT DESERVES ALL THE PRAISE AND HOOPLA SURROUNDING IT. IT WAS NAMED "BOOK OF THE YEAR" BY TIME MAGAZINE, FOR CRYIN' OUT LOUD!
FUN HOME IS ANOTHER STRONG BLOCK IN THE FOUNDATION OF THE GRAPHIC NOVEL AS AN ARTFORM. IT SHOWS THAT A GRAPHIC NOVEL CAN ADDRESS ANY TOPIC, NO MATTER HOW PERSONAL OR CONTROVERSIAL, AND DO IT WITH DEPTH AND SUBTLETY!
FUN HOME IS AN AUTOBIOGRAPHICAL SOUL LAID BARE...
I WAS SPARTAN TO MY FATHER'S ATHENIAN.
THE NUDE
KENNETH CLARK
ONLY FOUR MONTHS EARLIER, I HAD MADE AN ANNOUNCEMENT TO MY PARENTS.
I am a lesbian.
...AND BECHDEL HOLDS BACK NOTHING IN THE TELLING OF HOW HER (AND HER FATHER'S) SEXUALITY MANIFESTED AS IMPORTANT PARTS OF BOTH THEIR LIVES.
SO IMAGINE MY SURPRISE TO LOOK UP AT MY BOOTH AT THIS YEAR'S A.L.A. NATIONAL CONFERENCE IN WASHINGTON, D.C...
...TO SEE ALISON BECHDEL HERSELF, LOOKING AT STUFF IN OUR BOOTH!
OF COURSE, I INTRODUCED MYSELF TO HER, AS ONE CREATIVE PROFESSIONAL TO ANOTHER...
FUH-FUH-FUN HOME GOOD! CONGRAT...YOU ROCK. HERE MY BOOK! YOU TAKE? THANKS!
UHH, THANKS...
...NO DOUBT COMING OFF AS ONE COOL FELLOW ARTIST!
IT'S ALL TRUE!
SIZER2007
Illustration ©2007 Alison Bechdel, used by permission

Guest strip (c)2007 by Paul Sizer. Find out more about his work at www.paulsizer.com

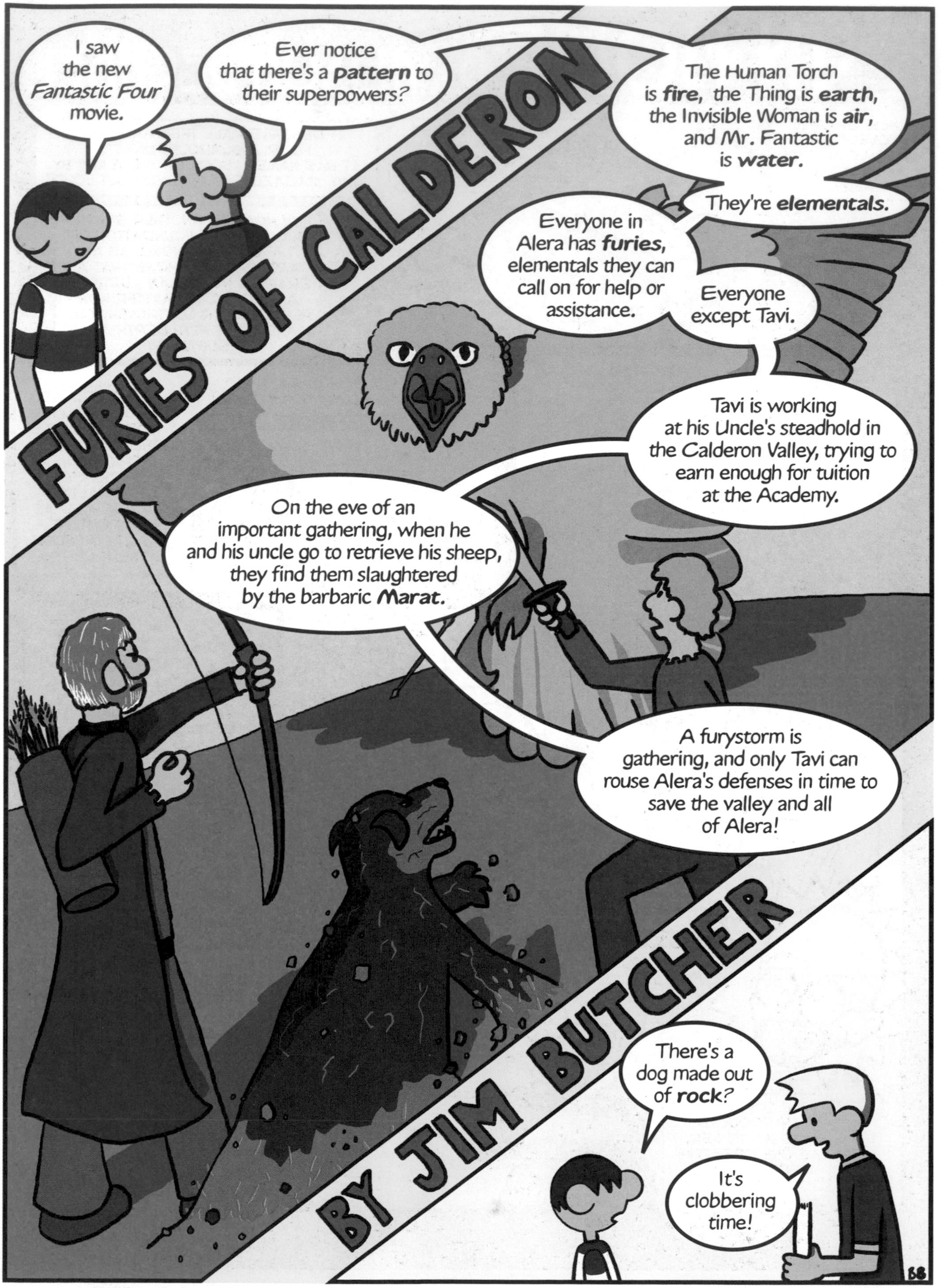

I saw the new *Fantastic Four* movie.
Ever notice that there's a **pattern** to their superpowers?
FURIES OF CALDERON
The Human Torch is **fire**, the Thing is **earth**, the Invisible Woman is **air**, and Mr. Fantastic is **water**.
They're **elementals.**
Everyone in Alera has **furies**, elementals they can call on for help or assistance.
Everyone except Tavi.
Tavi is working at his Uncle's steadhold in the Calderon Valley, trying to earn enough for tuition at the Academy.
On the eve of an important gathering, when he and his uncle go to retrieve his sheep, they find them slaughtered by the barbaric **Marat.**
A furystorm is gathering, and only Tavi can rouse Alera's defenses in time to save the valley and all of Alera!
BY JIM BUTCHER
There's a dog made out of **rock**?
It's clobbering time!
BB

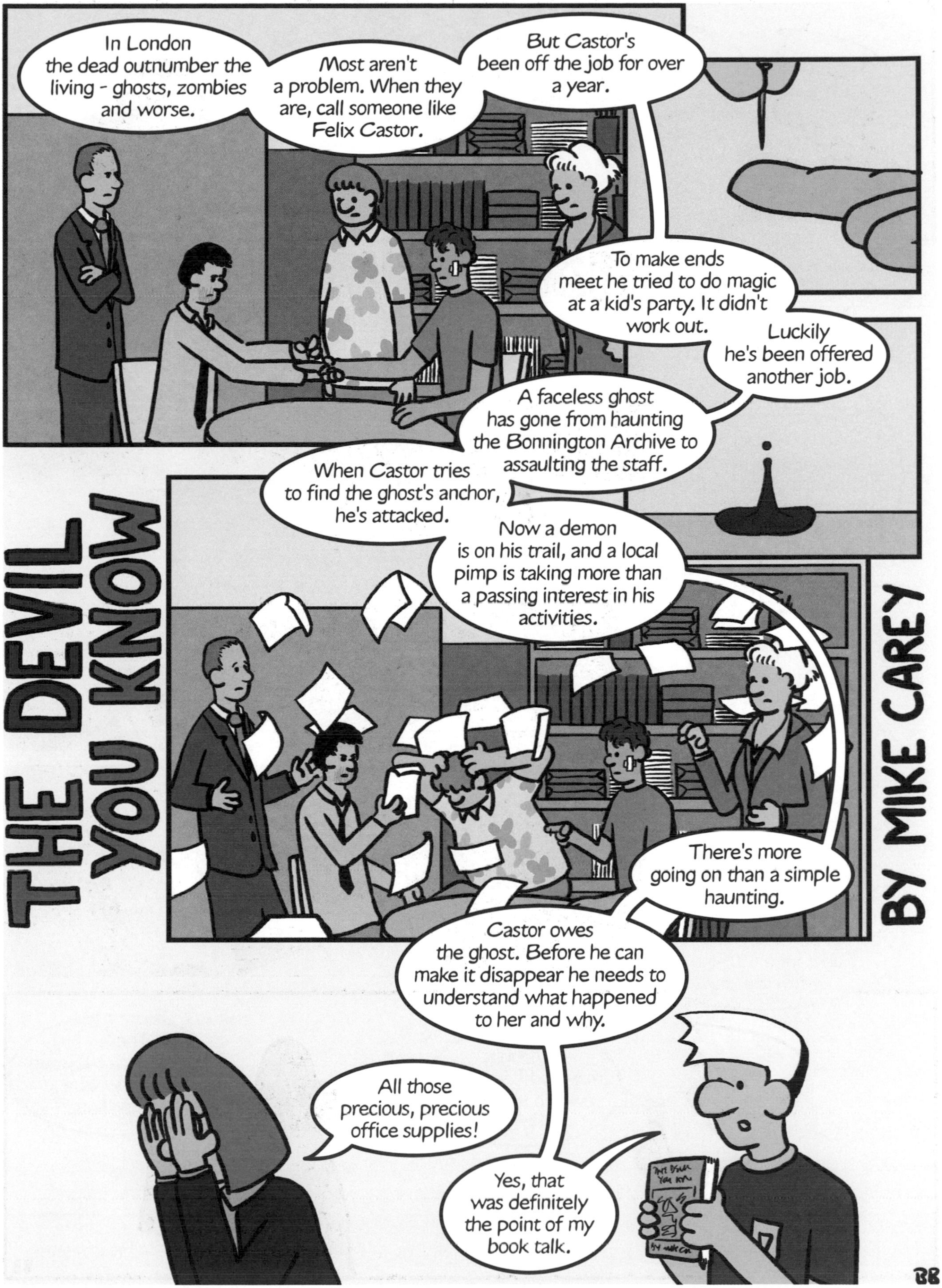
In London the dead outnumber the living - ghosts, zombies and worse.
Most aren't a problem. When they are, call someone like Felix Castor.
But Castor's been off the job for over a year.
To make ends meet he tried to do magic at a kid's party. It didn't work out.
Luckily he's been offered another job.
A faceless ghost has gone from haunting the Bonnington Archive to assaulting the staff.
When Castor tries to find the ghost's anchor, he's attacked.
Now a demon is on his trail, and a local pimp is taking more than a passing interest in his activities.
THE DEVIL YOU KNOW
BY MIKE CAREY
There's more going on than a simple haunting.
Castor owes the ghost. Before he can make it disappear he needs to understand what happened to her and why.
All those precious, precious office supplies!
Yes, that was definitely the point of my book talk.
BB

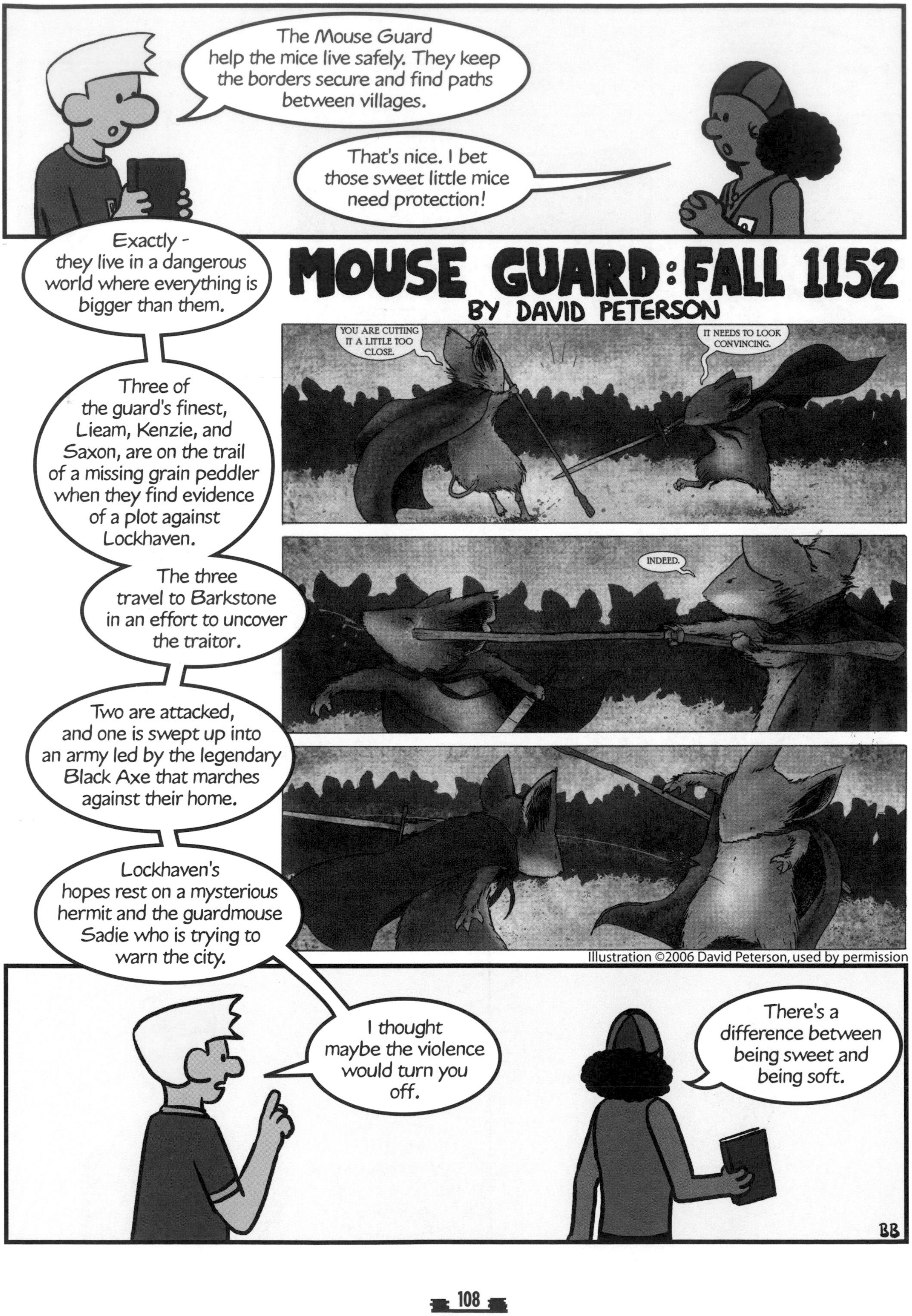
The Mouse Guard help the mice live safely. They keep the borders secure and find paths between villages.
That's nice. I bet those sweet little mice need protection!
Exactly - they live in a dangerous world where everything is bigger than them.
MOUSE GUARD: FALL 1152
BY DAVID PETERSON
YOU ARE CUTTING IT A LITTLE TOO CLOSE.
IT NEEDS TO LOOK CONVINCING.
Three of the guard's finest, Lieam, Kenzie, and Saxon, are on the trail of a missing grain peddler when they find evidence of a plot against Lockhaven.
The three travel to Barkstone in an effort to uncover the traitor.
INDEED.
Two are attacked, and one is swept up into an army led by the legendary Black Axe that marches against their home.
Lockhaven's hopes rest on a mysterious hermit and the guardmouse Sadie who is trying to warn the city.
I thought maybe the violence would turn you off.
There's a difference between being sweet and being soft.
BB
Illustration ©2006 David Peterson, used by permission

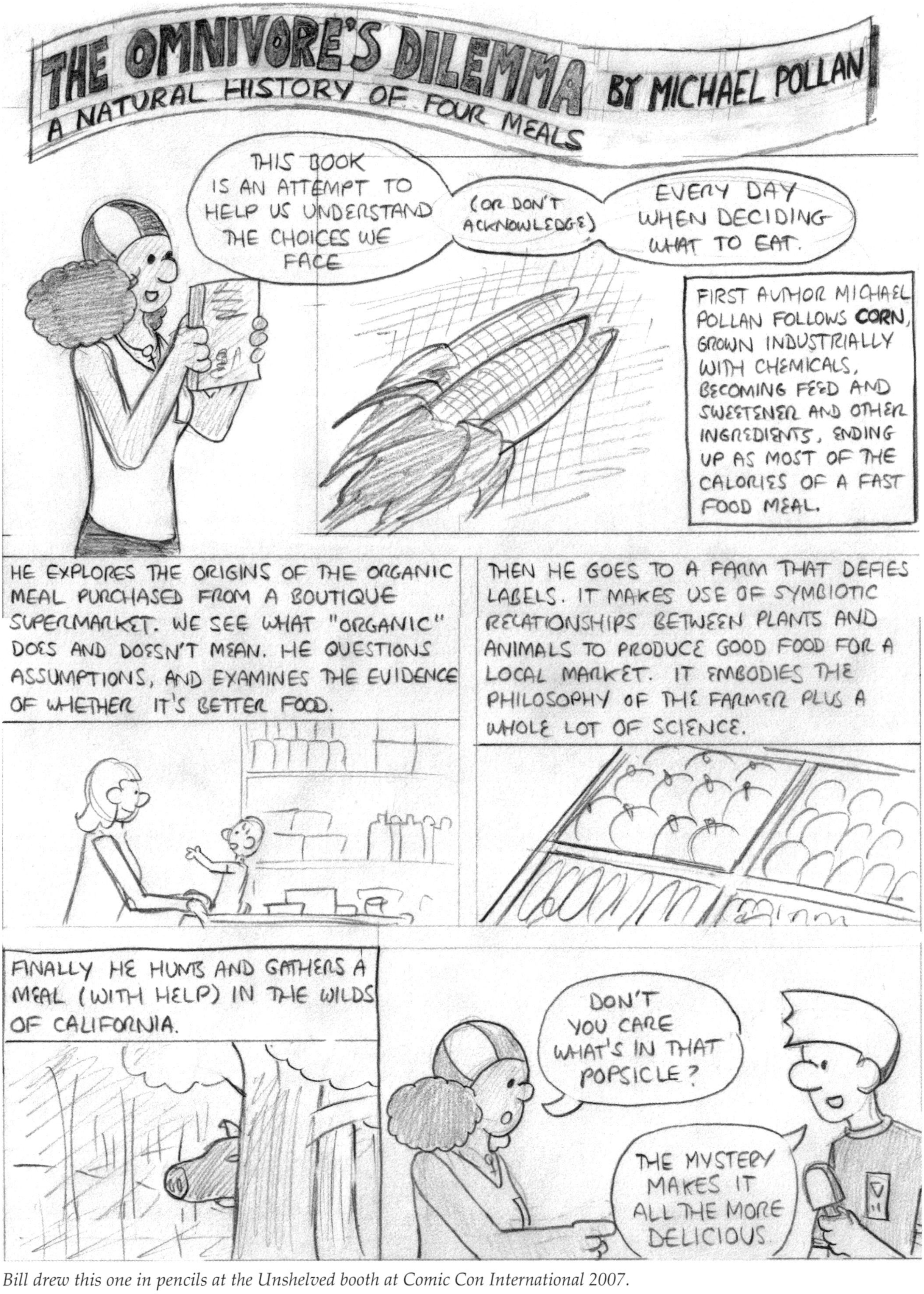
THE OMNIVORE'S DILEMMA
A NATURAL HISTORY OF FOUR MEALS
BY MICHAEL POLLAN
THIS BOOK IS AN ATTEMPT TO HELP US UNDERSTAND THE CHOICES WE FACE
(OR DON'T ACKNOWLEDGE)
EVERY DAY WHEN DECIDING WHAT TO EAT.
FIRST AUTHOR MICHAEL POLLAN FOLLOWS CORN, GROWN INDUSTRIALLY WITH CHEMICALS, BECOMING FEED AND SWEETENER AND OTHER INGREDIENTS, ENDING UP AS MOST OF THE CALORIES OF A FAST FOOD MEAL.
HE EXPLORES THE ORIGINS OF THE ORGANIC MEAL PURCHASED FROM A BOUTIQUE SUPERMARKET. WE SEE WHAT "ORGANIC" DOES AND DOESN'T MEAN. HE QUESTIONS ASSUMPTIONS, AND EXAMINES THE EVIDENCE OF WHETHER IT'S BETTER FOOD.
THEN HE GOES TO A FARM THAT DEFIES LABELS. IT MAKES USE OF SYMBIOTIC RELATIONSHIPS BETWEEN PLANTS AND ANIMALS TO PRODUCE GOOD FOOD FOR A LOCAL MARKET. IT EMBODIES THE PHILOSOPHY OF THE FARMER PLUS A WHOLE LOT OF SCIENCE.
FINALLY HE HUNTS AND GATHERS A MEAL (WITH HELP) IN THE WILDS OF CALIFORNIA.
DON'T YOU CARE WHAT'S IN THAT POPSICLE?
THE MYSTERY MAKES IT ALL THE MORE DELICIOUS.

Bill drew this one in pencils at the Unshelved booth at Comic Con International 2007.

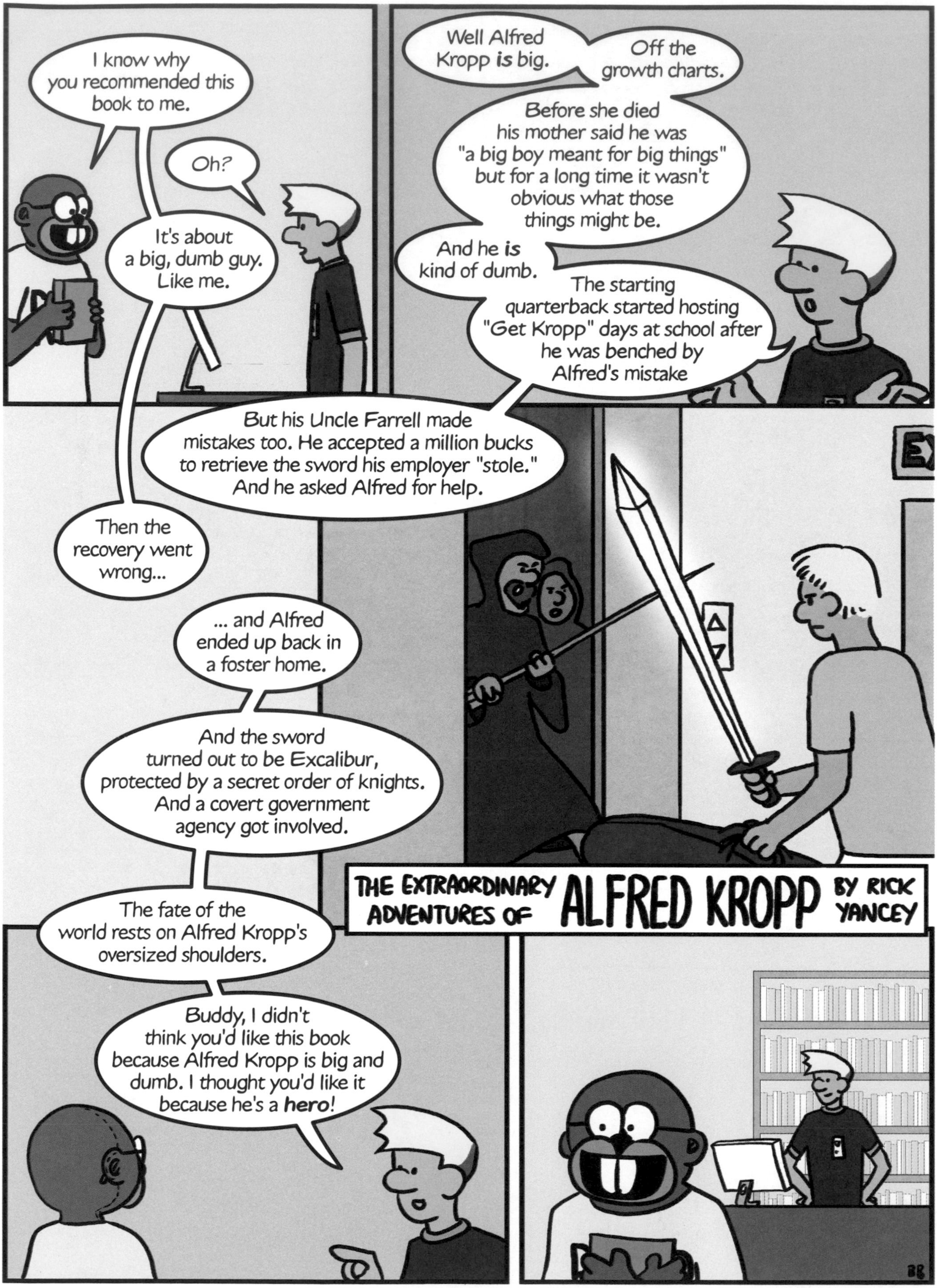
I know why you recommended this book to me.
Oh?
It's about a big, dumb guy. Like me.
Well Alfred Kropp **is** big.
Off the growth charts.
Before she died his mother said he was "a big boy meant for big things" but for a long time it wasn't obvious what those things might be.
And he **is** kind of dumb.
The starting quarterback started hosting "Get Kropp" days at school after he was benched by Alfred's mistake
But his Uncle Farrell made mistakes too. He accepted a million bucks to retrieve the sword his employer "stole." And he asked Alfred for help.
Then the recovery went wrong...
... and Alfred ended up back in a foster home.
And the sword turned out to be Excalibur, protected by a secret order of knights. And a covert government agency got involved.
THE EXTRAORDINARY ADVENTURES OF ALFRED KROPP BY RICK YANCEY
The fate of the world rests on Alfred Kropp's oversized shoulders.
Buddy, I didn't think you'd like this book because Alfred Kropp is big and dumb. I thought you'd like it because he's a ***hero***!

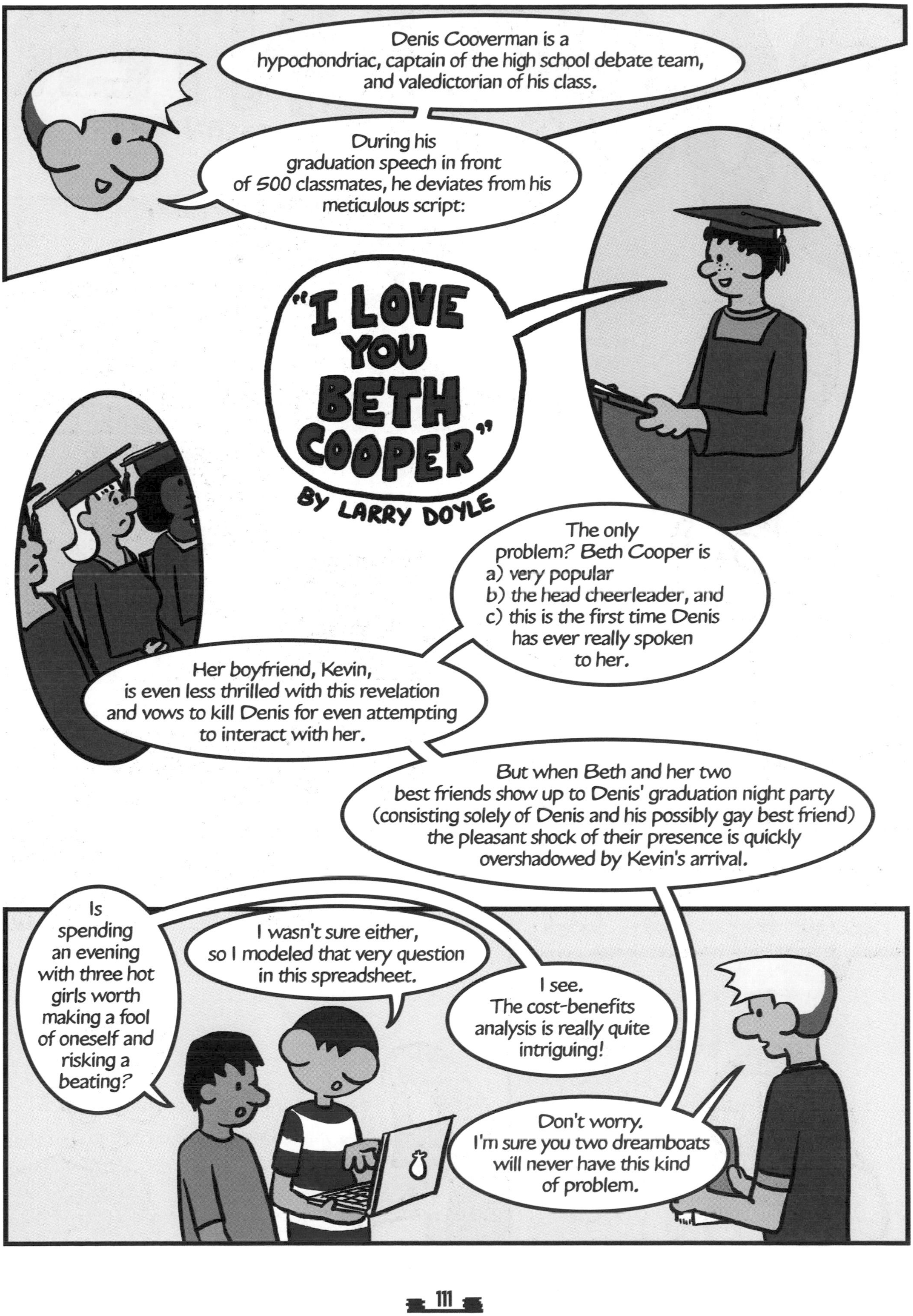
Denis Cooverman is a hypochondriac, captain of the high school debate team, and valedictorian of his class.
During his graduation speech in front of 500 classmates, he deviates from his meticulous script:
"I LOVE YOU BETH COOPER"
BY LARRY DOYLE
The only problem? Beth Cooper is a) very popular b) the head cheerleader, and c) this is the first time Denis has ever really spoken to her.
Her boyfriend, Kevin, is even less thrilled with this revelation and vows to kill Denis for even attempting to interact with her.
But when Beth and her two best friends show up to Denis' graduation night party (consisting solely of Denis and his possibly gay best friend) the pleasant shock of their presence is quickly overshadowed by Kevin's arrival.
Is spending an evening with three hot girls worth making a fool of oneself and risking a beating?
I wasn't sure either, so I modeled that very question in this spreadsheet.
I see. The cost-benefits analysis is really quite intriguing!
Don't worry. I'm sure you two dreamboats will never have this kind of problem.

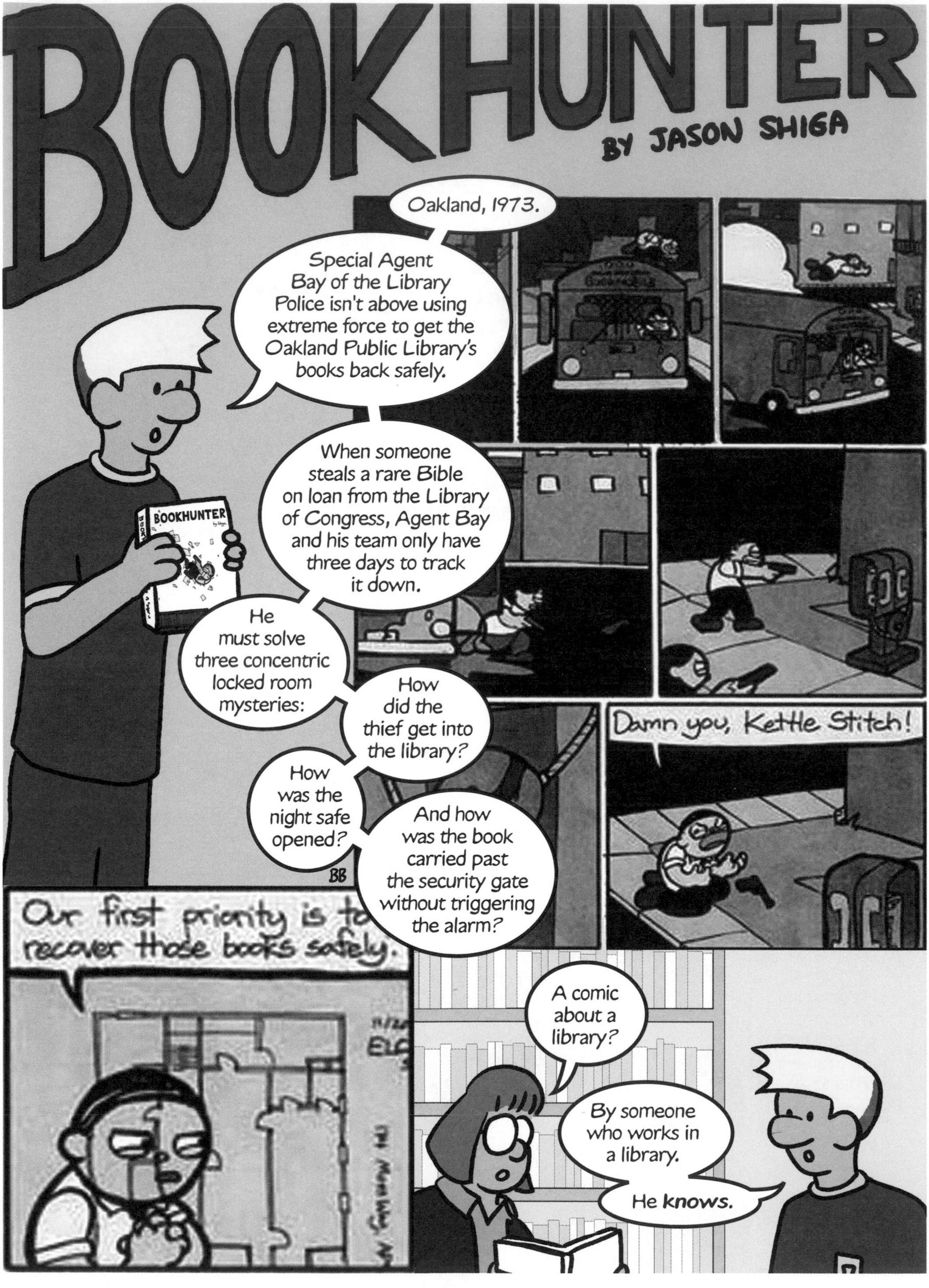

BOOKHUNTER
BY JASON SHIGA
Oakland, 1973.
Special Agent Bay of the Library Police isn't above using extreme force to get the Oakland Public Library's books back safely.
When someone steals a rare Bible on loan from the Library of Congress, Agent Bay and his team only have three days to track it down.
He must solve three concentric locked room mysteries:
How did the thief get into the library?
How was the night safe opened?
And how was the book carried past the security gate without triggering the alarm?
Damn you, Kettle Stitch!
Our first priority is to recover those books safely.
A comic about a library?
By someone who works in a library.
He **knows**.

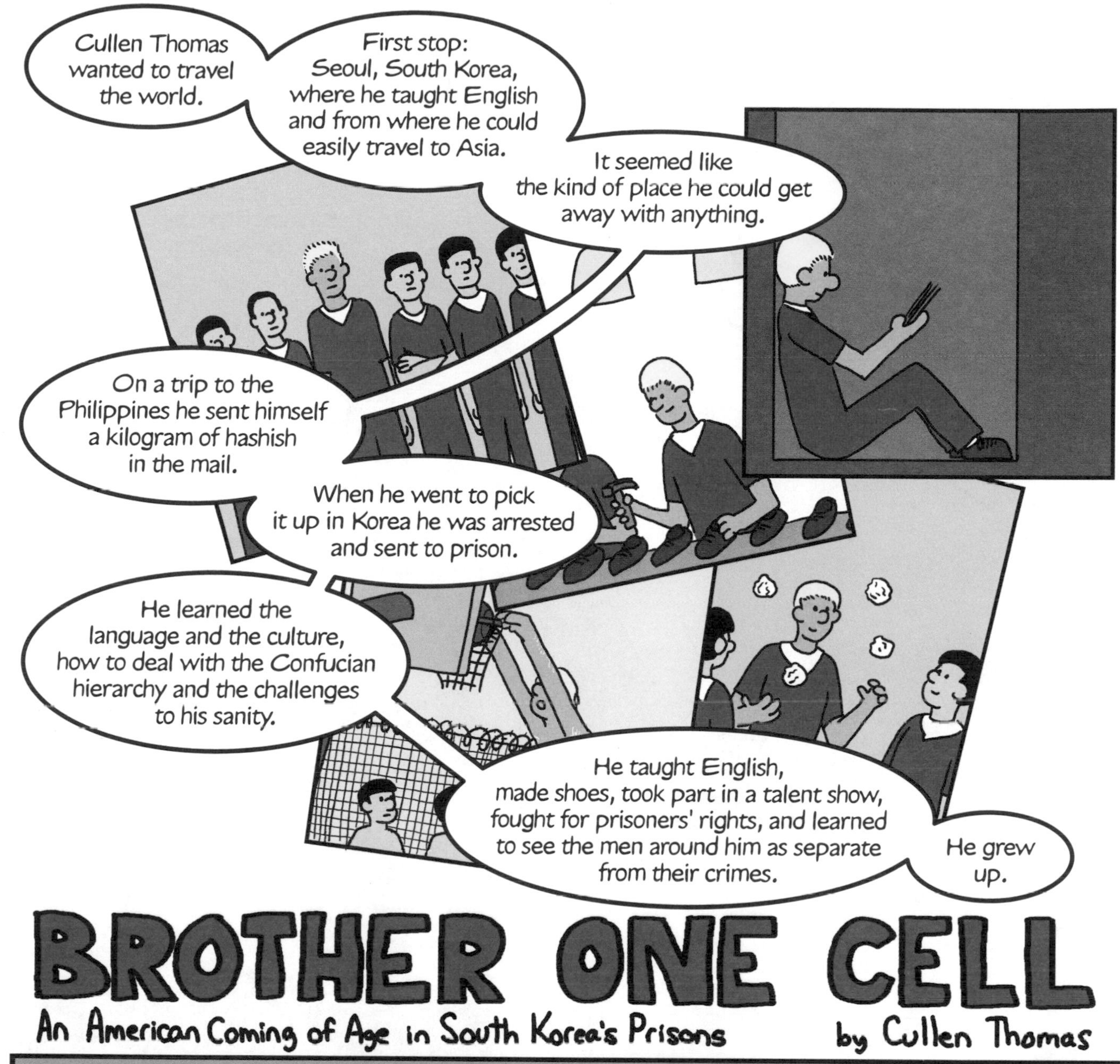
Cullen Thomas wanted to travel the world.
First stop: Seoul, South Korea, where he taught English and from where he could easily travel to Asia.
It seemed like the kind of place he could get away with anything.
On a trip to the Philippines he sent himself a kilogram of hashish in the mail.
When he went to pick it up in Korea he was arrested and sent to prison.
He learned the language and the culture, how to deal with the Confucian hierarchy and the challenges to his sanity.
He taught English, made shoes, took part in a talent show, fought for prisoners' rights, and learned to see the men around him as separate from their crimes.
He grew up.

BROTHER ONE CELL

An American Coming of Age in South Korea's Prisons

by Cullen Thomas

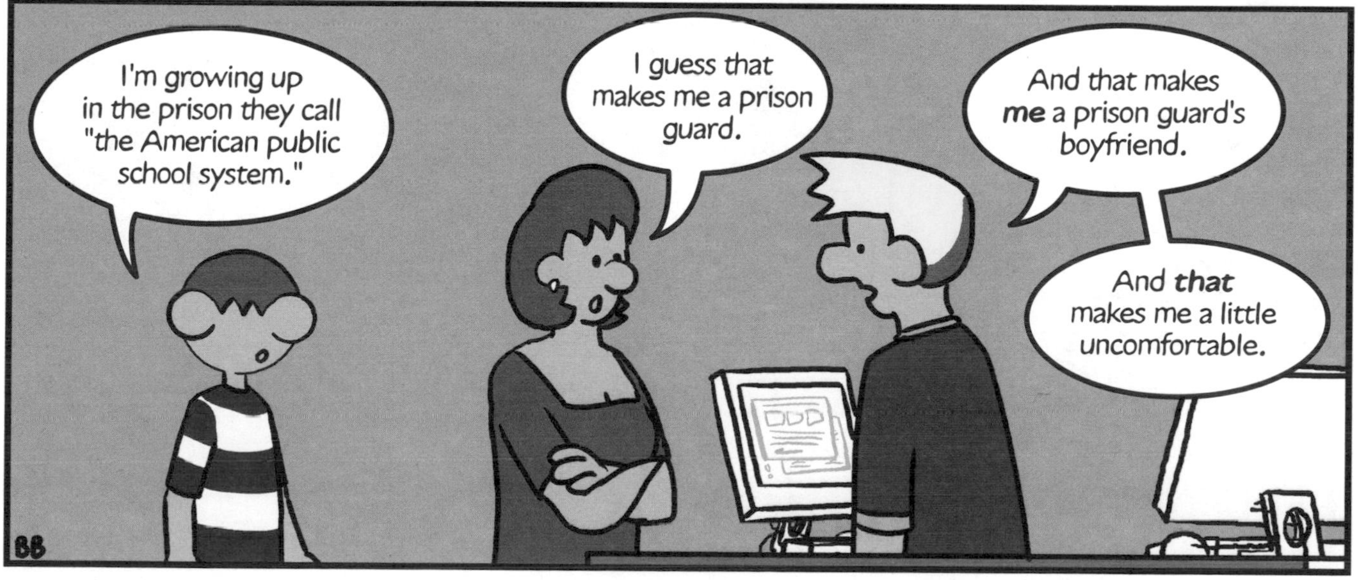
I'm growing up in the prison they call "the American public school system."
I guess that makes me a prison guard.
And that makes **me** a prison guard's boyfriend.
And ***that*** makes me a little uncomfortable.
BB

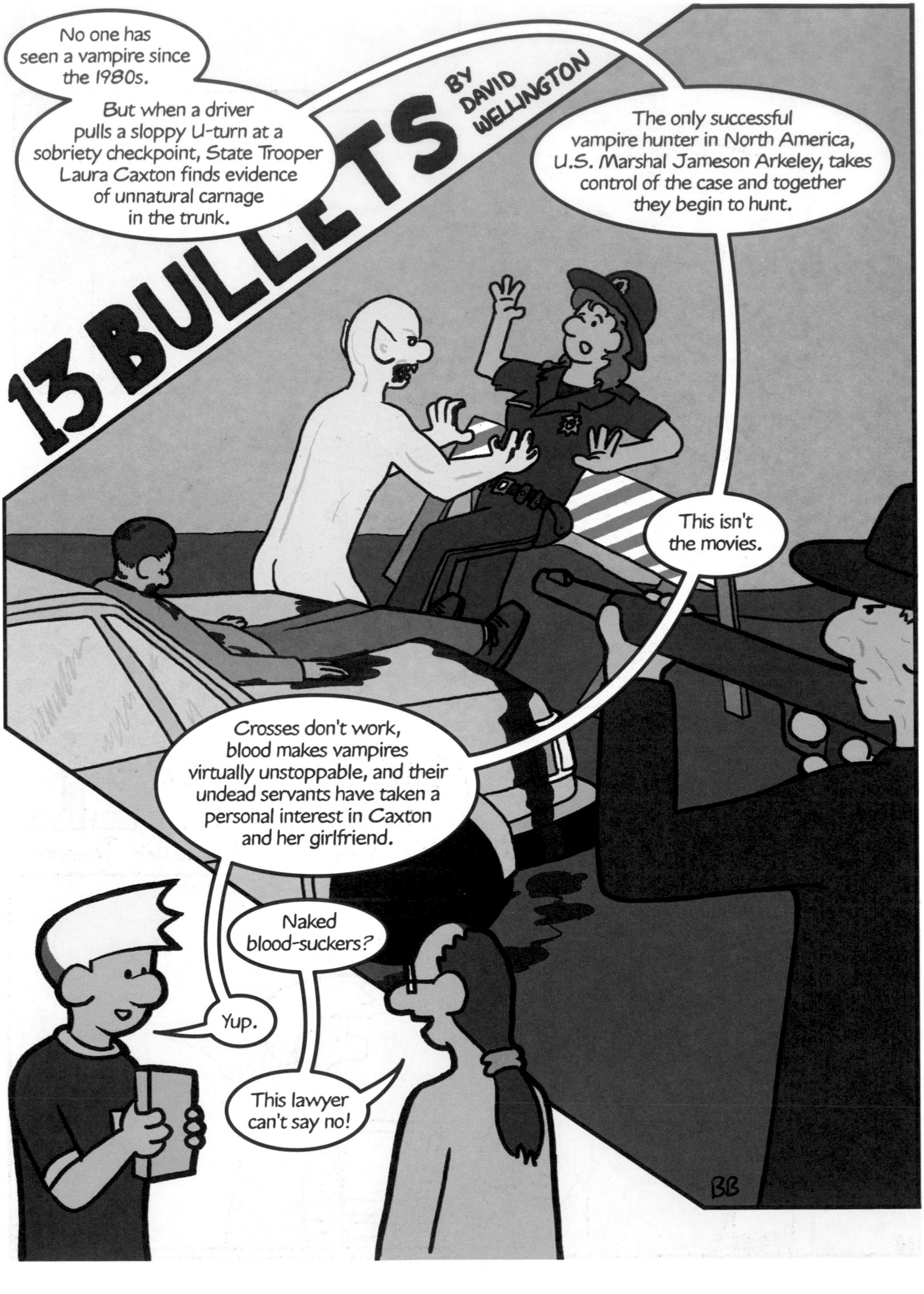
13 BULLETS
BY DAVID WELLINGTON
No one has seen a vampire since the 1980s.
But when a driver pulls a sloppy U-turn at a sobriety checkpoint, State Trooper Laura Caxton finds evidence of unnatural carnage in the trunk.
The only successful vampire hunter in North America, U.S. Marshal Jameson Arkeley, takes control of the case and together they begin to hunt.
This isn't the movies.
Crosses don't work, blood makes vampires virtually unstoppable, and their undead servants have taken a personal interest in Caxton and her girlfriend.
Naked blood-suckers?
Yup.
This lawyer can't say no!
BB

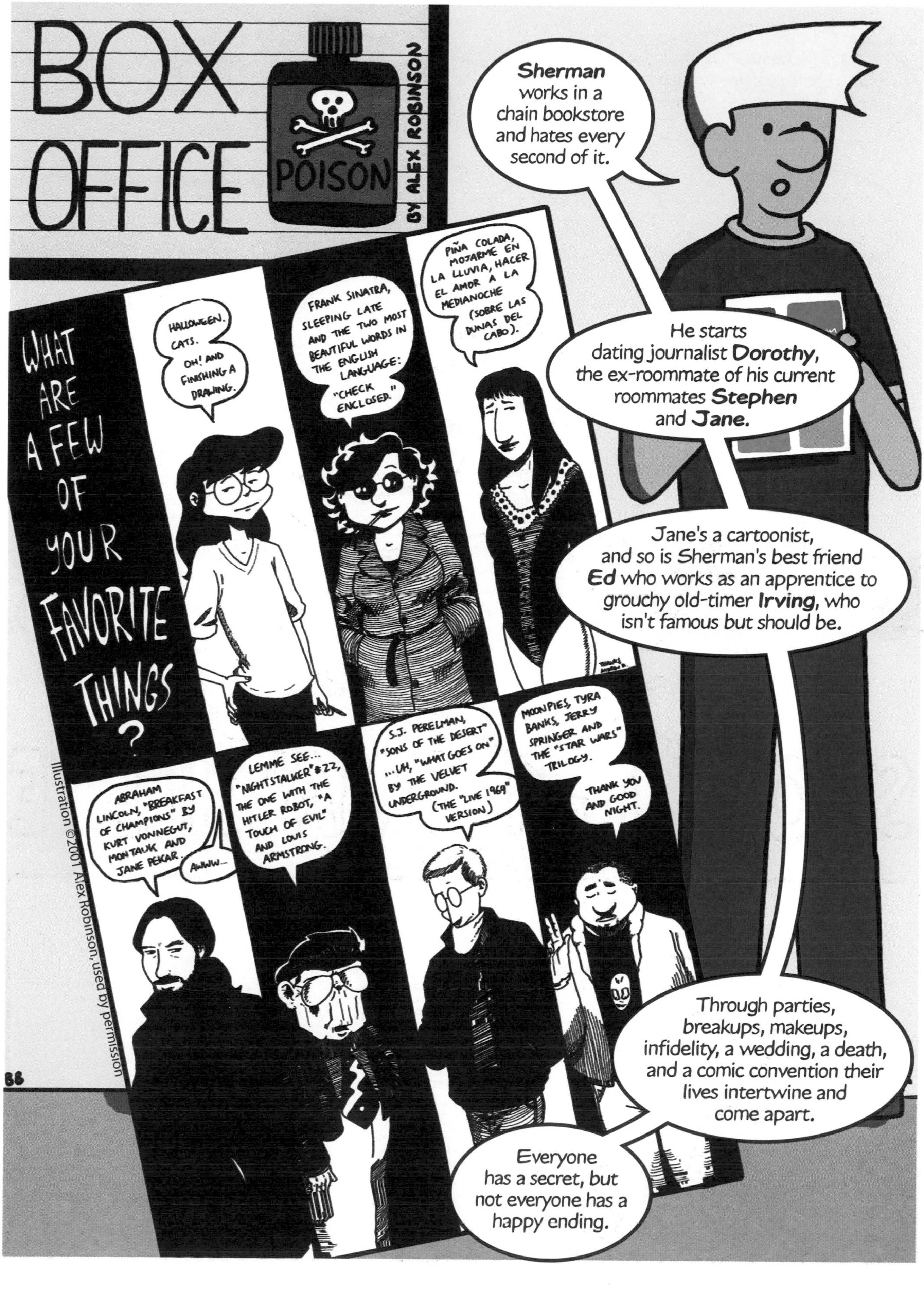
BOX OFFICE POISON
POISON
BY ALEX ROBINSON
Sherman works in a chain bookstore and hates every second of it.
WHAT ARE A FEW OF YOUR FAVORITE THINGS?
HALLOWEEN. CATS. OH! AND FINISHING A DRAWING.
FRANK SINATRA, SLEEPING LATE AND THE TWO MOST BEAUTIFUL WORDS IN THE ENGLISH LANGUAGE: "CHECK ENCLOSED."
PIÑA COLADA, MOJARME EN LA LLUVIA, HACER EL AMOR A LA MEDIANOCHE (SOBRE LAS DUNAS DEL CABO).
He starts dating journalist **Dorothy**, the ex-roommate of his current roommates **Stephen** and **Jane.**
Jane's a cartoonist, and so is Sherman's best friend **Ed** who works as an apprentice to grouchy old-timer **Irving**, who isn't famous but should be.
ABRAHAM LINCOLN, "BREAKFAST OF CHAMPIONS" BY KURT VONNEGUT, MONTAUK AND JANE PEKAR.
AWWW...
LEMME SEE... "NIGHTSTALKER" #22, THE ONE WITH THE HITLER ROBOT, "A TOUCH OF EVIL" AND LOUIS ARMSTRONG.
S.J. PERELMAN, "SONS OF THE DESERT" ...UH, "WHAT GOES ON" BY THE VELVET UNDERGROUND. (THE "LIVE 1969" VERSION.)
MOONPIES, TYRA BANKS, JERRY SPRINGER AND THE "STAR WARS" TRILOGY.
THANK YOU AND GOOD NIGHT.
Through parties, breakups, makeups, infidelity, a wedding, a death, and a comic convention their lives intertwine and come apart.
Everyone has a secret, but not everyone has a happy ending.

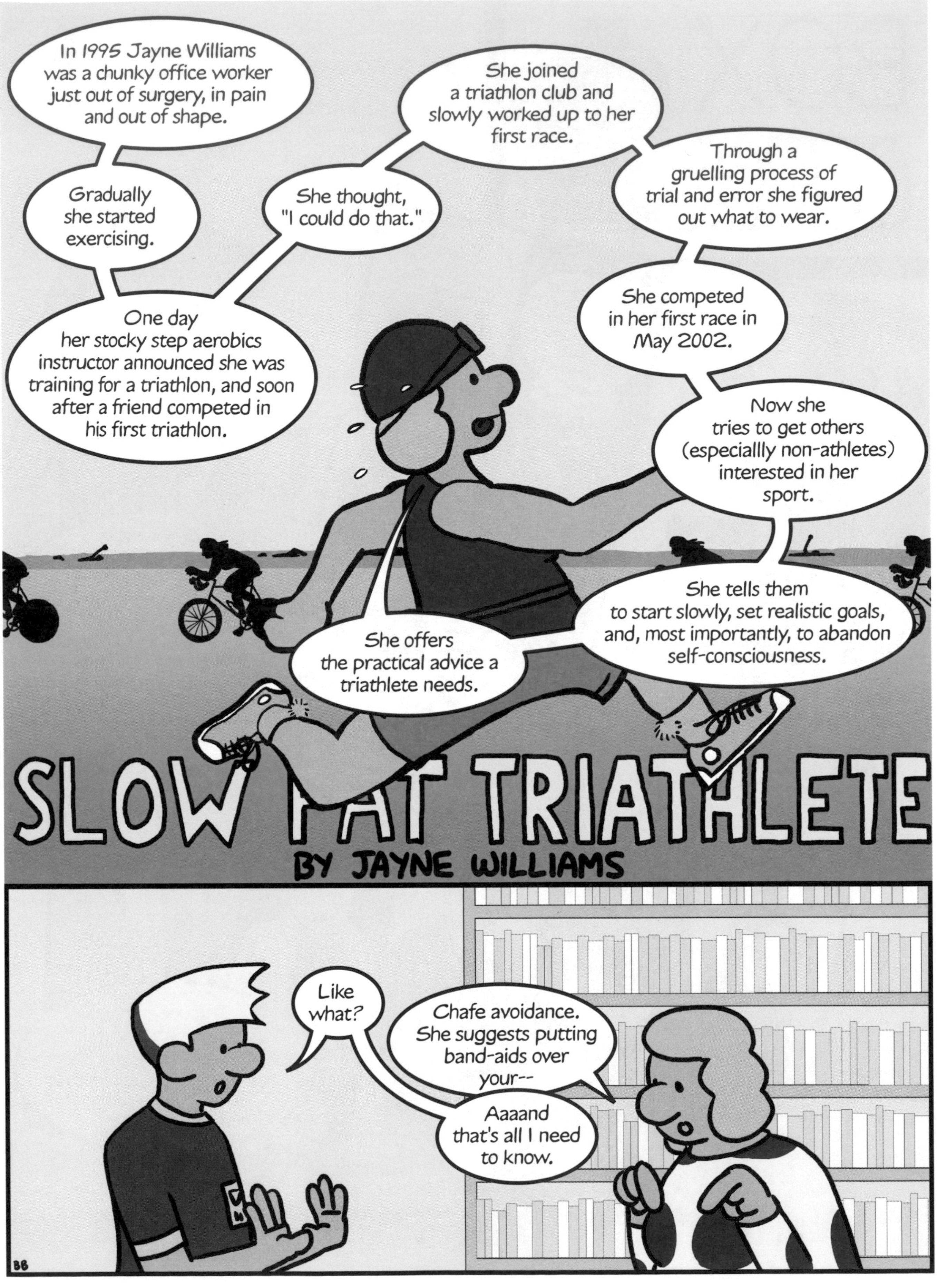
In 1995 Jayne Williams was a chunky office worker just out of surgery, in pain and out of shape.
Gradually she started exercising.
One day her stocky step aerobics instructor announced she was training for a triathlon, and soon after a friend competed in his first triathlon.
She thought, "I could do that."
She joined a triathlon club and slowly worked up to her first race.
Through a gruelling process of trial and error she figured out what to wear.
She competed in her first race in May 2002.
Now she tries to get others (especiallly non-athletes) interested in her sport.
She tells them to start slowly, set realistic goals, and, most importantly, to abandon self-consciousness.
She offers the practical advice a triathlete needs.
SLOW FAT TRIATHLETE
BY JAYNE WILLIAMS
Like what?
Chafe avoidance. She suggests putting band-aids over your--
Aaaand that's all I need to know.
BB

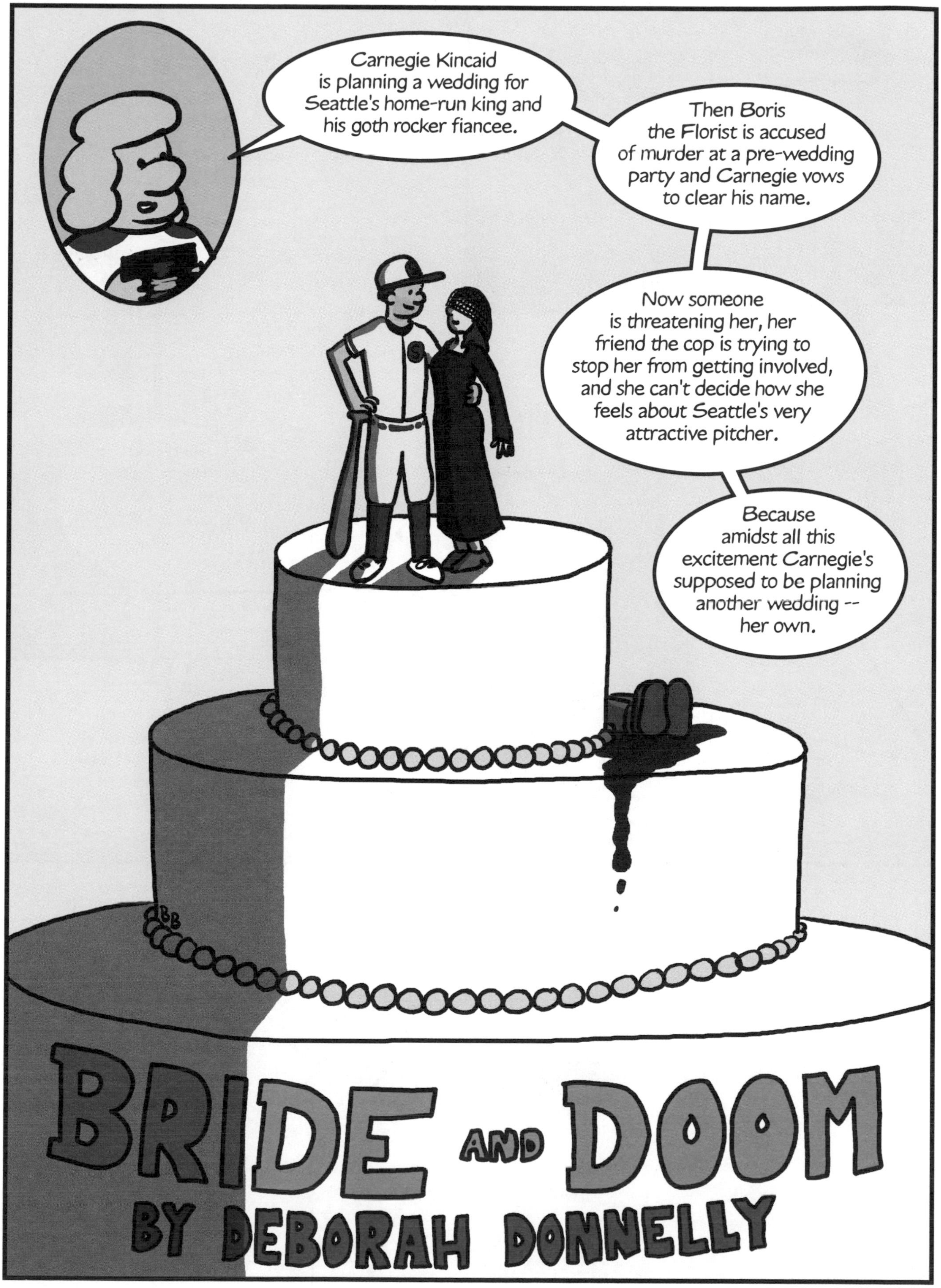
Carnegie Kincaid is planning a wedding for Seattle's home-run king and his goth rocker fiancee.
Then Boris the Florist is accused of murder at a pre-wedding party and Carnegie vows to clear his name.
Now someone is threatening her, her friend the cop is trying to stop her from getting involved, and she can't decide how she feels about Seattle's very attractive pitcher.
Because amidst all this excitement Carnegie's supposed to be planning another wedding -- her own.
BB
BRIDE AND DOOM
BY DEBORAH DONNELLY

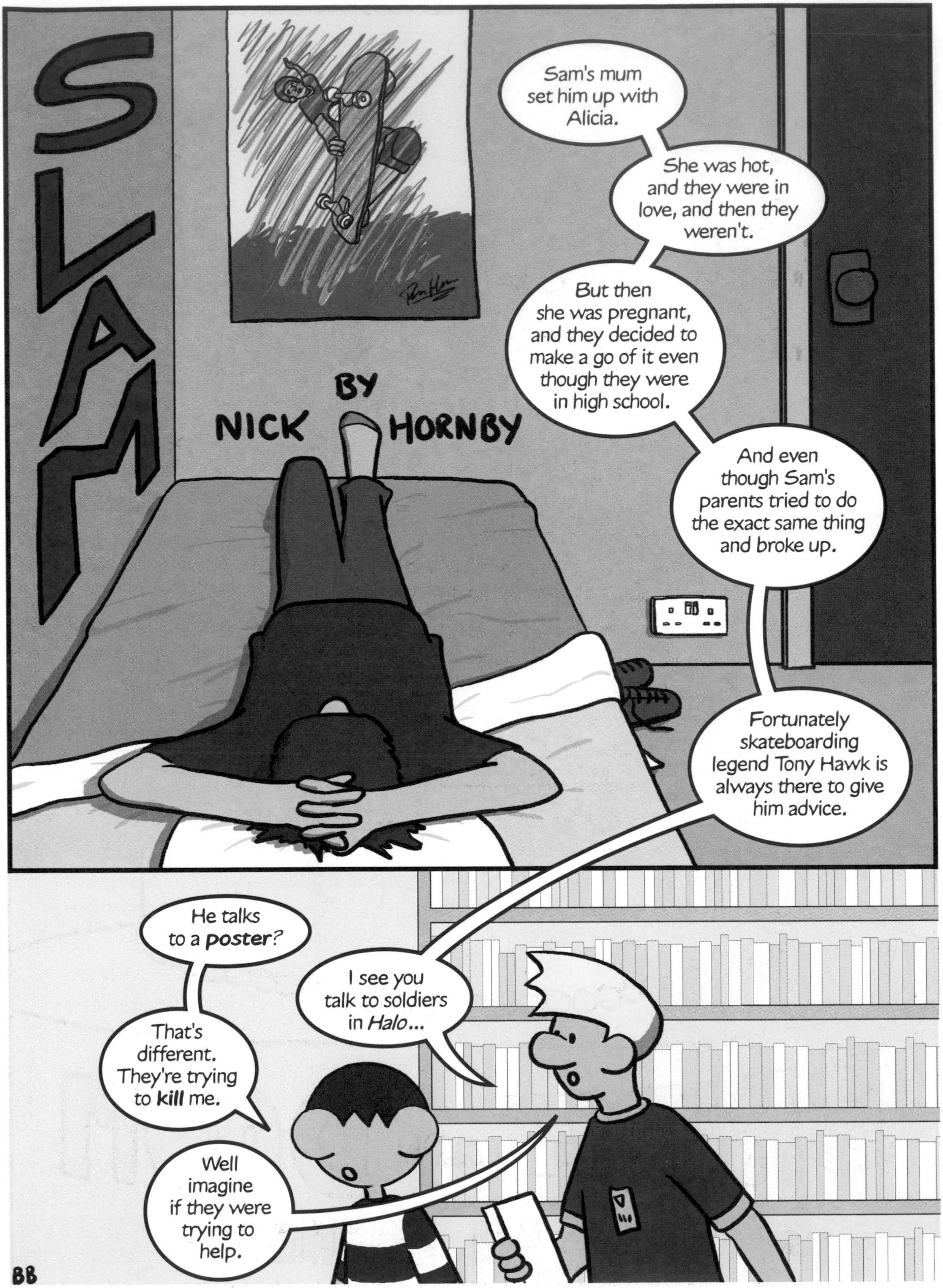

SLAM
BY NICK HORNBY
Sam's mum set him up with Alicia.
She was hot, and they were in love, and then they weren't.
But then she was pregnant, and they decided to make a go of it even though they were in high school.
And even though Sam's parents tried to do the exact same thing and broke up.
Fortunately skateboarding legend Tony Hawk is always there to give him advice.
He talks to a **poster**?
I see you talk to soldiers in *Halo*...
That's different. They're trying to **kill** me.
Well imagine if they were trying to help.
BB

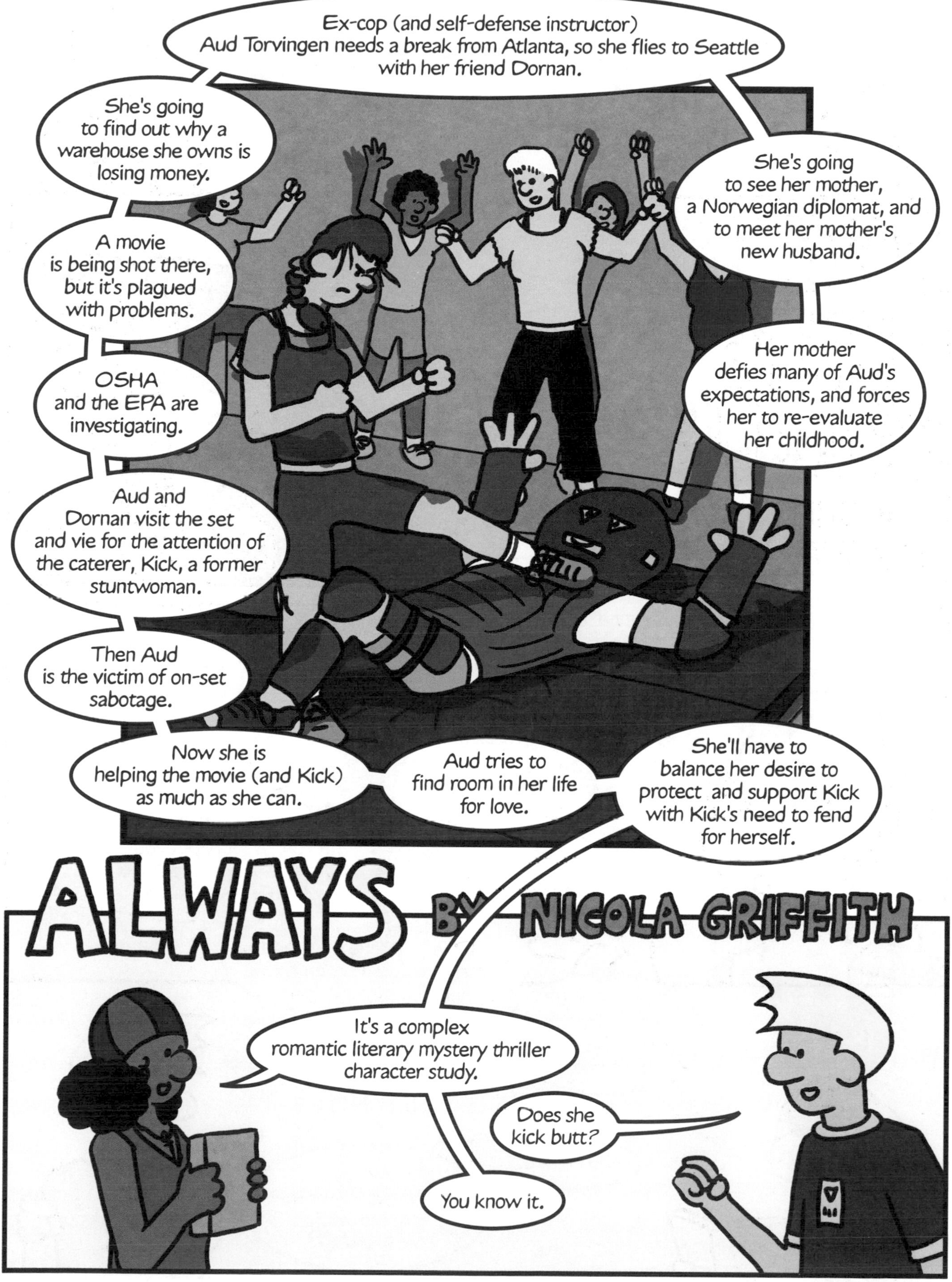
Ex-cop (and self-defense instructor) Aud Torvingen needs a break from Atlanta, so she flies to Seattle with her friend Dornan.
She's going to find out why a warehouse she owns is losing money.
A movie is being shot there, but it's plagued with problems.
OSHA and the EPA are investigating.
Aud and Dornan visit the set and vie for the attention of the caterer, Kick, a former stuntwoman.
Then Aud is the victim of on-set sabotage.
Now she is helping the movie (and Kick) as much as she can.
She's going to see her mother, a Norwegian diplomat, and to meet her mother's new husband.
Her mother defies many of Aud's expectations, and forces her to re-evaluate her childhood.
Aud tries to find room in her life for love.
She'll have to balance her desire to protect and support Kick with Kick's need to fend for herself.
ALWAYS BY NICOLA GRIFFITH
It's a complex romantic literary mystery thriller character study.
Does she kick butt?
You know it.

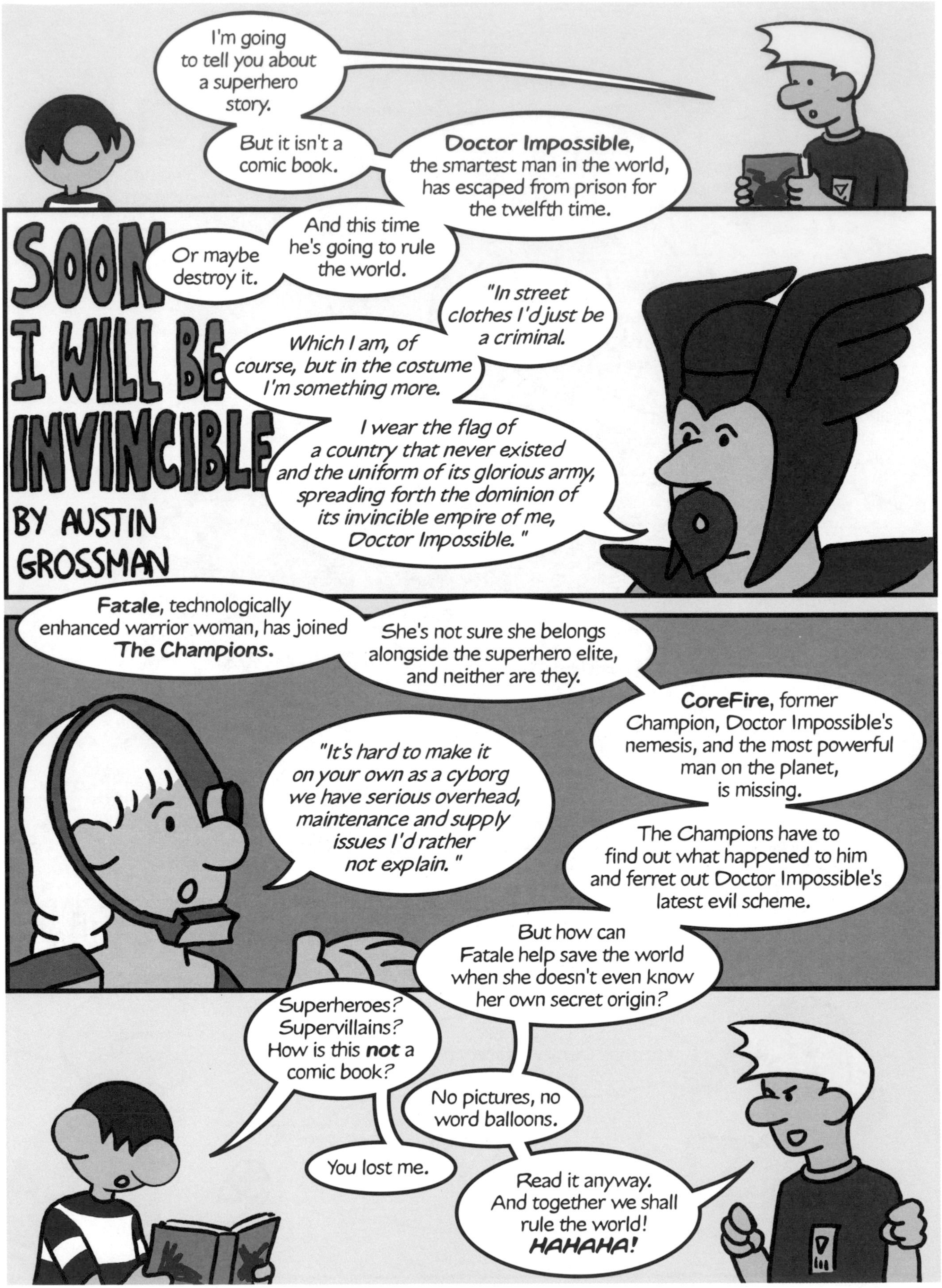
I'm going to tell you about a superhero story.
But it isn't a comic book.
Doctor Impossible, the smartest man in the world, has escaped from prison for the twelfth time.
And this time he's going to rule the world.
Or maybe destroy it.
SOON I WILL BE INVINCIBLE
BY AUSTIN GROSSMAN
"In street clothes I'd just be a criminal.
Which I am, of course, but in the costume I'm something more.
I wear the flag of a country that never existed and the uniform of its glorious army, spreading forth the dominion of its invincible empire of me, Doctor Impossible."
Fatale, technologically enhanced warrior woman, has joined **The Champions.**
She's not sure she belongs alongside the superhero elite, and neither are they.
CoreFire, former Champion, Doctor Impossible's nemesis, and the most powerful man on the planet, is missing.
"It's hard to make it on your own as a cyborg we have serious overhead, maintenance and supply issues I'd rather not explain."
The Champions have to find out what happened to him and ferret out Doctor Impossible's latest evil scheme.
But how can Fatale help save the world when she doesn't even know her own secret origin?
Superheroes? Supervillains? How is this **not** a comic book?
No pictures, no word balloons.
You lost me.
Read it anyway. And together we shall rule the world! ***HAHAHA!***

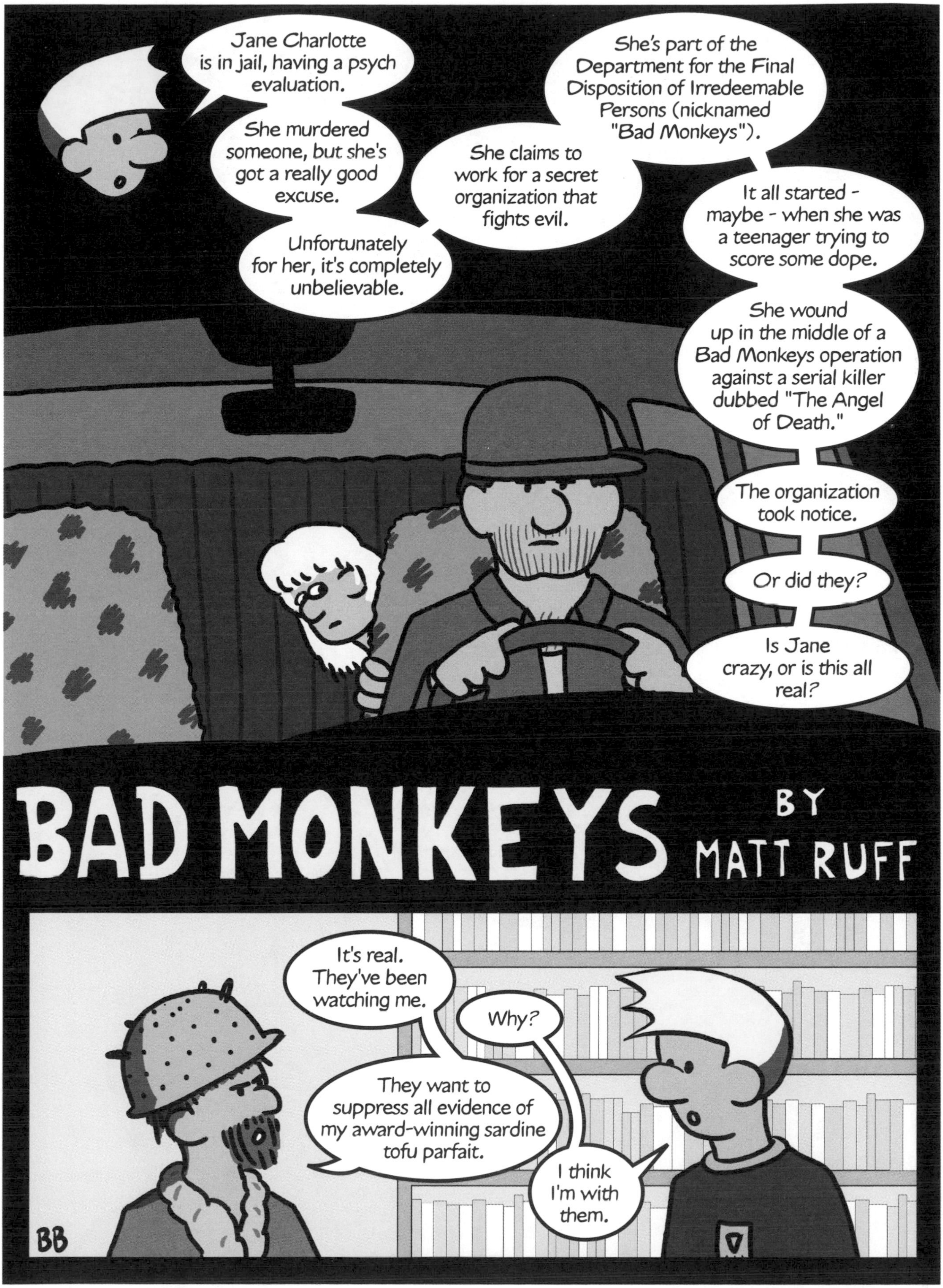
Jane Charlotte is in jail, having a psych evaluation.
She murdered someone, but she's got a really good excuse.
Unfortunately for her, it's completely unbelievable.
She claims to work for a secret organization that fights evil.
She's part of the Department for the Final Disposition of Irredeemable Persons (nicknamed "Bad Monkeys").
It all started - maybe - when she was a teenager trying to score some dope.
She wound up in the middle of a Bad Monkeys operation against a serial killer dubbed "The Angel of Death."
The organization took notice.
Or did they?
Is Jane crazy, or is this all real?
BAD MONKEYS BY MATT RUFF
It's real. They've been watching me.
Why?
They want to suppress all evidence of my award-winning sardine tofu parfait.
I think I'm with them.
BB

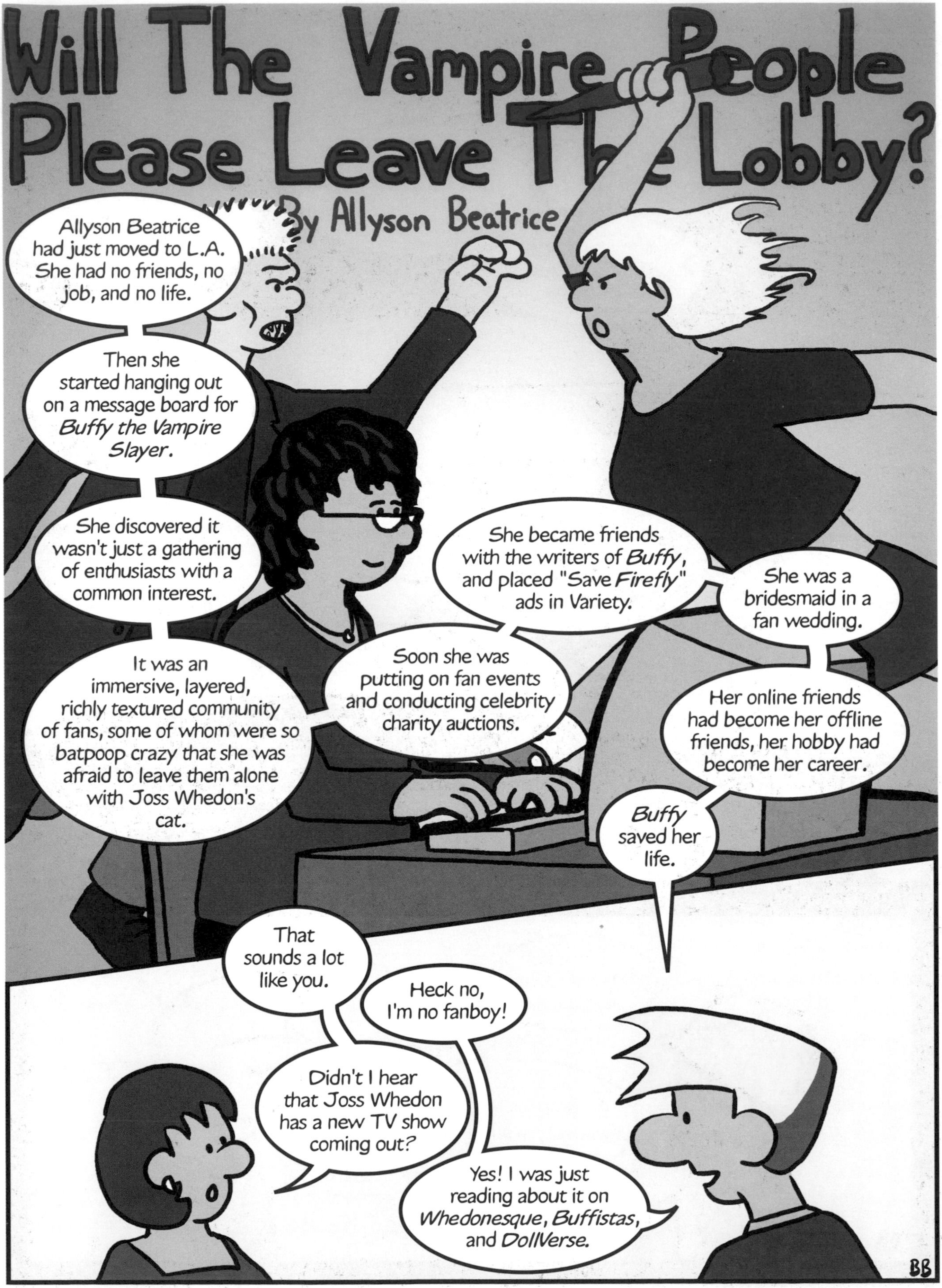
Will The Vampire People Please Leave The Lobby?
By Allyson Beatrice
Allyson Beatrice had just moved to L.A. She had no friends, no job, and no life.
Then she started hanging out on a message board for *Buffy the Vampire Slayer*.
She discovered it wasn't just a gathering of enthusiasts with a common interest.
It was an immersive, layered, richly textured community of fans, some of whom were so batpoop crazy that she was afraid to leave them alone with Joss Whedon's cat.
Soon she was putting on fan events and conducting celebrity charity auctions.
She became friends with the writers of *Buffy*, and placed "Save *Firefly*" ads in Variety.
She was a bridesmaid in a fan wedding.
Her online friends had become her offline friends, her hobby had become her career.
Buffy saved her life.
That sounds a lot like you.
Heck no, I'm no fanboy!
Didn't I hear that Joss Whedon has a new TV show coming out?
Yes! I was just reading about it on *Whedonesque*, *Buffistas*, and *DollVerse*.
BB

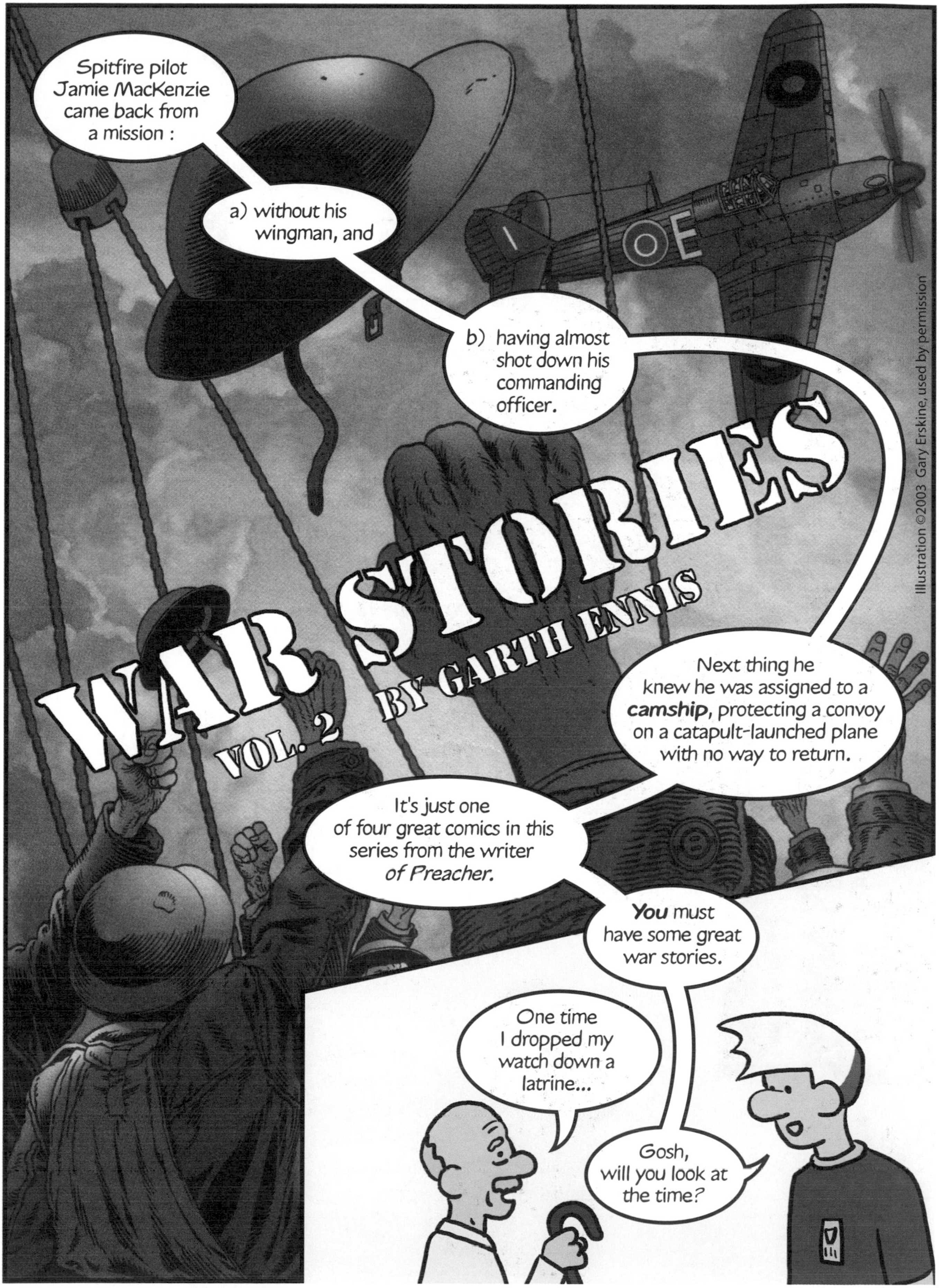

Spitfire pilot Jamie MacKenzie came back from a mission :
a) without his wingman, and
b) having almost shot down his commanding officer.
WAR STORIES VOL. 2
BY GARTH ENNIS
Next thing he knew he was assigned to a **camship,** protecting a convoy on a catapult-launched plane with no way to return.
It's just one of four great comics in this series from the writer of *Preacher.*
You must have some great war stories.
One time I dropped my watch down a latrine...
Gosh, will you look at the time?
Illustration ©2003 Gary Erskine, used by permission

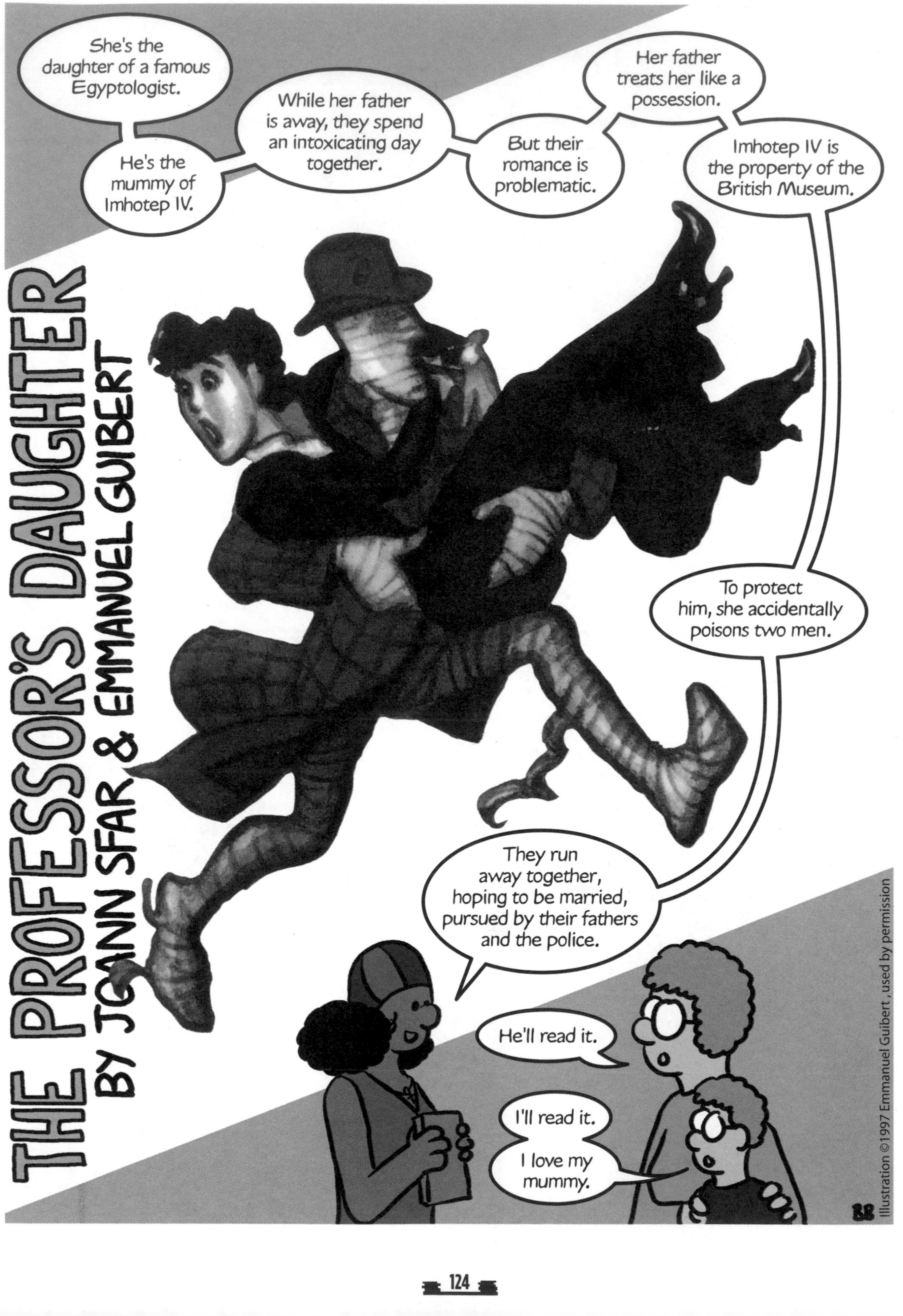

THE PROFESSOR'S DAUGHTER
BY JOANN SFAR & EMMANUEL GUIBERT
She's the daughter of a famous Egyptologist.
He's the mummy of Imhotep IV.
While her father is away, they spend an intoxicating day together.
But their romance is problematic.
Her father treats her like a possession.
Imhotep IV is the property of the British Museum.
To protect him, she accidentally poisons two men.
They run away together, hoping to be married, pursued by their fathers and the police.
He'll read it.
I'll read it.
I love my mummy.

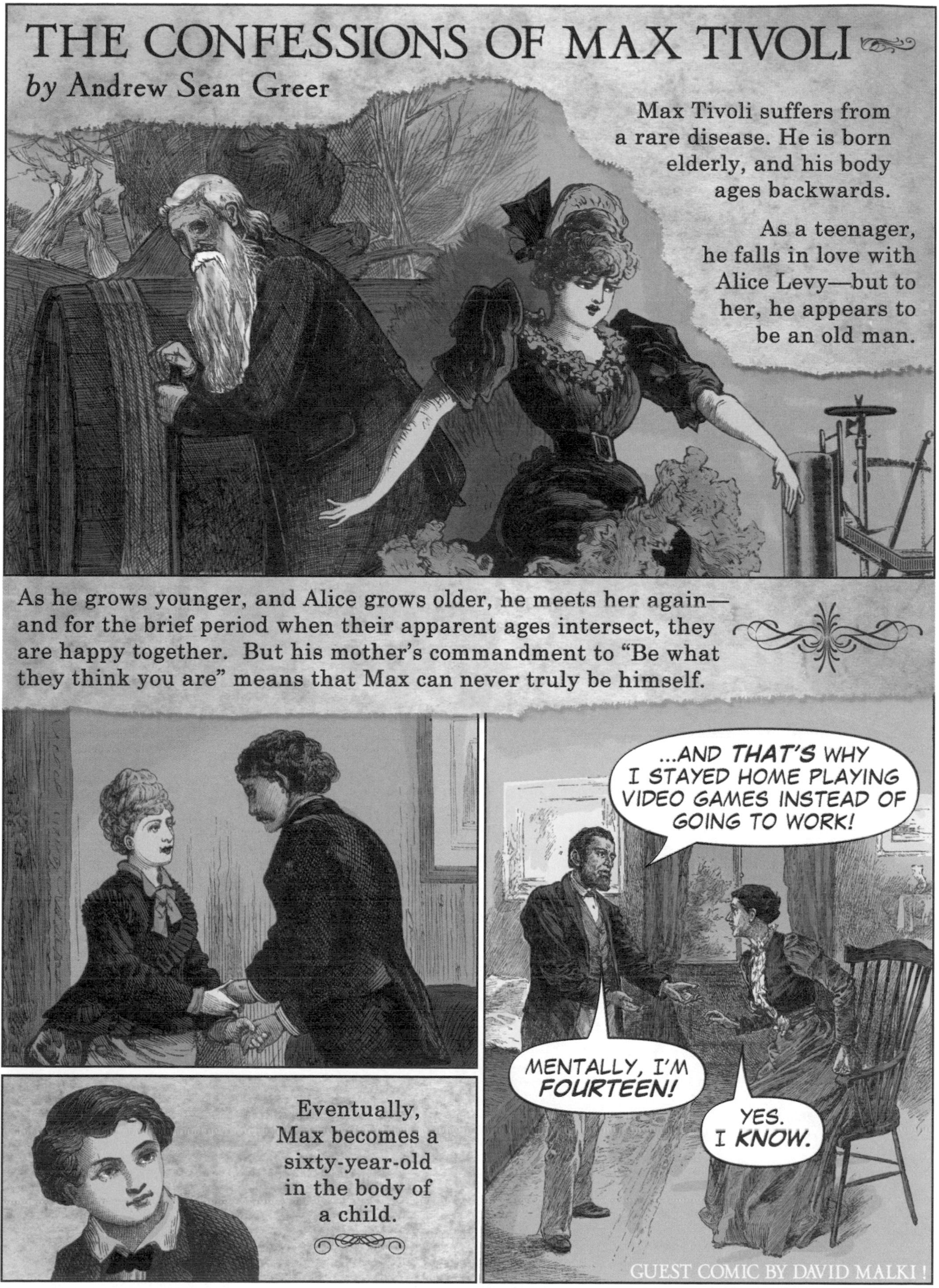
THE CONFESSIONS OF MAX TIVOLI
by Andrew Sean Greer
Max Tivoli suffers from a rare disease. He is born elderly, and his body ages backwards.
As a teenager, he falls in love with Alice Levy—but to her, he appears to be an old man.
As he grows younger, and Alice grows older, he meets her again—and for the brief period when their apparent ages intersect, they are happy together. But his mother's commandment to "Be what they think you are" means that Max can never truly be himself.
Eventually, Max becomes a sixty-year-old in the body of a child.
...AND THAT'S WHY I STAYED HOME PLAYING VIDEO GAMES INSTEAD OF GOING TO WORK!
MENTALLY, I'M FOURTEEN!
YES. I KNOW.
GUEST COMIC BY DAVID MALKI !

Guest strip (c)2008 by David Malki! For more wonderful madness, go to www.wondermark.com

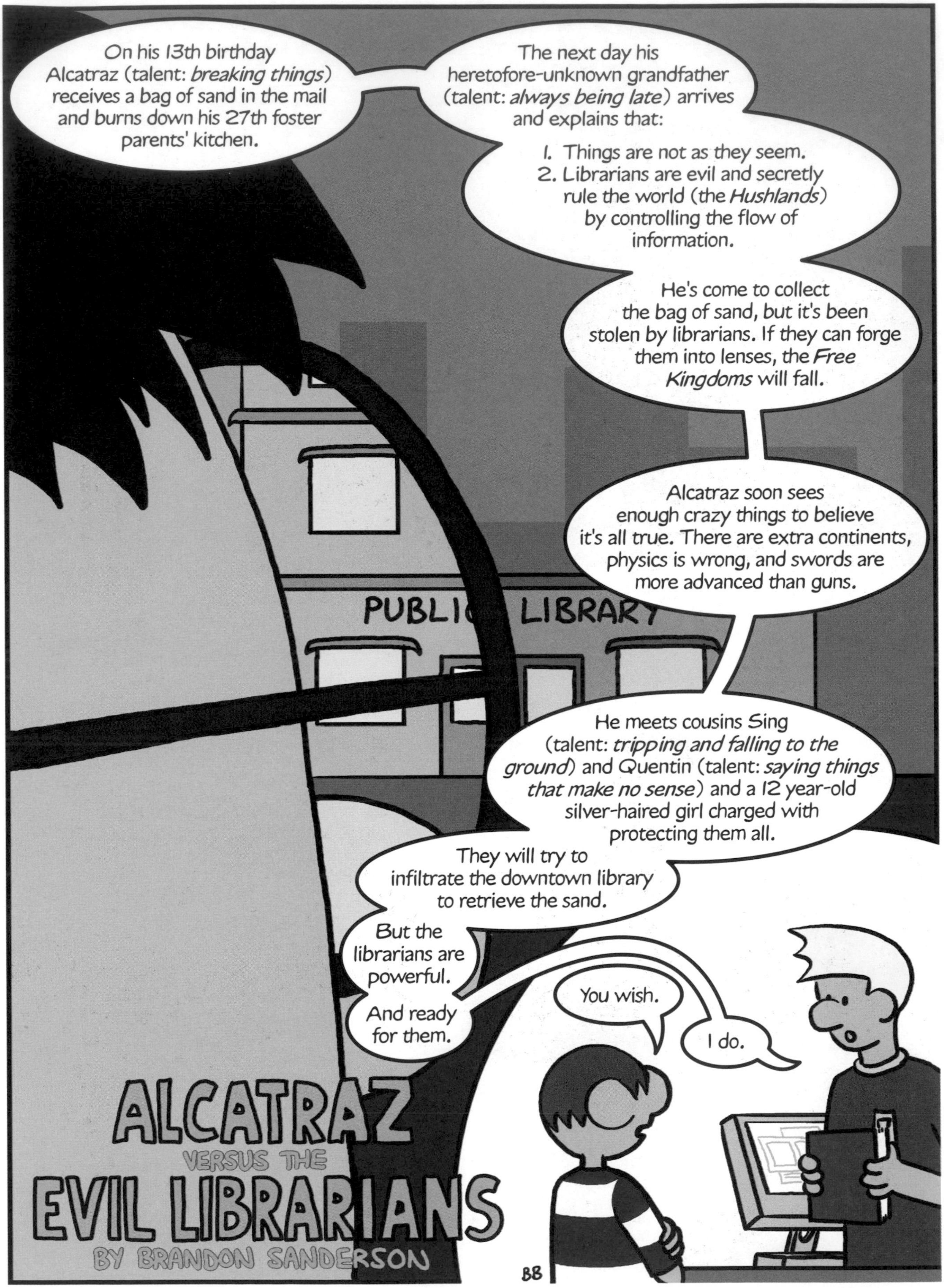
On his 13th birthday Alcatraz (talent: *breaking things*) receives a bag of sand in the mail and burns down his 27th foster parents' kitchen.
The next day his heretofore-unknown grandfather (talent: *always being late*) arrives and explains that:
1. Things are not as they seem.
2. Librarians are evil and secretly rule the world (the *Hushlands*) by controlling the flow of information.
He's come to collect the bag of sand, but it's been stolen by librarians. If they can forge them into lenses, the *Free Kingdoms* will fall.
PUBLIC LIBRARY
Alcatraz soon sees enough crazy things to believe it's all true. There are extra continents, physics is wrong, and swords are more advanced than guns.
He meets cousins Sing (talent: *tripping and falling to the ground*) and Quentin (talent: *saying things that make no sense*) and a 12 year-old silver-haired girl charged with protecting them all.
They will try to infiltrate the downtown library to retrieve the sand.
But the librarians are powerful.
And ready for them.
You wish.
I do.
ALCATRAZ VERSUS THE EVIL LIBRARIANS
BY BRANDON SANDERSON
88

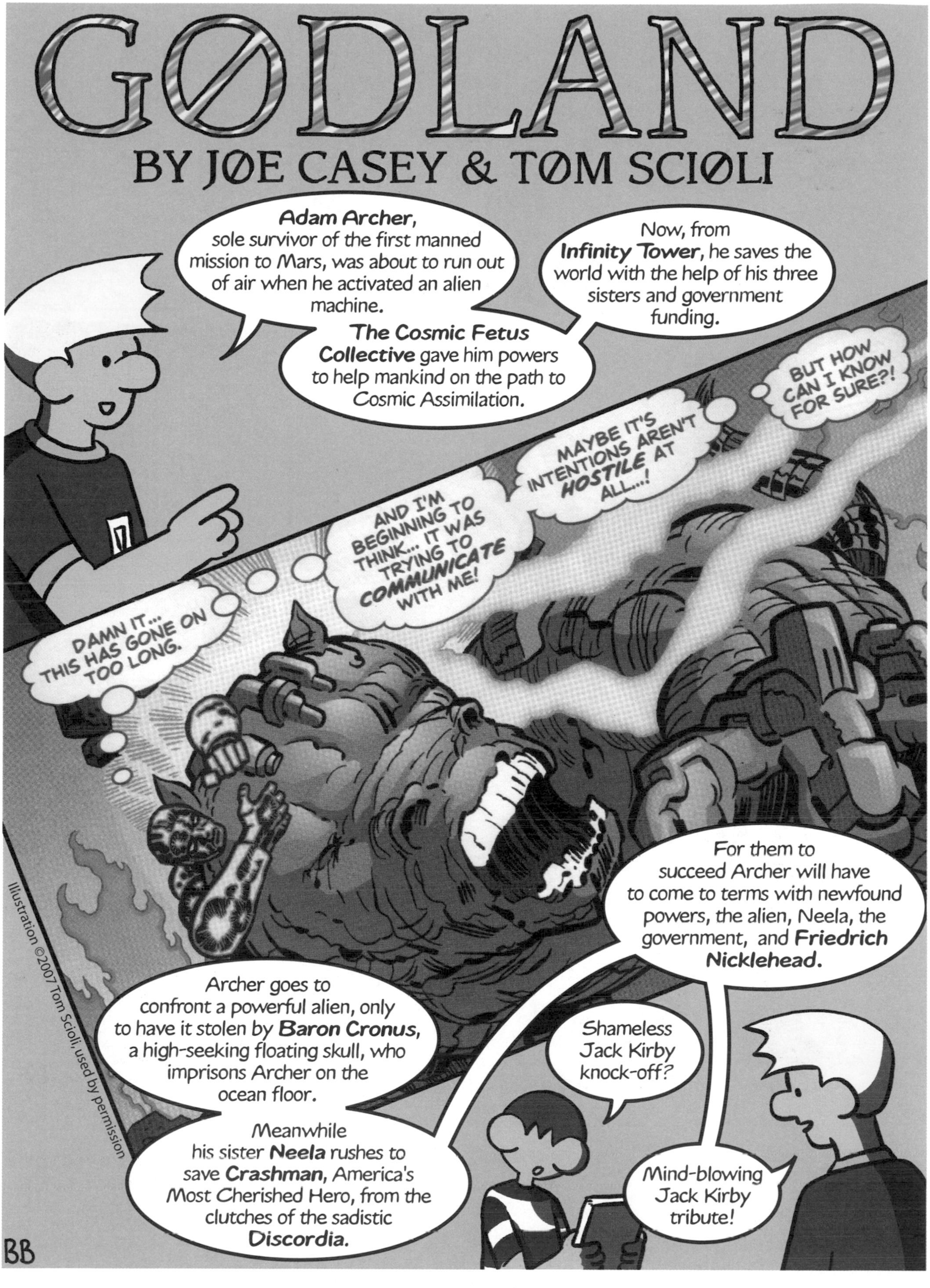
GØDLAND
BY JØE CASEY & TØM SCIØLI
Adam Archer, sole survivor of the first manned mission to Mars, was about to run out of air when he activated an alien machine.
The Cosmic Fetus Collective gave him powers to help mankind on the path to Cosmic Assimilation.
Now, from Infinity Tower, he saves the world with the help of his three sisters and government funding.
DAMN IT... THIS HAS GONE ON TOO LONG.
AND I'M BEGINNING TO THINK... IT WAS TRYING TO COMMUNICATE WITH ME!
MAYBE IT'S INTENTIONS AREN'T HOSTILE AT ALL...!
BUT HOW CAN I KNOW FOR SURE?!
Illustration ©2007 Tom Scioli, used by permission
For them to succeed Archer will have to come to terms with newfound powers, the alien, Neela, the government, and Friedrich Nicklehead.
Archer goes to confront a powerful alien, only to have it stolen by Baron Cronus, a high-seeking floating skull, who imprisons Archer on the ocean floor.
Meanwhile his sister Neela rushes to save Crashman, America's Most Cherished Hero, from the clutches of the sadistic Discordia.
Shameless Jack Kirby knock-off?
Mind-blowing Jack Kirby tribute!
BB

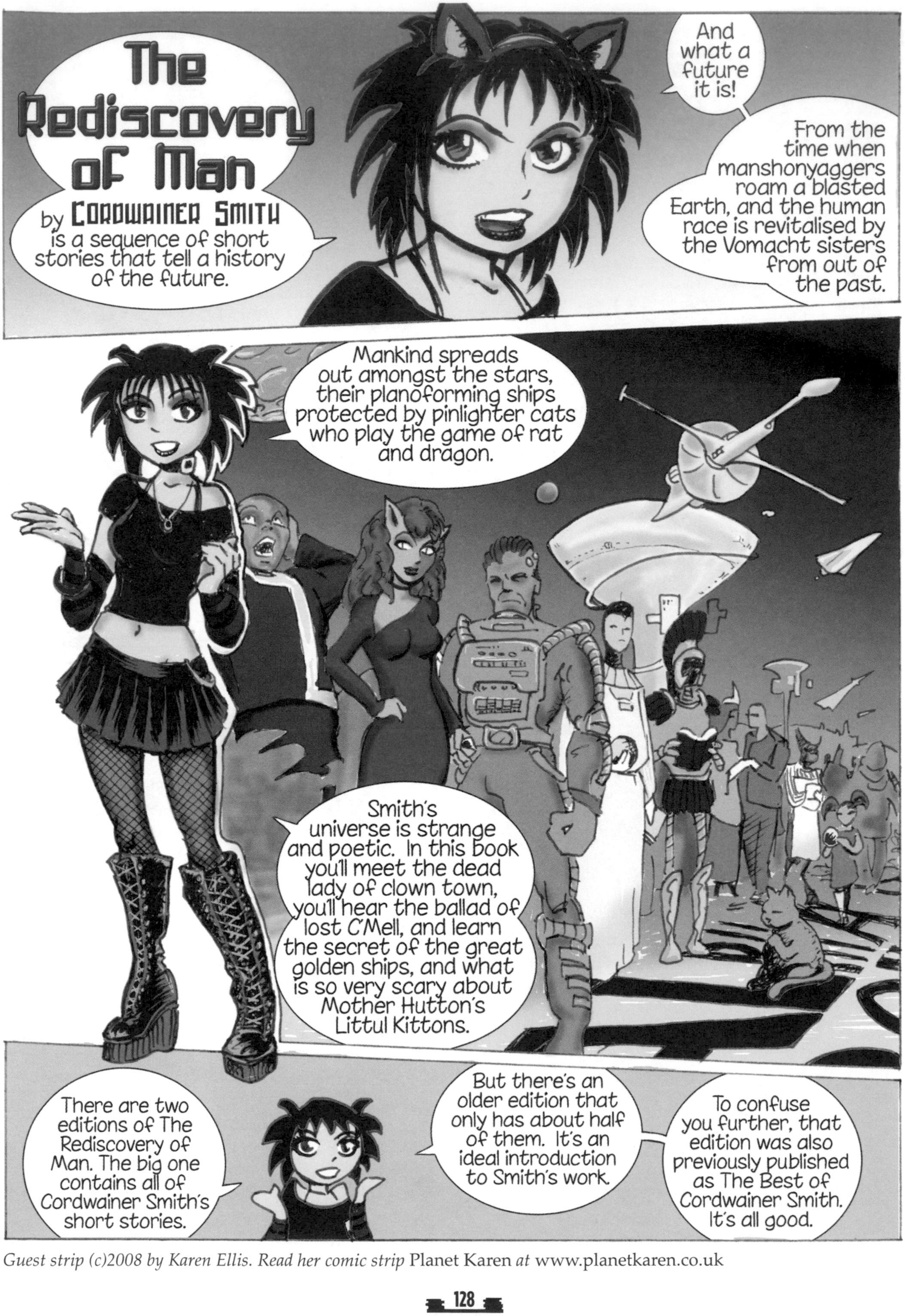
The Rediscovery of Man
by Cordwainer Smith is a sequence of short stories that tell a history of the future.
And what a future it is!
From the time when manshonyaggers roam a blasted Earth, and the human race is revitalised by the Vomacht sisters from out of the past.
Mankind spreads out amongst the stars, their planoforming ships protected by pinlighter cats who play the game of rat and dragon.
Smith's universe is strange and poetic. In this book you'll meet the dead lady of clown town, you'll hear the ballad of lost C'Mell, and learn the secret of the great golden ships, and what is so very scary about Mother Hutton's Littul Kittons.
There are two editions of The Rediscovery of Man. The big one contains all of Cordwainer Smith's short stories.
But there's an older edition that only has about half of them. It's an ideal introduction to Smith's work.
To confuse you further, that edition was also previously published as The Best of Cordwainer Smith. It's all good.

Guest strip (c)2008 by Karen Ellis. Read her comic strip Planet Karen *at* www.planetkaren.co.uk

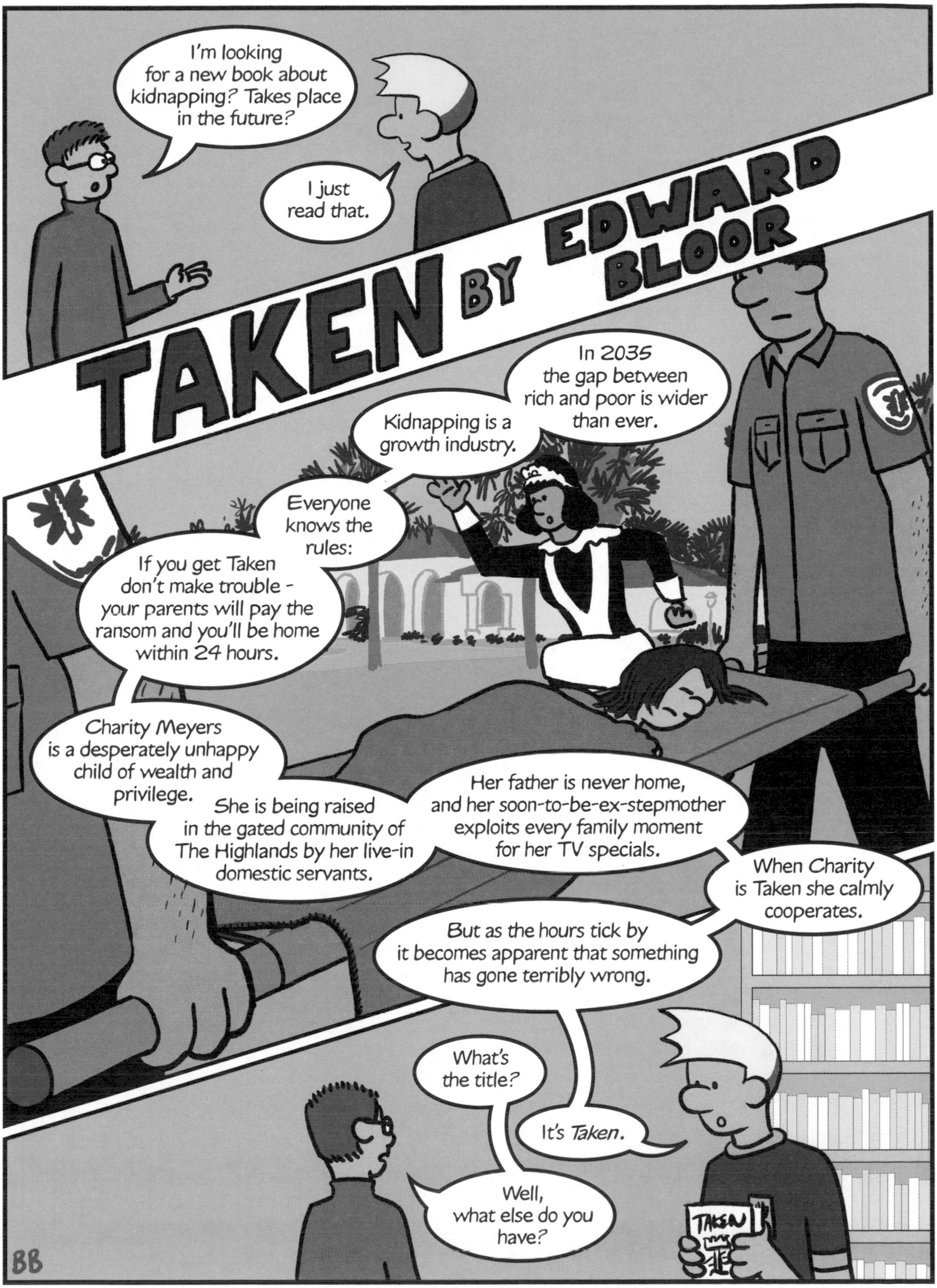
I'm looking for a new book about kidnapping? Takes place in the future?
I just read that.
TAKEN BY EDWARD BLOOR
In 2035 the gap between rich and poor is wider than ever.
Kidnapping is a growth industry.
Everyone knows the rules:
If you get Taken don't make trouble - your parents will pay the ransom and you'll be home within 24 hours.
Charity Meyers is a desperately unhappy child of wealth and privilege.
She is being raised in the gated community of The Highlands by her live-in domestic servants.
Her father is never home, and her soon-to-be-ex-stepmother exploits every family moment for her TV specials.
When Charity is Taken she calmly cooperates.
But as the hours tick by it becomes apparent that something has gone terribly wrong.
What's the title?
It's *Taken*.
Well, what else do you have?
TAKEN
BB

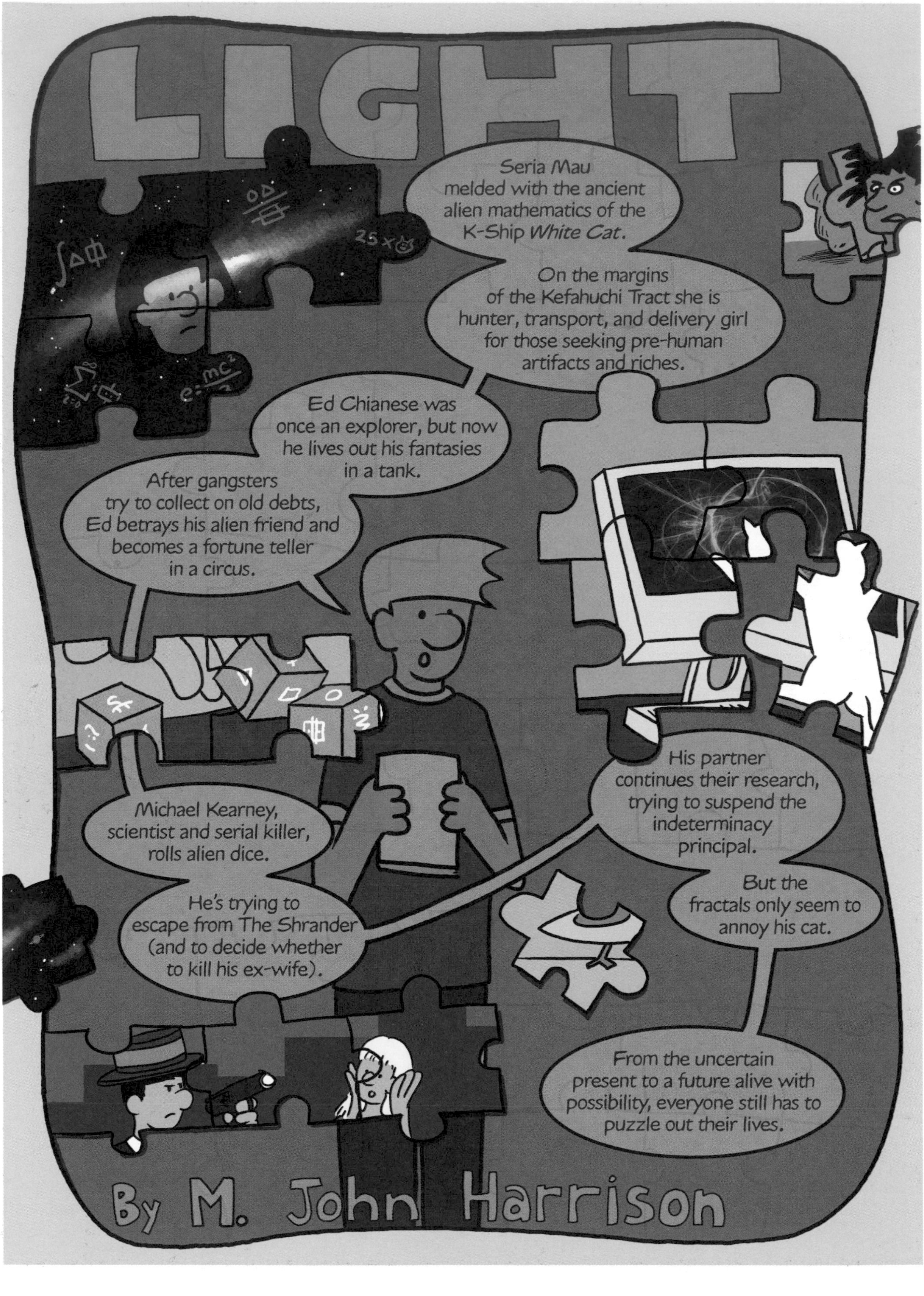
LIGHT
Seria Mau melded with the ancient alien mathematics of the K-Ship *White Cat*.
On the margins of the Kefahuchi Tract she is hunter, transport, and delivery girl for those seeking pre-human artifacts and riches.
Ed Chianese was once an explorer, but now he lives out his fantasies in a tank.
After gangsters try to collect on old debts, Ed betrays his alien friend and becomes a fortune teller in a circus.
Michael Kearney, scientist and serial killer, rolls alien dice.
He's trying to escape from The Shrander (and to decide whether to kill his ex-wife).
His partner continues their research, trying to suspend the indeterminacy principal.
But the fractals only seem to annoy his cat.
From the uncertain present to a future alive with possibility, everyone still has to puzzle out their lives.
By M. John Harrison

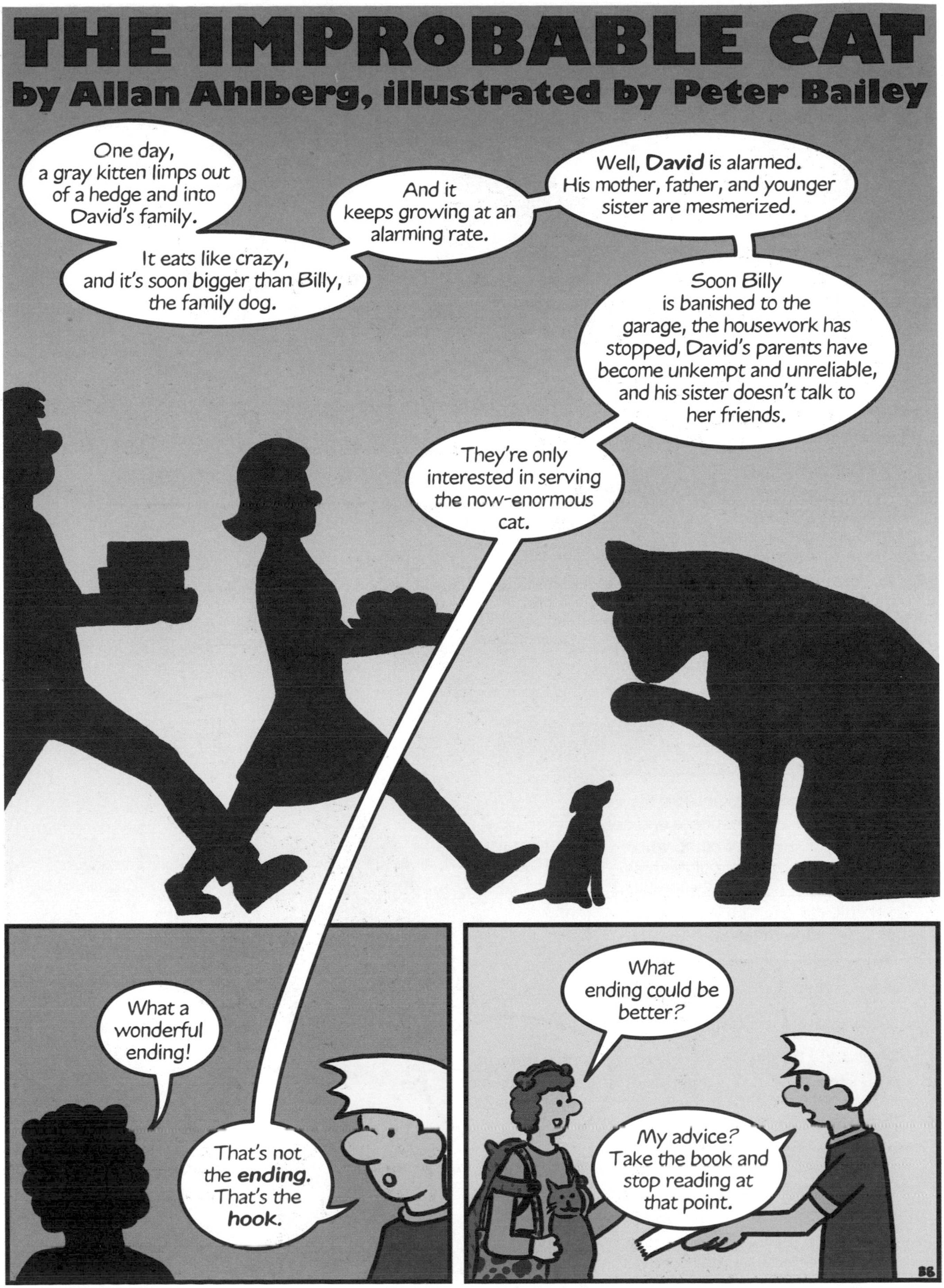
THE IMPROBABLE CAT
by Allan Ahlberg, illustrated by Peter Bailey
One day, a gray kitten limps out of a hedge and into David's family.
It eats like crazy, and it's soon bigger than Billy, the family dog.
And it keeps growing at an alarming rate.
Well, **David** is alarmed. His mother, father, and younger sister are mesmerized.
Soon Billy is banished to the garage, the housework has stopped, David's parents have become unkempt and unreliable, and his sister doesn't talk to her friends.
They're only interested in serving the now-enormous cat.
What a wonderful ending!
That's not the **ending**. That's the **hook**.
What ending could be better?
My advice? Take the book and stop reading at that point.
BB

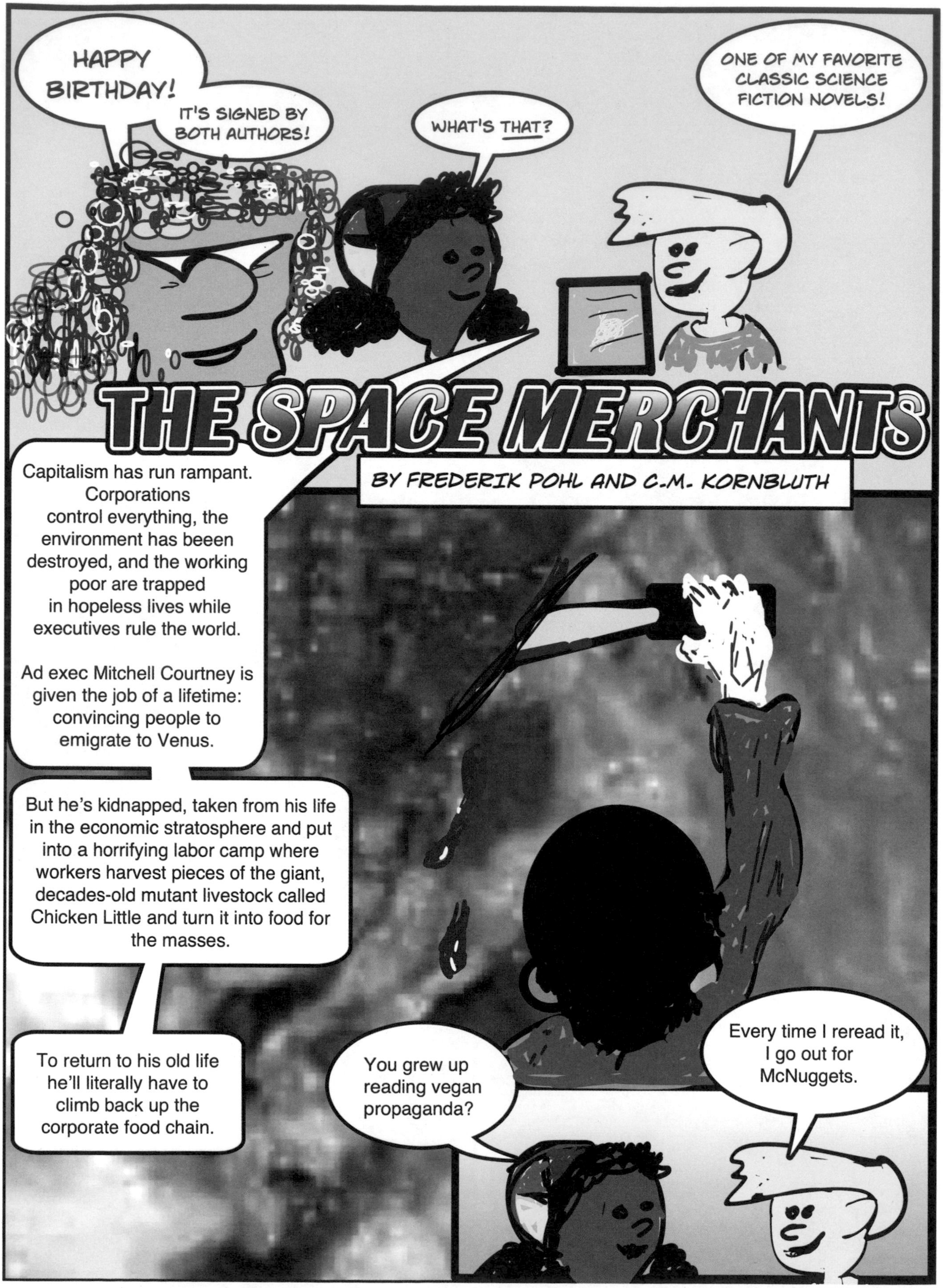
HAPPY BIRTHDAY!
IT'S SIGNED BY BOTH AUTHORS!
WHAT'S THAT?
ONE OF MY FAVORITE CLASSIC SCIENCE FICTION NOVELS!
THE SPACE MERCHANTS
BY FREDERIK POHL AND C.M. KORNBLUTH
Capitalism has run rampant. Corporations control everything, the environment has beeen destroyed, and the working poor are trapped in hopeless lives while executives rule the world.
Ad exec Mitchell Courtney is given the job of a lifetime: convincing people to emigrate to Venus.
But he's kidnapped, taken from his life in the economic stratosphere and put into a horrifying labor camp where workers harvest pieces of the giant, decades-old mutant livestock called Chicken Little and turn it into food for the masses.
To return to his old life he'll literally have to climb back up the corporate food chain.
You grew up reading vegan propaganda?
Every time I reread it, I go out for McNuggets.

Every year on Bill's birthday Gene draws the strip. This year was he able to make two great authors look bad too.

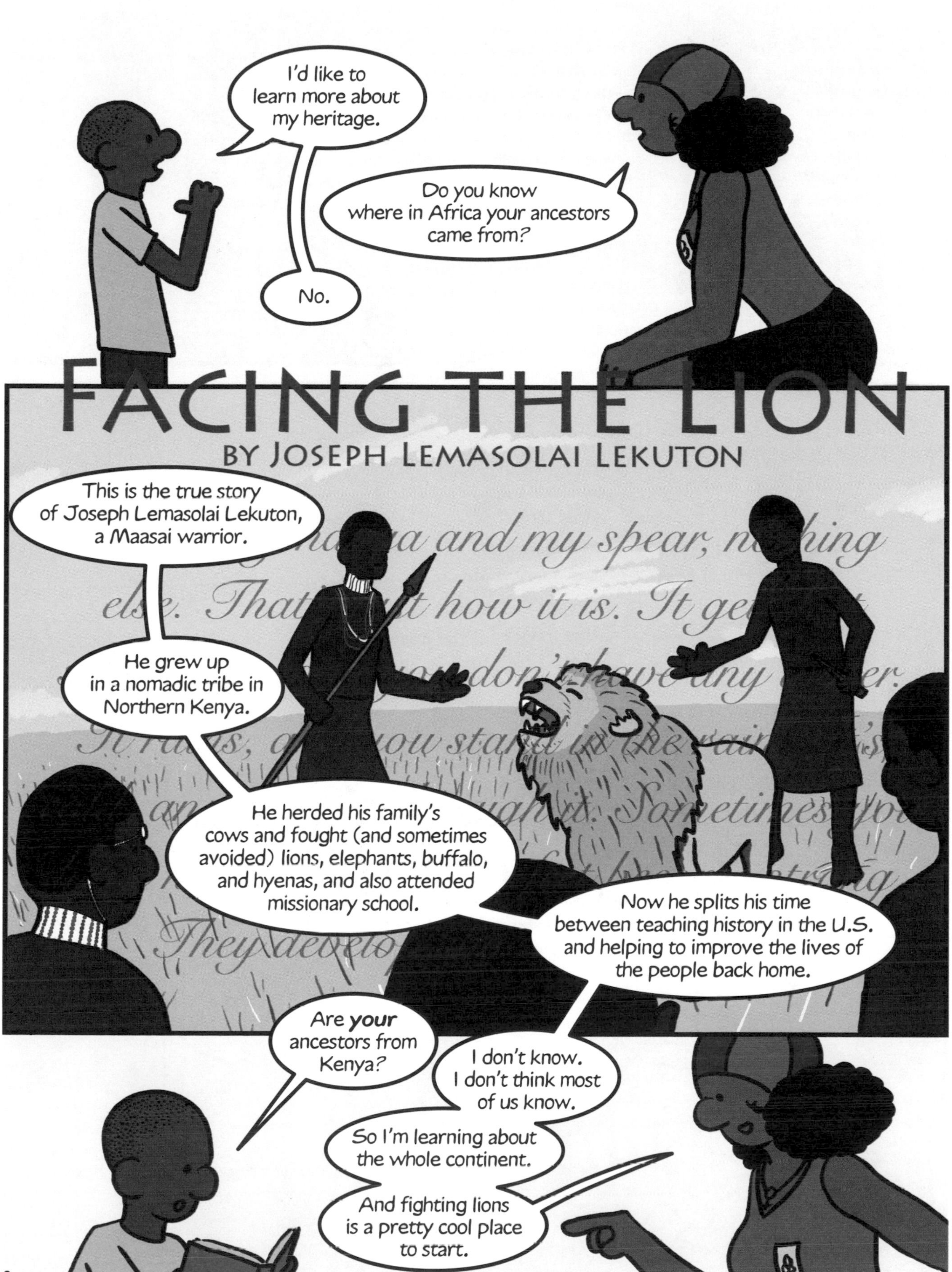
I'd like to learn more about my heritage.
Do you know where in Africa your ancestors came from?
No.
FACING THE LION
BY JOSEPH LEMASOLAI LEKUTON
This is the true story of Joseph Lemasolai Lekuton, a Maasai warrior.
He grew up in a nomadic tribe in Northern Kenya.
He herded his family's cows and fought (and sometimes avoided) lions, elephants, buffalo, and hyenas, and also attended missionary school.
Now he splits his time between teaching history in the U.S. and helping to improve the lives of the people back home.
Are **your** ancestors from Kenya?
I don't know. I don't think most of us know.
So I'm learning about the whole continent.
And fighting lions is a pretty cool place to start.

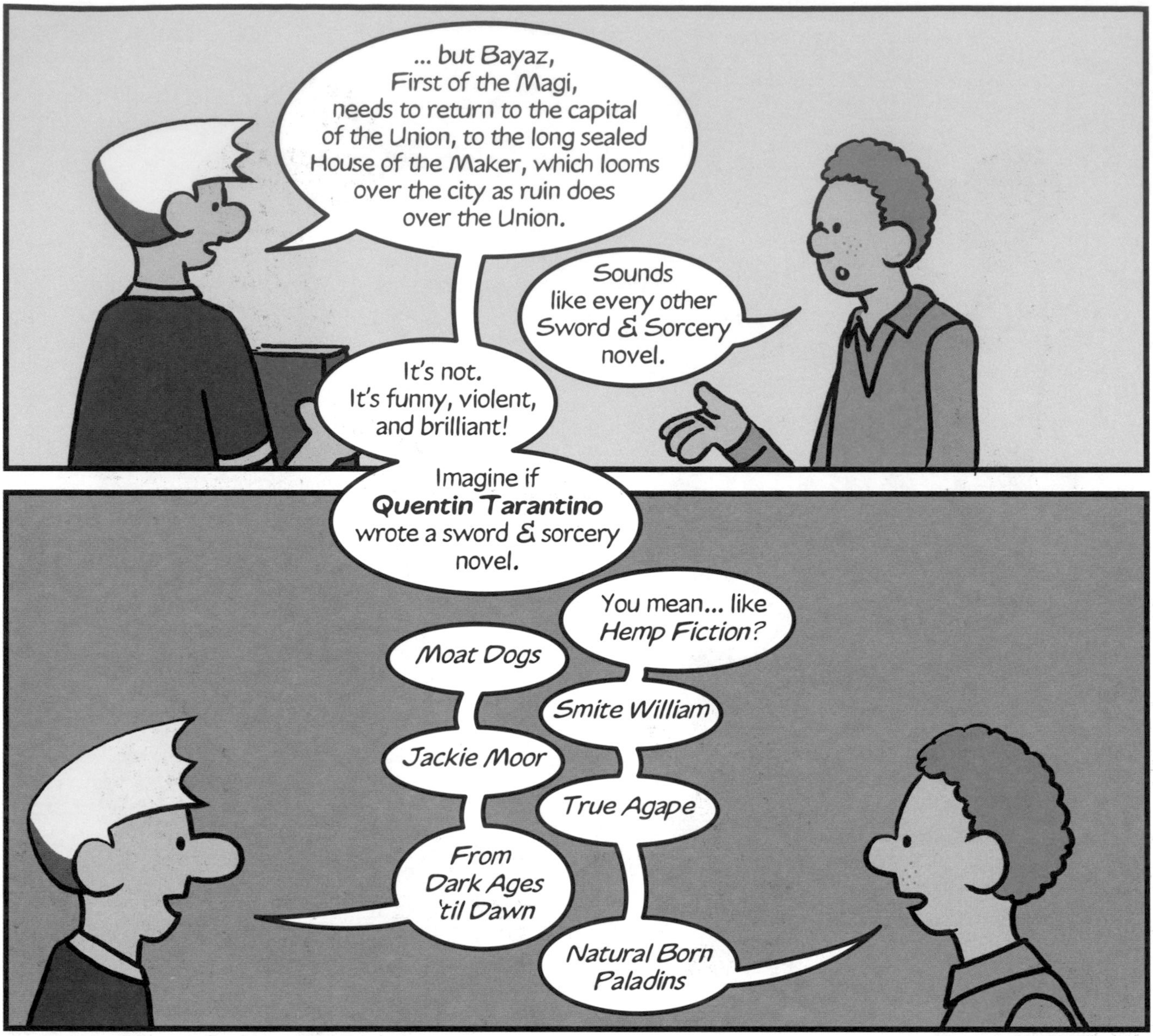
... but Bayaz, First of the Magi, needs to return to the capital of the Union, to the long sealed House of the Maker, which looms over the city as ruin does over the Union.
Sounds like every other Sword & Sorcery novel.
It's not. It's funny, violent, and brilliant!
Imagine if **Quentin Tarantino** wrote a sword & sorcery novel.
You mean... like *Hemp Fiction?*
Moat Dogs
Smite William
Jackie Moor
True Agape
From Dark Ages 'til Dawn
Natural Born Paladins

The Blade Itself by Joe Abercrombie

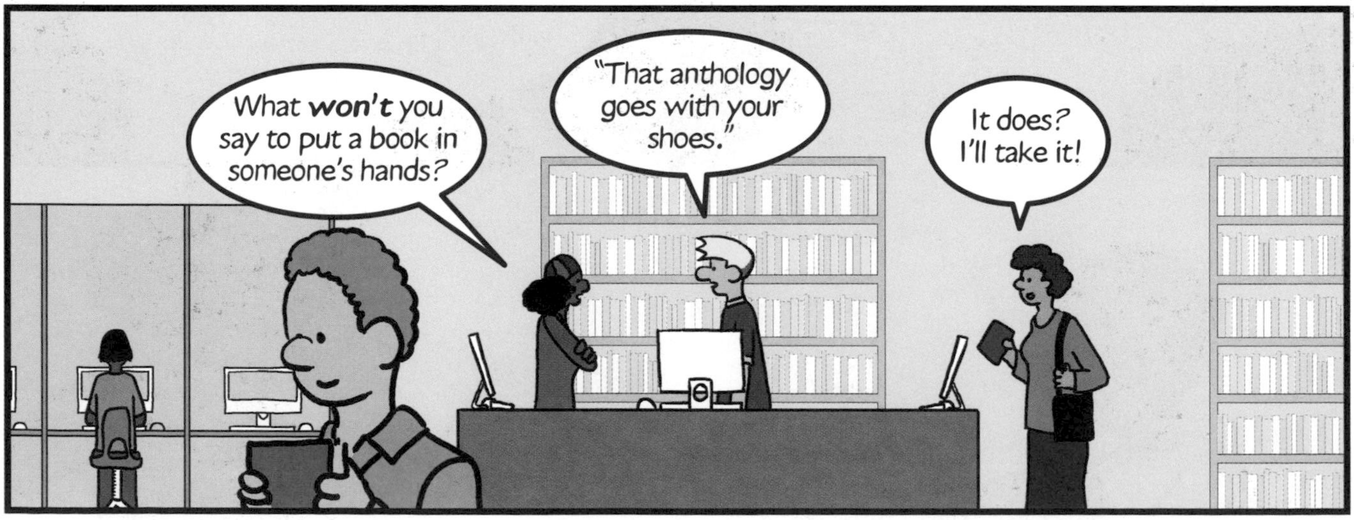
What **won't** you say to put a book in someone's hands?
"That anthology goes with your shoes."
It does? I'll take it!

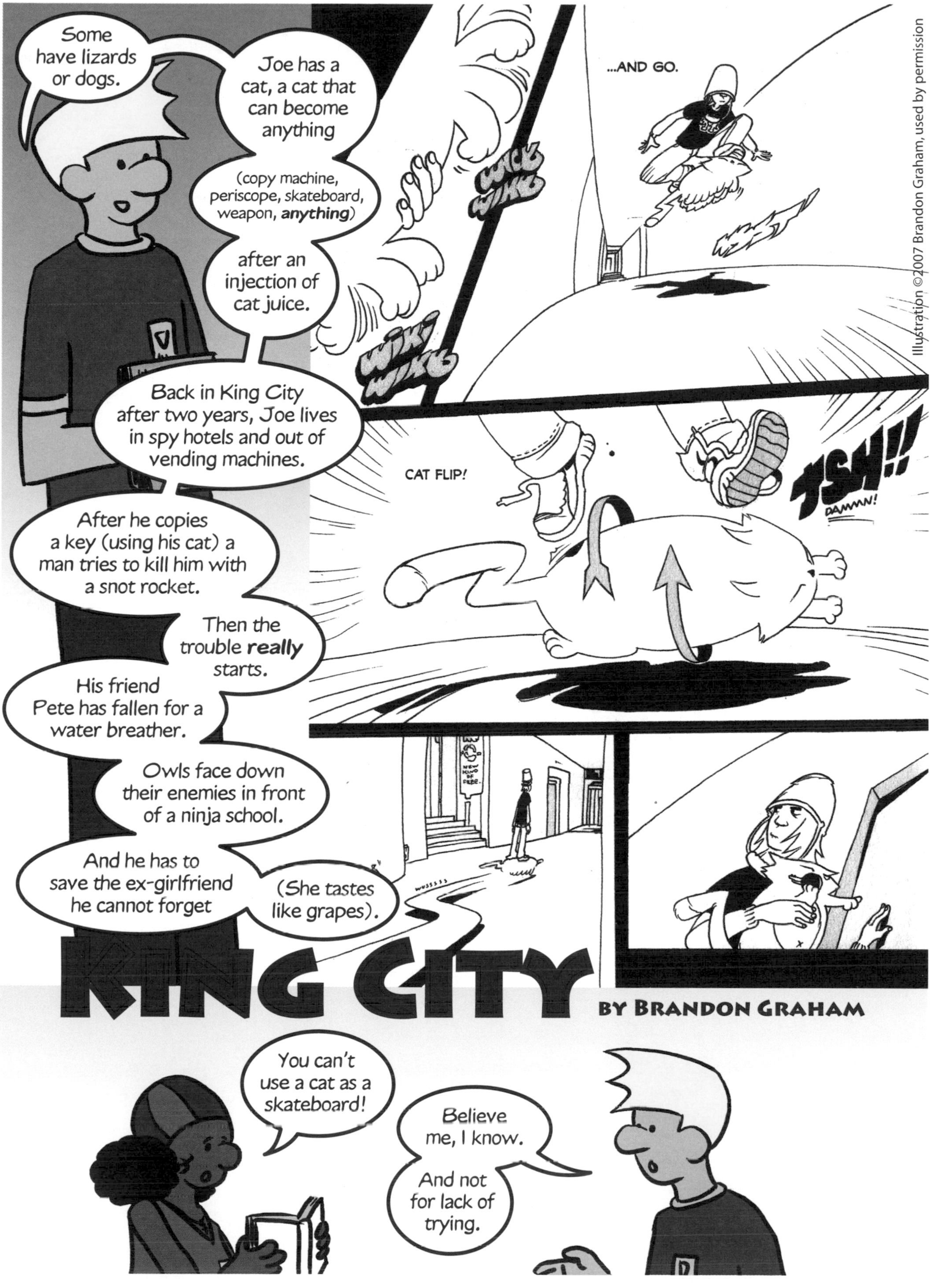
Some have lizards or dogs.
Joe has a cat, a cat that can become anything
(copy machine, periscope, skateboard, weapon, **anything**)
after an injection of cat juice.
...AND GO.
WIKI WIKI
WIKI WIKI
Back in King City after two years, Joe lives in spy hotels and out of vending machines.
CAT FLIP!
TSH!!
DAMMN!
After he copies a key (using his cat) a man tries to kill him with a snot rocket.
Then the trouble **really** starts.
His friend Pete has fallen for a water breather.
Owls face down their enemies in front of a ninja school.
And he has to save the ex-girlfriend he cannot forget
(She tastes like grapes).
KING CITY
BY BRANDON GRAHAM
You can't use a cat as a skateboard!
Believe me, I know.
And not for lack of trying.